More praise for
Public Budgeting in Context

"Katherine Willoughby's *Public Budgeting in Context* is an excellent textbook, and much more. Students and scholars alike worldwide will find it an authoritative text on American budgeting and an informed and up-to-date guide to the increasingly diverse research literature. Refreshingly, American practice is placed in an international comparative context. I intend to recommend the book to international colleagues for their teaching and research."

—James L. Chan, PhD, Professor Emeritus of Accounting,
University of Illinois at Chicago; Distinguished Overseas
Professor, Peking University, China

"This is a unique and comprehensive book that covers revenue and expenditure institutions and practices at all three levels of the US system using many comparative international examples. Eschewing jargon, it is written in readable and clear language for both introductory and more advanced students and practitioners. It is especially comprehensive, covering for example, the role of the courts in budgeting and efforts of the media and citizenry to make inputs in and monitor budget execution in the US and overseas contexts."

—George M. Guess, PhD, Adjunct Professor,
Department of Public and International Affairs,
George Mason University

"This book showcases Professor Willoughby's original research on budgeting by sovereign and subnational governments and adds a highly recommended, rich texture to our need for a renewed focus on the theory and practice of public budgeting."

—W. Bartley Hildreth, PhD, Professor, Andrew Young School
of Policy Studies, Georgia State University

"This book provides a practical and easy-to-read guide to government budgeting. It equips readers with a functional knowledge of the increasingly complex issues of budgeting at all levels of government in an international context. The text provides common sense examples of public budgeting that give students an understanding of how budget decisions by government shape all aspects of public policy and everyday life. Most fundamentally, it answers the question: Why study public budgeting?"

—Marilyn Rubin, PhD, Program Director,
Master of Public Administration, John Jay College,
City University of New York

Public Budgeting in Context

STRUCTURE, LAW, REFORM, AND RESULTS

Katherine G. Willoughby

Cover Design: Wiley
Cover Image: © Jon Boyes / Getty Images
Copyright © 2014 by John Wiley & Sons, Inc. All rights reserved.

Published by Jossey-Bass
A Wiley Brand
One Montgomery Street, Suite 1200, San Francisco, CA 94104-4594—www.josseybass.com

Jossey-Bass books and products are available through most bookstores. To contact Jossey-Bass directly call our Customer Care Department within the U.S. at 800-956-7739, outside the U.S. at 317-572-3986, or fax 317-572-4002.

Wiley publishes in a variety of print and electronic formats and by print-on-demand. Some material included with standard print versions of this book may not be included in e-books or in print-on-demand. If this book refers to media such as a CD or DVD that is not included in the version you purchased, you may download this material at http://booksupport.wiley.com. For more information about Wiley products, visit www.wiley.com.

Library of Congress Cataloging-in-Publication Data

Willoughby, Katherine G., 1958–
    Public budgeting in context : structure, law, reform, and results / Katherine G. Willoughby.
    1 online resource. — (Bryson series in public & NP management)
    Includes index.
    Description based on print version record and CIP data provided by publisher; resource not viewed.
    ISBN 978-1-118-91311-6 (pdf)
    ISBN 978-1-118-91310-9 (epub)
    ISBN 978-1-118-50932-6 (hardback)
      1. Budget—United States.   2. Budget—United States—States.   3. Finance, Public—United States.   I. Title.
    HJ2051
    352.4'80973—dc23
                                                                              2014021832

FIRST EDITION

HB Printing   10 9 8 7 6 5 4 3 2 1

CONTENTS

Dedicated to Dan

Bryson Series in Public & NP Management

PREFACE

This book examines public budgeting across levels of government in the United States and describes the legal foundations for budgeting and its practice in a few industrialized and developing countries around the world. To date, there are few books that investigate public budgeting across numerous governments with different legal, political, economic, and fiscal structures and capacities. The purpose of this book is to provide readers a clear picture of public budgeting in a sample of governments of various structures, fiscal capacities, and from continents all over the world. The reader is introduced to concepts related to the best practice of public budgeting and to several prominent theoretical perspectives about how public budgeting is actually conducted. Readers will be exposed to the obligations of and constraints on governments for budgeting that are produced in constitutions and established in code.

The audience for this book is upper-level undergraduate and graduate students of public policy, management, budgeting, and political science. This is not a nuts-and-bolts guide for conducting public budgeting. Rather, this book should help students to understand the complex and confusing context of government budgeting, especially surrounding the legal foundations for its practice and how the process and final budgets are affected by different governance structures and laws and the roles of various budget actors. Professors teaching in academic programs in these disciplines should find this book useful for engaging students in learning about public budgeting, considering several perspectives, finding public budgeting data, and conducting analyses about government budgets to actively bridge the gap between theory and practice.

In addition to describing the legal strictures that bind public budgets and the budgetary process, the budget powers and roles of important stakeholders of the process—those in the executive, legislative, and judicial branches of government, the bureaucracy, the public, and the media—will be exposed. Governance structures influence the budget powers of legislatures, chief executives, and the judiciary. Culture, tradition, economics, politics, innovation, and information technology affect how each branch operates within a governance structure in determining and making fiscal allocations. In light of worldwide fiscal malaise, especially during and since the Great Recession, this book illustrates the heightened complexity of the budgeting environment that pervades all governments today—industrialized or developing, large or small.

This book is designed to actively engage readers in the study and analysis of public revenues and expenditures, budgeting laws, processes, roles, and reforms. It is novel in providing extensive footnotes to direct readers to government portals, public agencies, budget offices, and to numerous research institutions, foundations, and professional organizations that study, collect, and analyze data on and consult about public budgeting and financial management. These footnotes offer entrée into a tremendous amount of data about government budgeting, providing readers an avenue to investigate public budgeting as practiced in virtually any government of interest to them.

Those who read the following chapters, investigate the information accessible via the footnotes, complete the chapter discussion questions, and conduct a healthy proportion of the exercises offered online, should come away with a good understanding of the context of public budget making. Students should also be able to make comparisons of the budgeting foundations, systems, and practices among governments. Students should gain skills in describing and explaining the technical nature of public budgeting, including the timetables and rules typically used at different levels of government and across a variety of countries; distinguishing political aspects of budgeting with rational methods of resource allocation in a variety of governments; explaining various budgetary reform efforts; assessing the budgetary management and fiscal status and trends of governments; and producing analyses and reports that effectively describe such status to others.

The book begins in chapter 1 by defining a budget, distinguishing between types of budgeting decisions and examining different theoretical perspectives about government budgets and the budgeting process. Chapter 2 presents descriptions of constitutional and statutory provisions for the conduct of budgeting in the selected governments around the world. Chapter 3 describes the legal foundations for budgeting in the US federal government. Chapters 4 and 5 present these foundations for budgeting in American state and local governments. The next section, chapters 6, 7, and 8, covers budget powers and influences of the executive, legislative, and judicial branches of government, with a special look at some of the governments of interest in each case. Chapter 9 regards budget execution in government bureaucracies, the input of customers, clients, and citizens to public budgets, and how the media influences government budgeting. Next, chapter 10 presents the mechanics of the budgeting process—budget types, timelines, and reforms. This discussion is followed in chapter 11 by consideration of taxes and other revenues available to governments, including an articulation of principles of sound tax policy and descriptions of predominant tax choices at every level of government in the United States and those in Guatemala, a developing country included in the sample of interest. Finally, chapter 12 is an accounting of the results of government budgets, recognizing an expanded interpretation of public budgeting as human rights budget work. How do the sample countries compare in these results, given differing governance structures and fiscal capacities? This chapter describes how budget results can be measured and compared across governments and highlights budget reform in one industrialized country in the area of health services.

ACKNOWLEDGMENTS

Writing is lonely, but in this case, I was never alone. I offer sincere thanks to my colleagues and dear friends Marilyn Rubin, Paul Posner, Tom Lauth, Jim Savage, and Jim Douglas. Each of you inspired me to keep studying and writing, as I examined your scholarship and with your encouragement, and by witnessing your continued excitement about the study and practice of public budgeting. To my colleagues and friends at Georgia State University, Cynthia Searcy, Carolyn Bourdeaux, Greg Streib, Jorge Martinez, Bart Hildreth, and Paul Benson: each of you in your own way energized me throughout the process—you have been interested in the book and asked about it, offered to help, and provided good insight. The substance of this book reflects your great support.

I am grateful to our superb graduate students, Sherman Cooper, Sarah Beth Gehl, Keegan Smith, and Sandy Zook. Sherman provided a wonderful start to referencing for the book and drafted sections and tables in chapter 2. Sarah Beth read every chapter, drafted discussion questions and some of the instructional materials, and provided astute feedback about numerous sections. Keegan drafted the section on local government bankruptcy in chapter 5 and developed several of the budget stories included throughout the book. Sandy prepared a prototype for the budget timelines presented in chapter 10. I appreciate the diligence that each of you exhibited in accommodating my requests for research along the way.

I owe genuine thanks to Alison and Emilie—my editors—as well as to my reviewers. You provided excellent perspective, critical analysis, and improving suggestions. Alison and Emilie, thank you for your gentle nudging to finish this book. Your expertise in dealing with writers was evidenced, tested, and worked.

Mostly, this book is a product of my own family foundations. Thank you to my mother and father—you listened daily to my blow-by-blow updates on the book. Your support remained upbeat even as you pressed me to keep an eye on the end result. To Forrest, Hart, and Anna, thank you three for your genuine interest in my work and tenderly coaxing me along the way. Of course, this book would never have come about without Dan. For decades now, whenever I have felt unsteady, I need only reach out my hand and yours is there to hold.

ABOUT THE AUTHOR

Katherine G. Willoughby is professor of public management and policy in the Andrew Young School of Policy Studies at Georgia State University in Atlanta, Georgia. She holds a Bachelor of Science degree in psychology from Duke University, a Master of Public Administration degree from North Carolina State University, and a PhD in public administration from the University of Georgia. Her dissertation, "The Decision Making Orientations of State Government Budget Analysts: Rational or Intuitive Thinkers?" received the NASPAA Dissertation Award for best dissertation in public affairs in 1991.

For the past twenty-five years, Katherine has taught undergraduate and graduate classes at Georgia State University in the Department of Public Management and Policy, including courses about public budgeting and financial management, public management systems and strategies, organizational theory, and research methods. She is a past recipient of her college's faculty achievement award for excellence in teaching. Her research appears in numerous academic journals, books, monographs, and reports and regards public budgeting and management, performance budgeting, E-governance, and public policy development. Her research foci include comparative budgeting, state and local budgeting and financial management, executive budgeting, budget reform, and performance budgeting. She is coauthor with Kurt Thurmaier of the book *Policy and Politics in State Budgeting*, which examines the decision strategies and influence of central budget office analysts in the budgetary process of US state governments. She is coauthor and coeditor with Marilyn Rubin of the forthcoming book *Sustaining the States: The Fiscal Viability of American State Governments*, which presents research by numerous scholars and experts about revenues, expenditures, and debt as well as the future financial and budget prospects of these governments.

Katherine is a research associate with the International Center for Public Policy of the Andrew Young School of Policy Studies at Georgia State University. In this capacity, she has lectured for and consulted extensively with different governments and public officials, budget and finance officers, and agency managers from around the world seeking information about best practices in public budgeting and financial management.

Katherine is a member of the American Society for Public Administration and the Association for Budgeting and Financial Management, the latter of which she chaired in 2009. She is on the editorial board of *Public Administration Review* and is a fellow of the National Academy of Public Administration.

Public Budgeting in Context

Overview of Modern Public Budgeting

Struggle and compromise are the very essence of the democratic process and are necessarily reflected in the budget.

—Harold D. Smith, director of the US Bureau of the Budget, 1944

LEARNING OBJECTIVES

After reading this chapter, you should be able to

- Define public budgets in several ways
- Distinguish between different types of public budgeting decisions
- Distinguish between public and private budgets
- Understand different perspectives about the role, growth, and size of government
- Compare several theoretical frameworks about public budgeting
- Conduct your own investigation of government size
- Distinguish budget principles applicable to the legislative and executive branches of government

It is an especially important time to study public budgeting and financial management. Grim examples of government fiscal austerity, from the global to local scene, are plentiful right now. In 2012, Greece suffered through the greatest sovereign debt restructuring in history; the United States has had to weather an embarrassing downgrade of its credit since 2011; the American states collectively have closed budget gaps of over $500 billion since 2009; and American local governments have cut more than 500,000 positions since 2008. The official end of the Great Recession is now over four years in the past, but the City of Detroit just declared bankruptcy (July 2013).

In fact, public officials, budgeters, finance ministers and directors, agency department heads, and managers in governments around the world are grappling with how to reform their budget systems in order to provide basic services, sustain current operations, and build and maintain public infrastructure given the very long, slow recovery from the economic downturn that ended in June 2009. Many recognize that governments are simply unable to sustain the levels and mix of services and programs that citizens have come to expect. Government budget decision makers are reaching the end of an ability to budget using (as stated in a March 30, 2012, telephone interview by the author with a state government auditor) "strategic seat-of-the-pants flying," whereby budget gaps are plugged with one-time funds. According to this auditor from a traditionally poor (fiscally) US state government, "We think (hope) the federal government will increase funding, we hope our revenues will increase, or that our Attorney General has a settlement coming. It has always worked out for the last decade. And, to us, a couple of million dollars is a huge amount of money. Our luck has helped us find ways to fill gaps to keep the status quo." But how long can governments budget on hope? And for which governments will such luck hold?

This introductory chapter provides an entrée into the complicated and confusing world of public budgeting, beginning with a review of the foundational aspects of budgeting systems, such as governmental structure and size. The chapter addresses the distinctiveness of public (governmental) and private (market) activities, introduces popular theoretical frameworks for better understanding public budgets and budgetary processes, and defines some enduring public budgeting principles. These concepts set the stage for the systems and results of public budgeting that will be examined throughout the book.

The rest of this book describes the foundations for public budgets and budget making in a few countries, with focused attention on those at every level in the

United States. Today, the interconnectedness of governments, businesses, non-profits, and individuals throughout the world makes it vital to understand how different communities function. Governments provide for the rule of law that structures the relationships among individuals in communities. Governments, by taxing and spending, have an impact on the strength of economies and the behaviors of inhabitants. The countries examined throughout this book were chosen to expose readers to examples from industrialized and developing nations, with different governmental structures and various fiscal capacities. This group is a purely judgmental sample of governments that includes the federal, state, and local ones in the United States (North America), one government each from Central (Guatemala) and South America (Brazil), one from Africa (Tanzania), one from Europe (Italy), one government from South Asia (India), and one from East Asia and Pacific (Australia). There has been no predetermination for selection into this sample that any of these governments consistently conducts budgeting either poorly or well.

WHAT IS A BUDGET?

Merriam-Webster's Dictionary (2013) defines "budget" in several ways:

1. Chiefly dialect: a usually leather pouch, wallet, or pack; also, its contents

2. Stock, supply

3. A quantity (as of energy or water) involved in, available for, or assignable to a particular situation; also, an account of gains and losses of such a quantity (the global carbon budget)

4. a. A statement of the financial position of an administration for a definite period of time based on estimates of expenditures during the period and proposals for financing them

   b. A plan for the coordination of resources and expenditures

   c. The amount of money that is available for, required for, or assigned to a particular purpose

These definitions yield important concepts about public budgets and budgeting—a pouch or wallet brings to mind *containment*, an entity *restricted* in the amount of loose change or paper bills that can be held within it; stock or supply implies *accounting* for quantities of things; accounting of gains and losses entails some sort of *balancing*. The fourth definition presents constraints of *time* and *resources*, and suggests a budget as *strategic*. Irene Rubin (2010), who has written and conducted research extensively about public budgeting, explains that government budgets are different from those of individuals or businesses because they are public or open to scrutiny, they engage public resources, and involve many stakeholders—politicians, government workers, taxpayers, the media, professional groups, clients and customers of government services, and citizens generally—and numerous institutions (budget laws, rules, protocols, and processes).

A couple of things should become apparent to you as you progress through the following chapters. Most important, there is really no way to determine which country or government has the best budget or budgets best. There is no attempt here to ferret out "leaders" or "laggards" in budgeting. There are over two hundred different countries around the world, some with multiple levels of government and with many governments at each level. Each government budgets a bit differently and there are a vast range of revenue capacities and spending categories among them. You will learn that a great way to gain understanding about a country or community, its people and traditions, is to examine its budget. Public budgets—what governments spend money on and the taxes that support this spending—provide a snapshot into the values, commitments, and interests of governments and the people who reside in them.

You will also learn that it is extremely challenging to study and compare governments and their budgets globally because every country is unique—each has its own social, cultural, legal, political, and economic histories and traditions that influence budget development, budget information, and format requirements, tax structures, expenditure categories, and in-country and external relationships with other governments. The *CIA World Factbook* lists information about 237 "world entities" on its website.[1] The July 2013 report on chiefs of state and cabinet members of foreign governments includes information about 198 countries, ranging from Afghanistan to Zimbabwe. This report includes developed (i.e., Australia and Italy) and developing countries (i.e., Brazil, Guatemala, India, Tanzania); governments in transition (i.e., Fiji, Guinea-Bissau, Lebanon, Madagascar, Mali, and Tunisia); those for which the United States has no diplomatic exchanges (Bhutan, Cuba, Iran, North Korea, and Taiwan); territories and colonies (Cook Islands and Bermuda, respectively); and the Holy See (Vatican City). Examining the *Factbook* is a quick and easy way to glimpse the breadth of governments that exist as well as compare data that characterize country budgets and populations.

For example, Table 1.1 presents expenditures for health, education, and military as a percent of gross domestic product (GDP or total annual production in the economy within country borders) for the countries we will investigate throughout this book. Examining this data, it is clear that the public and private expenditure for health care as a percent of GDP in the United States dwarfs that in all other countries—it is about twice the ratio evidenced in Italy, Australia, and Brazil, more than twice that in Guatemala and Tanzania, and more than four times India's ratio. Tanzania indicates the highest ratio for education spending, with Brazil, Australia, and United States falling behind. Public expenditures for education as a proportion of GDP trail in India and Guatemala. Military expenditures as a percent of GDP are lowest in Guatemala, followed by Tanzania, Brazil, Australia, and Italy. India's ratio is six times that of Guatemala; of the countries here, the United States has the largest ratio for this category of spending.

Table 1.1 provides information on a sample of countries about categories of expenditure and a measure of the size of these expenditures in relation to annual economic production. But the data do not give insight as to who gets services, coverage areas, service quality, or the results from such spending. In the case of health expenditures, you would need to dig further to determine what portion of total expenditures is public and what is private. Also, there is no way to tell if Brazil's health services are better than Guatemala's using these data alone. Nor can you determine from the data that people living in the United States are healthier than those living anywhere else. Although you can make some assessments about what governments and their citizens consider important by looking at ratios like these, you would have to collect more and different information to analyze and learn about the effects of these expenditures.

You are probably already realizing that governments will never be able to satiate the public's needs, desires, or expectations related to addressing community and individual problems. Public budgets represent the choices made about how to spend finite resources. As government budgets have grown to accommodate new and changing policies and problems, these choices have become more difficult to make and the results seem to be more painful to bear. Especially in periods of economic stasis or decline, addressing problems by creating new programs or expanding current ones often means that others must be trimmed,

Table 1.1
Expenditures as a Percent of GDP, by Country and Function[a]

	Health[b]	Date of Information	Education[c]	Date of Information	Military[d]	Date of Information
United States	17.9	2011	5.4	2010	4.4	2012
Italy	9.5	2011	4.5	2010	1.7	2012
Australia	9.0	2011	5.6	2010	1.7	2012
Brazil	8.9	2011	5.8	2010	1.5	2012
Tanzania	7.3	2011	6.2	2010	1.1	2012
Guatemala	6.7	2011	3.0	2012	0.4	2012
India	3.9	2011	3.2	2011	2.4	2012

Source: CIA World Factbook, Guide to Country Comparisons, People and Society and Military, available at https://www.cia.gov/library/publications/the-world-factbook/rankorder/rankorderguide.html

[a]Definitions of all terms and measures, available at https://www.cia.gov/library/publications/the-world-factbook/docs/notesanddefs.html

[b]According to the *CIA World Factbook,* for the measure total expenditure on health as a percentage of GDP, health expenditures are defined as "activities performed either by institutions or individuals through the application of medical, paramedical, and/or nursing knowledge and technology, the primary purpose of which is to promote, restore, or maintain health."

[c]According to the *CIA World Factbook,* this is a measure of "public expenditure on education as a percent of GDP."

[d]According to the *CIA World Factbook,* this is a measure of "spending on defense programs for the most recent year available as a percent of GDP; the GDP is calculated on an exchange rate basis, i.e., not in terms of purchasing power parity (PPP). For countries with no military forces, this figure can include expenditures on public security and police."

cut back significantly, or even shut down entirely. In such times, new revenue sources must be tapped or traditional revenue sources reconsidered. As you advance through this book, you will learn about how governments attempt to solve public problems and keep up with growing demands within the constraints of foundational laws.

MACRO- AND MICRO-BUDGETING

Studying budgets is difficult because the process of budgeting involves choices that represent the uniqueness and commonness of human behavior in a certain context (Golembiewski and Rabin 1983). In a most elemental sense, public budgets are the result of the judgments of those legally responsible for requesting, recommending, appropriating, and spending public money. Much of the complexity of public budgets today concerns the fact that they represent the culmination of conflict, negotiations, and decisions made among many elected officials, public agency and department heads, managers, staff, program clients, taxpayers, and the public, more generally.

The process of budgeting includes macro- and micro-budgetary decisions.

- Macro-budgeting decisions are visible, overarching policy decisions that determine the size and role of government in an economy.

- Micro-budgeting decisions are less visible, trade-off decisions made to carry out policies determined by macro-budgeting decisions.

"Macro-budgeting involves setting large policy targets for both fiscal and political purposes" (Thurmaier and Willoughby 2001, 50). Macro-budgeting decisions are those that result in the mix of tax and spending policies determined largely in the political arena and by elected officials. These decisions result in government-wide policy objectives—to advance economic opportunity, to have an educated and healthy citizenry, to maintain safe communities, to foster a clean environment. Elected officials responsible for macro-budgetary decisions receive information from many stakeholders, including high-level political appointees, political parties, business, professional, and other organized interests, the public, and even the media. John Kingdon (1984, 1995) classifies this group as a visible cluster of actors in his theoretical consideration of public policy development. He describes a chaotic policy agenda setting process as a swirl of solutions and problems in which a hidden cluster of actors feeds the visible cluster of actors information about policy alternatives (policies that could address specific problems). The hidden cluster of actors includes bureaucrats, agency and program staff, analysts, and researchers from think tanks, universities, and colleges. Kingdon adds that predictable and unpredictable windows of opportunity afford the chance for the hidden cluster of actors to push certain policy alternatives. In the end, however, everything must come together for success—an identified problem must be matched to the policy alternative, and the political climate must be right for change to occur.

Micro-budgeting decisions are those made to square with or accommodate macro-budgeting ones. Whereas macro-budgeting often entails strenuous debate about a few very high-profile budget issues such as more money for defense versus health care, micro-budgeting entails making tradeoffs among agencies and programs to fulfill policies that have been decided upon earlier (promoting an educated society, for example). The decision makers, mostly in the hidden cluster, take their cues from the macro-budgeting decision arena that has already occurred. That is, it is important for these actors to understand the revenue and expenditure mix that has already been determined at the top in order to figure out how government programs, services, and activities will be conducted. Kingdon's model of policy agenda setting in the United States has crossover benefits for understanding budgetary processes. His model presents policy development as time bound, yet evolutionary, meaning that there are elements of top-down and bottom-up decision making, and change may come about in very gradual or cataclysmic ways.

PUBLIC AND PRIVATE BUDGETING

Public budgets are different from those of individuals or private companies. Individuals cannot spend more resources than they are able to secure through their own labors, by borrowing, or perhaps through bequests. A recent letter writer to advice columnist "Dear Abby" explains typical individual budgeting behaviors well:

> Dear Abby:
> After years of enduring overdraft charges and dodging bill collectors, I have finally gotten my financial house in order. I pay all of my bills, and I pay them on time. However, I have very little money left over at the end of the week. Many of my friends have two-income

households or use credit cards when they go out to eat or to the movies, which is often. I want them to know that because I decline their invitations does not mean I'm antisocial—I just can't afford it. I have said so at times, but I hate to be a broken record.

—**On Track But Still Broke in Maine,** *Atlanta Journal-Constitution,* **July 30, 2013, D2**

Whereas the public budgeting process results in legislative appropriations that set the legal limits on spending for a future fiscal year or years, the letter above illustrates how private budgets are more malleable and the timing is different. Private budgets are financial plans that are open to change more frequently, and certainly can be changed more quickly, than public budgets. Also, the profit motive of private companies leads to actions and activities that promote the adage "buy low, sell high" in terms of their market transactions, often necessitating nimble actions. Governments are usually unable to make budget changes on a dime in the way that private companies can. On the other hand, although there may seem to be limitless income amounts possible for individuals and private corporations to realize, there are short-run constraints—the bottom line for individuals is paying the bills when due; that line for private corporations is maximizing profits while minimizing costs.

Governments, however, operate differently, because they are public and not private entities. Governments provide goods and services that do not necessarily generate profits. This discussion acknowledges that many of the services provided by governments today are available through fee for service. Also, governments contract with private companies to conduct public business. Still, the public or communal aspect that undergirds government work necessitates attention to different objectives from private ones. Part of this relates to understanding the nature of public goods. For example, it is difficult to put a price on national defense, an example of a public good. Also, the provision of national defense cannot be contained to specific individuals or communities. In the United States, whether you pay federal taxes or not, you receive the same national defense services as your neighbor. In the most ideal form, a public good or service has two qualities—non-rivalry and non-excludability. Non-rivalry relates a bit to the pricing problem—that is, that the value of the good or service is not affected by how many people receive the good or service. Non-excludability relates to the other point, that no one can be excluded from consuming the good or service.

Governments engage in activities to address market failures or to address externalities that can arise from an imperfect market economy. Importantly, governments can incur deficits to provide public goods and services and to pursue policy goals that address such failures and externalities.

In the United States, policy decisions (macro-budgeting decisions) that influence how large a presence government is in the economy (i.e., federal spending as a percent of GDP) are made at the federal level. Theoretically, national fiscal policy can be used to counteract a changing economy. That is, when the economy is on the decline, the government can initiate tax cuts and spend money through transfers and grants for services, programs, and infrastructure to spur growth. A balancing component to this perspective would be to increase taxes and pull back on spending when the economy surges—but historically this has been more problematic to do, at least in the United States. The US federal budget does not have to balance—it can use borrowed funds in addition to tax receipts, fees, and charges to cover expenditures. Spending that outpaces revenues can cause a budget deficit (the gap between expenditures and revenues in one year) and increase government debt (the total amount of borrowed funds, to date). The decisions that determine the size and role of government in the economy are macro-budgetary ones.

The budgeting decisions of subnational governments are similar to those made by the federal government in terms of setting policy direction for their citizens; however, taxing and spending by these entities are not expected to have nationwide economic impact. Also, at least in the United States, state and local government budgets must balance—the chief executive's budget proposal must balance, the appropriation bill or bills passed by the legislature must balance, the budget must balance at year-end, or some combination of balancing requirements exists. Though the definition of balance varies, subnational governments in the United States cannot conduct deficit financing to support operating budgets.

THE ROLE AND SIZE OF GOVERNMENT

Economists James Buchanan and Richard Musgrave participated in a seminal weeklong discussion at the University of Munich in March, 1998 that has been recorded in *Public Finance and Public Choice: Two Contrasting Visions of the State* (1999). These scholars present their perspectives about government budget growth in the twentieth century by debating principles of efficiency and justice related to their theories of public choice and public finance, respectively. These theories represent opposing views of government taxing and spending (macro-budgetary decisions). Musgrave presents government as beneficent—viewing its allocation, distribution, and stabilization roles as appropriate. He defines democratic governance as problem solving, with the distributive role of government guided by a democratically determined "social welfare function" (Buchanan and Musgrave 1999, 46). Though he considers government and its agents as positive forces of justice and efficiency, he recognizes that *redistributive* politics will "guarantee class conflict" (85–86), which is the antithesis of his vision for a more equitable state through government expansion.

Buchanan, on the other hand, distrusts the state, believing it has become a Leviathan (monolithic) given the self-interested behaviors of political agents (elected officials and bureaucrats). He considers that these agents must be curbed through constitutional rules. Whereas Musgrave views government as an elixir to market failures and inequality, Buchanan views justice as reachable through a well-working market economy and limited government.[2] Both men contemplate if the public sector has grown too large by the mid- to late-twentieth century. Musgrave recognizes this growth as "the share of gross national product (GNP)[3] flowing through public budgets" (Buchanan and Musgrave 1999, 64) and as ranging among governments from 10 to 60 percent. Buchanan considers a 10 to 12 percent share of GDP "devoted to financing public goods as justifiable" (Buchanan and Musgrave 1999, 84).

What does the size of government look like today, using similar measures? The International Monetary Fund (IMF) collects government finance indicators and other measures for countries around the world that allow for some comparability of government size vis-à-vis the economy. According to the IMF in their World Economic Outlook Database (April 2013), average general government revenues as a percent of GDP for countries around the world increased from 28.2 percent in 2002 to 32.4 percent in 2012 (estimated). Average general government expenditures as a percent of GDP increased from 31.1 percent to 34.0 percent and average gross debt to GDP decreased from 74.8 percent to 50.0 percent, for the same decade. As you would suspect, however, averages can mask outliers.

Table 1.2 presents data from the IMF Economic Outlook Database (April 2013). This table indicates how many countries fall into each category of the fiscal measures of interest—general government revenues, expenditures, and gross debt, each as a proportion of GDP. The countries that will be examined throughout the rest of this book are noted where they fall in this table, too. Table 1.2 shows that over half of countries (52.4 percent) have revenues as a

Table 1.2
Number of Countries by Measure of Government Size, 2012

	General Government Revenues as % of GDP n=187 (# of countries)	General Government Expenditures as % of GDP n=187 (# of countries)	General Government Gross Debtas % of GDP n=174 (# of countries)
less than 20%	(28) Guatemala India	(20) Guatemala	(26)
20% to <30%	(70) Tanzania	(59) India Tanzania	(18) Australia Guatemala
30% to <40%	(45) Australia Brazil United States	(53) Australia	(36)
40% to <50%	(28) Italy	(39) Brazil United States	(24) Tanzania
50% to <60%	(7)	(11) Italy	(21)
60% or more	(9)	(5)	(49) Brazil India Italy United States

Source: International Monetary Fund, World Economic Outlook Database, April 2013.

Note: Data for 2012 for some countries may be an estimate.

percent of GDP less than 30 percent; well over half of countries (70.6 percent) indicate expenditures as a percent of GDP at 40 percent or less. Over half of countries (54 percent) indicate debt as a percent of GDP at 40 percent or more; 28 percent of countries indicate a debt to GDP ratio over 60 percent. In 2012, a dozen countries have or estimate this ratio to be over 100 percent—Japan indicates the highest debt ratio at 237.9 percent and of the countries we will examine, Italy stands at 127.0 percent and the United States at 106.5 percent. This data attests to an underlying principle of public budgeting—people want services, programs, and support, but they do not want to pay the full costs associated with conducting the work or the support. Governments borrow and seek grants or donor funds to fill gaps between revenues and expenditures.

MODELING THE BUDGETARY PROCESS

Research about public budgeting that attempts to develop predictive models falls into different camps. *Normative research* is prescriptive, recommending solutions to budget problems that are based on values and not necessarily what happens in actual practice. The primary question addressed through such research is, "what *should* be done?" In the early part of the twentieth century, during the Progressive movement, budget reformers, public administrators, and economists pressed for greater efficiency of government operations and decision making. This normative approach to budgeting focused on rationalizing the business of government. In strong reaction to corruption in governments at all levels in the United States at the time, some reformers sought more limited government as well as a means to good government; that is, government efficiently conducted and economic in results (Rubin 1990, 1993). The public choice and public finance theories discussed above present different "amounts" of government as efficient—public choice theory reaching efficiency through individual choice behaviors that constrain government growth and public finance theory suggesting government spending to realize the greatest possible return for the public.

On the other hand, *descriptive studies* seek observable proof of trends, sequences, and patterns of events to determine cause. The primary question addressed through this type of research is "What *is* done?" Around the mid-twentieth century, incrementalism became the predominant budget theory, having mushroomed from disciplines of political science, economics, and decision sciences. Using descriptive studies of budgetary decisions, processes, and relationships as well as statistical analyses of budget expenditures, the theory offered (at the time) a realistic consideration of public budgeting. Incrementalism was different from normative theories of budgeting that focused on the science of government operations. Nonetheless, Berry (1990), Rubin (1990), and others clarify why incrementalism lost favor as a good explanation for public budgeting by the latter part of the twentieth century. The theory's tenets of the regularity of relationships, simple decision rules, and an insularity of process simply did not hold up. Especially at the US federal level, as the budget and its components grew more complicated, as the process of budgeting became more jumbled, as conflict among stakeholders amplified, and as budget imbalance expanded, new perspectives poured forth. Following incrementalism, punctuated equilibrium and real-time budgeting (RTB) are two theoretical perspectives that take root as viable predictive models of public budgeting.

Each of these theories is described in more detail below. In the following chapters, you will read about how budget processes have developed in different countries around the world and at the local, state, and federal levels in the United States. You should find that governmental budgeting today, wherever practiced, is an evolving process that is difficult to explain with one theoretical framework or through one research lens.

Branch and Root Methods of Decision Making

Incrementalism is a theoretical perspective used to describe government budget growth around the middle of the twentieth century in the United States. Aaron Wildavsky (1964) explained a framework in which budget development is backward looking, based on history and past policy. That is, current budget deliberations are anchored on past agreements, thereby keeping conflict to a minimum. Budget allocation is based on political promises of goods and services to be provided. Rather than representing any grand scheme for government, the budget was the result of successive limited comparisons or consideration at the margins—the most important determinant of next year's budget was this year's budget.

This perspective of budgeting regarded a process in the United States at the time that was routine. There were annual, repetitive roles among the president, executive (central) budget examiners, agency heads, and budget and program officers in terms of developing spending requests, and the congressional committee and subcommittee members in terms of determining appropriations. Receipts from the national income tax that grew significantly after World War II provided a ready resource to federal agencies in accommodating the burgeoning expectations of the public for new or expanded services. Ever-growing revenues, a routine budget cycle, and consistent roles among budget actors allowed Wildavsky (1964) to tease out the calculations made and strategies used by these actors throughout the process. Cabinet secretaries and agency heads pushed for expansive budgets to carry out programs and services demanded by clients and constituents; central budget examiners culled requests to fit with the president's budget and policy agendas and later in the process provided central clearance for agency spending. Congressional committee and subcommittee members (Appropriations) acted as naysayers in the House—cutting back agency budget requests in their traditional service as guardians of the public purse. Senators, however, traditionally offered some recourse to agencies to recoup cuts made by House members. According to Wildavsky (1984), "[a] member of the Senate Appropriations Committee is likely to conceive of his proper role as the responsible legislator who sees to it that the irrepressible lower House does not do too much damage either to constituency or to national interests" (51). Incrementalism was a good explanation of budgeting in its day. It accommodated consistent, slow growth of the federal budget and the distinctive roles but routine negotiations of budget actors who recognized and engaged in a sense of the budget base and fair share in terms of the budget pie.

Incrementalism is often juxtaposed with more rational methods of budgeting. In his research about policy development, Charles Lindblom (1959) compares what he terms the branch (successive limited comparisons) and root (rational comprehensive) methods of decision making. The most distinctive aspect of the branch method is that agreement among decision makers determines which policy or policies to pursue. The most distinctive feature of the root method is its comprehensiveness—the determination through means-end analysis of every possible policy to tease out the most valuable one to be pursued. The root method requires that "every important relevant factor is taken into account" (Lindblom 1959, 81), whereas the branch method requires that "important possible outcomes, alternative potential policies and affected values are neglected" (81).

The root method or rational comprehensive theory is normative and certainly in its ideal form, unrealistic for humans to conduct (see Simon 1957). On the other hand, incrementalism (successive limited comparisons) is heavily descriptive, recognizing roles among budget actors in a routine process, requiring the restriction of possible alternatives to reduce conflict, and in fact, determining that complete information and comprehensive analyses are impracticable and even undesirable.

Punctuated Equilibrium

Eventually, incrementalism became "too many things to too many people to be useful" (Berry 1990, 182) as a concept or theoretical framework for understanding public budgeting. Frank Baumgartner and Bryan Jones (1991, 1044–1045), like Kingdon, develop a theory of policy development founded upon agenda setting that accounts for periods of both "extreme stability" as well as "bursts" of dramatic change to policy. James True (1995) considers policy intervention and its effects on budgeting in the United States, examining federal budget authority from 1969 to 1993 to tease out significant budget changes. True determines that some dramatic changes to the US national budget can be explained by policy intervention. Then, Jones, Baumgartner, and True (1998) investigated periods of budget stability or stasis versus change, comparing annual percentage changes in US federal budget authority for domestic spending across time to identify significant budget epochs. They identify three epochs:

1. From the end of World War II to 1956, characterized as high variability among budget categories, but no consistent trend of budget growth or decline
2. From 1956 to 1974, characterized as substantial budget growth
3. Since 1976, characterized as "slower budget growth"

These scholars are able to rule out partisan control of government, changes in the economy, and the public mood as determining budget changes. They explain that finding significant budget change across time knocks traditional incrementalism out as a good predictive model of public budgeting. Both incrementalism and punctuated equilibrium recognize the limits of human decision making. But punctuated equilibrium allows for "shifts in selective attention" that can bring about dramatic changes to policy and budgets (Jones, Baumgartner, and True 1998, 23). These authors point to punctuated equilibrium as a better model of budgetary change, though they conclude that much more data must be collected and analyzed to accurately predict the results of extremely complicated interactions among numerous variables inherent to budgeting. Nonetheless, their framework, in line with Kingdon's ideas about budgets as evolutionary and the possibilities for cataclysmic change, offered up a new way of thinking about public budgets and the budgeting process.

Real-Time Budgeting

Rubin's real-time budgeting (RTB) (2010) is a celebration of the complexity of the budgetary process that concentrates heavily on timing and the intersection of budget streams, including revenues, process, expenditures, balance, and implementation. RTB is important for highlighting budgeting as nonsequential and composed of overlapping processes, each with its own timing, budget actors, and context. Each stream produces decisions that affect other streams. Budgets are the result of intersections of these different budget streams, though intersections do not occur at the same time or consecutively.

Each stream regards a vital component of public budgeting. The revenue stream produces decisions about government resources and availability. Tax structures result from this stream, engaging the public, taxpayers, interest groups, and politicians who negotiate and determine the fiscal resources available for government to spend. The process stream regulates who has access to budgeting decisions and presents the rules of the game. This stream provides the framework for how decisions will be made, who will make them, and any constraints to budgetary decision making. Examining a government to determine its process stream would involve investigating budget rules and institutions. Some questions that would need to be answered include

- What spending (programs) are legally required to be provided by the government?
- What tax and expenditure limits are applicable to the government?
- What is the fiscal year for the government?
- Who or what office is responsible for developing the budget?
- What is the required budget format?
- When must the chief executive present the budget to the legislative branch?
- How long does the legislative branch have to deliberate about the budget?
- Are public hearings required to be held to discuss the budget?
- Must the budget balance? If so, how is balance defined?

- What type of veto power, if any, does the chief executive have?
- What accountability, evaluation, and reporting rules exist regarding funds in particular and the budget more generally?

These questions indicate how constraining a budget process can be for decision makers and stakeholders. For instance, requirements in federal law related to health care for the poor (Medicaid) have a dramatic impact on US state governments—most that have statutory or constitutional requirements to balance their budgets. Eligibility rules and matched funding requirements can (and do) constrain the ability of state government budgeters to spend for other services and programs.

The expenditures stream recognizes the significant difficulties in determining public spending categories and amounts. The result of decisions in this stream is the mix and level of goods and services provided by a government. Competition in this stream is extremely high. Budget actors strive to protect and expand their preferred goods and services. Many of the strategies that budget actors engage in this stream are reminiscent of Wildavsky's calculations discussed earlier regarding budgeting in the US federal government. According to Rubin, however, modern budgeting is characterized by strong efforts on the part of budget actors to "lock up" (2010, 157–164) expenditures—earmarking revenues, establishing entitlements, stipulating automatic increases—so as to reduce conflict and avoid having to compete for funding in the first place.

The balance stream considers the basic budgeting equation, in which revenues (should) equal expenditures. RTB recognizes that governments at all levels and around the world operate in constrained circumstances—a limited supply of revenues must support seemingly limitless demands for spending. The US federal government does not have a legal requirement to balance, though its credit downgrade in 2011 was a nod by some about the effects of runaway national borrowing. It is within the balance stream that conflict arises about the size and reach of government and the appropriateness of deficit spending. For example, in the following chapters, you will read about constitutional and statutory requirements that some national governments have put in place to promote budget balance or some deficit or debt reduction. Many of these rules have been unsuccessful in disciplining governments in terms of actually reaching balance. But the existence of these laws reflects the ongoing struggle in societies regarding the scope and impact of government. On the other hand, US state and local governments do have requirements to balance, as noted earlier.

These subnational governments are often referred to as "revenue driven," given that they technically cannot spend more than they bring in through pooled tax receipts, fees, charges, grants, and borrowed funds.

RTB wraps up the budgeting framework by including the implementation stream or budget execution. Once the budget is passed, the real work begins—that is, the spending of public funds for the conduct of government work. Just as every stream has constraints, in the form of budget actors, degrees of access, laws, rules, regulations, standard operating procedures, and traditions, this one also can be immediately and severely affected by changes in revenue forecasts, numbers served, and costs as well as cataclysmic events such as a hurricane, forest fire, drought, the outbreak of a disease, or any sort of international conflict. For example, the State of Louisiana's Revenue Estimating Conference indicated a reduction of $34.7 million in that state's fiscal 2014 budget because of changes in corporate income tax receipts during the year. In spite of the fact that Louisiana's Commissioner of Administration noted the ability to make up the deficit with other excess funds, the governor instituted a hiring freeze in certain executive agencies to account for the dip in revenues (Baker 2014).

Though Rubin points out that most budgets are implemented "as passed," with little deviation, the implementation stream hones in on the balance (or lack thereof) between control and discretion. In addition to any outside forces that can compromise budget execution, the degree of flexibility that the chief executive, department heads, program managers, and staff have for managing the flow of funds into and out of government also determines how smoothly the budget will be implemented.

Rubin's RTB comes close to being a comprehensive theory of public budgeting. It recognizes the special nature of the individual budget streams, the distinctive budget actors, and the complexity of circumstances and relationships within each, as well as the external factors that can easily divert a stream in midflow. Timing and nonlinearity are important components of this perspective. In Rubin's own words, "'real time' refers to the continual adjustment of decisions in each stream to decisions and information coming from other streams and from the environment" (2010, 283). Nonlinearity refers to the fact that the five streams do not flow into each other sequentially. Streams flow together at different times and for different periods of time. Budget actors in any stream may have to look forward, backward, or both into other decision streams to access the information that they need to make a decision.

BUDGET PRINCIPLES

It is hard to provide a definitive list of public budgeting principles that, if followed, will meet with budget success. However, Harold Smith (1944), director of the US Bureau of the Budget (now the Office of Management and Budget) from 1939 to 1946, determines the public budget to be "the very core of democratic government" (181) and discusses a number of budgetary precepts that should exist to promote democracy. His tenets span the work of the legislative and executive branches of government. Budget principles to support legislative control include publicity, clarity, comprehensiveness, unity, specification, prior authorization, periodicity, and accuracy (Smith 1944). Public budgeting should be conducted in the open (publicity). The information in the budget should be understandable (clarity). All revenues, expenditures, and debt for all that government does should be included in the budget (comprehensiveness). Government funds should flow through one general fund, with earmarked and special funds kept to a minimum (unity). Legislative appropriations should be specific, not overly broad (specification). Authorization to spend should be made before budget implementation (prior authorization). Spending should be confined to a specified period of time (periodicity). Revenue and expenditure estimates should be correct (accuracy).

On the executive side, Smith (1944) considers eight budget principles, including executive programming and responsibility, reporting, tools, procedures, executive discretion, flexibility in timing, and a "two-way budget organization" (184). The budget represents the chief executive's budget and policy agenda, representative of the government-wide work program (programming). The chief executive has the obligation to execute the budget as passed by the legislature (responsibility). The executive branch is responsible for full disclosure of the finances and flow of funds of government (reporting). The chief executive needs staff and authority to execute the budget and spend funds (tools). The executive branch should be allowed to budget differently for a variety of activities (capital versus operating; businesslike activities versus traditional government administration) (procedures). Some choice should be afforded to the executive branch in the conduct of government operations (discretion). The executive branch should be able to adjust the budget to accommodate changing circumstances (flexibility in timing). The final commandment regards a two-way budget organization and calls for budget offices within executive agencies along with a central or executive budget office. The flow of information should not be one-way from the central budget office to agencies, but also from agency budget offices to the central office. According to Smith, "budgeting is not only a central function but a process that should permeate the entire administration structure" (185).

Admittedly, it is difficult to reconcile some of these principles across the branches. The legislative commandments address traditional fears of an omnipotent monarchy and so press for strict control of the executive and the ability of this branch to make changes to what the legislature has decided. According to Smith (1944), the executive management tenets promote "the responsible executive who must be equipped to deal with the difficult political, economic and social problems of our time" (183). Smith further suggests that the principles themselves are "dynamic" and recognizes the budget "not as an incomprehensible book but as a living process of democratic policy formation and policy execution" (188). Important to modern budgeting, Smith's tenets do not include the role of the judiciary in making and changing budgets. A later chapter in this book considers how the courts influence government taxing, spending, and programming.

CONCLUSION

This chapter has introduced you to the living process that is public budgeting. Public budgets grow, decline, and change. There continues to be strong debate worldwide about the appropriate reach and impact of government on individuals, communities, and societies. Understanding public budgeting requires knowledge of the many things that are involved in the process and various components that constrain it. For example, considerations of revenue sources and their restrictions must be addressed along with any requirements for balance, if they exist. Theoretical frameworks for understanding public budgeting have evolved with the process itself to recognize the complexities of decisions and relationships among numerous budget actors in distinctive circumstances and across time. As you proceed, you should come to realize that understanding public budgeting requires talking with budgeters, reading budget documents, examining numbers, memos, and reports, examining government websites, following budgets as they develop in real time, making calculations and, most important, asking questions.

DISCUSSION QUESTIONS

1. Why do governments budget?

2. Consider the different definitions of "budget" presented in this chapter. Do you think any of the definitions are more important or relevant than others? Explain your answer.

3. What can you learn about a government by examining its budget?

4. Why is it difficult to compare the quality of public services provided by different governments using only expenditure data? How would you measure the quality of a government service?

5. Define and explain the differences between macro- and micro-budgeting. How do macro-budgeting decisions inform micro-budgeting ones? How do micro-budgeting decisions influence macro-budgeting ones?

6. Kingdon highlights visible and hidden clusters of actors involved in the budgeting process. Define the scope of each cluster and its respective influences on macro- and micro-budgeting.

7. How does public budgeting differ from private budgeting?

8. Explain what you consider to be most distinctive about the perspectives of Musgrave and Buchanan regarding government growth. Justify your response.

9. Explain why the development of normative and descriptive theories is important for understanding public budgeting. How do the budgeting theories discussed here inform your understanding of the process?

10. Consider Smith's budget principles for the legislative and executive branches of government. Are these commandments relevant for public budgeting today? Justify your ideas about principle relevancy and modern budgeting.

NOTES

1. Available at http://www.cia.gov/library/publications/the-world-factbook/index.html

2. In a classic debate about administrative responsibility and democratic accountability, Carl Friedrich (1940) and Herman Finer (1941) discussed

their opposing views of the appropriate checks on bureaucratic judgment. Friedrich considered that bureaucrats could be held in check through professional association. By virtue of the technical specialization required of work in public agencies, bureaucrats as professionals would be held accountable by fellow specialists. Finer believed such checks must come through institutions such as the courts, agencies themselves, or spelled out by legislative directive. Though regarding different concepts, Buchanan similarly called for institutional checks (rules) as a check on state behavior.

3. Gross national product includes gross domestic product and income earned by residents from overseas investments but excludes income earned within the domestic economy by overseas residents.

REFERENCES

Baker, D. 2014. "State Announces Strategic Plan After Adjustment of Revenue Forecast." State of Louisiana, *Department of Administration News*, January 15. Available at http://www.doa.louisiana.gov/doa/PressReleases/Strategic_Plan_after_Revenue_Forecast_Adjustment.htm

Baumgartner, F. R., and B. D. Jones. 1991. "Agenda Dynamics and Policy Subsystems." *Journal of Politics* 53 (4): 1044–1074.

Berry, W. D. 1990. "The Confusing Case of Budgetary Incrementalism: Too Many Meanings for a Single Concept." *Journal of Politics* 52 (1): 167–196.

Buchanan, J., and Musgrave, R. 1999. *Public Finance and Public Choice: Two Contrasting Visions of the State.* Cambridge, MA: MIT Press.

Finer, H. 1941. "Administrative Responsibility in Democratic Government." *Public Administration Review* 1 (4): 335–350.

Friedrich, C. J. 1940. "The Nature of Administrative Responsibility." *Public Policy* 1: 3–24.

Golembiewski, R. T., and Rabin, J., eds. 1983. *Public Budgeting and Finance: Behavioral, Theoretical, and Technical Perspectives,* 3rd ed. New York: Marcel Dekker.

International Monetary Fund. 2013. World Economic Outlook Database, April 2013. Available at https://www.imf.org/external/pubs/ft/weo/2013/01/weodata/index.aspx

Jones, B. D., J. L. True, and F. R. Baumgartner. 1997. "Does Incrementalism Stem from Political Consensus or from Institutional Gridlock?" *American Journal of Political Science* 41 (4): 1319–1339.

Kingdon, J. W. 1984. *Agendas, Alternatives, and Public Policies.* Boston: Little Brown.

_____. 1995. *Agendas, Alternatives, and Public Policies,* 2nd ed. New York: HarperCollins.

Lindblom, C. E. 1959. "The Science of 'Muddling Through.'" *Public Administration Review* 19 (2): 79–88.

Merriam-Webster Dictionary. 2013. Accessed on January 12, 2013. Available at http://www.merriam-webster.com/dictionary/budget

Rubin, I. S. 1990. "Budget Theory and Budget Practice: How Good the Fit?" *Public Administration Review* 50 (2): 179–189.

_____. 1993. "Who Invented Budgeting in the United States?" *Public Administration Review* 53 (5): 438–444.

_____. 2010. *The Politics of Public Budgeting*, 6th ed. Washington, DC: CQ Press.

Simon, H. A. 1957. *Models of Man.* New York: Wiley.

Smith, H. D. 1944. "The Budget as an Instrument of Legislative Control and Executive Management." *Public Administration Review* 4 (3): 181–188.

Thurmaier, K. M., and K. G. Willoughby. 2001. *Policy and Politics in State Budgeting.* Armonk, NY: M. E. Sharpe.

True, J. L. 1995. "Is the National Budget Controllable?" *Public Budgeting & Finance* 15 (2): 18–32.

Wildavsky, A. B. 1964. *The Politics of the Budgetary Process.* Boston: Little Brown.

_____. 1984. *The Politics of the Budgetary Process*, 4th ed. Boston: Little Brown.

Budget Foundations in Selected Countries

chapter
TWO

When it comes to classifying countries according to their level of development, there is no criterion (either grounded in theory or based on an objective benchmark) that is generally accepted.

—Lynge Nielsen, *Classifications of Countries Based on Their Level of Development: How It Is Done and How It Could Be Done*

LEARNING OBJECTIVES

After reading this chapter, you should be able to

- Understand various ways of measuring and categorizing level of development of different countries

- Distinguish ways scholars and others measure and compare budgeting systems of governments globally

- Compare governance structures and budgeting precepts of sample countries as provided through constitutions and budget laws

- Quantify the application of "rule of law" in a country

- Conduct your own investigation of constitutional budget provisions

- Find and access data and information about public budgeting as conducted in countries around the world

---

25

The previous chapter defined a budget, discussed characteristics of public versus private budgets, and presented several theories and various concepts to consider when studying government budgets. You should have some sense of the many decisions made and decision makers involved in the budgetary process as well as the nonlinear, eclectic manner in which budgets are developed. You have been exposed to two different economic perspectives regarding government size and function, and to a sample of government fiscal data that is available to you to conduct your own studies of government budgets.

This chapter will delve deeper into the foundations for budgeting in a select group of industrialized and developing countries that includes Australia, Brazil, Guatemala, India, Italy, and Tanzania. As noted in the first chapter, these countries were chosen as they represent different governance structures, fiscal capacities, and development status and are from regions all around the globe. The first part of the chapter considers how to distinguish emerging versus pioneer countries, then explains different ways to measure development status and makes a few comparisons. Next, various ways of comparing budgeting systems are described. Finally, the chapter describes constitutions and laws that influence the budgetary processes in the select countries that are considered throughout this book.

DEVELOPING VERSUS INDUSTRIALIZED COUNTRIES

Distinguishing countries according to level of development is a first step in making comparisons of their budgeting systems. Lynge Nielsen (2011) points out that there has been much research attempting to categorize countries along continuums of developing to industrialized, poor to rich, emerging to advanced, low-, middle-, to high-income, Third World to First World, and so on. In an attempt to come up with a better measure of levels of development, Nielsen examines development taxonomies created by the United Nations Development Programme (UNDP), the World Bank (WB), and the International Monetary Fund (IMF). The UNDP created its Human Development Index (HDI) which incorporates measures of longevity of life and attained educational and income levels.[1] The index is calculated by making within-country comparisons of actual values for these measures to maximum and minimum thresholds. HDI values fall between zero and one and the UNDP classifies countries as low, medium, high, or (more recently) very high in human development.

Table 2.1 presents the HDI for the countries of interest in this book. Comparing this index across countries suggests relatively high standards of living, on average, in Australia, Italy, and United States; reduced average life spans, educational and income levels in Brazil, lower still in Guatemala and India; with shortest average life spans and lowest educational and income levels, on average, evidenced in Tanzania. Table 2.1 also presents various governance indicators representative of levels of citizen freedoms, governmental effectiveness, and corruption in government. Australia and United States indicate the highest levels of

		Perceptions of Governance (as of 2011) Percentile Rank: 0 (lowest) to 100 (highest)		
	HDI 2012	Voice and Accountability[a]	Government Effectiveness[b]	Control of Corruption[c]
Australia	0.938	95.3	95.3	96.7
Brazil	0.730	63.8	55.5	63.0
Guatemala	0.581	36.2	28.0	36.5
India	0.554	59.2	54.5	35.1
Italy	0.881	74.6	66.4	57.3
Tanzania	0.467	45.5	36.5	36.0
United States	0.937	85.9	88.6	85.3

Table 2.1
Social Indicators: Selected Countries

Sources: Human Development Index (HDI): United Nations Development Programme, *Human Development Report 2013,* available at http://hdr.undp.org/en/media/HDR_2013_EN_complete.pdf Perceptions of Governance: The World Bank Group, *Worldwide Governance Indicators Project,* available at http://info.worldbank.org/governance/wgi/index.aspx#home

Notes: The Worldwide Governance Indicators (WGI) project defines perceptions of governance indices accordingly:
[a]*Voice and accountability* captures perceptions of the extent to which a country's citizens are able to participate in selecting their government, as well as citizens' freedom of expression, freedom of association, and a free media.
[b]*Government effectiveness* captures perceptions of the quality of public services, the quality of the civil service and the degree of its independence from political pressures, the quality of policy formulation and implementation, and the credibility of the government's commitment to such policies.
[c]*Control of corruption* captures perceptions of the extent to which public power is exercised for private gain, including both petty and grand forms of corruption, as well as power over the state by elites and private interests.
All definitions and information about other governance indices. Available at http://info.worldbank.org/governance/wgi/index.aspx#home

citizen freedoms, quality and effectiveness of government, and control of corruption. Italy and Brazil fall to a second tier on these measures, with Italy besting Brazil in voice, accountability, and government effectiveness and Brazil seemingly better than Italy at combating corruption. India, Tanzania, and Guatemala receive lower scores—Guatemala indicates the lowest scores of this group of countries regarding voice, accountability, and government effectiveness. India receives the lowest score regarding its ability to control corruption.

The WB and IMF have created indices for both operational (to qualify countries as developing for purposes of preferred borrowing and other resource support) and analytical (data collected from member countries for analysis, sharing, and dissemination) classification purposes. Also, these organizations use absolute rather than relative development thresholds—absolute or judgmental thresholds are chosen ones versus relative ones that are established based on observed data. By 2010, the UNDP and WB determined the share of countries worldwide designated as developed to be 25 and 26 percent, respectively, while the IMF share is 17 percent. All three organizations have established subcategories of the much larger share of developing countries, subcategories that span low- to middle-income or emerging (WB and IMF) and low-, medium-, or high–human development countries (UNDP). Nielsen (2011) claims there are problems with using absolute thresholds, the use of equal country weights for some indices, and lack of clarity in how categories of countries are determined, in some cases. Nielsen (2011) develops a more "data-driven" classification scheme that breaks down countries into three categories—lower, middle, and higher development countries—using relative thresholds and accounting for the "highly uneven" world population because "China and India account for more than a third of the world's total population" (32).

Table 2.2 presents the WB 2012 classifications by level of income of the selected countries of interest in this book. The GNI is gross national income that the WB calculates by summing production within country, accounting for relevant taxes, and determined income from outside the country, dividing by mid-year population, and then converting the measure from the country's national currency to US dollars.[2] Notice that the proportion of countries defined as developed (high income) by the WB has increased from 26 percent in 2010 to 35 percent by 2012. Each category of income level is represented by at least one country of interest here. Australia, Italy, and United States are classified by the WB as high income (developed). The rest are classified as developing countries

Table 2.2
World Bank Classification of Countries by GNI Per Capita*

World Bank Classification	GNI per capita in US $	# of Countries Meeting WB Classification	% of Countries by WB Classification	Countries of Interest by WB Classification
High Income	>$12,615	76	35.3	Australia, Italy, United States
Upper Middle Income	$4,086–$12,615	55	25.6	Brazil
Lower Middle Income	$1,036–$4,085	48	22.3	Guatemala, India
Low Income	<= $1,035	36	16.7	Tanzania
Total Countries Examined		**215**	**100.0**	

Source: The World Bank, *A Short History.* Accessed on August 30, 2013; historical classifications in Excel format available for download at http://data.worldbank.org/about/country-classifications/a-short-history

*GNI is gross national income, converted to US dollars using the World Bank Atlas method. More information about the calculation of this measure is available at http://data.worldbank.org/indicator/NY.GNP.PCAP.CD

by the WB, Brazil as upper middle income, Guatemala and India as lower middle income, and Tanzania as low income. Although 65 percent of countries are categorized by the WB as developing, by 2012, less than one fifth (~17 percent) are classified with Tanzania as low income.

Table 2.3 presents several economic indicators that measure national production, government size, level of debt and trade balances; these measures offer additional means for comparing the countries of interest. The data for this table is from the IMF World Economic Outlook Database (October 2013), which provides the most recent information collected for each country, by measure and year. It is important to understand that some data for 2012 may be estimated by IMF staff based on information from previous years. All measures for years 2013 and 2014 are estimates provided by IMF staff. At the bottom of this table, countries are listed from highest to lowest in value for each measure, using 2014 estimates.

Table 2.3

Selected Economic and Government Indicators, by Country and Across Years

	GDP, Constant Prices, % Change			GDP Based on PPP, Per Capita*			General Government Revenues, % GDP			General Government Total Expenditures, % GDP			General Government Gross Debt, % GDP			Current Account Balance, % GDP		
	2012	2013	2014	2012	2013	2014	2012	2013	2014	2012	2013	2014	2012	2013	2014	2012	2013	2014
Australia	3.7	2.5	2.8	41,954	43,042	44,406	33.3	33.9	34.4	37.1	37.0	36.7	27.9	29.1	29.2	−3.7	−3.4	−3.5
Brazil	0.9	2.5	2.5	11,747	12,118	12,528	37.7	37.0	37.0	40.4	40.0	40.2	68.0	68.3	69.0	−2.4	−3.4	−3.2
Guatemala	3.0	3.3	3.4	5,153	5,265	5,398	11.7	12.1	12.3	14.1	14.3	14.6	24.4	24.9	25.7	−2.9	−2.9	−2.9
India	3.2	3.8	5.1	3,843	3,991	4,209	19.4	19.6	19.7	27.3	28.0	28.2	66.7	67.2	68.1	−4.8	−4.4	−3.8
Italy	−2.4	−1.8	0.7	29,812	29,598	30,218	47.7	47.9	48.0	50.6	51.1	50.0	127.0	132.3	133.1	−0.7	0.0	0.2
Tanzania	6.9	7.0	7.2	1,627	1,713	1,812	21.9	23.0	23.5	26.9	28.4	28.0	40.8	42.5	43.6	−15.3	−14.9	−14.1
United States	2.8	1.6	2.6	51,704	52,839	54,609	30.4	32.5	33.0	38.8	38.3	37.7	102.7	106.0	107.3	−2.7	−2.7	−2.8

Countries Listed Highest to Lowest by Measure, 2014 Estimate

	GDP, Constant Prices, % Change	GDP Based on PPP, Per Capita*	General Government Revenues, % GDP	General Government Total Expenditures, % GDP	General Government Gross Debt, % GDP	Current Account Balance, % GDP
Highest	Tanzania	United States	Italy	Italy	Italy	<Tanzania>**
	India	Australia	Brazil	Brazil	United States	<India>
	Guatemala	Italy	Australia	United States	Brazil	<Australia>
	Australia	Brazil	United States	Australia	India	<Brazil>
	United States	Guatemala	Tanzania	India	Tanzania	<Guatemala>
	Brazil	India	India	Tanzania	Australia	<United States>
Lowest	Italy	Tanzania	Guatemala	Guatemala	Guatemala	Italy

Source: The International Monetary Fund, World Economic Outlook Database, October 2013. Available at http://www.imf.org/external/pubs/ft/weo/2013/02/weodata/index.aspx. Report generated for each measure, by country and year.

*Gross domestic product based on purchasing power parity (PPP), per capita, in current international dollars. Information about the calculation of this measure is available at http://data.worldbank.org/indicator/NY.GDP.PCAP.PP.CD
**<Brackets> indicate current account balance deficit.

Note: Figures for 2012 may be IMF staff estimates, depending upon latest data availability for specific country. Figures for 2013 and 2014 all are IMF staff estimates.

Examining the measures separately would present an incomplete comparison of national capacity among this group of countries. For example, if an annual change in GDP (constant prices) from 3 to 5 percent is considered a stable, growing economy, it seems that Tanzania, India, and Guatemala are beating out all other countries in their production. But we would want to dig deeper to understand these numbers. Specifically, what is the nature of production in each country? Services as a percent of total GDP predominate in the United States and Australia, whereas agricultural production predominates in Tanzania (gold mining). India's economy is mixed, heavily in services and industry with a strong dose of agricultural production. Brazil's economy is service and industrial based; Italy and Guatemala have economies heavily dependent on their respective service and agricultural production. A country's chief means of production influences how quickly and well it can respond to global financial upswings and downturns. Many countries with economies heavily dependent on service production have suffered the most from the recent Great Recession that officially began in December, 2007 and ended in June, 2009 (National Bureau of Economic Research 2012). This might explain the slower-growth countries in this group.

The second measure, GDP per capita, is considered an indicator of national prosperity or standard of living. All the industrialized nations in this select group indicate higher standards of living than developing ones. Still, compare how the countries stack up for this measure with how they rank using the HDI. What might explain any differences?

Remember from the first chapter that government revenues and expenditures per capita offer evidence of the size of government vis-à-vis the nation's economy. Among this group of countries, Italy's government has the largest presence in its economy; Brazil, the United States, and Australia are next. The smallest governments in terms of size as measured here include Guatemala, Tanzania, and India. The debt to GDP measure shows us that of this group of countries, Italy has the highest level of debt and Guatemala has the lowest. Although this measure allows you to compare debt levels across countries, it is difficult to determine how much debt is too much. Researchers with the National Bureau of Economic Research (NBER) have labeled the decade from the onset of the Great Recession in December, 2007 to 2017 as the "decade of debt" (Reinhart and Rogoff, 2011, 3). Surges in debt are to be expected with international conflict (war), banking crises, and with the drops in government revenues from taxes and the attendant increased spending needs that come with recessionary periods.

Carmen Reinhart and Kenneth Rogoff (2011) compare the cumulative increase in real public debt of selected countries from 2007 to 2010, finding the crisis countries' average increases to equal 88 percent (includes United States, Greece, and Iceland, among others) while the average for other selected countries equals 65 percent (includes Australia, Brazil, Germany, Japan, and India, among others). They explain that high public debt levels contribute to slower growth, negatively affecting government ability to react well to future fiscal shocks.

Current account balance as a percent of GDP measures a nation's balance of payments on goods and services (imports and exports), and includes transfer payments. Measures here indicate that most countries have a negative trade balance; Italy is the lone country to have a positive trade balance. Italy is a member of the European Union (EU),[3] and one explanation for the positive balance might be that transfer payments from the EU may be pushing this country's current account balance into the black.

COMPARING BUDGETING SYSTEMS

In their research about public financial systems around the world, Martin Cihak et al. (2012) explain that well-functioning systems can advance long-run economic growth. Their results indicate that strong public financial systems can make up for market imperfections—transaction costs, externalities, imperfect information, and the often murky preferences of individuals. Cihak et al. (2012) measure and study financial institutions and markets in a range of high-, middle-, and low-income countries around the world and determine that these systems are multidimensional (no one variable can be used to fully define or compare systems). They find that vast differences exist in system capacities across regions and income groups, and there are wide disparities across countries and within regions.

In fact, studies about budgeting in developing countries, in particular, tease out that political concerns overshadow economic ones for budgeting to be conducted successfully. That is, effective public finance and budgeting rests on establishing government legitimacy—at a basic level, this means establishing consent of the governed through political institutions such as a federal republic or constitutional democracy. James Boyce and Madalene O'Donnell (2007) discuss the importance of understanding a country's political and legal histories in order to gain insight into their budget processes; their economies and cultures have an impact on the mix of public resources used and expenditures rendered.

Naomi Caiden (2009) explains that in postwar countries especially, but also in developing countries generally, corruption, nepotism, and cronyism severely compromise transparency, accountability, and control—the last three concepts being recognized principles vital for effective budgeting (see also, Caiden and Wildavsky 2003).

George Guess and Lance LeLoup (2010) examine budgeting in a number of different countries and develop a framework for comparison that includes the size and wealth of a nation, centralization of authority, legal and political institutions, and the budget and policy contexts. These scholars use financial indicators that quantify country wealth, as well as the size of the public sector, public debt, and social expenditures. They distinguish between presidential and parliamentary systems; coalition, majority party, and single-party regimes; and unified and divided government. They reference the Government Finance Officers Association (GFOA) principles of budgeting to define budget systems—including relationships among budget guardians and spending advocates, centralization or decentralization of processes, budget fragmentation, and intergovernmental fiscal relationships (Guess and LeLoup 2010). They round out their comparative framework by outlining a number of policy issues that challenge modern public budgets—sustaining social security and pension systems; providing for health and welfare services while controlling costs; national defense; energy, natural resources, and climate change; taxation; government ownership, privatization and intervention in the economy; and agriculture policy and trade.

A. Premchand (1999) discusses budgeting in Australia, New Zealand, the United Kingdom, and the United States, distinguishing countries along a continuum from those with strong to weak legislative branches in terms of their roles in budget making and approval. Some, like the United States and Italy, have strong legislative bodies that react to executively developed budgets; these bodies might even create their own budgets that the president may sign or veto. Legislative budgetary powers are weaker in countries with parliamentary or Westminster systems. These systems exist in slightly different forms in Australia, Canada, New Zealand, and the United Kingdom—the executive branch is responsible for budget development and execution and the legislature (or Parliament) is responsible for passing appropriations, with responsibility for evaluating and auditing public spending. Legislatures in other countries have unique foci as well. In France, the legislature concentrates on new spending over the continuation budget. Countries like Germany, Norway, Finland, Denmark, and Japan use a medium-term framework (MTEF) or investment budgets that force a multiyear budget orientation.[4] In countries like China, the legislative branch (People's Congress) is not powerful and there are others in which budgets are issued "through royal decrees and the public has little access to them" (Premchand 1999, 86).

Charles Menifield (2011) compiles case analyses of budget histories and practices in eighteen countries around the world, representing the North and South Americas, Africa, Asia, Europe, and the Middle East. This author concludes that Wildavsky's institutional model (2002) together with Rubin's real-time budgeting perspective (2010) are both useful frameworks for understanding and comparing public budgeting systems around the world. Although political institutions are important, culture determines how successful budgeting will be in any particular country. Menifield acknowledges that the technical aspects of public budgeting, such as modern attempts to move to accrual accounting[5] and to engage in performance budgeting[6] are ubiquitous. Still, the manner in which these types of techniques are implemented is determined more by culture and human behavior than by adherence to formally established rules and regulations. A culture of corruption, for example, may not be able to be overcome with the establishment of sound budget principles through constitutional amendment, legislation, regulations, or standard operating procedures.

The very complexity of public budgeting systems around the world is related to the fact that the framework for any particular system may be established solely in a nation's constitution or through a mix of constitutionally specified requirements, laws, agreements, executive mandates, administrative rules, or regulations. Some countries only have constitutionally determined budget systems. Others have established their budgeting systems through their constitutions and also by way of organic laws—these are higher-order laws that require super majorities or even unanimity among legislators and in both houses for passage. Some countries, like the United States, have systems with frameworks spelled out in a constitution but also requirements and timelines established in regular laws, executive mandates, standard operating procedures, administrative rules, or regulations. Many budget system requirements, often those established by law, lack specificity, thereby opening up the process to interpretation. Just because a process is framed by law does not mean that it is implemented according to the letter of the law. Also, no matter how a public budgeting framework may be initially prescribed and even installed, the systems and budgets that result from such frameworks evolve over time. It is for this reason that Ian Lienert and Israel Fainboim (2010) explain the impossibility of formulating model budget law or of pointing to any nation or nations as engaging the best budget laws, framework, or system.

The following section examines the legal foundations for budgeting in the select group of countries that includes

- Australia
- Brazil
- Guatemala
- India
- Italy
- Tanzania

Constitutional and statutory law regarding budgeting in the United States will be considered in chapter 3. For each of these other countries, we present a brief description of the current governmental structure and legal system as practiced and then review constitutional provisions. Significant budget system framework components are explained as related to these few countries. The comparison of budgeting systems among these countries is interesting, given their distinctive histories, political structures, cultures, and resources. Keep in mind, though, that none of these countries (or the United States) have systems that can be termed best, ideal, or even model.

Each section ends with assessment of the country's level of adherence to rule of law as determined by the World Justice Project (WJP). The WJP measures the degree to which rule of law operates effectively in surveyed countries. The WJP is a research effort that couples survey data from a sample of people from the three largest cities in a country, with survey data of experts on the laws, criminal justice system, and public health of the country to quantify the degree to which national governments ascribe to a rule of law. The WJP is premised on the vitality of laws to the successful functioning of governance and for economic and social advancement of a society. WJP (2014) applies four universal principles regarding the rule of law:

1. Government and its officials and agents, individuals, private and other entities are accountable under the law.

2. Laws are clear, public, stable and just; evenly applied; and protect individual rights, property and person.

3. The enactment, administration and enforcement of laws are public, fair and efficient.

4. Justice is delivered without undue delay by proficient, ethical, independent and neutral representatives of their communities; are of sufficient number and have adequate resources to conduct this work. (4)

The WJP (2014) has developed 47 measures to quantify the following dimensions of rule of law:

- The extent to which government officials are held accountable for their decisions and actions

- The absence of corruption, defined as use of public power for private gain that includes bribery and the misappropriation of funds

- The degree to which laws are publically developed, publicized, and exposed through open public meetings

- The advancement of fundamental rights, many that are articulated in constitutions such as equality and equal protection under the law; due process; right to life and security of person and property; freedom of opinion, expression, belief, and religion; right of privacy; freedom of assembly; this measure also considers labor rights such as right to collective bargaining, the prohibition of forced labor, and discrimination

- Order and security including level of crime, degree of political unrest, and socially acceptable ways of seeking conflict resolution

- Regulatory enforcement free from corruption, effectively enforced, with due process in administrative proceedings and just compensation with government expropriation

- Impartial, accessible, and affordable civil and criminal justice, free of discrimination and corruption; includes alternative dispute resolution

- Corruption-free, public, fair, and efficient informal justice which refers to customary law often applied in rural areas of various countries as well as law based on culture and tradition

In its most recent study of rule of law in 99 countries, the WJP (2014) found criminal justice declining worldwide with twenty countries indicating appreciable decline in their scores for this measure from last year; no country indicated appreciable improvement in criminal justice from last year. On the other hand, twenty-five countries indicate measurable improvement in order and security and only seven had scores for this measure that decreased from last year. Overall, the WJP found that four factors improved, on average (absence of corruption, open government, order and security, and regulatory enforcement), while four became worse (constraints on government powers, fundamental rights, civil justice, and criminal justice). The WJP does examine informal justice, but does not include these scores in global assessments or when calculating the rule of law index. Scores of the rule of law index by country ranged from 0.88 (Denmark and Norway) to 0.31 (Venezuela). Figure 2.1 presents rankings of best to worst performers in the WJP index that include the countries of interest in this book. Generally, industrialized countries and those with higher scores on HDI (from Table 2.1) have higher scores for rule of law.

Figure 2.1
World Justice Project Rule of Law Index and Rank, by Country

Best Performers / Worst Performers	Rank	Country	WJP Index
	1	Denmark	0.88
	2	Norway	
	8	Australia	0.80
	9	Germany	
	19	United States	0.71
	29	Italy	0.63
	42	Brazil	0.54
	43	Senegal	
	64	El Salvador	0.48
	65	Vietnam	
	66	India	
	67	Dominican Republic	0.47
	68	Ukraine	
	69	Tanzania	
	70	Zambia	
	71	Kazakhstan	
	82	Iran	0.44
	83	Guatemala	
	84	Sierra Leone	
	99	Venezuela	0.31

Source: The World Justice Project, "WJP Rule of Law Index 2014." Washington, DC. Available at http://worldjusticeproject.org/

Australia

Australia is a federated constitutional monarchy, one of sixteen sovereign states that comprise the Commonwealth realm. Made up of six states and ten territories, Australia realized independence from the United Kingdom's federation of colonies in January, 1901, the Australian Constitution having been drawn up in the previous year. As part of the realm, Australia's chief of state is England's Queen Elizabeth (referred to as Queen of Australia, Elizabeth II) though the governor-general serves in this capacity as the Queen's representative. The leader of the majority party or coalition in parliament serves as the head of government.[7] The prime minister recommends the governor-general, who is formally appointed by the monarch. Parliament is composed of a Senate (76 members) and a House of Representatives (150 members). Australia's Senate is directly elected, which is not the case in other Westminster systems. Within the executive branch, a cabinet is formally appointed by the governor-general upon recommendation by the prime minister; cabinet members are also appointed as members of parliament. Like the United States, Australia engages a common law legal system based on the English model.[8]

The Commonwealth of Australia Constitution Act (July 1900) establishes the powers, duties of, and relationships among the three branches of government; stipulates elections, membership, and salaries of public officials and chamber members; and specifies taxation and appropriation bill responsibilities. (According to this constitution, "proposed laws appropriating revenue or moneys, or imposing taxation, shall not originate in the Senate.") Policies related to Commonwealth finances found in the constitution include the creation of the nation's Consolidated Revenue Fund and the statement, "no money shall be drawn from the Treasury of the Commonwealth except under appropriation made by law." The constitution ascribes to the states revenue from the Commonwealth resulting from the imposition of taxes, financial assistance, and auditing requirements of such funds. Trade among the states is outlined as well. Chapter 5 of Australia's Constitution saves the power of state constitutions, legislatures and laws, although "when a law of a State is inconsistent with a law of the Commonwealth, the latter shall prevail, and the former shall, to the extent of the inconsistency, be invalid."

As with other Westminster systems, Australia's budgetary authority is concentrated in the hands of the prime minister and members of the cabinet; the parliament does not have budget powers equal to the United States Congress.

Executive authority determines public revenues and expenditures while the parliament most often approves the executive budget as is (Blöndal et al. 2008). The budget powers of Australia's Parliament are limited by constitutional strictures, political traditions, a strong two-party system, and because relatively few budget expenditures are submitted to the annual budget process (80 percent of total budget expenditures are special or permanent and not considered annually).

Australia's budget process has evolved since the first issue of the Budget Reform White Paper in 1984. Jón Blöndal and colleagues (2008) outline the transition from early reforms to limit central directives and improve administrative flexibility to the adoption of MTEF outlooks and an improved cabinet committee process. Additional reforms include the adoption of an accrual accounting basis for budgeting, the passage of the Australian Charter of Budget Honesty Act (1998) and, more recently, a fiscal transparency and accountability platform coined "Operation Sunlight."

Institutional Authority: Executive Leads, Parliament Follows   Two cabinet committees with overlapping membership have significant budget roles—the Pre-budget Expenditure Review Committee[9] (Pre-ERC) and the Expenditure Review Committee (ERC). The deputy prime minister and the treasurer chair the Pre-ERC and relevant cabinet members attend meetings. This committee sets strategic direction for the government through the budget and makes recommendations regarding budget management in periods of economic improvement or decline (Blöndel et al. 2008). The deputy prime minister and treasurer also chair the ERC which makes budget trade-off decisions, such as which ministerial proposals will receive funding and the amounts each will receive. Both committees serve as guardians of the public purse—the Pre-ERC through its budget management orientation across changing economies and the ERC by maintaining a conservative spending approach and a sense of fiscal stewardship (10).

Constitutional parameters prohibit the Australian Parliament from proposing new expenditure during the budget process, hindering this body from anything more than the approval of or reductions to executive proposals. Blöndel and colleagues (2008) point out that political precedent and historical party discipline in Australia limit the likelihood of amendments to proposed budgets. Westminster protocol considers such amendments to be a vote of no-confidence in the existing government.

Accrual Output Budgeting, the Charter of 1998, and Operation Sunlight The 1990s brought substantial changes to Australia's budgetary framework including a shift from cash basis of accounting to accrual output budgeting. The accrual output budgeting framework created a market-like structure in which the central government acts as a purchaser of goods and services from its ministerial departments. Acting as "quasi-independent businesses," each department records central government funds received as a revenue transaction and maintains a balance sheet (Robinson 2002, 81). Each department's profit-and-loss results serve as strategic performance measures. Such measurement has opened up the spending process, making it easier to hold departments accountable for budget-related performance.

Following the change to accrual output budgeting, parliament passed the Charter of Budget Honesty Act in 1998. This law presented a framework in which national fiscal policy was to be conducted and prescribed the accomplishment of two goals—development of a national fiscal strategy and oversight of the strategy through reporting. Principles of sound fiscal management[10] articulated in the Act include

1. A requirement to manage the Commonwealth's financial risks and maintain general government debt "prudently"
2. An assurance that national fiscal policy supports achievement of sufficient national savings and moderate cyclical change in economic activity
3. Pursuit of taxing and spending policies consistent with stability and predictability in resulting tax burdens
4. Maintenance of a reliable and honest tax system
5. Recognition of the long term effects of national policy decisions

The law requires some extensive reporting throughout the year, including an *Economic and Fiscal Outlook, Mid-Year Economic and Fiscal Outlook*, and *Final Budget Outcome Report*. It also requires a report at least ten days prior to calling of elections (*Pre-Election Economic and Fiscal Outlook*) and another at least every five years that examines the fiscal sustainability of current policy (*Intergenerational Report*).

Additional tenets to the Charter are included in the 2006 release of "Operation Sunlight-Enhancing Budget Transparency," which outlines Australia's reform to bolster budget and financial management transparency and encourage good governance practices.[11] Broad objectives of the platform include pressing for a "results orientation" and long-term perspective, improving budget clarity, readability, and the transparency of estimates, and expanding the reach of budget reporting (Tanner 2008).

According to the WJP, Australia ranks eighth best in terms of adherence to rule of law. Of all nations examined in this book, Australia ranks highest on all dimensions measuring observance of the rule of law. Its rankings for all measures fall within the top 15 worldwide of all 99 countries surveyed. It ranked highest for regulatory enforcement (7), then constraints on government powers (8) and absence of corruption (8). Australia received its lowest ranking from WJP for order and security (14) with rankings for the rest of the dimensions (open government, fundamental rights, civil and criminal justice) falling between the highest and lowest ranked ones. The WJP indicates that corruption in this country is minimal; Australia does well in protecting fundamental rights, though it falters when compared to other high-income countries regarding equal treatment under the law, mostly related to immigrants and the poor (World Justice Project 2014).

Brazil

Brazil is a federal republic, having declared independence from Portugal in 1822. Brazil currently operates under its 1988 constitution. Within the Brazilian federal framework, power is divided between the central government, 26 states, and one federal district. The president serves as chief of state and head of government; the president and vice president are elected on the same ticket. The president appoints the cabinet. Brazil engages a legal system based on civil law; in 2002, new civil law code replaced that from 1916.[12]

Brazil's Constitution is highly detailed, listing expansive social policy objectives of government. It presents the country's self-governing framework, outlining the powers, duties, and relationships of the different branches of government, the election of public officials, and the development and maintenance of a national military. The constitution articulates Brazilian rights and freedoms, specifying those related to education, health, food, work, housing, leisure, public safety, and security, and even "protection of motherhood and childhood." The document delineates the organization and public administration of the Union as well as those of the states and municipalities. Subnational governments are governed by the constitution, though states have "powers not prohibited to them" by it, whereas municipalities are governed by organic law. This constitution indicates ability of each level of government to raise revenues, with the attendant responsibilities associated with accountability, transparency, and timeliness of budgeting by these governments. Brazil's Constitution establishes a national tax system and presents principles of economic order as well as national policies associated with urban development; agriculture and land reform; and social welfare, including education, health, social security, the environment, national and regional cultures, sports, science and technology, and the media. A section of the document relates expectations of public budgets and budgeting standards.

Marcus Melo, Carlos Pereira, and Saulo Souza (2010) explain Brazil's political power balance between the executive and legislature, given the propensity for "multi-party presidential regimes where coalition governments are formed for purposes of post-election bargaining" (3). Prior to the push toward a more democratic system of government in the mid-1980s, budget authority in Brazil was concentrated in the presidency with congressional action a proverbial rubber stamp on executive proposals. The 1988 constitution sought enhanced budgetary authority in Brazil's bicameral Congress, an 81-member Senate and 531-member House of Representatives. For example, on the one hand, constitutional law provides that it is the prerogative of the Senate to determine the debt limits of states and municipalities and to approve international financial operations. Such law also articulates the role of the House in supervising revenues collected from the polity.[13] On the other hand, in most of the 13 Latin American countries studied by Teresa Curristine and Maria Bas (2007), budget powers of the executive are stronger than legislative ones. Brazil's Constitution includes numerous sections that frame budget responsibilities among the three branches of government as well as mandate government spending at all levels; collectively these constrain legislative budgetary powers. The constitution also restricts government borrowing, which cannot exceed spending for capital (Lienert and Fainboim 2010).

Power leans to the executive in other ways. For example, continuity across executive administrations is bolstered through the Plano Pluri-Annual (PPA), a strategic four-year fiscal plan. In the first year of office, a new president applies the fourth year of the PPA from the previous administration and then prepares a new four-year plan that will overlap with the subsequent administration. Also, Brazil's Congress approves its budget at the subprogram level, which is the highest level of detail of all the Latin American countries indicated in the study by Curristine and Bas (2007). This provides some flexibility in spending to the executive. Brazil's Congress is restricted in the changes it can make to the president's budget proposal—it can reallocate funding only if there is no net change in total deficit or surplus results (2007). Also, although the Congress generates an excessive number of amendments to proposed budgets (compared to other Latin American legislatures), these reflect efforts by the Brazilian Congress to make decisions about supplementary funds, or are amendments developed by coalitions of different party members to enhance the regional impact of outputs. Total spending affected by the numerous amendments is really quite small—no more than 5 percent. Brazil's chief executive has both the line-item and package veto powers. Especially compared to the Guatemalan legislature, which we will examine in the next section, Brazil's is relatively weak vis-à-vis the president in terms of budget powers and determining final budget numbers.

Brazil's Constitution and its organic and annual budget laws and regulations collectively determine budget roles, the budget timeline (annual), budget form and structure, budget formulation and execution, and stipulations related to independent auditing of government accounts. Law No. 4320, 1964 and the Fiscal Responsibility Law No. 101, 2000 are both organic laws that cannot be modified by lower-order or ordinary laws. These laws are efforts to enforce constitutional directives. Law No. 4320 established financial and accounting standards for all levels of government in Brazil and the Federal District (the nation's capital), as well as budget development, management accountability, and financial and budget reporting requirements. The law spells out required financial statements (balance sheet, statement of financial performance, statement of cash performance, and budgetary statement) but is not explicit about the accounting basis. The 2000 law tweaks some parts of the 1964 law (Vieira, 2011). The Fiscal Responsibility Law applies budgetary constraints at all levels of government, provides for the exclusive right of the federal government to determine debt and expenditure limits, and expressly prohibits federal financing of state governments. The law instructs that enforcement of its provisions be managed by Brazil's Federal Court of Accounts (Tribunal de Contas da União). The Court is charged to act preemptively to warn subnational governments as they approach legally prescribed debt and expenditure limits as well as to identify any infringement on program cost and results compliance issues.[14] Budget guidelines that set the stage for passing Brazil's budget are established in annual rather than organic law.

According to the WJP, Brazil ranks 42nd out of 99 countries in terms of adherence to rule of law. It received its best ranking for constraints on government powers (32), then fundamental rights (35) and open government (36). Brazil received its lowest rankings for order and security (71), and its criminal (69) and then civil justice systems (50). Regulatory enforcement (39) and absence of corruption (45) are ranked within the best and worst ranked dimensions. The WPJ finds Brazil to be the third-best performer of adherence to rule of law in its region, behind Chile and Uruguay. Its governance system adequately constrains executive power and fundamental rights are upheld. High crime rates contribute to its low ranking for order and security; its criminal justice system has numerous problems, poor capacity for criminal investigations, adjudication and due process, and inadequate correctional facilities. Government corruption in this country remains problematic (World Justice Project 2014).

Guatemala

Guatemala is a constitutional democratic republic, realizing independence from Spain in September, 1821. Guatemala currently operates under its constitution originating on May, 1985, and effective in 1986.[15] In 1993, this constitution was suspended, reinstated, and then amended. Within the republic, power is divided between the central government and 22 departments, subnational governmental entities similar to provinces that are further divided into municipalities. The president serves as chief of state and head of government; the president and vice president are elected on the same ticket. Legislative powers are vested in a unicameral Congress in which 158 members are elected by party via a proportional representative system.[16] Like Brazil, Guatemala engages a legal system based on civil law.

Like Brazil, the Guatemalan Constitution promises a wide range of social rights including the equality of children, recognizes the importance of maternity and adoption, and government responsibility to "take measures of prevention, treatment and rehabilitation" to combat "alcoholism, drug abuse and other causes of family disintegration." Also, constitutional provisions specify government expenditure for education (including "religious education without discrimination"), sports and physical education, and social programs regarding the health, safety, and welfare of citizens, stipulating that "the health of the inhabitants of the Nation is a public good."[17] Regarding sport, the document states that "custodial assignment will go no less than three percent of the general budget of the State Revenue." In this assignment, "50 percent will go to federated sport sector through its governing bodies; 20 percent to physical education, school sports and recreation, and 25 percent to the sport not federated." Policy related to indigenous communities is included in one section; later in the document bilingual education services are expressed as preferred "in schools located in areas of predominantly indigenous population." Guatemala's Constitution also specifies the establishment, responsibilities, and budgets of public universities. The document outlines individual rights to work as well as the rights of state workers. It recognizes municipalities as autonomous entities, with the power to elect their own government officials, collect and manage their own resources, and attend to public services. The constitution directs that the central government manage the "national economy to achieve the use of natural resources and human potential, to increase wealth and pursue full employment and fair distribution of national income."

Following thirty years of internal warfare, democratic governance was established in Guatemala with the constitution as described and the election of a president in 1985. A recurring theme of the Guatemalan Constitution is the protection of the citizenry against overreach by the state. Boyce and O'Donnell (2007) point out that the Guatemalan Constitution is much stricter than those of other Latin American countries regarding the government's ability to tax; taxes must be "fair and just" and "structured according to the capacity to pay" (101). In fact, the revenue-raising ability of the Guatemalan government is restricted and hinders policy execution.

In 1996, then President Alvaro Arzu successfully brokered an agreement with the guerrillas (Guatemala National Revolutionary Unity or GNRU) to pursue a commitment to peace (Boyce and O'Donnell 2007). This peace agreement followed a dozen others negotiated between 1994 and 1996 which collectively present a framework for state building in the aftermath of sustained in-country warfare. The accords establish timetables to reach and maintain peace. They also present policy directions regarding human rights, the legal recognition and resettlement of specified communities, constitutional reforms, and electoral processes. At the time, costs to carry out accord directives were estimated to reach 2.6 billion in United States dollars, 30 percent to be covered by the Guatemalan government and 70 percent to be covered by external, international organizations. The ambitiousness of the accords is evidenced by the policies expressed in them that require

- A focus on building up Guatemala's human capital—the social, educational, health and welfare of its people
- Establishing a "fair, equitable and progressive" tax system
- Meeting clear targets for government revenue and expenditure (Boyce and O'Donnell 2007)

A combination of constitutional provisions, organic and annual budget laws, and regulations provide the legal framework for the Guatemalan budget process and the responsibilities of the executive and legislature. This includes the organic budget law passed in 1997. According to Curristine and Bas (2007), the Guatemalan legislature approves budget appropriations in more detail than does Brazil. Also, of the thirteen countries they studied, Guatemala is the only one in which there are no restrictions on the ability of its legislature to change the executive budget proposal. Still, these scholars explain that, realistically, the Guatemalan legislature makes few changes to the president's budget as the proportion of spending in the budget affected by such changes is below 5 percent (like in Brazil). Brazil and Guatemala both claim legislatures with strong legal powers to influence the budget—Guatemala indicates that actual legislative powers equal legal ones, whereas in Brazil, the actual powers of the Congress trail its legal ones.

In Guatemala, the president does not have a line item veto power, but is able to veto the entire budget as passed. There are some limited restrictions on the ability of the president to make changes to the budget once passed, though legislative approval varies depending on the requested change. Unlike Brazil, which has fiscal rules limiting debt and annual deficits (or surpluses), Guatemala has no such rules. But both Brazil and Guatemala have legal requirements to engage MTEF.

Guatemala's government adopted subsequent law realigning original revenue and expenditure targets to accommodate more feasible timelines. Also, successive legislatures and presidential administrations have pushed for a tax system that could adequately support the ambitious priorities of the Peace Accords as well as meet constitutional edicts for fairness. This developing country continues to grapple with significant problems, however, including a substantial black market, lax or crooked tax administration, a culture of tax evasion, and ongoing violence related to gangs and the drug trade within and across its borders (Boyce and O'Donnell 2007). To combat recent violence, for example, the 2013 budget passed by the Congress hiked defense spending by 23 percent from the previous year, though citizens have questioned this strategy (McDonald, 2012).

According to the WJP, Guatemala ranks 83rd out of 99 countries in terms of adherence to rule of law, the lowest ranking of the countries examined here. It received its best ranking for open government (57) and respect for fundamental rights (57), then constraints on government powers (59). Still, rankings for the rest of the dimensions that measure observance of the rule of law are dismal. Absence of corruption (76) and regulatory enforcement (85) fall between this country's best and worst rankings. Order and security is ranked 92 of 99; Guatemala's civil and criminal justice systems were each ranked 93. Guatemala scores in the lower half of other Latin American countries on most of the rule of law measures. Although the country indicates respect for fundamental rights and scores well on government accountability, its civil and criminal justice systems have low capacity, and security in Guatemala is further compromised by a high level of government corruption (World Justice Project 2014).

India

India is a federal republic, a union of twenty-eight states and seven territories. India declared independence from the United Kingdom in August, 1947. The country operates under a constitution that has been amended many times since inception in 1949. According to the constitution, India is a Sovereign, Socialist, Secular, Democratic Republic.[18] The chief of state is the president, who is elected by an electoral college composed of members of parliament and state legislatures. A vice president is separately elected by parliament, and the prime minister by the majority party of parliament. The prime minister recommends and the president appoints a Union Council that serves as the cabinet and, effectively, the *real* executive power. The two-house parliament (Sansad) is composed of a Council of States (Rajya Sabha) with 245 members and a People's Assembly (Lok Sabha) with 545 members.[19] India's legal system is based on common law of the English model, though separate personal law codes apply to people of different faiths.

According to India's Constitution, the Union must "strive to minimize the inequalities in income, and endeavor to eliminate inequalities in status, facilities and opportunities, not only amongst individuals but also amongst groups of people residing in different areas or engaged in different vocations." Principles of central government policy span equal pay for equal work among men and women to the promotion of international peace and security. The constitution details a framework for governing that divides revenue capacity and service responsibilities of the central and state governments, and includes the organization of territories, as well as the establishment and duties of local governments (the districts or panchayats, and municipalities). Regarding the central and state governments, some responsibilities are concurrent, in that responsibilities are shared (such as for education, welfare, and employment) whereas others are relegated to central or state responsibility only (health and rural development are state responsibilities).

Jos Mooij and S. Mahendra Dev (2004) point out that the Government of India (GOI) is likely to be involved in most functions or what are termed "schemes," given the strength of India's unitary system and the strong policy direction and significant financial support (loans, grants, and transfers) that flow from the central to subnational governments. Whereas Guatemala's Constitution focuses on averting the overreach of the state, India's originally sought to forestall "the divisive forces operating in the economy" (Sowani 2012, 1). In fact, constitutional provisions allow India's central government "to transform itself into a unitary state" in periods of emergency, and, vis-à-vis the states, affords the GOI "vast powers over the collection and distribution of revenues" (Jain 2001, 1303). India's Constitution also creates a finance commission that determines the revenue distribution between the Union and states, and the Office of Comptroller and Auditor General to audit accounts of these governments (1306).

India's annual budget is divided into Plan and non-Plan components. Plan expenditures are developed through work groups and ministries and flow to a Planning Commission. Plan spending is considered to be new, or spending in excess of non-Plan expenditures that include past obligations or required outlays such as interest payments on debt, government personnel, grants, loans and subsidies, and any general government administrative work such as tax collection. Timing also plays a role in how expenditures are labeled, however, and further confuses budget process and outcomes. Anand Gupta (2005) outlines a number of problems with budgeting and fiscal policies in India, suggesting that the distinction between Plan and non-Plan expenditures be "abolished" (Gupta 2005, 51).

Nonetheless, the Indian public budgeting process requires the generation of five-year expenditure plans and annual budgets. Decision making authority is primarily concentrated in the hands of the prime minister who is chair of India's Planning Commission (of which the finance minister is also a member), which is responsible for the development of Plan expenditures. The Commission is responsible for examining country resources and needs, establishing a framework for the use of resources to accommodate needs, and determining impediments to reaching goals (Mooij and Dev, 2004). Despite efforts at inclusiveness in the development of five-year plans and in the budget process, more generally (by including external experts, interest groups as well as local citizens), the process is strongly centralized. Also, legislative input in this annual planning process may be slim to none "because of lack of interest or expertise, or because the parliamentary session is dominated by other issues" (Mooij and Dev 2004, 112).

According to the WJP, India ranks 66th out of 99 countries in terms of adherence to rule of law. It received its best ranking for open government (30), then constraints on government (35). Its criminal justice system is ranked 48 of 99. Scores on other dimensions are less favorable—respect for fundamental rights (63) and absence of corruption (72) fall between this country's best and worst rankings. Its worst rankings are for regulatory enforcement (81), civil justice (90), and order and security (95 of 99). According to the WJP (2014), India's governance system of checks and balances is "robust, ranked 35th worldwide and first in the South Asia region" (54) of the countries included in this study. However, the bureaucracy is "slow and ineffective" (hence the low ranking for regulatory enforcement) and its civil justice system experiences tremendous backlog, contributing to significant delays in case processing and problems with the enforcement of laws. Government corruption is a significant problem in India; attendant high crime rates, civil conflicts, and political violence all contribute to this country's very poor ranking on order and security (World Justice Project 2014).

Italy

The Kingdom of Italy was declared in March, 1861, though the country was not unified until 1870. This republic is divided into fifteen regions and five autonomous regions. Italy operates under a constitution passed in December, 1947, which has been amended many times since inception.[20] The president is the chief of state of Italy, elected by an electoral college made up of Parliament and specially elected regional representatives. The president appoints the prime minister, who is confirmed by Parliament and serves as the head of government. Italy's bicameral Parlamento includes a Senate with 315 members, and a

Chamber of Deputies with 630 members. The prime minister selects members of a Council of Ministers, who are confirmed by the president. Italy engages a legal system based on civil law.

The Italian Constitution provides for a framework of governance with powers, duties, and relationships across three branches of government, as well as devolution of authority to subnational governments (municipalities, provinces, metropolitan cities, and regions). These governments have revenue-raising abilities and a system of fiscal decentralization is presented. Most of the countries studied here do not have obligatory military service. Italy's Constitution indicates conscription, though this was suspended in 2004.

This constitution provides for individual rights similar to the others examined here—freedom of religion, expression, a secure home, and a free press; the right to work; and the proviso that "every citizen has the duty, according to capability and choice, to perform an activity or function that contributes to the material or spiritual progress of society." Separation of the Catholic Church from the State is declared. Specific provisions indicate cultural traditions and social policy; for example, Article 30 states that "it is the duty and right of parents to support, raise and educate their children, even if born out of wedlock. In case of incapacity of the parents, the law shall provide for the fulfillment of their duties. The law shall ensure to children born out of wedlock every form of legal and social protection that is compatible with the rights of the members of the legitimate family." Further, this constitution provides for "rules and limitations for the determination of paternity."

State policy evidenced in the document also includes government support of individual health and free education, with a promise to provide higher education financial support to individuals and families that have submitted to a competitive examination process. The right to work is expressed, and specifically, "working women have the same rights and are entitled to equal pay for equal work," while "workers have the right to a weekly rest day and paid annual holidays," a right that cannot be waived.

Concerning taxing and spending, the Italian Constitution determines that every individual will contribute to a progressive tax system (Article 53). Article 81 constrains the government to an annual, balanced budget and "any law involving new or increased expenditure shall provide for the resources to cover such expenditure." Other subnational governments must also realize balanced budgets and engage debt prudently, "in accordance with EU law."

Italy's budget process was ranked by the European Union in 2003 as weakest in centralization, followed by budgetary procedures and then overall quality. Centralization of budgeting procedure regards top-down budgeting; budgetary procedure is an all-encompassing index of several characteristics such as centralization, prudent economic assumptions, and performance budgeting; and quality in terms of budgetary transparency, multiyear perspective, prudent economic assumptions, and performance budgeting (Ranalli and Giosi 2011).

Luigi Pacifico and Maria Laura Sequiti (2000) describe the evolution of budgeting in Italy, clearly illustrative of a resulting mismatch between established law and practical application. They point to a number of problems with the budget system that arose by 1978—constitutional constraints can be skirted; formula-based social welfare spending, financed through debt, is overwhelming the budget; poor, inept, corrupt public management; ineffective controls; a fractured tax system with high evasion; and weakening local governments that are highly dependent upon central government financing for service delivery.

Budget reform legislation in 1978, modeled after the US Congressional Budget and Impoundment Act of 1974 (which you will read about in the next chapter), created a reconciliation-like procedure in which the Italian Parliament developed a Finance Act early in the budget process to frame budget decisions going forward. Another budget reform law passed in 1988 stipulating limits on the Finance Act and a focus on current account budget balance. Italy has also attempted to accommodate EU strictures of a budget deficit not in excess of 3 percent of GDP and a ratio of public debt to GDP not in excess of 60 percent. By the 1990s, Italy was pursuing New Public Management reforms, some to be considered later in this book. Relevant to the discussion here, these reforms reoriented the focus of decision makers on fiscal discipline and greater efficiency of operations. Accordingly, the Italian Parliament develops a macro-economic, multiyear framework of public spending that conforms to EU standards, for comparability with other member governments. Law in 1997 (Law No. 94 and Legislative Decree No. 279) sought to meet considerations of reform internally as well as conform to these EU (external) pressures.

Pacifico and Sequiti (2000) claim that Italy was able to improve its budgeting during this period, given tax increases, expenditure cuts, through creative accounting, and because of the deadlines imposed by the EU.[21] Evolution of the budgeting process in Italy has been organizational and procedural. Preparation of the budget has been centralized with the merging of the Ministry of the

Treasury and the Ministry of Budget and Economic Planning. Ministry appropriations are structured by function, responsibility center, and basic budget unit.

Francesco Ranalli and Alessandro Giosi (2011), however, indicate that coupled with more recent reforms in 2008 and 2009 (Accounting and Public Finance Law 196), there remains room for progress for Italian budgeting. They claim a "partially evolved" system that "remains very complex" (38). While internal budget planning has been strengthened, the several documents and budgets (the Multiyear Budget, the Political Budget and the Administrative Budget) and parallel budget systems (the political and the administrative) contribute to this complexity. It is hard for this country to shed a highly legalist cultural tradition.

According to the WJP, Italy ranks 29th out of 99 countries in terms of adherence to rule of law. It received its best ranking for respect for fundamental rights (22), for the criminal justice system (24), and for its system of checks and balances that provides adequate constraints on government (26). Italy's worst rank is for order and security (50). The rest of the dimensions (regulatory enforcement, absence of corruption, civil justice, and open government) have scores between these best and worst rankings. The WJP (2014) finds that Italy's "administrative agencies are effective in enforcing regulations and the civil justice system is independent but slow" (59). The country's lowest ranking for security and next lowest for open government are "attributable to an increasing use of violence to express discontent and to perceived difficulties in petitioning the government accessing official information, respectively"(59). Corruption and discrimination against the disadvantaged are problem areas for Italy, too (World Justice Project 2014).

Tanzania

A Sub-Saharan African country, Tanzania is a republic operating under a constitution that originated in April 1977 and then underwent significant revisions in October 1984.[22] Tanzania (originally Tanganyika) realized independence from a United Nations' trusteeship in 1961, united with newly independent Zanzibar in 1964, and was renamed the United Republic of Tanzania that same year. Within the republic there are 30 regions, 25 on mainland Tanzania, and five on Zanzibar islands off the east coast of the country. These regions are further subdivided into districts or local authorities (there are 113 local government authorities or LGAs). The president serves as chief of state and head of government; the president and vice president are elected on the same ticket. Legislative powers are vested in a unicameral body, the "Bunge" or National Assembly, in which almost a third of the membership (102 of 357) is designated for women nominated by the president. The president of Tanzania appoints cabinet members, selecting members from the National Assembly. Zanzibar, established as the Revolutionary Government of Zanzibar in the Tanzanian Constitution, has a separately elected president who is the chief executive of this government. The Zanzibar House of Representatives is made up of 50 members who represent the people within Zanzibar only. This country engages a legal system based on common law of the English model.

The Constitution of the United Republic of Tanzania of 1977 presents foundational policies of the government; fundamental rights and duties of citizens; the power and duties of the executive, legislative, and judicial branches of government; provision for and control of the military; and the establishment of the Revolutionary Government of Zanzibar, its Revolutionary Council, House of Representatives; and the authority for it to tax.

Tanzania's Constitution provides for the financial operations of the country, creating a Consolidated Fund (Joint Finance Account) into which all money provided by both Tanzania and Zanzibar flows. The constitution establishes a commission of seven members with duties to analyze government revenues and expenditures, and to oversee the government's fiscal system as well as the fiscal relationship (contributions and allocations) between the Tanzania and Zanzibar. However, according to Luc Noiset and Mark Rider (2011), the Joint Finance Commission "was only recently constituted and staffed with technical experts and, to date, has made little progress and exercised little influence on such matters" (475). They also explain an ongoing distrust between the two governments, as Zanzibar's authoritarianism contrasts with Tanzania's multiparty politics.

The constitution specifies conditions for payments of funds from the Consolidated Fund by virtue of an appropriation by parliament and "for the purpose of expenditure unless and until such expenditure has been approved by the controller and auditor-general." A Contingency Fund is established as well, from which the government can borrow in emergencies; public debt is secured on the Consolidated Fund. The position of controller and auditor general is aligned with the executive rather than the legislative branch of government.

In Tanzania, the constitution establishes an executive budget system in which the president is responsible for preparing and submitting a budget to the National

Assembly annually. The National Assembly approves spending estimates and develops an appropriations bill. Supplementary appropriation bills may be necessary in cases when the National Assembly has approved such spending. If the Appropriation Act has not passed by the start of the fiscal year, the president can authorize expenditures from the Consolidated Fund to pay the government's bills for essential services, programs, and obligations. These funds can be spent for the first four months after the start of the fiscal year or until an appropriations bill has passed, whichever occurs first.

Like some of the other constitutions described earlier, Tanzania's defines local government authorities and assigns their revenue and expenditure capacities. Similar to other developing countries and unified governments, Tanzania's central government holds significant power over its subnational governments in making these assignments, determining the grant and transfer system, and regulating the ability of subnational governments to borrow. In fact, in Tanzania, the central government recruits and employs local government employees (Noiset and Rider 2011). The Local Government Acts of 1982 assign responsibility for most basic services to local governments, including primary education, healthcare, agricultural and livestock services, water, public works, sanitation, and local public markets. Most of the funding for these services and activities is provided by block grants from the central government (Boex and Martinez-Vazquez 2003). Amendments to these laws passed since 2003 have constricted the possible revenue sources that Tanzanian LGAs can use to fund their budgets.

Noiset and Rider point out that aggregate own-source revenues of the LGAs make up only 10 percent of local resources to pay for public services and activities; the rest includes central government transfers and grants from international donors. They also explain that the central government in Tanzania has the ability to use broad-based, high-yielding taxes such as sales and income, but its local governments have the responsibility to provide resource-intensive functions. The Act of 1982 also created a Local Government Loan Board (LGLB) that presumably provides financial support to LGAs. However, its capitalization is weak, it holds sway in the choice of which local projects to fund, and it is predisposed to direct funds to poorer, rural areas, which have weaker capacity for mounting and completing projects.

Over the years, at the request of external donors, to meet grant stipulations or to pursue best practices, Tanzania has incorporated various new components into the budget process, such as its Poverty Reduction Strategy (PRS) and MTEF. PRS initiatives seek to establish and promote national policies to advance economic performance and quality of life, reduce poverty, and generate improved government accountability. MTEF involves economic and budget planning and multiple year estimating that links with PRS initiatives. Frans Ronsholt and colleagues (2003) discuss problems with data validity and reliability of these components as well as coordination of the processes themselves that compromise budgeting in Tanzania. "Considering that the budget is the government's main tool for policy implementation, it is unfortunate that the political level (legislature) enters into the process only at that very late stage and leaves strategic decisions on expenditure allocations to the administration"(14).

On the other hand, Alta Fölscher (2006) writes about African countries that have instigated reforms somewhat successfully and includes Tanzania with South Africa and Uganda as having worked to better clarify the rules and procedures of budgeting. For example, Tanzania uses annual public expenditure reviews which involve "sector working groups" for more open discussions about government spending (Fölscher 2006, 2). In this way, better information is included in the decision process. Noiset and Rider (2011), in their description of fiscal decentralization in Tanzania, claim that the features of Tanzania's budget and fiscal arrangements (described earlier) present "union preserving federalism" (483). That is, they determine that Tanzania's extreme poverty, weak governmental institutions and human resource capacities, low-mobility population, high ethnic rivalries, and strong competition for natural resource rents necessitate an accommodation of the traditional tenets of efficient fiscal decentralization.

According to the WJP, Tanzania ranks 69th out of 99 countries in terms of adherence to rule of law. It received its best rankings for its criminal justice system (44) and for adequate constraints on government (52). The country's worst ranking is for order and security (90). The rest of the dimensions (civil justice, respect for fundamental rights, open government, absence of corruption, and regulatory enforcement) have scores between these best and worst rankings. The WJP (2014) places Tanzania in the upper half of low-income countries regarding observance of the rule of law, finding its bureaucracy, "although not without problems, to be slightly more efficient that those in other countries in the region" (57). Tanzania's judiciary must contend with significant corruption; a high crime rate and the continuance of vigilante justice contribute to poor security in this country. Government transparency is lacking as well (World Justice Project 2014).

CONCLUSION

There is a tremendous amount of research and practical application efforts to develop, enhance, and sustain public budgeting and financial management systems in governments around the world. A great deal of this information has been collected through traditional academic research, but much has also been gleaned from the significant efforts by various institutions to advance best (really, better) practices in developing countries or in more developed countries that may have faltered. These institutions are made up of funding agencies, development consultants, advocacy groups, nongovernmental organizations (NGOs), foundations, and many other entities that provide support through direct funding and loans, training, personnel support, consulting and research, advocacy, or project and infrastructure development. Some of these institutions that are referred to in this book include

- Organization for Economic Cooperation and Development (OECD)
- World Bank (WB)
- International Monetary Fund (IMF)
- United Nations (UN)
- UK's Department for International Development (DFID)
- European Union (EU)
- International Budget Partnership (IBP)
- International Consortium on Governmental Financial Management (ICGFM)

Among these organizations, there is recognition that strong public budgeting and financial management systems are vital for country health and growth, not just to ensure better public money management, but also for more effective government operations and to promote the long-term vibrancy of nations.

This chapter offers just a glimpse into the legal foundations for budgeting in six countries that can be placed along a continuum from low income and developing to high income and industrialized. The constitutions of these countries evidence wide variety—some are concise relative to others. India's prescribes the establishment and structure of its subnational governments in detail, Guatemala's spell outs specific budget amounts for physical sport, and Italy promises government support for children born out of wedlock. Laws in these countries have further influenced processes—tightening or loosening the strictures that these governments have to meet regarding promises originally made and those since made. Adherence to the rule of law is considered to support democratic principles and promote a strong economy. Research about these governments and their observance of the rule of law indicates their rankings from strongest adherence (Australia) to weakest (Guatemala). The lofty policies evidenced in law set each government on a path. Adherence to the rule of law contributes to governments' ability to reach policy goals in the struggle to make good on national promises.

DISCUSSION QUESTIONS

1. Scholars have argued that there is not a best model for budgeting for all governments. At the same time, governments are pressed adhere to universal tenets (like Smith's presented in the last chapter), adopt approaches like MTEF, or implement reforms like performance-oriented budgeting. How can these two concepts (global "best practices" versus local or context-driven practice) be reconciled? Or can they?

2. Would you expect the budget law and practices of developing countries to be different from those in developed countries? Why or why not?

3. Characterizing governments according to economic status (industrialized versus developing) is one possible grouping for studying international budgeting practices. What are other ways of characterizing governments? Discuss the advantages and disadvantages of the characterizations that you come up with.

4. Considering the Worldwide Governance Indicators presented in Table 2.1 of this chapter, why is freedom of expression and a free media important to governmental budgeting? Also, how would you measure the credibility of government commitment to budget policies?

5. How does the nature of production of a country affect its budget?

6. Explain why a nation's adherence to the rule of law might have an impact on its budgeting process and its budget.

NOTES

1. The HDI has been reformulated over time; in 2010, the income component changed to Gross National Income per capita (GNI/population), "with

local currency estimates converted into equivalent US dollars using the purchasing power parity index (PPP)," that provides relative comparison of different currencies (Nielsen 2011, 8).

2. For information about the WB application of its "special Atlas method" for converting dollars to advance comparability, see http://data.worldbank.org/indicator/NY.GNP.PCAP.CD

3. The European Union is a collective of twenty-eight countries that pursues "peace, stability and prosperity" for its member nations. Originally created in 1958 as the European Economic Community, the name of the organization was changed in 1993 to the European Union (EU). The EU is not a federal government, but does pool the powers if its member nations to engage in work based on agreements (laws) established democratically; the EU has a single currency, the Euro, that supports mobility and the conduct of economic transactions freely across all member nation borders. EU member countries are expected to uphold all charters, treaties, and other agreements related to its governance, fiscal accountability, budget and debt management, human rights, and social equality. For more information about the EU, see http://europa.eu/index_en.htm and for information about significant treaties for EU governance, membership, and policy, see http://europa.eu/eu-law/treaties/index_en.htm

4. MTEF is a strategic attempt to reconcile government spending with resource constraints. Estimates of the resources available to a government are developed as are those of the costs associated with spending policies. Much work goes into determining the drivers or causes of government spending across functions, such as demographics, technology, or policy changes. Revenues and expenditures are reconciled to produce plans that seek to match overarching macro-economic concerns (stabilizing the economy) with more micro ones such as concerns about spending for defense and social programs. Estimates of revenues and expenditures are provided across several years and periodically reconsidered to accommodate changing circumstances.

5. Basis of accounting determines when financial transactions are recognized and recorded. Cash basis of accounting records revenues when received and expenditures when paid; there is no avenue to record receivables or payables

(future transactions) using this basis of accounting. (Think of a simple cash box in which revenues are recognized and recorded when cash goes into the box; expenditures are recognized and recorded when cash is taken out of the box.) Accrual accounting calls for recording revenues when earned or measureable. Expenditures are recorded when incurred, if measurable. In both instances, the transaction is recognized even though there may not have been actual receipt of revenue or any outlay of expenditure. Modified accrual accounting, a form of accounting traditionally used by governments for recording current finances, recognizes revenues when available and measurable (or collected in time to pay current liabilities) and expenditures when the liability is incurred (accrual basis).

6. There are different definitions of "performance budgeting"; some will be examined in more detail in chapter 4, which considers American state government performance budgeting laws, and in chapter 10, which discusses various budget reforms.

7. To access information about the legal systems and constitutions of various countries, see US Library of Congress. For information about Australia, for example, see http://www.loc.gov/law/help/guide/nations/australia.php or see the Australian Constitution, http://foundingdocs.gov.au/resources/transcripts/cth1_doc_1900.pdf

8. Common law is uncodified in that precedent (past judicial decisions) is considered in subsequent, relevant cases. Common law pits two sides against each other before a judge and involves a jury of peers (those who may or may not have any legal training) who make a determination of outcome based on the facts of the case as presented by both sides. The judge then hands down a sentence, based on the jury's verdict. Civil law is codified by legislators, legal scholars, and others. In a system of civil law, the judge determines the facts of the case and applies appropriate code.

9. The Pre-budget Expenditure Review Committee replaced the Strategic Priorities and Budget Committee in the 2011–2012 national budget cycle. For access to current and past Australian budgets, see http://www.budget.gov.au/2013-14/

10. From the Charter of Budget Honesty Act 1998, Commonwealth of Australia.

11. Operation Sunlight can be accessed via the Australian government Department of Finance and Deregulation website. Available at http://www .finance.gov.au/financial-framework/financial-management-policy-guidance /operation-sunlight/

12. For more information about Brazil's legal system, see US Library of Congress, http://www.loc.gov/law/help/guide/nations/brazil.php

13. See Constitution of the Federal Republic of Brazil 1988, http://www .planalto.gov.br/ccivil_03/Constituicao/Constituicao.htm

14. See Official Website for the Tribunal de Contas da União, http://portal2.tcu .gov.br/portal/page/portal/TCU/english/inside/fiscal_responsibility_act

15. See US Library of Congress, http://www.loc.gov/law/help/guide/nations /guatemala.php

16. A proportional system to elect members of a legislature requires that party make-up in the body is equal to proportion of votes received. If 25 percent of voters support one particular party, then 25 percent of the legislature will be members of that party.

17. See The Republic of Guatemala Constitution of 1985 with the 1993 reforms, http://pdba.georgetown.edu/Constitutions/Guate/guate93.html

18. See Constitution of India, http://indiacode.nic.in/coiweb/welcome.html or US Library of Congress, http://www.loc.gov/law/help/guide/nations /india.php

19. See The National Portal of India, http://india.gov.in/my-government /indian-parliament

20. See US Library of Congress, http://www.loc.gov/law/help/guide/nations /italy.php or see Costituzione Della Repubblica Italiana, http://www .camera.it/application/xmanager/projects/camera/attachments/upload_file /upload_files/000/000/002/costituzione.pdf

21. The Stability and Growth Pact of the EU includes limits on government budget deficits and sanctions for excessive deficits of member states. Member governments must also accommodate their budget, accounting, and reporting systems to an EU template to support comparability of data across participants. To read more about this Pact, see http://ec.europa.eu /economy_finance/economic_governance/sgp/index_en.htm

22. See, US Library of Congress, http://www.loc.gov/law/help/guide/nations /tanzania.php or Constitution of the United Republic of Tanzania, http://www .tanzania.go.tz/constitution.html

REFERENCES

Australian Charter of Budget Honesty Act. (Cth) 22 Stat. 1998. Retrieved July 30, 2013. Available at http://www.comlaw.gov.au/Details/C2004C00949

Blöndal, J. R., D. Bergvall, I. Hawkesworth, and R. Deighton-Smith. 2008. "Budgeting in Australia." *OECD Journal on Budgeting* 8 (2): 1–64.

Boex, J., and J. Martinez-Vazquez. March 2003. "Local Government Reform in Tanzania: Considerations for the Development of a System of Formula-Based Grants." Working Paper 03–05. International Studies Program, Andrew Young School of Policy Studies, Georgia State University. Available at ideas.repec.org/p/ays/ispwps/paper0305.html

Boyce, J. K., and M. O'Donnell (eds.). 2007. *Peace and the Public Purse: Economic Policies for Postwar Statebuilding.* Boulder, CO: Lynne Rienner.

Caiden, N. 2009. "Extreme Budgeting Reform: Going Beyond Transitional Economics to Postconflict Nations." *Public Budgeting & Finance* 29 (2): 137–144.

Caiden, N., and A. B. Wildavsky. 2003. *Planning and Budgeting in Poor Countries.* New Brunswick, NJ: Transaction Publishers. (Originally published 1974.)

Cihak, M., A. Demirguc-Kunt, E. Feyen, and R. Levine. August 2012. *Benchmarking Financial Systems around the World.* Policy Research Working Paper 6175. Washington, DC: The World Bank. Retrieved May 12, 2013. Available at https://openknowledge .worldbank.org/handle/10986/12031

Curristine, T., and M. Bas. 2007. "Budgeting in Latin America: Results of the 2006 OECD Survey." *OECD Journal on Budgeting* 7 (1): 1–37.

Fölscher, A. 2006. "Introduction: African Experience with Budget Reform." *OECD Journal on Budgeting* 6 (2): 1–16.

Jain, R. B. 2001. "Towards Good Governance: A Half Century of India's Administrative Development." *International Journal of Public Administration* 24 (12): 1299–1334.

Guess, G. M., and L. T. LeLoup. 2010. *Comparative Public Budgeting.* Albany, NY: SUNY Press.

Gupta, A. P. 2005. "Reforming Management of the Government of India's Expenditures: Some Thoughts." *Indian Journal of Public Audit and Accountability* 1 (1): 41–53.

Lienert, I., and I. Fainboim. January 2010. *Reforming Budget System Laws.* Technical Notes and Manuals. Fiscal Affairs Department, International Monetary Fund.

McDonald, M. 2012. "Guatemala 2013 Budget Foresees Boost for Defense." *Reuters,* October 23.

Menifield, C. E. (ed.). 2011. *Comparative Public Budgeting: A Comparative Perspective.* Sudbury, MA: Jones and Bartlett Learning.

Melo, M., C. Pereira, and A. Souza. February, 2010. "The Political Economy of Fiscal Reform in Brazil: The Rationale for the Suboptimal Equilibrium." Inter-American Development Bank. IDB Working Paper Series No. IDB-WP-117.

Mooij, J., and S. M. Dev. 2004. "Social Sector Priorities: An Analysis of Budgets and Expenditures in India in the 1990s." *Development Policy Review* 22 (1): 97–120.

National Bureau of Economic Research (NBER). April 23, 2012. "U.S. Business Cycle Expansions and Contractions." Cambridge, MA: National Bureau of Economic Research. Accessed on September 20, 2012. Available at http://www.nber.org/cycles/US_Business_Cycle_Expansions_and_Contractions_20120423.pdf

Nielsen, L. February 2011. *Classifications of Countries Based on Their Level of Development: How It Is Done and How It Could be Done.* IMF Working Paper, WP/11/31.

Noiset, L., and M. Rider. 2011. "Tanzania's Fiscal Arrangements: Obstacles to Fiscal Decentralization or Structures of Union-Preserving Federalism?" In *Decentralization in Developing Countries*, edited by Francios Vaillancourt and Jorge Martinez-Vazquez, 465–499. North Hampton, MA: Edward Elgar Publishing.

Pacifico, L., and M. L. Sequiti. 2000. "Reform: Budgeting and Financial Management." *International Journal of Public Administration* 23 (2&3): 367–81.

Premchand, A. 1999. "Budgetary Management in the United States and in Australia, New Zealand, and the United Kingdom." In *Handbook of Government Budgeting*, edited by Roy T. Meyers, 82–115. San Francisco: Jossey-Bass.

Ranalli, F., and A. Giosi. 2011. "New Perspectives on Budgeting Procedures in Italy." *International Journal of Public Administration* 34 (1–2): 32–42.

Reinhart, C. M., and K. S. Rogoff. February 2011. *A Decade of Debt.* NBER Working Paper Series, Working Paper 16827. Cambridge, MA: National Bureau of Economic Research. Available at http://www.nber.org/papers/w16827

Robinson, M. 2002. "Financial Control in Australian Government Budgeting." *Public Budgeting & Finance* 22 (1): 80–93.

Ronsholt, F., with R. Mushi, B. Shallanda, and A. Paschal. March 2003. "Results-Oriented Expenditure Management Country Study—Tanzania." Working Paper 204. London: Overseas Development Institute.

Rubin, I. S. 2010. *The Politics of Public Budgeting: Getting and Spending, Borrowing and Balancing,* 6th ed. Washington, DC: CQ Press.

Sowani, S. V. 2012, "Pragmatic Approach of Fiscal Federalism in India." *Indian Streams Research Journal* 2 (11): 1–4.

Tanner, L. December 2008. "Operation Sunlight-Enhancing Budget Transparency." Commonwealth of Australia. Retrieved July 30, 2013. Available at http://www.finance.gov.au/sites/default/files/operation-sunlight-enhancing-budget-transparency.pdf

Vieira, L. M. December 2011. "Government Financial Reporting in Brazil and in the U.S.: A Comparative Study of Governance Frameworks." George Washington

University, Institute of Brazilian Issues, XXX Minerva Program—Fall 2011. Available at http://www.gwu.edu/~ibi/minerva/Fall2011/Laercio.pdf

Wildavsky, A. B. 2002. *Budgeting: A Comparative Theory of Budgetary Processes*, 2nd ed. New Brunswick, NJ: Transaction Publishers. (Originally published 1986.)

World Justice Project (WJP). 2014. "WJP Rule of Law Index 2014." Washington, DC. Available at http://worldjusticeproject.org/sites/default/files/files/wjp_rule_of_law_index_2014_report.pdf

Budget Law and History of the US Federal Government

As the United States starts down the road toward third-world budgeting practices, who knows what will happen next?

—Rudolph G. Penner, former director, Congressional Budget Office, 2013

LEARNING OBJECTIVES

After reading this chapter, you should be able to

- Understand the constitutional foundations for US federal budgeting
- Be familiar with the history of budget law and process of the US federal government
- Explain growth of the US federal government over time
- Distinguish congressional from executive budgeting in the US federal government
- Describe modern budgeting at the federal level of government in the United States
- Find and access data about the US federal budget

The previous chapter introduced the constitutions, statutes, and budget processes in six countries. Each system operates within a distinct governmental framework; budgeting laws in the various countries present challenges and opportunities for realizing the budgetary concepts introduced in the first chapter. Adherence to the rule of law contributes to the ability of a government to operate well. Chapter 3 explains budgeting and significant constitutional and statutory laws relevant to federal budgeting in the United States. The history of budgeting in this country is a story of power struggles between the executive and legislative branches of government, with strong, periodic influence from the judiciary. What began as a disaggregated decision making system in the nineteenth century, became strongly centralized, with some attempted rebalancing, in the twentieth century, and has devolved into an "ad hoc, fragmented and opaque" process in the twenty-first century (Rubin 2007, 608). By studying this history, you will find that rather than evolving with time into a disciplined process that meets various tenets of good budgeting, the process in this industrialized nation has indeed tumbled toward that practiced in some developing countries, as mentioned by a former budget director in this chapter's epigraph.

EARLY BUDGETING

The first constitution of the United States, the Articles of Confederation, was ratified by thirteen states in March, 1781, and created a "loose confederation" in which state powers overshadowed those of a weak central government. Though the Articles provided a framework for state and federal relationships, the limited powers of the central government, most especially its inability to secure revenues, led to the development of a new governmental arrangement and powers. In 1787, a Constitutional Convention held in Philadelphia began with the intent to amend the Articles, but eventually created the US Constitution that was operational in March, 1789.

This Constitution provides for a federal system of government with separation of powers among three branches—executive, legislative, and judicial—affording "checks and balances" of governance and representing a democratic tradition.[1] The US Constitution gives the federal government the power to collect revenue and incur debt, and to use these resources to carry out the business of government. Constitutional provisions included in Article 1, Sections 7 through 9, determine that

- All revenue bills originate in the House (Section 7)
- Congress has the "power to lay and collect taxes, duties, imposts and excises, pay the debts, provide for the common defense and general welfare of the

United States; to borrow money on the credit of the United States; and to coin money and regulate the value thereof" (Section 8)

- "No money shall be drawn from the Treasury except in consequence of an Appropriation made by law" (Section 9)

The third clause of Article 1, Section 8 of the US Constitution gives Congress the power "to regulate commerce with foreign Nations, and among the several States, and with the Indian Tribes." The Commerce Clause has been interpreted by the courts differently over time—the clause has most recently been examined given passage of the Patient Protection and Affordable Care Act (ACA) of 2010 which has a requirement that individuals purchase health insurance. In a decision in June, 2012, the US Supreme Court ruled that Congress did not have the power to mandate that individuals purchase health insurance under the Commerce Clause. According to the decision:[2]

> Construing the Commerce Clause to permit Congress to regulate individuals precisely because they are doing nothing would open a new and potentially vast domain to congressional authority. Congress already possesses expansive power to regulate what people do. Upholding the Affordable Care Act under the Commerce Clause would give Congress the same license to regulate what people do not do. The Framers knew the difference between doing something and doing nothing. They gave Congress the power to regulate commerce, not to compel it. Ignoring that distinction would undermine the principle that the Federal Government is a government of limited and enumerated power.

Still, the Court upheld the mandate commanding individuals to purchase health insurance as falling within congressional power to "lay and collect taxes."

US state government tax authority is affected by the Commerce Clause as well—these governments, though afforded sovereignty through the US Constitution, cannot impose policies regarding commerce across state lines or internationally that conflict with this federal power.

The Bill of Rights include the first ten amendments to the Constitution, spelling out individual rights such as freedom of religion, various legal protections, and the powers reserved to the states and the people. The rest of the seventeen amendments make changes to different sections of the Constitution, including establishment of the Electoral College system of electing the president, presidential tenure and removal, the abolition of slavery and the extension of the right to vote to women and eighteen-year-olds, and the power to tax income. The prohibition on "intoxicating liquors" (the Eighteenth Amendment) was repealed with the Twenty-first Amendment. Like some of the countries examined in chapter 2, the United States operates within an English common law tradition versus a legal system based on civil law.

The first departments of the US federal government included Foreign Affairs (State), War, and Treasury. These represent vital responsibilities of the new nation—diplomacy, protection, and ability to secure and manage fiscal resources. The Act of Congress passed on September 2, 1789, which created the Treasury Department, delineated financial management and reporting responsibilities among the Treasury Secretary, Assistant Secretary, Controller, Auditor, Treasurer, and Register, and included controls on payments made by Treasury and its reporting to Congress of "a true and perfect account of the state of the Treasury."[3]

Federal budgeting in this early period was legislatively based and founded primarily on commercial transactions. The United States government had a relatively small presence in the economy. Revenue sources included customs, duties, and tariffs predominantly and spending was mostly for administrative purposes (salaries of government employees). Lump-sum appropriations covered a few areas of spending—warrants (payments of public funds made by the Treasury), the civil list (government workers), the Department of War, and other expenditures. On the legislative side, the House Ways and Means Committee, which determines revenue and tax policy, was established as a permanent committee in 1802; the Senate Finance Committee, which considers these issues in the upper chamber, was made permanent in 1816. In 1837 and then in 1850, a two-step authorization-appropriation process was established in the House and Senate, respectively. The federal fiscal year (July 1 to June 30) was created in 1842. Separate, permanent appropriations committees to determine spending were established in the House (1865) and in the Senate (1867). Previously, House Ways and Means and Senate Finance Committees considered both revenue and spending issues. Late in the nineteenth century, the Dockery Act (1884) established financial accounting practices, central auditing, and the federal financial management system.

Throughout the nineteenth century, Congress was mainly concerned that all spending by the federal government conform to law. Toward this end, Congress replaced lump-sum appropriations with detailed ones. Object of expenditure, or line-item appropriations, provide distinct categories of spending and amounts, such as for salaries, supplies, and postage; this type of budget format affords great control over spending to the legislative branch and less flexibility to chief executives and agency personnel. That is, the executive branch has little discretion in spending funds except for the specific purposes expressed in the spending bill. Congress continued to constrict executive spending discretion throughout this period. For example, in 1868 Congress banned transfers between accounts to stop commingling of appropriations and the ability of executive agency managers to use unexpended balances for purposes other than those specified by Congress. In 1870, Congress curbed "coercive deficiencies," which is the ability of agencies to spend in advance of or more than appropriated funds and then return to Congress for additional funds to continue operating. In 1905, the Anti-Deficiency Act (31 U.S.C. §1341–1342, §1511–1519)[4] was passed (and has since been amended); it bans federal employees from spending money in excess of or in advance of an appropriation, an apportionment, or a reapportionment.[5] Also empowering to Congress, members approved supplemental appropriations to support Union efforts during the Civil War. As we shall see, this practice, which is not part of the normal appropriations process, is used today by Congress often to get around the normal, annual appropriations process.

AN EXECUTIVE BUDGET PROCESS IS BORN

Arthur Eugene Buck (1934) explains that the United States government did not have an established budget system at the beginning of the twentieth century. Reforms that centralized budgeting and empowered chief executives bubbled up from local and state governments. The Progressive Movement pressed for opening up a system of spoils in government to professionalizing public management. For example, the New York Bureau of Municipal Research in 1907 conducted studies of municipal conditions and sought an efficient and engaged citizenry that would hold public officials and bureaucrats accountable for ethical and efficient public service. In 1910, President William Taft created a Commission on Economy and Efficiency that drafted a framework for a national budget in which the president would develop and recommend a budget to Congress that would be inclusive of the president's budget message and policy initiatives. The Commission also recommended that Congress be provided a consolidated financial report from Treasury and annual financial reports from individual agencies.

Federal laws in 1913 and 1917 were important to future budgeting as practiced in the United States as well. In 1913, the US Constitution was amended (Sixteenth Amendment) to empower Congress to tax income. Revenue acts by Congress during the Civil War and again in 1894 had provided Congress the ability to tax personal income, but the first law was repealed after a decade, and the second was ruled unconstitutional just one year after its passage. You will find out later in this book that the personal or individual income tax quickly becomes the most significant source of revenue for the United States federal government.

Also in 1913, Congress passed the Federal Reserve Act which created the nation's central banking system with the power to coin and regulate money. Banking in the United States, like budgeting in this country, has a chaotic history. A national bank had been chartered from 1791 to 1811, and again in1816, only to expire in 1836. After that, the United States went through a period characterized as "free banking" in which state legislatures chartered banks which operated with no federal oversight. With many different state banks and currencies, the banking system nationally was highly unstable. Federal banking laws in 1863 and 1864 sought a more coordinated system along with providing for war expenditures. Still, continued financial panics and the inability of banks to secure credit to weather such runs (especially in 1907) led Congress to develop and debate what became the Federal Reserve Act that was signed into law by President Woodrow Wilson at the end of 1913. The Act established "The Fed" with the responsibility for developing and monitoring monetary policy—the amount and flow of currency in the economy. The system includes a Board of Governors centralized in Washington, DC, and twelve regional banks. "The Board and Reserve Banks share responsibility for supervising and regulating certain financial institutions and activities, for providing banking services to depository institutions and the federal government, and for ensuring that consumers receive adequate information and fair treatment in their business with the banking system" (Board of Governors of the Federal Reserve System 2005, 3).

The Liberty Bonds Acts of 1917 and subsequent amendments to them are important for extending flexibility of borrowing money to the executive branch.

The Second Liberty Bond Act of 1917 lifted some constraints on United States bond maturities and redemptions. Over the next twenty years, Congress further enhanced the ability of the Treasury to issue debt. In 1939, Congress created a cap on all public debt; this provided the Treasury greater flexibility to manage federal debt (Austin and Levit 2013). The debt ceiling has often been increased to fund war efforts and reduced at the end of such conflicts. In 1945, the debt ceiling was $300 billion; it was reduced to $275 billion after World War II, subsequently lowered and increased over the next 20 years, reaching $300 billion again in 1962. Since then, Congress has changed the debt limit 77 times. Since 1993, the United States debt ceiling has been increased, suspended or temporarily exempted 18 times (Austin and Levit 2013).[6]

The Budget Act of 1921

The 66th Congress ended on March 4, 1921, with Democratic President Woodrow Wilson having vetoed the Executive Budget Act, a bill sponsored by Republicans Senator Medill McCormick and Representative James Good (both from Illinois). Proponents of the Act determined that the law would spark greater coordination of the federal budget process and a more efficient budget. At the closing of the congressional session, Representative F. W. Mondell stated,

> The Congress began its labors in the trying period of readjustment immediately following [World War I] and has carried out its programs of legislation and appropriations handicapped by serious differences of opinion existing between the Congress and the Administration. The great reductions in Government expenditure which the Congress accomplished were undertaken and carried out in the face of extravagant expenditure and enormous estimates made by the Administration.
>
> —"No Jollification as House Ends Session,"
> *The New York Times*, March 5, 1921

New winds swept in Republican rule—GOP members outnumbered Democrats in both houses of Congress from 1919 to 1931, and the next three presidents were Republicans, Warren Harding (1921–1923), Calvin Coolidge (1923–1929), and Herbert Hoover (1929–1933). Harding signed the Budgeting and Accounting Act into law on June 10, 1921, "to provide a national budget system and an independent audit of Government accounts" (Congressional Digest 1940, 37). This Act

- Requires the President to submit an annual budget to Congress
- Creates the Bureau of the Budget (BOB) within the Department of Treasury to support executive budget development, evaluation, and central clearance
- Creates the General Accounting Office (GAO, renamed Government Accountability Office in 2004) as an independent audit agency of executive agencies

In addition to helping the president develop the budget, the Bureau would be responsible for central clearance and control of agency fund management, research about agency programs, management and efficiency reviews, coordination of federal statistical services, and advice to the president regarding proposed legislation and policy initiatives (Congressional Digest 1940). Now, instead of agencies providing budget estimates to the Treasury and the Treasury collecting a "Book of Estimates" to present to Congress, the president would be responsible for developing a national budget and delivering to Congress the "Budget Message of the President" to include "his general fiscal policy for the period in question." Instead of individual agencies meeting with the Appropriations Committees or their subcommittee members about budget requests in an ad hoc fashion, committee members are to stay "in constant touch with the officials of the Bureau of the Budget" as well as executive agencies, as these committee members consider the president's plan (Congressional Digest 1940, 39–40). The first BOB employed about forty-five people and was directed by Charles Dawes who imprinted on the agency a strict orientation of control and where efficiency, not policymaking, was the chief concern (Berman 1979).

The federal executive budget system continued to gain strength from its inception in 1921 and for the next fifty years. The Reorganization Act of 1939 enhanced the president's reorganization powers, created the Executive Office of the President (EOP), and transferred the BOB from Treasury to the EOP. Together with several other reorganization plans, changes included the consolidation and reorganization of selected federal agencies as well as an extension of budget control requirements of the 1921 Act to independent and regulatory boards and commissions. BOB became a strong arm of control for the president and a centralizing conduit for a national budget.

Government Spending Growth and the Employment Act

The fifty-year period after creation of the US executive budget system was one of great expansion in federal revenues, expenditures, and programming. In the 1930s and 1940s, Democratic President Franklin D. Roosevelt and Congress pressed for new and enlarged federal government programs and spending. This period brought an alphabet soup of new federal activities as well as the United States' participation in World War II (WWII). Federal spending, at $4 billion in 1931, reached $92.7 billion by 1945. The deficit that year was $47.6 billion (over one-half trillion dollars, if inflation is taken into account). New Deal programs, support during the economic downturns throughout the period, the newly created Social Security system (1935), and the war effort collectively drove up federal spending. The year after the end of WWII, outlays dropped to $55.2 billion and stayed below this level for the next five years. However, by the early 1950s, government spending began a steady creep upwards; federal outlays were 15.6 percent of GDP in 1950, 17.8 in 1960, 19.3 in 1970, 21.7 in 1980, and 21.9 in 1990.[7]

An important law passed by Congress in 1946 was the Employment Act. This Act stipulated that the president and Congress must promote full employment, stable prices, and steady economic growth. The law also created a Council of Economic Advisors that would provide policy direction and expertise to the president concerning a range of economic issues relevant to the advancement of these goals. This law represents the influence of economic theory espoused by John Maynard Keynes (1936) throughout the Great Depression and WWII. In very simple terms, Keynesian theory considers that fiscal policy can be used effectively to make market corrections. Specifically, in periods of economic downturn, government spending (an infusion of money into the economy) can boost production and help pump the economy. During economic surges, in theory (and sometimes in practice), taxes should be increased and government spending cut back to slow the economy. The passage of the Employment Act indicates the agreement about macro-economic policy among public officials at the time—that federal government was responsible for promoting a strong and vibrant economy and could accomplish this (or at least influence the economy) through taxing and spending.

CONGRESS STRIVES FOR CREDIBILITY

By the mid-1960s, the executive budget office (up to this point, the Bureau of the Budget or BOB) was being questioned as an effective resource for the president, given the ever-extending reach and complexity of government programs and spending. A self-study of the agency in 1967 expressed a need for change to better "serve the President in the context of today's problems" (Memorandum cited by Berman 1979, 101). Early in 1970, President Richard Nixon issued a reorganization plan (number 2) that reconfigured BOB to bolster its capabilities and further strengthen presidential ability to manage the government. On July 1, 1970, BOB's name was changed to the Office of Management and Budget (OMB) and its director, George Shultz, proclaimed that the agency would now be able to "implement the President's desire for strong, effective, and responsive management" (Berman 1979, 113).

Congress at this time was viewed as a fractious body, labeled "fiscally irresponsible" by President Nixon, and more often than in the past, unable to adhere to the federal timetable for passing the budget (passing appropriation bills by the start of the fiscal year) (US National Archives and Records Service 1974, 587). Study committees in Congress attempted to quell member frustrations with the president's criticisms and desires for even more executive spending discretion. Congress as a whole realized a need to regain its power of the purse, to have access to better information for making budget decisions, and to engage a more coordinated process that would support timely budget passage. Most members of Congress considered that in order to maintain institutional credibility, the body "had to equip itself with the means of arriving at its own coherent budgetary decisions" (Dumbrell 1980, 485). In the declaration of purposes of new budget law, Congress determined that "it is essential to establish national budget priorities" (Public Law 93–344, 88 Stat., July 12, 1974, 298).

The Congressional Budget and Impoundment Control Act (hereafter referred to as the Congressional Budget Act or CBA) that Congress passed in 1974 was significant because it fundamentally changed the US federal budget process for a second time. Important components of this law included

- Changed the federal fiscal year to October-September
- Created Congressional Budget Office (CBO)
- Created Budget Committees in the House and Senate
- Changed the budget process to include two budget resolutions and reconciliation

- Required additional (a) analytics for budget review, (b) data in budget presentations, and (c) review of federal programs
- Tightened presidential impoundments

Upon signing the billing July 1974, President Nixon bemoaned inflation as the number one problem in the United States at the time and that

> a major cause for inflation is overspending by government, when government spends more than it takes in . . . this bill addresses that particular part of the problem because as we work together to keep down the cost of government, it means that we can help keep down the cost of living for every American.
> **—National Archives and Records Service, 1974**

Nixon did sign this bill just prior to his August 1974 resignation in response to impending impeachment for the Watergate scandal; he effectively had no power left.

Members of Congress, however, considered the bill necessary to stem presidential attempts to overreach budget powers by redirecting appropriated funds to military initiatives in Vietnam and impounding those funds that Congress had directed to environmental, housing, and other domestic programs. The CBA was an attempt by Congress to pull back power from what some termed the "Imperial Presidency" in light of Nixon's efforts to amass budget and war powers. The law can also be understood as an effort to curtail the growth of "backdoor spending," or government spending occurring outside of the annual appropriations process. Such spending could involve authorizations by Congress for an agency or government entity to loan money, engage in contracts, or any other sort of allowance that obligates government funding in the future.

This law has a number of components that were expected to solve problems with congressional budget making and power vis-à-vis the president. The start of the budget year was extended to October 1, presumably to allow Congress more time to deliberate and to be able to pass the budget on time. The CBO would provide the legislative branch with its own technical and analytical arm for budget and economic analysis, just like the president had the OMB. Budget Committees would now provide a holistic view of the budget that the president had by virtue of developing a national budget, but which had been missing from

Congress. That is, House Ways and Means and Senate Finance considered revenue issues only and Appropriations Committees considered spending issues only. Consideration of budget balance or the relationship between revenues and expenditures by Congress was essentially nonexistent. Now, Budget Committees were made responsible for developing and passing a first budget resolution (by April 15) that included estimates of total revenues, budget outlays, new budget authority, surplus, or deficit and an "appropriate" level of public debt using estimates developed by the CBO. This concurrent resolution provided parameters for standing committees for developing their revenue and spending bills and resolutions—these committees had to develop legislation that fell within resolution parameters. "The concurrent resolution can take the president's budget proposal as a guide, or it can make substantial changes in the president's priorities and totals, but it must be identical" in the House and Senate (Rubin 2007, 609). By September 15, Congress needed to pass a second budget resolution that affirms or revises the first concurrent resolution. Any work of standing committees must be reconciled with the budget resolution—to make sure that what standing committees are recommending in bills and resolutions equates with the framework established by the first, then revised or affirmed by the second budget resolutions. While the CBA created this new process, it did not prescribe ceilings for revenues, spending, or debt. The idea of ceilings would surface in later law.

The CBA also reined in the president's ability to stop funds from being spent after Congress appropriated them. The CBA redefined impoundments as rescissions or deferrals. Rescissions, a presidential request to stop funds from being spent, were automatically cancelled (and the money spent accordingly) unless Congress approved the impoundment within forty-five days. Deferrals, a presidential request to delay funds from being spent, would proceed (and the money delayed) unless the impoundment was cancelled by Congress.

BUDGET BALANCE AND MANAGEMENT IMPROVEMENT

Ronald Reagan's presidency in the early 1980s is remembered for his agenda of tax, red tape, and expenditure cuts. President Reagan adhered to supply-side economics—the theory that tax cuts would incentivize individuals and businesses to work more, which in turn would stimulate the economy. In spite of his tax cut success, the Economic Recovery Act of 1981, the sixteen-month economic downturn that lasted from July, 1981 to November, 1982, set the country on a course of increasing deficits that kept the public nervous and searching for blame. Congress reacted with legislation in 1985 and throughout the 1990s to stem a growing federal budget deficit as well as to impose some degree of fiscal discipline on members of the legislative branch of government.

In 1997, Congress was able to revert to protective strategies with the first budget surplus in almost thirty years. But the events of September 11, 2001, then pushed budget balance down the totem pole of important policy concerns; national security needed to be addressed. The Great Recession from 2007 to 2009 brought on federal stimulus programs with attendant federal funding to subnational governments to pump the national economy. However, the recovery limped along and partisan bickering reached new heights. An obstructionist stance of Congress vis-à-vis the president contributed to the first-ever credit downgrade for the United States. A full forty years after CBA, budgeting by brinksmanship has become an art form in this country.

Gramm-Rudman-Hollings of 1985

The 1980s were characterized as a period of fiscal restraint on the part of Congress. The deficit as a percent of GDP hovered around 2.5 from 1977 to 1981 and then doubled to 5 percent from 1982 to 1985. Though spending continued to increase in every year from 1979 to 1983, President Ronald Reagan's tax cuts brought a dramatic drop in receipts (as a percent of GDP, these were 19.2 in 1982 and 17.5 the following year). Phil Gramm, a Democratic Representative from Texas at the time, was pushing a balanced budget amendment. In 1983, he switched parties and as a Senator—along with Warren Rudman, a Republican from New Hampshire, and Ernest "Fritz" Hollings, a Democrat from South Carolina—developed and successfully navigated through Congress the Balanced Budget and Emergency Deficit Control Act (Public Law 99–177 and hereinafter referred to as Gramm-Rudman-Hollings or GRH). Though it started as a bill to increase the debt limit, the focus of the law that passed was on deficit reduction. GRH made some changes to the congressional budget process, such as cutting out one budget resolution and requiring resolution reports and points of order in adopted resolutions. But chiefly the law reoriented congressional focus on deficit reduction, establishing a five-year timeframe to reduce the deficit to zero by 1990. If Congress could not meet targets for deficit reduction in any given year, an automatic trigger—sequestration—would be applied to spending to bring it in under the targets. Realistically, however, most government spending (i.e., Social Security, Medicare, and various other entitlement programs) was exempted from sequestration. Essentially, Congress developed an automatic trigger that would make cuts that congressional members found too difficult to make. In any case, the timeframe to reach balance went unmet. Cuts to discretionary spending were implemented, but the amount of spending affected by the law was so small (relative to exempted spending) and Congress was able to engage smoke-and-mirrors strategies, such selling assets or other accounting tricks to wiggle out of the sequester process. Outlays as a percent of GDP remained at or above 21 from 1987 to 1990. The deficit as a percent GDP was 3.2 in 1987 and 3.9 in 1990.

In 1986, the United States Supreme Court ruled that a section of the GRH violated separation of powers and was unconstitutional. The original law stipulated that the Comptroller General, the head of the GAO, an arm of Congress, was responsible for initiating sequesters. But execution of the law lies with the executive branch; thus in 1987 an amended GRH placed sequester responsibilities with the OMB and extended the timeline for deficit reduction (still to zero) to 1992. By 1990, however, frustration on all sides with the inability to meet targets engendered a budget summit between then President George H. W. Bush and congressional leaders to agree on a budget. From this summit, the Budget Enforcement Act of 1990 was born.

Budget Enforcement Act and Chief Financial Officers Act of 1990

Title XIII of the Omnibus Budget Reconciliation Act of 1990 (BEA) attempted to reinforce fiscal policy to realize budget balance through new rules and triggers. BEA maintained the GRH concept of maximum deficit amounts and across-the-board spending cuts (sequesters). This law addresses deficit control through adjustable deficit targets and limits on categories of appropriations— defense, international, and domestic.[8] In this case, if spending in any of these categories topped established targets, the spending would be sequestered, a trigger that could be implemented at any point in the budget process. The law also established Pay-As-You-Go (PAYGO), which requires that budget legislation be deficit neutral, in the aggregate—if spending increases or revenue decreases are proposed, then spending cuts or revenue increases must be coupled with these proposals to assure a zero-sum game. That is, those suggesting entitlement increases or cuts in taxes must come up with the difference(s) somewhere else, although any such changes due to shifts in the economy were not subject to

PAYGO. Supplemental appropriations, unless emergency, were held to PAYGO, as well.

Also in 1990, Congress passed Public Law 101–576, the Chief Financial Officers (CFO) Act. Although the role of the bureaucracy in the federal budget process will be examined in a later chapter, it is important to mention this particular law here as it provided financial management leadership capacity to the OMB. This Act added chief financial officers in twenty-three federal agencies; OMB would establish standards for these CFOs, who were made responsible for agency financial management. The law also called for a new deputy director for management to oversee information and procurement policies, property, and productivity improvements in the federal government. Finally, the CFO Act placed an Office of Federal Financial Management within the OMB to oversee federal financial management activities government-wide (US Government Accountability Office 1991).

Balanced Budget Act of 1997

President Bill Clinton and Congress agreed to the Balanced Budget Act (BBA) in the summer of 1997. The president rejoiced at the imminent flip to a federal budget surplus,[9] as well as the "largest investment in higher education since the G.I. Bill in 1945, the largest investment in health care for children since 1965, and tax relief for 27 million working families."[10] The overarching budget goal of the times involved protecting Social Security. "The budget was to remain balanced, excluding the surpluses in the Social Security trust funds. In budget speak, this meant running unified budget surpluses equivalent to these trust fund surpluses" (Joyce 2005, 20). Later, when President George W. Bush took office, protecting the Social Security surplus served as a budget constraint as he pushed for tax cuts and Medicare Part D. But September 11 and the 2001 recession meant that "the long-term security for the country and its citizens" and tax cuts "in the name of economic stimulus, trumped budgetary balance as the primary goal of fiscal policy" (21).

The Great Recession, Federal Stimulus, the 2011 Budget Act, and a Partial Shutdown

The official start of the Great Recession, the most dramatic economic downturn experienced in the United States since the Great Depression, was December 2007 (National Bureau of Economic Research 2012). By this time, the go-go economy of the 1990s was long gone and governments at all levels had barely recouped, if at all, from the 2001 recession. Housing values nationwide plummeted and, given the extent of subprime loaning activities, a tsunami of foreclosures resulted. Congress passed the Troubled Asset Relief Act (TARP) in October 2008, which eventually provided $475 billion in federal funds to insurers, car companies, as well as investment firms and banks, to stabilize the industries and advance credit markets.[11] In February 2009, Congress passed the American Recovery and Reinvestment Act (ARRA) to quickly inject federal funds into local communities. Stimulus funds included those to create and save jobs, pump the economy, and support shovel-ready infrastructure projects; the ARRA included tax cuts and other benefits, funding for unemployment benefits, and other entitlement programs, too.[12]

The 1974 Congressional Budget Act required Congress to complete action on an annual budget resolution by May 15 of each year (by April 15 after 1986). But in the first decade of the new century, Congress did not adopt a budget resolution "for FY2003 in 2002, for FY2005 in 2004, for FY2007 in 2006, for FY2011 in 2010, or for FY2012 in 2011" (Heniff and Murray 2012, 28). The federal deficit in 2011 was $1.3 trillion, an uptick from 2010, two years following the official end of the Great Recession (June 2009), and in spite of the TARP and stimulus money that had been pumped into the economy.[13] From June, 2002 to August, 2011, when the Budget Control Act (BCA) is passed, the statutory limit on federal debt was increased 11 times. By the end of FY2011, gross federal debt as a percent of GDP is 98.9; it tips over 100 by the following year.[14]

The Budget Control Act passed on August 2, 2011, is complex legislation that attempted to deal with numerous components of the federal budget. Bill Heniff, Elizabeth Rybicki, and Shannon Mahan (2011) explain that the law:

- Increased the federal debt limit in three installments
- Established ten-year caps on discretionary spending that cannot be waived by either chamber; if caps are compromised, sequester triggers across-the-board "cancellation of budgetary resources"
- Created a Joint Select Committee on Deficit Reduction to develop budget deficit reduction law—by $1.5 trillion by FY2021
- Specified that if deficit reduction does not occur by January 15, 2012, an automatic spending reduction process is triggered

- Each chamber must vote on a balanced budget amendment to the Constitution
- Made cuts and changes to federal student aid programs
- Established procedures for expedited consideration of a resolution disapproving any debt increase, the joint committee bill, and a balanced budget amendment passed by the other chamber

Quickly following passage of the BCA in August, Standard & Poor's downgraded the sovereign (long-term) credit of the United States from AAA to AA+, indicating concern about the country's fractious policymaking process, its debt level, and overall fiscal performance. According to Nikola Swann and John Chambers (2013), the downgrade represented problems with the increasing partisanship of elected officials and "fundamentally opposing views by the two main political parties on the optimal size of government and the preferred mix between expenditure and revenue measures" to reach budget balance. These analysts point to the failures of both the 2010 National Commission on Fiscal Responsibility as well as the Joint Select Committee on Deficit Reduction to effect any budget agreements.

In March 2013, sequester per BCA 2011 was triggered (having been delayed from January 2013). This sequester stipulates billions of dollars in annual spending cuts for a decade. Though spending for entitlements like Medicaid and the Children's Health Insurance Program (CHIP), Social Security, veterans' benefits, and the like are exempt from sequester, defense and nondefense spending and most discretionary appropriations are subject to the trigger.

Brinksmanship Brings Government Shutdown

More recently, the effects of federal budgeting by brinksmanship were evidenced. After Congress failed to reach agreement on a budget by October 1, 2013, the US federal government was shutdown (partially). Congress approved and the president signed law to end a government shutdown on October 16, 2013.[15] This law increases the debt limit (again) until January, 2014. What began as an effort by Republicans to tie agreements about the budget and debt with defunding or delay in implementation of the Patient Protection and Affordable Care Act (ACA) of 2010, ended in a scramble to make sure that the country could pay its bills. This agreement required that Congress reach a budget deal by December 13, 2013 that presents "a long-term blueprint for tax and spending policies over the next decade" (Weisman and Parker 2013). Budget negotiations were headed by Representative Paul Ryan of Wisconsin and Senator Patty Murray of Washington. By December 26, 2013, President Barack Obama had signed a budget deal negotiated by Representative Ryan and Senator Murray that eased up on triggered cuts and averted another shutdown. Then, a deal was struck in January 2014 on a budget to fund the government through September 30, 2014, and to avoid an imminent government shutdown as the stopgap measure from December 2013 ran out.

THEN AND NOW, BUDGET NUMBERS

Table 3.1 illustrates how the federal budget of the United States has changed in the last 70+ years. The largest increase in spending as a percent of total federal outlays is for human resources—this spending grew from 43.7 percent of total outlays in 1940 to 70 percent estimated by 2018; this 26.3 percent increase indicates 61 percent growth from 1940. Human resources spending includes that for education and training and employment services, health, Medicare, income and Social Security programs, as well as benefits and services for the nation's veterans. For the same period, spending for physical resources—made up of energy, natural resources, environmental, commerce-related, and transportation and community development programs—indicates the greatest decline in outlays as a percent of the total (86 percent), followed by all other functions combined (42 percent). Spending for national defense— the primary function of the national government at its inception—decreased as a share of total outlays by 24 percent from 1940 to 2018 (estimated).

Figure 3.1 presents US revenues, outlays, and debt held by the public as a percent of GDP and by budget law period. Most remarkable about this data are the periods of growth in government borrowing, particularly from 1980 to 1994, and then again after 2007. The strong economy and implementation of PAYGO (BEA 1990) may explain some of the downturn in debt as a percent of GDP after 1994; the 2001 recession and the expiration of PAYGO in 2002 coincide with another ascent in the debt level, which then spikes at the onset of the Great Recession in December 2007. Alan Auerbach (2008) claims that this spike confirms that since 2009, "Congress has acted essentially without budget rules" (62), though sequesters and ten-year PAYGO have been imposed

Table 3.1
Outlays by Superfunction and Function, 1940 to 1980

Superfunction and Function	1940	1950	1960	1970	1980	1990	2000	2010	2018 Estimate
As Percentages of Total Federal Outlays									
National defense	17.5	32.2	52.2	41.8	22.7	23.9	16.5	20.1	13.3
Human resources	43.7	33.4	28.4	38.5	53.0	49.4	62.4	69.0	70.4
Physical resources	24.4	8.6	8.7	8.0	11.2	10.1	4.7	2.6	3.5
Net interest	9.5	11.3	7.5	7.4	8.9	14.7	12.5	5.7	10.4
Other functions	8.2	18.7	8.4	8.8	7.6	4.8	6.4	5.0	4.8
Undistributed offset-ting receipts	−3.4	−4.3	−5.2	−4.4	−3.4	−2.9	−2.4	−2.4	−2.3
Total Federal Outlays	**100.0**	**100.0**	**100.0**	**100.0**	**100.0**	**100.0**	**100.0**	**100.0**	**100.0**
(On-budget)	100.2	98.8	88.2	85.9	80.7	82.0	81.5	84.0	79.0
(Off-budget)	−0.2	1.2	11.8	14.1	19.3	18.0	18.5	16.0	21.0
As Percentages of GDP									
National defense	1.7	5.0	9.3	8.1	4.9	5.2	3.0	4.8	2.8
Human resources	4.3	5.2	5.0	7.4	11.5	10.8	11.4	16.6	14.9
Physical resources	2.4	1.3	1.5	1.5	2.4	2.2	0.9	0.6	0.7
Net interest	0.9	1.8	1.3	1.4	1.9	3.2	2.3	1.4	2.2
Other functions	0.8	2.9	1.5	1.7	1.7	1.1	1.2	1.2	1.0
Undistributed offset-ting receipts	−0.3	−0.7	−0.9	−0.9	−0.7	−0.6	−0.4	−0.6	−0.5
Total, Federal outlays	**9.8**	**15.6**	**17.8**	**19.3**	**21.7**	**21.9**	**18.2**	**24.1**	**21.2**
(On-budget)	9.8	15.4	15.7	16.6	17.5	17.9	14.8	20.2	16.7
(Off-budget)	(−*)	0.2	2.1	2.7	4.2	3.9	3.4	3.9	4.4

Source: The Budget of the United States Government, Fiscal Year 2014, Historical Tables, Table 3.1. Data aggregated by decade from raw data. Available at http://www.whitehouse.gov/omb/budget/Historicals

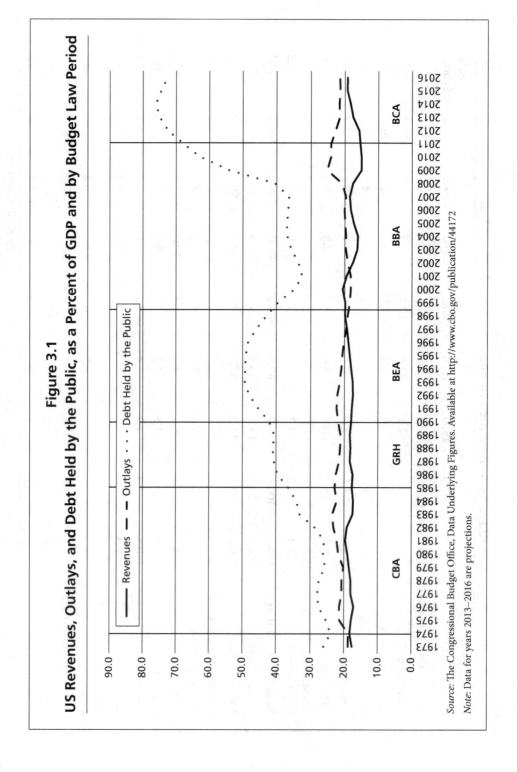

Figure 3.1
US Revenues, Outlays, and Debt Held by the Public, as a Percent of GDP and by Budget Law Period

Source: The Congressional Budget Office, Data Underlying Figures. Available at http://www.cbo.gov/publication/44172

Note: Data for years 2013–2016 are projections.

during this time. For example, modern sequester brought about 10 percent cuts in 2013.

Philip Joyce (2005) reviews federal budgeting after the terrorist attacks in the United States on September 11, 2001, and emphasizes that congressional deference to the president and increasing discretionary defense spending have been traditional reactions to such crises in the past. He explains a confluence of other circumstances such as President George W. Bush's tax cuts, the 2001 economic downturn, and the expiration of budget rules (like PAYGO) as shifting the collective focus (of Congress, the president, and the public) away from fiscal discipline and budget balance and onto the war on terrorism. This new focus is more opaque than in the past; that is, Joyce explains, success in a war on terrorism is difficult to define, completion dates are elusive, and a cohesive strategy to conduct the work may be impossible to develop as circumstances change. Joyce points out that federal budgeting dysfunction may be most evident by the consistent inability of Congress to pass a budget on time. According to Jessica Tollestrup (2012), from 1977 to 2012, there are eleven years when not even one regular appropriations bill was passed by the start of the fiscal year (October 1), necessitating the employment of continuing resolutions (CRs) to keep the federal government operating.[16] Joyce considers that the continuing high level of uncertainty portends a federal budget process that is slapdash and random in the future.

Rubin (2007, 608) concurs with this assessment and claims that the "unraveling" of federal budgeting in the United States has severely compromised democracy, accountability, transparency, and predictability. She explains that lost revenues from the Bush tax cuts contributed more to federal deficits early in the twenty-first century than did increased spending for homeland security, the war effort, discretionary spending, or for entitlements. Rubin (2007) emphasizes that although the 1990 BEA was not perfect, "the law strengthened the norm of balance by increasing the expectation that increases in one area had to be offset by decreases somewhere else" (609). The period of surpluses in the 1990s allowed Congress to fall off the wagon and then, when PAYGO lapsed in 2002, the process became highly variable and unpredictable. Congress was unable to pass concurrent resolutions, thus the legislative branch was not meeting the president's budget with any sort of comprehensive framework of its own—that is, aggregate totals that would have been included in a concurrent resolution disappeared and instead totals were determined appropriation by appropriation.

According to Rubin (2007, 614), each of the problems below adds to a fractured, "opaque" process that is highly unpredictable:

- The breakdown of discipline on the part of Congress to pass annual spending bills
- The use of supplemental appropriations
- Enhanced reprogramming by the executive (moving money around programs within an appropriation) with limited or no reporting
- Tax expenditures (revenue foregone by the government through tax breaks)
- Growth of the "black budget" (secret spending for intelligence and defense weaponry)
- Contracting out
- Earmarking and pork

All of these factors contribute to increased borrowing by the United States to close budget gaps. Rubin emphasizes that by 2007, interest on the debt became the fourth largest expenditure by the federal government, following Social Security, defense spending and Medicare. In contemplating how to "motivate those who benefit from the status quo" from this process, Rubin (2007, 615) suggests reform through embarrassment. That is, public officials need to be held accountable, reminded of their promises when taking office and discussing budget issues, and embarrassed into considering generational rather than party equity.

ADHERENCE TO RULE OF LAW

Chapter 2 described budgeting in six countries and provided the World Justice Project (WJP 2014) ranking for each country in terms of adherence to the rule of law. You may recall that the WJP conducted in-country surveys, developing a number of measures to rank nations on various dimensions of strength of observance of the rule of law. According to the WJP, the United States ranks 19th out of 99 countries in terms of adherence to rule of law, behind Australia in the rankings, but ahead of the rest of the countries of interest here. The United States received its best ranking for open government (17) and then for order and security (18). Its lowest rankings include those measuring respect for fundamental rights (27) and the civil justice system (27). Rankings for the rest of the dimensions (constraints on government powers, absence of corruption, regulatory enforcement, and criminal justice) fall between the country's best and worst rankings.

According to the WJP results, the United States rankings across dimensions, along with Australia's, are more consistent (the difference between the highest and lowest ranking is 7 for Australia and 10 for the United States) than those of the other countries—Italy (28), Brazil (39), Guatemala and Tanzania (both 46), and India (65). Higher values indicate wider disparity in rankings across the eight dimensions of adherence to rule of law (World Justice Project 2014). In comparison to these countries, the United States scores well on its system of checks and balances, open government, and security. Regarding respect for fundamental rights, the WJP (2014) finds the United States "strong with regard to the rights of association, opinion and expression, and freedom of religion . . . but underperforming when compared to peers in the protection of right to privacy, due process of law and labor rights" (60). The United States has an independent judiciary that is relatively corruption-free. Equal treatment afforded to the disadvantaged and minorities lags as compared to peers, however, and civil legal assistance is cost prohibitive for many poor citizens, contributing to the United States' lowest ranking on this dimension (World Justice Project 2014).

CONCLUSION

Like other countries, the United States has an extensive overlay of constitutional and statutory laws, rules, regulations, and court decisions that influence how budgeting is conducted and the results of the process. Originally, the American states provided for a federal government but showed hesitancy in affording it considerable powers. Tracking the taxing and spending of this government over time, however, indicates that the United States today yields considerable powers to generate revenues and an extensive reach as evidenced through its expenditures.

Modern budgeting in the United States has turned into a game of brinksmanship in which teams of rivals hold fast to party ideologies about the size of government, the make-up of federal spending, taxes, and levels of deficit and debt. Especially in the last decade, budget laws and rules that serve as the foundations for government to develop a national budget view have been ignored, twisted, or simply dropped. In the past few years, short-term budget deals have kept uncertainty levels extremely high. The budget deal of October 16, 2013, ended a two-week partial shutdown of the government. Then, several stopgap measures were agreed to before a budget was set in January 2014 that provides funding through the fiscal year. Though some agencies and programs are exempt from shutdowns or may be able to stay open through a shutdown (using fees and charges, carryover, or reserve funds), shutdowns and stopgap budgeting create an unstable situation that interrupts the work of federal employees and quickly trickles down to state and local governments that receive federal dollars for a wide array of programs, services, and projects. In these periods, the routine of the budget process that has been mapped in constitutions, laws, and traditions is disrupted.

The United States ranks well among nations worldwide and when compared to the sample countries of interest here, given its adherence to the rule of law as studied by the World Justice Project. In terms of government transparency, security, low corruption, constraints placed on government, regulation enforcement, and the criminal justice system, the United States indicates relatively strong performance. On the other hand, according to the WJP, in the United States, respect for fundamental rights and equal access to civil justice falters a bit.

DISCUSSION QUESTIONS

1. How do recent discussions about the US federal budget reflect the contrasting views of Musgrave and Buchanan (see chapter 1) about the size of government?

2. What are the consequences of uncertainty in the national budget process?

3. What are the implications of an increasing proportion of federal outlays to human resources that include transfer payments to individuals?

4. Budget laws in the United States illustrate the power struggle between the executive and legislative branches of government. Are there advantages and disadvantages to this ongoing tension between branches regarding budget powers?

5. What, if any, are the budget implications for the United States should it attempt to improve in the areas of respect for fundamental rights and its civil and criminal justice system?

6. Explore media accounts of the most recent budget negotiations of the US Congress and the president. Do these negotiations mirror past discussions? Explain any changes that you uncover that either exacerbate or

remedy the unraveling of the budget process that has been highlighted in this chapter.

7. Discuss the differences between the US federal budgeting process and the parliamentary process in Australia (see chapter 2). How do power and decision making about the budget differ in these two governments?

NOTES

1. There are numerous places to go to access a copy of the US Constitution, Bill of Rights, and other historical documents related to the United States, including the Library of Congress at http://www.loc.gov/rr/program/bib/ourdocs/Constitution.html or the National Archives at http://www.archives.gov/historical-docs/

2. The law (2010) and the US Supreme Court decision (2012) about the Patient Protection and Affordable Care Act are available at http://www.hhs.gov/healthcare/rights/law/index.html. Or, look up opinions at http://www.supremecourt.gov/opinions/11pdf/11-393c3a2.pdf

3. See Chapter XII, Section 4, at http://www.treasury.gov/about/history/Pages/act-congress.aspx

4. See US GAO, Antideficiency Act Background at http://www.gao.gov/legal/lawresources/antideficiencybackground.html

5. **Appropriations** are laws passed by Congress and signed by the president that authorize spending public funds. **Apportionment** is the distribution of these funds by the executive budget office (today, the Office of Management and Budget) to agencies. Apportionment is usually made in specific periods (quarterly) during a fiscal year and for particular projects and programs. **Allotment** is the approval by an agency head to lower-level managers to incur obligations or spend money in amounts no larger than that apportioned by the executive budget office.

6. **Deficit** results when government revenues cannot cover its expenditures in one fiscal year; a **surplus** occurs if revenues exceed expenditures in one fiscal year. A deficit is measured on a cash basis. **Debt** is the total accumulated borrowing by government across years. Total federal debt is made up of external debt or debt held by the public (public purchase of Treasury

notes, bills, and bonds) and internal debt or debt held by government trust funds (like Social Security, Medicare, and Transportation trust funds). The United States issues debt to the public to "finance a deficit"—that is, to close any negative gap between revenues and expenditures, to pay its obligations, and to keep government operating (see Austin and Levit 2013).

7. See US Office of Management and Budget, Historical Tables, Table 1.3—Summary of Receipts, Outlays, and Surpluses or Deficits in Current Dollars, Constant (FY 2005) Dollars and as Percentages of GDP: 1940–2018.

8. Federal spending is discretionary or mandatory (direct). Discretionary spending is provided through annual appropriations; mandatory spending is provided through permanent appropriations. Mandatory spending is nondiscretionary; eligibility and other formulas determine how much money the federal government must spend to cover these obligations. Mandatory spending includes about half of all federal expenditures and includes Social Security, Medicare, Medicaid, and interest on federal debt. Today, there are twelve annual appropriation bills that cover spending for defense and protection services (about two-thirds of discretionary spending) and for all other domestic programs such as education, housing, parks, energy, and transportation (about a third of discretionary spending). You can read about the status of appropriations bills by accessing Thomas at http://thomas.loc.gov/home/approp/app14.html. This is where the United States Library of Congress provides easy access to the work and output of the Congress.

9. Table 1.1—Summary Receipts, Outlays, and Surpluses or Deficits (–): 1789–2018 provided by the US Office of Management and Budget, Historical Tables, available at http://www.whitehouse.gov/omb/budget /historicals, indicates that by 1998, a $69.3 billion surplus emerged that grew to $236.2 billion by 2000, dropped to $128.2 billion in 2001 and then headed back into a deficit of −$157.8 billion by 2002.

10. See *The White House at Work*, Thursday, July 31, 1997. Available at http://clinton2.nara.gov/WH/Work/073197.html

11. See US Department of Treasury, TARP Programs. Available at http:// www.treasury.gov/initiatives/financial-stability/TARP-Programs/Pages /default.aspx#

12. To read the Act, go to http://www.gpo.gov/fdsys/pkg/BILLS-111hr1enr/pdf/BILLS-111hr1enr.pdf

13. See US Office of Management and Budget, Historical Tables, Table 1.1.

14. See US Office of Management and Budget, Historical Tables, Tables 7.1 and 7.3.

15. This partial government shutdown lasted two weeks and two days in October, 2013. Of the eighteen budget funding gaps experienced by the US federal government since 1976, the last and longest shutdown was from December 16, 1995 to January 6, 1996, lasting three weeks. Federal activities and programs in permanent law, such as Social Security, and functions, such as national defense, continue operating during shutdowns. It is the programs and activities that are funded through the annual appropriations process that are most significantly affected during shutdowns. For a recent discussion about the causes of US federal shutdowns, see Brass (2010).

16. When regular appropriation bills are not passed by the start of the fiscal year (October 1), then Congress must resort to continuing resolutions (CRs) to keep government agencies operating and avoid a government shutdown. CRs can include different specifications of timing for spending (full or partial year), activities funded, and the like. According to Rubin (2007), budgeting by CR greatly reduces the predictability of the federal budget process, given that these resolutions provide for appropriations of different funding levels and time periods for spending. After the CBA was passed in 1974, all appropriations bills were passed on time in 1977, 1989, 1995, and 1997. Since FY1977, an average of six CRs per year has been enacted to keep the government open. "During the past 15 fiscal years, Congress provided funding by means of a CR for an average of more than four months (126.6 days) each fiscal year" (Tollestrup 2012, 14).

REFERENCES

Auerbach, A. J. 2008. "Federal Budget Rules: The US Experience." *Swedish Economic Policy Review* 15: 57–82.

Austin, D. A., and M. R. Levit. 2013. "The Debt Limit: History and Recent Increases." Congressional Research Service Report for Congress, 7–5700 RL31967, October 15. Available at http://www.fas.org/sgp/crs/misc/RL31967.pdf

Berman, L. 1979. *The Office of Management and Budget and the Presidency, 1921–1979.* Princeton, NJ: Princeton University Press.

Board of Governors of the Federal Reserve System. June 2005. "The Federal Reserve System Purposes and Functions." Washington, DC: Federal Reserve System.

Brass, C. T. 2010. "Shutdown of the Federal Government: Causes, Processes, and Effects." Congressional Research Service Report for Congress (7–5700), September 27.

Buck, A. E. 1934. "Taxation in the New Social State II. Public Budgeting." *The Nation*, October 24, 139 (3616): 472–474.

Congressional Digest. 1922. "Digest of the Budget and Accounting Act, 1921." *Congressional Digest* 2: 39–40.

Congressional Digest. 1940. "The Practical Operation of the Federal Budget System." *Congressional Digest*, February: 37–40.

Dumbrell, J. 1980. "Strengthening the Legislative Power of the Purse: The Origins of the 1974 Budgetary Reforms in the US Congress." *Public Administration* 58 (4): 479–496.

Heniff, B., Jr., E. Rybicki, and S. M. Mahan. 2011. "The Budget Control Act of 2011." R41965, August 19. Washington, DC: Congressional Research Service. Available at http://www.fas.org/sgp/crs/misc/R41965.pdf

Heniff, B., Jr., and J. Murray. 2012. "Congressional Budget Resolutions: Historical Information." RL30297, March 13. Washington, DC: Congressional Research Service. Available at http://www.senate.gov/CRSReports/crs-publish.cfm?pid='0E%2C*PLS2%23%20%20%20%0A

Joyce, P. G. 2005. "Federal Budgeting after September 11th: A Whole New Ballgame, or Is It Déjà Vu All Over Again? *Public Budgeting & Finance* 25 (1): 15–31.

Keynes, J. M. 1936. *The General Theory of Employment, Interest, and Money.* London: Macmillan.

National Bureau of Economic Research (NBER). 2012. "US Business Cycle Expansions and Contractions." April 23. Cambridge, MA: National Bureau of Economic Research. Accessed on September 20, 2012. Available at http://www.nber.org/cycles/US_Business_Cycle_Expansions_and_Contractions_20120423.pdf

Penner, R. G. 2013. "The Folly of the Debt Ceiling," *CNN Money*, October 9. http://money.cnn.com/2013/10/09/news/economy/debt-ceiling-commentary/

Rubin, I. 2007. "The Great Unraveling: Federal Budgeting, 1998–2006," *Public Administration Review* 67 (4): 608–617.

Swann, N. G., and J. B. Chambers. 2013. "United States of America 'AA+/A-1+' Ratings Affirmed; Outlook Revised to Stable on Receding Fiscal Risks." Standard & Poor's Ratings Services, June 10. Available at http://www.standardandpoors.com/ratings/articles/en/us/?articleType=HTML&assetID=1245352834859

Tollestrup, J. 2012. "Continuing Resolutions: Overview of Components and Recent Practices." Congressional Research Service Report for Congress (7–5700), August 6.

US Census Bureau. 2012. "2012 Census of Governments: Organization Component Preliminary Estimates." Available at http://www2.census.gov/govs/cog/2012/formatted _prelim_counts_23jul2012_2.pdf

US Government Accountability Office. September 1991. "The Chief Financial Officers Act: A Mandate for Federal Financial Management Reform." GAO/AFMD-12.19.4. Available at http://www.gao.gov/special.pubs/af12194.pdf

US National Archives and Records Service. 1974. Federal Register Division, Public Papers of the Presidents of the United States, Richard Nixon. Washington, DC: Government Printing Office, 586–587.

US Public Law 93–344, 88 Stat., July 12, 1974. Available at http://www.gpo.gov/fdsys /pkg/STATUTE-88/pdf/STATUTE-88-Pg297.pdf

Weisman, J., and A. Parker. 2013. "Republicans Back Down, Ending Crisis Over Shutdown and Debt Limit." *The New York Times*, October 15. Available at http://www .nytimes.com/2013/10/17/us/congress-budget-debate.html?_r=0

World Justice Project (WJP). 2014. "WJP Rule of Law Index 2014." Washington, DC. Available at http://worldjusticeproject.org/sites/default/files/files/wjp_rule_of_law_ index_2014_report.pdf

Budget Foundations in US States

The powers not delegated to the United States by the Constitution, nor prohibited by it to the States, are reserved to the States, respectively, or to the people.

—Amendment X, US Constitution

LEARNING OBJECTIVES

After reading this chapter, you should be able to

- Understand the history of state government budget growth and the importance of this level of government in the United States

- Articulate the different legal constraints on US state government budgeting

- Distinguish between and among the constitutions, amendment procedures, and budgeting provisions of US states

- Investigate US state government budget rules and institutions and assess their impact on budgets

- Understand the legal foundations for performance budgeting in US state governments

- Understand the roles and importance of credit ratings, standards-setting agencies, and professional associations to state budgeting in the United States

---

Chapters 1 through 3 have introduced you to the truly unique systems of government and foundations for budgeting that exist around the world. The United States federal system of governance is distinctive in that thirteen colonies initially got together in 1787 to reform the Articles of Confederation, but then ratified a new Constitution that recognizes states and the central government as sovereign powers. As self-governing entities, states can develop and implement their own budgets by raising their own revenues, including borrowing money, to pay for services and programs as well as capital projects. The relationship of the national, state, and local governments in the United States has changed dramatically over the last 225 years. Today, in spite of the very real strength and influence of the federal government, the states have evolved as James Madison predicted in 1778 in the Federalist Papers, Number XLV: "the powers reserved to the several States will extend to all the objects which, in the ordinary course of affairs, concern the lives, liberties, and properties of the People" (Madison [1778] 2012, 461).

This chapter examines the legal foundations for budgeting in the US states. In this chapter, you will learn about the diversity of the fifty states, their constitutions and laws. This chapter also covers details about specific constitutional provisions and code—that is, the budget rules and institutions that directly affect state budgeting and budget outcomes. We will also consider the effects of credit ratings, public financial management, and reporting standards-setting and professional associations on state budgets as well.

THE FISCAL LANDSCAPE OF STATES: TWO CENTURIES OF GROWTH

As noted in the previous chapter, from early on the US national government maintained a relatively small presence in the ordinary course of affairs of its people. From 1800 to 1830, US federal revenues (per capita, in current dollars) exceeded those of the states by four to five times (Wallis 2000). However, during this time, it was state investment in public assets and banks that helped to advance local and regional economies. Development of the country's transportation grid—through waterways, roadways, and railroads—was primarily funded or initiated by the states. For example, Peter Samuel and Geoffrey Segal (2007) explain that during this period, many states leveraged private investment through long-term contracts, charters, and privatization initiatives for the development of roads and highways. In Pennsylvania alone, "some 199 turnpike companies were incorporated from 1800 to 1830 and the money raised from investors to build roads during that period amounted to over six percent of the state's GDP" (Samuel and Segal 2007, 3). Eric Zolt (2008–2009) concentrates on the relationship between economic equality and the size of state and local governments in the country noting that during the nineteenth century, spending for education and then insane asylums were the top two expenditure categories of states. According to Zolt (2008–2009), prior to the 1930s, many states "provided services to a substantial portion of the population in excess of the amounts paid in taxes" (447).

John Joseph Wallis (2000) accounts for US federal and state government revenues in current dollars per capita from 1800 to 1830, adding in local government revenues from 1840 to 1900. His data indicate that state revenues made up 9 percent of total government revenues in 1800 and inched up to 10 percent by 1830. State share then jumped to 24.4 percent of total government revenues in 1840, but declined to 13.7 percent by 1900. Local receipts made up the lion's share of total government revenues by 1900, at 49.9 percent. According to Wallis' data, revenues from state and local governments combined made up 63.7 percent of total government revenues in 1900. As Wallis (2000) explains, fiscal federalism in the United States has been fostered by the generation of revenues "at the least costly level of government" coupled with spending at "the level generating the greatest benefit" (65).

From mid-1800 until about 1930, local governments held sway vis-à-vis states and the federal government, using property taxes to provide basic services such as education, roads, and utilities (Wallis 2000). An economic recession in the 1840s precipitated some state defaults and allowed local governments to gain a more influential foothold in the development of public infrastructure across the nation. As you read in the previous chapter, throughout the nineteenth century, the federal government's commerce-related revenues remained plentiful even though this level of government maintained a relatively small presence in the economy. Federal revenues supported administration costs (personnel) predominantly, rather than grants, transfers, or the like to subnational governments. With the arrival of the twentieth century, "local government debt was roughly eight times state government debt" (Wallis 2000, 62) and local revenues made up the greatest share of all US government revenues (Zolt 2008–2009). The property tax became the predominant source of local revenue. This tax had slipped in importance for states, given their stronger reliance on commerce-related revenues (Wallis 2000).

The 16th Amendment to the US Constitution, which empowers Congress to tax income (1913), and legislation establishing a central bank (1913) as well as that regarding borrowing money (1917) serve as the foundations for a growing federal influence that spans the twentieth century. State and local government own-source revenues rise steadily throughout the century as well. In 1948, state and local government receipts made up 25 percent of total government revenues (in current dollars) compared to 75 percent in federal receipts. By 1968, state and local receipts comprised 33 percent of total government revenues. Today, US subnational receipts make up almost 40 percent of total government revenues with the federal share at 60 percent of these revenues.[1]

According to Randall Holcombe and Russell Sobel (1997), state expenditures as a percentage of GDP doubled from the 1950s to the 1960s and then increased "as much during the five years from 1988 to 1992 as during the entire period from 1970 to 1988" (4). Federal grants contribute to state influence as well. Federal grants as a percent of total government expenditures were 3.6 percent in 1948 and 9.7 percent by 2011.[2] Wallis (2000) points out that "national grants now account for roughly a third of state and local revenues. A system of central revenue collection and decentralized expenditure and administration became the standard model for administering programs in education, highways, water and sewage systems, and public welfare" (72). Table 4.1 presents US federal grants to state and local governments from 1940 to 2012 and estimated to 2018. These grants as a percent of GDP have grown over four and a half times since 1940. In 2011, federal support made up almost a quarter of state and local general revenue; states received over $574 billion in federal funding that year (Barnett and Vidal 2013; The Book of the States 2013, Table 2.5). Still, federal funds as a portion of state budgets vary considerably by state. For example, in fiscal year 2012, federal revenues made up 18 percent of total governmental funds in Wyoming and 49 percent of total governmental funds in Mississippi.[3]

LEGAL FOUNDATIONS FOR STATE BUDGETING

US state government budgets and their budgeting processes are interesting to study because there are fifty of them and each is unique. The following section examines state constitutions that structure the relationships and responsibilities

Table 4.1
US Federal Grants to State and Local Governments, 1940 to 2018 (Estimated)

Fiscal Year	In Millions of Dollars				In Billions of Constant (FY 2005) Dollars				Total Grants as % of GDP
	Total	Payments for Individuals	Capital Investment	Remainder	Total	Payments for Individuals	Capital Investment	Remainder	Total
1940	872	298	442	132	13.2	3.5	6.0	3.7	0.9
1980	91,385	32,619	22,570	36,196	227.0	71.1	44.9	111.1	3.4
1990	135,325	77,264	27,185	30,876	198.1	107.6	37.6	53.0	2.4
2000	285,874	182,592	48,655	54,627	326.7	203.1	56.5	67.0	2.9
2010	608,390	384,480	93,274	130,636	532.5	344.0	76.0	112.5	4.2
2011	606,766	387,806	96,546	122,414	519.7	339.6	76.9	103.2	4.1
2012	544,569	360,058	85,212	99,299	455.7	307.6	66.4	81.7	3.5
2013 est.	560,987	382,154	83,113	95,720	459.9	320.1	63.0	76.7	3.5
2014 est.	643,269	421,287	92,691	129,291	513.7	345.3	68.1	100.3	3.8
2015 est.	654,658	448,279	104,966	101,413	510.4	359.6	74.6	76.1	3.6
2016 est.	673,309	476,817	102,846	93,646	513.1	374.2	70.8	68.1	3.6
2017 est.	685,794	496,045	95,438	94,311	510.9	380.9	63.6	66.4	3.4
2018 est.	702,127	512,343	93,711	96,073	510.9	385.0	60.4	65.5	3.3

Source: US Office of Management and Budget, Historical Tables, Table 12.1—Summary Comparison of Total Outlays for Grants to State and Local Governments: 1940–2018 (in Current Dollars, as Percentages of Total Outlays, as Percentages of GDP, and in Constant [FY2005] Dollars). Available at http://www.whitehouse.gov/omb/budget/historicals

of government to the public. How state constitutions are amended and the nature of budget provisions that are included in them influences the capacity of states to finance public programs, services, and projects. The section that discusses budget institutions reviews the various strictures on the states for budget making, including balanced budget requirements, tax and spend limitations, debt limits, and legislative voting requirements regarding revenue changes and the budget, generally. The section closes with an overview of performance budgeting laws in the states—indicative of the very strong application of New Public Management to budgeting that is evident at this level of government in the United States.

State Constitutions

Marvin Krislov and Daniel Katz (2008) explain that "constitutions are important precisely because they are semi-permanent institutions robustly designed to restrict the current and future domain of possibilities" (327). The word "robust" implies strength, whereas "semi-permanent" suggests immutable, though with the possibility for transformation. US state government constitutions are forceful documents that provide the foundations for community life within their borders, though they are amended periodically. Collectively, these constitutions present a cornucopia of amendment methods and results that are indicative of the variety of traditions, cultures, and interpretations of democracy on the part of these governments and their voters. Table 4.2 presents information about the number of constitutions each state has had and the dates of adoption. Fewer than half of states (19) have had just one constitution; twenty-five states have had from two to five. Alabama, Florida, and Virginia have had six constitutions each; South Carolina, seven; Georgia, ten; and Louisiana currently operates under its eleventh constitution. Massachusetts' sole constitution was adopted in 1780 and is the oldest American state constitution. New Hampshire adopted its second and present constitution in 1784 and Vermont had three constitutions by the end of 1793. Rhode Island has the youngest constitution—the state adopted its second constitution in 1986 at the only state constitutional convention to be held for the past twenty-seven years. A computer word count indicates that Alabama's constitution is the wordiest with 376,006 words. This constitution is recognized as the longest in the world; the state's constitution still allows for local amendments that could regard just one county government (Dinan 2013). Alternatively, Vermont's constitution is quite terse at just 8,565 words.

There are many different ways that states provide for constitutional changes and promote "direct democracy," or the participation of the public. These avenues are not as limiting as those regarding changes to the US Constitution, however. Krislov and Katz (2008) point out that "many states provide multiple avenues to constitutional change and permit extensive citizen involvement in the constitutional amendment process" (298). These scholars further (302–303) describe the range of options that states provide to their citizens for making constitutional changes, including

The Public and No Legislature

Popular Referenda whereby the public petitions for voters to approve or reject legislation that has already been passed by the legislature

Direct Statutory Initiative whereby the public puts statutes before voters to approve or reject

Direct Constitutional Initiative whereby the public puts constitutional changes before voters to approve or reject

The Public with Legislative Consideration

Indirect Statutory Initiative whereby the public submits statutes to the legislature to consider before they go to ballot for voters to approve or reject

Indirect Constitutional Initiative whereby the public submits constitutional changes to the legislature to consider before they go to ballot for voters to approve or reject

Legislature to the Public

Statutory Legislative Referenda whereby legislators put statutes before voters to approve or reject

Constitutional Legislative Referenda whereby legislators put constitutional changes before voters to approve or reject

These methods vary regarding legislative role, with popular referenda and direct statutory and constitutional initiative methods being the most direct means for citizens to have a voice regarding their government and its powers and operation. Of direct ballot measures put forward to citizens in 49 states from 1977 to 2006, Krislov and Katz (2008) found that the constitutional legislative referenda by far the predominant method of change in law. Nonetheless, for

Table 4.2
State Constitutions by Effective Date of Present Constitution

State	# of Constitutions	Effective Date of Present Constitution	Dates of Adoption
Massachusetts	1	October 25, 1780	1780
New Hampshire	2	June 2, 1784	1776, 1784
Vermont	3	July 9, 1793	1777, 1786, 1793
Maine	1	March 15, 1820	1819
Wisconsin	1	May 29, 1848	1848
Ohio	2	September 1, 1851	1802, 1851
Indiana	2	November 1, 1851	1816, 1851
Iowa	2	September 3, 1857	1846, 1857
Minnesota	1	May 11, 1858	1857
Oregon	1	February 14, 1859	1857
Kansas	1	January 29, 1861	1859
Nevada	1	October 31, 1864	1864
Maryland	4	October 5, 1867	1776, 1851, 1864, 1867
Tennessee	3	February 23, 1870	1796, 1835, 1870
West Virginia	2	April 9, 1872	1863, 1872
Arkansas	5	October 30, 1874	1836, 1861, 1864, 1868, 1874
Nebraska	2	October 12, 1875	1866, 1875
Texas	5	February 15, 1876	1845, 1861, 1866, 1869, 1876
Colorado	1	August 1, 1876	1876
California	2	July 4, 1879	1849, 1879
North Dakota	1	November 2, 1889	1889
South Dakota	1	November 2, 1889	1889
Washington	1	November 11, 1889	1889
Idaho	1	July 3, 1890	1889
Wyoming	1	July 10, 1890	1889

State	No.	Effective date	Dates of adoption
Mississippi	4	November 1, 1890	1817, 1832, 1869, 1890
Kentucky	4	September 28, 1891	1792, 1799, 1850, 1891
New York	4	January 1, 1895	1777, 1822, 1846, 1894
South Carolina	7	January 1, 1896	1776, 1778, 1790, 1861, 1865, 1868, 1895
Utah	1	January 4, 1896	1895
Delaware	4	June 10, 1897	1776, 1792, 1831, 1897
Alabama	6	November 28, 1901	1819, 1861, 1865, 1868, 1875, 1901
Oklahoma	1	November 16, 1907	1907
New Mexico	1	January 6, 1912	1911
Arizona	1	February 14, 1912	1911
Missouri	4	March 30,1945	1820, 1865, 1875, 1945
New Jersey	3	January 1, 1948	1776, 1844, 1947
Alaska	1	January 3, 1959	1956
Hawaii	1	August 21, 1959	1950
Michigan	4	January 1, 1964	1835, 1850, 1908, 1963
Connecticut	4	December 30, 1965	1818 (f), 1965
Pennsylvania	5	1968	1776, 1790, 1838, 1873, 1968 (r)
Florida	6	January 7, 1969	1839, 1861, 1865, 1868, 1886, 1968
Illinois	4	July 1, 1971	1818, 1848, 1870, 1970
North Carolina	3	July 1, 1971	1776, 1868, 1970
Virginia	6	July 1, 1971	1776, 1830, 1851, 1869, 1902, 1970
Montana	2	July 1, 1973	1889, 1972
Louisiana	11	January 1, 1975	1812, 1845, 1852, 1861, 1864, 1868, 1879, 1898, 1913, 1921, 1974
Georgia	10	July 1,1983	1777, 1789, 1798, 1861, 1865, 1868, 1877, 1945, 1976, 1982
Rhode Island	3	December 4, 1986	1842, 1986

Source: Created from *The Book of the States*, Chapter 1. Table 1.1: General Information on State Constitutions (as of January 1, 2013). Excel file available at http://knowledgecenter.csg.org/kc/content/book-states-2013-chapter-1-state-constitutions

every one of these methods, voters are the final arbiter of changes. And "in virtually all states, any constitutional amendment must be ratified through a statewide vote" (Krislov and Katz 2008, 325).

Eighteen states allow their constitution to be amended by citizen initiative. The signatures necessary on an initiative petition vary in number and specificity—from 15 percent of total votes cast for all candidates for governor in the last election (Arizona) to 8 percent such votes in (Oregon) to 4 percent of the population of the state (North Dakota). The distribution of signatures ranges from "none specified" or not in effect (ten states) to some proportion of the state's counties or congressional districts (eight states). Most of these states require a majority vote on the amendment put forward to voters, though a few provide further qualifiers such as including at least 30 percent (Massachusetts), 35 percent (Nebraska), or not less than 40 percent (Mississippi) of votes cast at the election. Florida requires three-fifths of the vote on such amendments except those for any new state tax or fee not in effect November 7, 1994, which require two-thirds of the vote in the election. Oregon law stipulates a majority vote on amendment, except in cases where a supermajority voting requirement is contained in the proposed amendment. Nevada's initiative process requires a majority vote on the amendment in two consecutive general elections (*The Book of the States* 2013, Table 1.3).

John Dinan (2013) finds that "all state constitutional amendments on the 2012 ballot were formally proposed either by legislatures or the initiative process, with a passing rate of 72.6 percent for legislatively proposed amendments; the passing rate of amendments proposed through citizen initiative compares at 38.9 percent" (3). Most changes to state constitutions in the last five years regard finance and taxation, with the second most popular type of amendment regarding individual rights (including same-sex marriage, affirmative action, property rights, right to bear arms, freedom of religion, voting for union representation, voter identification, and those related to mandatory health insurance per passage by Congress of the Patient Protection and Affordable Care Act of 2010) (Dinan 2013).[4]

A sampling of the constitutional provisions that have an impact on the budget process is provided for three states. Beware that determining the meaning of constitutional provisions or statutes is not an exact science. The following discussion about state budget rules and institutions will clarify why this is so.

Missouri   Article IV of Missouri's constitution[5] presents requirements of the executive branch of government. Section 27 of the article gives the governor responsibility for the rate of spending during budget execution "by allotment or other means." The governor is allowed to reduce state spending below appropriations "whenever actual revenues are less than the revenue estimates upon which the appropriations were based." Section 27 (a) (as adopted in 1986 and amended in 2000) establishes the state's budget reserve fund, allowing the commissioner of administration to make transfers from the fund into "the general revenue fund or any other state fund without other legislative action if he determines that such amounts are necessary for the cash requirements of this state." This section also states that

> In any fiscal year in which the governor reduces the expenditures of the state or any of its agencies below their appropriations or in which there is a budget need due to a disaster, as proclaimed by the governor to be an emergency, the general assembly, upon a request by the governor for an emergency appropriation and by a two-thirds vote of the members elected to each house, may appropriate funds from the budget reserve fund to fulfill the expenditures authorized by any of the existing appropriations which were affected by the governor's decision to reduce expenditures or to meet budget needs due to the disaster. Such expenditures shall be deemed to be for "budget stabilization purposes." The maximum amount which may be appropriated at any one time for such budget stabilization purposes shall be one-half of the sum of the balance in the fund and any amounts appropriated or otherwise owed to the fund, less all amounts owed to the fund for budget stabilization purposes but not yet appropriated for repayment to the fund.

Other components of this provision in Missouri's constitution determine amounts that should remain in the balance of the fund, amounts that can be transferred or spent from the fund, in what circumstances funds may be transferred or spent, and the time periods of such transactions.

South Carolina   South Carolina's constitution[6] does press for budget balance, too. Article 10, section 7 of this constitution expresses the limitation on annual expenditures of the state and number of state employees and makes stipulations about the annual budgets and expenses of political subdivisions and school districts (we will learn more about local governments in the next chapter).

Specifically, this section states that "the General Assembly shall provide by law for a budget process to insure that annual expenditures of state government may not exceed annual state revenue."

Wisconsin   Article VIII of Wisconsin's constitution[7] presents rules regarding (1) taxation, appropriations, and limitations, and (2) state credit and borrowing authority and limits. Article VIII, section 6 considers public debt for extraordinary expenses, stating:

> For the purpose of defraying extraordinary expenditures the state may contract public debts (but such debts shall never in the aggregate exceed one hundred thousand dollars). Every such debt shall be authorized by law, for some purpose or purposes to be distinctly specified therein; and the vote of a majority of all the members elected to each house, to be taken by yeas and nays, shall be necessary to the passage of such law; and every such law shall provide for levying an annual tax sufficient to pay the annual interest of such debt and the principal within five years from the passage of such law, and shall specially appropriate the proceeds of such taxes to the payment of such principal and interest; and such appropriation shall not be repealed, nor the taxes be postponed or diminished, until the principal and interest of such debt shall have been wholly paid.

Provisions in section 7 of this article provide allowances for borrowing to fund specific things—the state can borrow "to repel invasion, suppress insurrection, or defend the state in time of war." Also, the state can borrow to pay for capital projects, equipment, and veterans' housing loans. Further constitutional requirements specify debt levels, legislative responsibilities for debt determinations and repayment, leasing and contracting, and recognition that "the full faith, credit and taxing power of the state are pledged to the payment of all public debt created on behalf of the state."

State Budget Institutions and Rules

The rules and institutions found in state constitutions and code provide the decision making structures and responsibilities and powers of the elected officials, managers, and staff for determining and executing the budgets of these governments. Important budget rules and institutions in the states include balanced budget requirements, debt limitations, tax and expenditure limitations, and supermajority voting requirements related to taxes and state finance. Table 4.3 aggregates data from several sources about these foundations for state budgeting.

As mentioned earlier, it is often difficult to understand the meaning of legal provisions in constitutions or code. Because of this, it is hard to provide definitive numbers for each type of budget rule or institution that exists in every state. The National Conference of State Legislatures (NCSL 2010) highlights the problems in determining with certainty which states have what provisions—it depends upon state history and tradition, to whom you talk, judicial precedent, and individual interpretation. For example, you are likely to get different answers about the legal foundations for state government budgeting if you talk to those who practice in the field, such as executive budget staff, state agency personnel, state legislators and their staff, or the governor versus those who study these systems and structures, such as academic scholars and researchers in evaluation agencies that include the US Government Accountability Office as well as the National Association of State Budget Officers (NASBO) and the NCSL. The NCSL (2010) explains the problems with pinning down the legal provisions for balanced budgets in North Dakota as follows:

> Executive budget staff [from North Dakota] reported to NASBO that the constitution requires that the governor submit, the legislature enact, and the governor sign a balanced budget. For this [NCSL] report, legislative fiscal staff cited Article X, Section 13 of the state constitution as the source of the state's balanced budget requirement. Hou and Smith (2006), however, report a complete absence of balanced budget requirements in the North Dakota Constitution and statutes, and point out that Article X, Section 13, is a general limitation on debt. A restriction of debt can certainly imply that annual or biennial budgets have to be balanced, but clearly is open to differing interpretations by observers. (5)

Balanced Budget Rules The NCSL (2010) describes the balanced budget rules found in the fifty states, the distinction between constitutional and statutory provisions, and state success in complying with such rules. The Conference explains the importance of understanding what part or parts of the budget must balance and who is responsible for developing and providing for a balanced budget. For example, most state budget balance provisions regard the general fund that is a governmental fund supported predominantly by taxes imposed by the state to pay for the general operations of the government.[8] Thus, most balance requirements in the states are only applicable to a portion of the budget. State balanced budget requirements range in stringency with the strictest being that the governor submit a balanced budget to the legislature, the legislature pass a balanced budget (the appropriations bill), the governor sign a balanced budget into law, and the state end the fiscal year in balance. Alternatively, states may be obligated to any kind of mix of these requirements—laws may stipulate that the governor must submit a balanced budget (general fund only), but there may be no legal requirements that the legislature pass a balanced budget or that the budget be balanced at the end of the fiscal year.[9]

Examination of Table 4.3 indicates that most states have legal provisions that the governor submit a balanced budget to the state legislature (the weakest constraint), but fewer require that the legislature pass a balanced budget, and fewer still require the governor to sign a balanced budget into law. Most states have some sort of legal requirement banning a budget deficit from being carried forward into the next fiscal year, an end-of-year balance requirement that is the most stringent of these rules. According to NASBO (2008), just over half of states (26) have constitutional or statutory laws that hold the government to all four balanced budget components.

Debt Limitations States issue debt (sell bonds) mostly to fund expensive capital projects that will provide benefits to residents and others over the long term, as opposed to paying for operations that provide services and programs during the fiscal year. The NASBO (2008) summarizes the debt provisions in states, indicating that just five states do not have any policy to limit debt (Alaska, Arkansas, California, Montana, and Oklahoma), although in Arkansas, "statutory limits can exist" (43). Alaska is an interesting outlier. The state has a constitutionally established "Permanent Fund" funded by revenues from mining oil reserves. The revenues in this fund are invested with earnings from investments available for the legislature to appropriate and dividends from the account paid to state residents annually.[10] In Alaska, general obligation (GO) bonds are passed by law and approved by voters (Montague and DeRose 2011). The consulting firm Montague and DeRose finds that just three states do have not any debt limits or guidelines (Maine, Michigan, and Montana). In each of these states, there

Table 4.3
US State Government Budget Rules, Number of States by Type

Type of Budget Constraint	Constitutional and Statutory	Type of Law or Policy				
		Constitutional	Statutory	Legal Requirement	Policy	Total
Governor must submit balanced budget	15	18	10			43
Legislature must pass balanced budget	10	22	8			40
Governor must sign balanced budget	12	18	5			37*
No carry forward of deficit into next year				37		37
Limit authorized debt		35	5		7	47
Revenue limitation		4	1			5
Expenditure limitation	5	7	15			27
Supermajority vote to pass revenue increase				15		15
Voter approval to pass revenue increase				3		3
Supermajority vote on all or part of state budget				9		9

Sources: Data compiled from Kioko 2011; Montague and DeRose and Associates, LLC 2011; NASBO 2008, 40; NCSL 2010, 3; NCSL 2008.

*From NASBO 2008, Table 11. Balanced Budget Requirements, 40, which does not indicate type of constraint (legal or policy) for two states with the requirement, New York and Utah.

are no legal restrictions on these governments regarding the issuance of general obligation (GO) debt (Montague and DeRose 2011). This firm, which consults with governments about capital investments, debt, and other public finance issues, finds that thirty-five states either have a debt limit or prohibit debt. For example, Indiana's constitution prohibits debt "except to meet casual deficits in revenue, pay interest on state debt, or to provide funds for public defense" (Montague and DeRose 2011, 2). Nebraska's constitution constrains the state "from pledging its credit as sole payment for debts incurred for state operations" (Montague and DeRose 2011, 2). In both Oklahoma and Oregon, there are no legal provisions that restrict state issuance of GO debt that can only be incurred by constitutional amendment. Generally, state government borrowing may be limited to specified dollar amounts, require approval by the legislature or voters, or may be subject to review by a debt management committee or commission. Eighteen states indicate no (or informal only) policy limiting debt service or the costs associated with borrowing (NASBO 2008).

Dwight Denison and Robert Greer (2014) conclude that most states have some sort of limit on GO debt, whereas just four states limit revenue or non-guaranteed debt (debt is paid back with revenues generated by the bonded project). In their discussion of state competition for debt resources, Denison and Greer point out that over a dozen states have "umbrella policies" that regard both GO and nonguaranteed debt (87). States also are limited informally regarding debt issuance through the credit ratings applied related to their debt quality. Debt quality is analyzed in terms of affordability, or the level of debt a government can finance, and capacity or "the level of debt or debt service relative to current revenues that an issuing entity could support without creating undue budgetary constraints that might impair the issuer's ability to repay outstanding bonds or make timely debt service payments" (Denison and Greer 2014, 87).

Tax and Expenditure Limitations   Bert Waisanen (2010) provides an overview of the tax and expenditure limitations (TELs) that exist in 30 states, finding four states with taxing limits, 23 with spending limits, and three that have both types. Three states require voter approval of tax increases; 15 require supermajority voting of both chambers of the state legislature to approve tax increases. Sharon Kioko (2011) lumps state tax and expenditure limitations together, referring to such measures as "general fund limitations" given their effects on tax receipts into or appropriations out of the general fund. As indicated in

Table 4.3, four states have constitutionally based tax limitations and just one state (Massachusetts) has this type of limitation in statute. According to Kioko (2011), most spending limitations are found in state code (15); seven states provide such limits in their constitution, and five have both constitutional and statutory expenditure limits.

Many states tie tax and expenditure limits to an index of inflation, personal income, or population, or some combination of these measures. Most states engage some sort of mixture of limitations. Waisanen's list (2010) of the pros and cons of these limitations presents such laws as double-edged swords. On the one hand, voters generally feel more secure that their taxes will be lower and government will be smaller, that their tax dollars will be more efficiently allocated, and the state budget will be more transparent and accountable, given the existence of TELs. On the other hand, TELs move decisions about state finances away from elected officials. Possibly more important, TELs can severely restrict the ability of a state to manage well (or even marginally) through an economic downturn. During a recession, state revenues shrivel up as income and sales taxes and other revenue receipts drop, and expenditures increase with expanding public demand for services and support.

Supermajority Voting Requirements Voting strictures related to tax increases and appropriations influence state budgets as well. Supermajority voting requirements of state legislators stipulate passing laws for new taxes or tax increases by three-fifths, two-thirds, or three-fourths, rather than by a simple majority. The NASBO (2008) indicates that eleven states require more than a simple majority of legislators to approve revenue increases. The NCSL (2010) counts fifteen states with supermajority voting requirements to pass tax increases and three states—Colorado, Missouri, and Washington—that engage the more stringent voter approval requirement for tax increases. Some states also require supermajority voting by legislators to pass appropriation bills, in part or in whole. According to an updated brief by the NCSL (2008), nine states have such requirements related to the budget. Arkansas, California, and Rhode Island require a supermajority vote to pass appropriation bills each fiscal year; Connecticut, Hawaii, Illinois, Maine, Mississippi, and Nebraska stipulate the supermajority vote under certain conditions that may relate to specific state functions, regard local interests, as exceptions when the budget is not passed on time, or if a budget gap exists (NCSL 2008).

There is no consensus on the effects of the budget rules and institutions discussed above. Although the states serve as "laboratories" in the sense that they offer up a very rich variety of budget structures and processes, this variety has been problematic to determining exactly what constitutional provision, law, or policy will consistently lead to a state's fiscal discipline, thriving economy, and happy residents. "Few generalities can be drawn from [the research about TELs] because no two TELs are exactly the same" (Stallman and Deller 2011, 113). As suggested earlier, the common perception is that restrictions on government taxing and spending will help to impose fiscal restraint on the part of states to balance their budgets, conduct work efficiently, and foster a strong business climate.

James Poterba (1996) has found that budget rules such as those described earlier orient decision makers to be alert to deficit reduction and fiscal conservatism; debt limits keep state borrowing low and pressure states to work through public authorities to conduct certain services and to develop infrastructure. Such constraints keep debt and taxes low; as Poterba (1996) writes, "constitutional or legislative provisions that make it more costly to balance the budget in a given fashion, by raising taxes or by issuing long-term debt, appear to have real effects in discouraging these fiscal actions" (40). Poterba and Kim Rueben (1995) have found that TELs can effectively limit government spending. Poterba (1996) adds that voter mobility might work in conjunction with these rules to pressure states to engage in fiscal discipline. That is, voters can move to states that provide the mix of services they want and collection of taxes and other charges and fees that they are willing to bear.

In summarizing research about balanced budget rules, Robert Inman (1996) determines that more stringent rules advance greater deficit control in the states. This scholar presents certain conditions for more effective balanced budget rules, including constitutional provision for the rule (making it harder to amend), a requirement of balance at the end of the fiscal year (the "no carry over" provision that bans a deficit to carry forward into the next fiscal year), transparent enforcement of the rule by an independent agency (state courts), and assignment by this agency of significant penalties (such as court control over an agency's budget) should the rule be broken (Inman 1996).

In a study that examines the relationships between TELs, state business climates, and economic performance, Judith Stallman and Steven Deller (2011) measure limitations along a continuum from most restrictive to nonexistent.

Their model also includes numerous measures of economic performance, strength of the business climate, and development capacity. They find that there are no real differences among states, given the varied levels of constraint imposed by TELs. They determine that more restrictive TELs are not related to a better business climate and economic performance. "From a policy perspective, the results suggest that TELs by themselves are not associated with higher levels of business climate and economic performance by states" (Stallman and Deller 2011, 134–135).

Performance Budgeting Laws in the States

In governments, performance-based budgeting, or what is perhaps better termed performance-*informed* budgeting (Joyce 2003), is a reform that requires developing, using, and reporting measures of agency performance and program outcomes throughout the budgeting process. The idea of injecting rationality into what is a highly political process has been considered in the United States for over a hundred years. For example, in the federal government, in 1905, the Keep Commission (technically, the Committee on Department Methods) was made up of appointees by then President Theodore Roosevelt to examine government operations, measure and evaluate these activities, and determine how work could be conducted more efficiently. Oscar Kraines (1970) studied the development of and results from the Keep Commission and reports that upon its creation, President Roosevelt said, "I do not want merely to know that things are bad; I want to know what is bad and what is to be done to make it better, so that if legislation is necessary I can recommend it" (6). The Commission, which existed until 1909, investigated corrupt practices of federal agencies and departments (Agriculture, Government Printing Office, and Interior, for example), examined federal classification systems and positions, analyzed federal procurement, coordinated the collection of statistics (recommended a central statistics agency), and assessed records management and agency accounting (for instance, the Commission's examination of the US Treasury accounting practices led to the adoption of double-entry bookkeeping in federal accounting) (Kraines 1970). In the end, the Commission's work resulted in significant savings to taxpayers through efficiency measures and the reduction of corruption in administration. According to Kraines, "one of its major accomplishments was to change the connotation of the word "administration" from its long-held simple meaning of the personnel of the executive departments to the art of managing the public business" (52–53).

State governments have been at the forefront of public budgeting reforms and we will examine some of these in more detail in a later chapter of this book. For now, it is important to understand the legal foundations of this reform in the US states. Yi Lu, Katherine Willoughby, and Sarah Arnett (2009) present a comprehensive list of performance budgeting laws in thirty-nine of these governments, defining such laws broadly as "code that stipulates measurement of government performance and the application of such measurement to the budgeting process" (270). Examination of their listing of laws (2009, 271–272) includes the oldest in Hawaii (Hawaii Revised Statutes Chapter 37–63, 1970) to more recent code in New Jersey (New Jersey Statutes, Title 52, 52:15C-8, 2007). The following are sections of each of these laws:

Hawaii Revised Statutes, Title 5. State Financial Administration
37. Budget

§37–63 Statement of policy. It is the purpose of this part to establish a comprehensive system for state program and financial management which furthers the capacity of the governor and the legislature to plan, program and finance the programs of the State. The system shall include procedures for:

(1) The orderly establishment, continuing review and periodic revision of the state program and financial objectives and policies.

(2) The development, coordination and review of long-range program and financial plans that will implement established state objectives and policies.

(3) The preparation, coordination and analysis, and enactment of a budget organized to focus on state programs and their costs, that authorizes the implementation of the long-range plans in the succeeding budget period.

(4) The evaluation of alternatives to existing objectives, policies, plans and procedures that offer potential for more efficient and effective use of state resources.

(5) The regular appraisal and reporting of program performance. [L 1970, c 185, §3]

New Jersey Statutes, Title 52, 52:15C-8, 2007

(3) The State Comptroller shall establish objective criteria for undertaking performance and other reviews authorized by this act, which criteria shall weigh relevant risk factors, including, but not limited to: (a) the size of the entity's budget, (b) the entity's past performance, (c) the frequency, scope, and quality of any audits or reviews that have been performed regarding the entity's financial condition or performance, (d) assessments or evaluations of the entity's management, performance or financial condition such as those undertaken as part of the New Jersey Quality Single Accountability Continuum for school districts, and (e) other credible information which suggests the necessity of a review.

Lu and Willoughby (2012) explain that Pennsylvania most recently passed performance budgeting legislation in 2011. State of Pennsylvania (2011) **Title 71, Chapter 41, §4104** enumerates the duties of the independent fiscal office to include

- Preparation of revenue estimates, including projected revenue surplus or deficit for a given fiscal year

- By November 15 of each year, assessment of the state's current fiscal condition and projection of the fiscal condition for next five years

- Performance measures for executive programs and departments and evaluation of performance measures and results, including measures that are outcome based, including activity cost analysis, measures of status improvement of recipient populations, economic outcomes, and performance benchmarks against similar state programs

- Analysis of all tax and revenue proposals submitted by the governor or the Office of the Budget

- Analysis of existing sales and use tax law and recommendations to the governor and the General Assembly for amending the tax

- Discretionary activities can include the development and use of econometric models to forecast state revenues; analysis of the executive budget, including budgetary projections, economic outlook, and economic impact that can include performance recommendations to secure greater efficiency and economy; assessment of state and national economies and the impact of the existing or emerging economic trends on revenue performance for the current year, and the forecasted revenue collections for the budget and succeeding years

As you can tell, performance budgeting law looks different in the various states. To date, forty states have laws that require some degree of performance measurement use for budgeting. These laws indicate a wide range of components applicable to a budgeting system. Possible requirements might include assignment of responsibilities regarding performance measurement development and/or the review and revision of program goals and objectives; establishment of benchmarks and/or long-range or other strategic plans; assessment of costs; the conduct of trend analysis; evaluation of alternatives; consideration of efficient and effective use of resources; and periodic evaluation, performance auditing, and/or measurement and results reporting. By 2012, just ten states did not have performance budgeting law: Arkansas, Kansas, Maine, Massachusetts, New Hampshire, New York, North Carolina, North Dakota, South Dakota, and West Virginia. These states may have systems in place through executive mandate, or they may have had systems legislated in the past that have since been repealed. Some may have a tradition of using measures for budgeting, but the practice is not required by law to be conducted.

The research about performance budgeting and its impact on state budgets, like that of TELs and other such rules and institutions, is inconclusive. For example, there is little evidence that public officials establish budgets and pass appropriation bills based strictly on measures of agency or program performance. Lu, Willoughby, and Arnett (2009) examined performance budgeting laws and the reform's practice in the states, determining that states with laws that are more specific about how measurement must be used and integrated into the budget process are more likely to make strong use of performance information for resource allocation decisions. States with strong budgeting for performance systems have more comprehensive laws requiring shared responsibilities (across executive and legislative branches) related to using performance measures in the budget process (Lu, Willoughby, and Arnett 2009). In later research comparing states that have performance budgeting laws to those without such laws, Lu, Willoughby, and Arnett (2011) find that states with robust performance budgeting systems "are more likely to have legal foundations that incorporate a broader array of performance measurement development, protocols and oversight" (91) for budgetary decision making. These states are also more likely to have laws that require development of a government-wide strategic plan and input from citizens into the budget process. This research provides a good case for developing laws that are specific (for example, assigning responsibility for measurement development, review, and reporting) as well as comprehensive (requiring performance measurement reporting and assessment throughout the budget process). More recently, Lu and Willoughby (2012) controlled for political, social, and economic factors across states with performance budgeting laws and found that

- States with a longer history of having performance budgeting law on the books indicate higher current ratios (liquidity) and lower expenditures per capita (service-level solvency).
- States with the strongest performance budgeting systems (as practiced) indicate lower long-term liability ratios.

Together, these findings suggest some long-term benefits to state fiscal health, given law and the consistent practice of performance budgeting. Scott Pattison (2011), executive director of the NASBO, has commented that performance budgeting in the states does add value to the decision arena. Performance information more fully differentiates between effective and ineffective government operations, programs, and services and can provide stronger justification for public officials when making budgetary trade-offs.

If you think back to the different theoretical approaches to public budgeting mentioned in chapter 1, each of the theories recognizes the real, substantial, and even rational aspects of the *politics* of the budgetary process. It would be impossible to take the politics out of the public budgeting process. On the other hand, the legal requirements for developing and using performance information in the budget process result in the addition of specific, important, and relevant data for making decisions about the use of public resources. Also, the structures and responsibilities laid out in these laws influence how public officials, budget and finance officers, managers, citizens, and others will interact throughout the budget process.

CREDIT RATINGS, GASB STANDARDS, AND PROFESSIONAL GUIDELINES

In addition to the laws, rules, and institutions that bind states in their budget making, as discussed, other factors structure budgeting systems and practices.

Credit rating agencies judge the risk of investing in states that borrow for infrastructure and other reasons. The Governmental Accounting Standards Board (GASB) provides standards for financial accounting and reporting that states (and US local governments) must follow to justify their adherence to strong accountability and transparency—which are part of what credit rating agencies consider when assessing government credit risk. Also, numerous professional organizations provide best practices that can help states to strengthen their budgeting and financial management. Evidence of the execution of such practices can assist states when going to market for funding in addition to advancing their budgeting more generally. Each of these factors is explained below.

Credit Ratings

As noted earlier, state governments generally borrow to pay for capital projects. Unlike the United States federal government, which has national fiscal policy responsibilities (economic stabilization and growth) that necessitate the use of debt primarily to finance budget deficits, US subnational governments consider credit and use debt differently. When state governments need to borrow money, they issue debt securities that must be rated for credit risk; a state's credit rating or the rating on a particular issue will determine the rate of interest paid—the higher the credit rating, the lower the cost of borrowing.[11] Therefore, credit ratings are very important to state budgets.

Credit rating agencies conduct analyses of this risk, determining the likelihood that the government is fiscally healthy enough to pay back the debt with interest and over time. Analysts with these agencies examine the characteristics of governments across a number of factors, including political framework and stability; economic aspects such as tax laws, bases, and rates; current and future prospects of revenue sources and availability; population characteristics and wealth; budgetary management and health; and debt burden, management policies, and practices.[12] Although you can join and search the databases of the three credit rating agencies to find the ratings of specific governments and debt issues, The Pew Charitable Trusts (2012) offers a graphic display of Standard & Poor's credit ratings for the fifty states from 2001 to 2012.[13] This display shows that thirteen states have the highest rating, AAA, from Standard & Poor's. Alaska's positive move from AA in 2003 to AAA in 2012 is attributed to the state's management of its oil revenues, while California's A– rating is indicative of its budget problems since strict tax limits were passed there in 1978. Missouri, North Carolina, Virginia, and Utah have held their AAA credit rating for forty-six years or more (The Pew Charitable Trusts 2012). Eight states have the coveted "Triple-Triple" credit rating—Aaa from Moody's and AAA from both Standard & Poor's and Fitch. These states include Delaware, Georgia, Iowa, Maryland, Missouri, North Carolina, Utah, and Virginia. Illustrative of the importance that governors (and others) attach to a state's credit rating, Georgia's Governor Nathan Deal has mentioned his state's pristine rating in every budget he has submitted to the General Assembly in the last three years. In his fiscal year 2014 budget recommendation, he proclaimed:

> Solid fiscal stewardship and steady economic growth allowed us to finish Fiscal Year 2012 in a strong position, growing the rainy day fund for the third straight year, increasing it to more than $378 million, and maintaining the prestigious triple-A bond rating with all three rating agencies (State of Georgia, The Governor's Budget Report, Fiscal Year 2014, 4).

GASB Standards and Professional Guidelines

Governments in the United States and around the world are subject to various accounting, financial management, and performance reporting standards that have an impact on their budgets and budgeting processes. Private accounting standards are set by the International Accounting Standards Board (IASB) that publishes International Financial Reporting Standards (IFRS), formerly called International Accounting Standards (IAS). Public accounting standards are developed by the Public Sector Committee of the International Federation of Accountants (IFAC PSC) in New York that produces International Public Sector Accounting Standards (IPSAS). Globally, governments have various research institutions, foundations, and professional associations that provide budgeting, financial management, and accounting guidelines as well. These include the International Budget Partnership, the World Bank, International Monetary Fund, and the European Group for Public Administration, to mention a few. Governments that issue debt, of course, are subject to credit assessment by credit rating agencies, such as Standard & Poor's.

Figure 4.1

Standards-Setting and Oversight of Financial Management and Accounting in US Governments

Federal Government	State and Local Governments
• Office of Management and Budget (OMB)	• Governmental Accounting Standards Board (GASB) (1984)
• Statements of Federal Financial Accounting Standards	Codification of governmental accounting and financial reporting standards; recognizes GAAP and the principles that guide public accounting for state and local governments
• Circular A-123* (revised 2004; effective 2006) re: federal internal controls	
• Circular A-127* (revised and effective 2009) re: federal financial management systems	• State Auditors and Comptrollers
• Circular A-134* (issued 1993) re: provides for adoption of financial accounting principles and standards	• GAO and OMB related to grant monies
	Professional Organizations
• Deputy Director for Management Office of Federal Financial Management headed by Controller	• Government Finance Officers Association Formerly the National Council on Governmental Accounting that produced Blue Book, GAAFR (Governmental Accounting, Auditing, and Financial Reporting) now produced by GFOA
Chief Financial Officers Act (1990) created similar offices and CFOs in major government agencies	• American Institute of Certified Public Accountants
• Government Accountability Office (GAO)	• American Accounting Association
• 1982 Federal Managers' Financial Integrity Act (amends 1950 Accounting and Auditing Act)	*Private Sector Organizations*
Agencies must establish internal accounting and administrative controls in accordance with GAO standards; agencies must conduct annual reviews to assess compliance with standards	• Financial Accounting Standards Board (FASB)
	• Accounting Firms
• Financial Systems Integration Office (closed 2010) formerly JFMIP	Deloitte
• Federal Accounting Standards Advisory Board (FASAB) (1990) Advisory; helps support JFMIP to develop consensus on accounting procedures and standards for federal financial management practices	Ernst & Young (EY)
	KPMG
	PricewaterhouseCoopers (PwC)

*Check http://www.whitehouse.gov/omb/circulars_default for updates to federal circulars.

Figure 4.1 presents standard-setting and oversight organizations of the federal and subnational governments in the United States. These institutions, circulars, offices, and firms provide accounting and financial management (and in some cases performance-related) reporting requirements, pronouncements, guidelines, and best practices that affect how budgeting is conducted. Accounting standards regard how the flow of money into and out of public agencies is recognized and recorded. The US federal government receives its guidance from a mix of offices—including the Office of Management and Budget (OMB), the Office of Federal Financial Management, the Government Accountability Office (GAO), the Federal Accounting Standards Advisory Board (FASAB), and the discontinued Financial Systems Integration Office (FSIO) and its predecessor, the Joint Financial Management Improvement Program (JFMIP)—and laws such as the Federal Managers' Financial Integrity Act and the Chief Financial Officers Act, and numerous circulars that provide very specific requirements for financial accounting, management, auditing, and reporting. The federal financial accounting system in the United States is extremely complex and involves the intersection of history, laws, policies, practices, and technologies.

State and local governments in the United States look to the Governmental Accounting Standards Board[14] (GASB) for concepts statements and guidelines regarding financial accounting and (now) financial performance reporting. GASB contributes to the generally accepted accounting principles (GAAP) that these governments use when accounting for and managing fund flows. Important changes to how these subnational governments account and report on their resources include GASB Statement No. 34, which introduced basic rather than general purpose financial statements, emphasized major versus non-major funds rather than fund types, and the presentation of government-wide governmental fund financial statements in modified and full accrual basis of accounting formats. In 2012, GASB approved Statements 67 and 68 to update financial reporting practices related to state and local government pension plans. State and local governments are now working to meet these guidelines that were developed to promote greater clarity of public pension obligations and more accurate measurement of these liabilities (and thus governments' future obligations).

State budgeting is also affected by the pronouncements of professional associations, such as the Government Finance Officers Association[15] (GFOA), which develops research, training, and conferences regarding the many subtopics within public budgeting and financial management. The policy statements, alone, that are produced by this association cover

- Accounting, auditing, and financial reporting
- Budgeting and financial management
- Intergovernmental relations and federal fiscal policy
- Public employee pension and benefits administration
- Tax-exempt financing and the municipal bond market
- Treasury and investment management

In addition, this association produces research reports, conducts training, and holds conferences to disseminate information to public budgeting and finance officers about the state of the practice and innovations in the field.

CONCLUSION

By now, you should realize the constrained circumstances of budgeting in state governments. The history of state government growth and the changing relationships between states and the federal government provide some evidence of state dependability. That is, states have certainly remained involved in the ordinary lives of their people. The states are beholden to a cornucopia of budget rules and institutions—no two are alike. The provisions in constitutions and the laws that require budget balance; that limit taxing, borrowing, and spending; or that require more than a simple majority approval for revenue changes contribute to lean governments but also restrict choices. Laws that require the use and reporting of agency and program performance measures contribute to the structure of budgeting relationships and can add value to budgeting processes—thus supplying information that can clarify the costs and the results of government operations and activities to elected officials, public managers, and citizens. In addition, states are bound to manage their credit risk seriously if they seek to reach and maintain strong fiscal health, for their borrowing costs are directly related to this risk. Standards-setting agencies like the GASB and GFOA provide foundations for public budgeting and financial management that further structure how budgeting and financial management are conducted in US state governments.

DISCUSSION QUESTIONS

1. What are some of the differences and similarities between national and state budget laws in the United States? What do you think accounts for these differences and similarities?

2. Explain some of the possible benefits and challenges for public officials working in a ballot initiative state in terms of developing, appropriating, and executing a budget.

3. Discuss the advantages and disadvantages of tax and expenditure limitations vis-à-vis public budgeting. Specifically address how these laws affect various budget makers and stakeholders.

4. Several US presidents who previously served as state governors have claimed expertise in budgeting because they have had to balance their state's budgets according to law. What does this mean? Do you think that balancing a US state budget can be equated with balancing the US federal budget? Explain your response.

5. Why is US state government attention to its credit risk so important for budgeting at this level of government?

NOTES

1. See the US Federal Budget, 2013, Historical Tables, Table 15.1. Available at http://www.whitehouse.gov/omb/budget/historicals

2. See the US Federal Budget 2013, Historical Tables, Table 15.2. Available at http://www.whitehouse.gov/omb/budget/historicals

3. See Statement of Revenues, Expenditures, and Changes in Fund Balances in State of Mississippi, Comprehensive Annual Financial Report for the Fiscal Year Ended June 30, 2012, prepared by Department of Finance and Administration, page 32. Available at http://www.dfa.state.ms.us /Offices/OFR/BFR%20Files/CAFR%20Files/2012%20CAFR.pdf. Also see State of Wyoming Comprehensive Annual Financial Report for Fiscal Year Ended June 30, 2012, prepared by CAFR Division of State Auditor's Office, page 38. Available at http://sao.state.wy.us/cafr/2012_Report /cafr2012.pdf

4. The law (2010) and the US Supreme Court decision (2012) about the Patient Protection and Affordable Care Act are available at http://www.hhs.gov/healthcare/rights/law/index.html. The final version of the law, as passed, is available at http://housedocs.house.gov/energycommerce/ppacacon.pdf; for one summary explanation, see http://www.dpc.senate.gov/healthreformbill/healthbill04.pdf

5. Missouri's constitution is available at http://www.moga.mo.gov/const/moconstn.htm

6. South Carolina's constitution is available at http://www.scstatehouse.gov/scconstitution/scconst.php

7. Wisconsin's constitution is available at http://legis.wisconsin.gov/rsb/unannotated_wisconst.pdf

8. Governments use fund accounting to account for the flow of money into and out of the public treasury. Specific types of funds are associated with particular revenues and expenditures. Governmental funds include general, special revenue, capital projects, and debt service funds—each has a specific stream of revenues and explicit spending associated to it. Revenues result from government imposition of taxes, grants, and borrowing. The general fund supports the general operations of the government and government tax receipts flow into this fund. Proprietary funds include enterprise and internal services funds—revenues that flow into these funds result from the fees and charges associated with businesslike activities, such as water-sewer, cable, or electricity services. Finally, fiduciary funds include trust and agency funds—revenues in these funds result from pension contributions and investments and certain court and other funds held in trust for specified purchases and payouts.

9. Fiscal year refers to the accounting period used for management and reporting of fund flow by a government. The fiscal year is typically an annual, twelve-month period and may be referred to as the budget year. Annual appropriations cover a twelve-month period; biennial appropriations cover a twenty-four-month period. States have different fiscal years, budgets, appropriation coverage and sessions—thirty-one states hold annual legislative sessions and have annual (twelve-month) budgets; fifteen states hold annual sessions and have biennial (twenty-four-month)

budgets; four states hold biennial sessions (every two years) and have biennial budgets (NCSL 2011). As you would expect, there is some variety within these categories, too. That is, in some states classified as having a biennial budget, there may be specified agencies that have annual rather than biennial appropriations. Or, in one state, the legislature may pass appropriations for the next two years, whereas in another, the legislature passes two separate appropriations bills to cover the next two years. In most states, the fiscal year begins July 1 and ends June 30, covers a twelve-month budget and the legislature meets annually. However, several states deviate from this fiscal year—Alabama and Michigan have fiscal years that match that of the US federal government, October 1 to September 30; New York operates under an April 1 to March 31 fiscal year, and Texas has a September 1 to August 31 fiscal year (see NASBO 2008). We will review some of this in a later chapter on budget mechanics, including budget types and timelines.

10. Information about Alaska's Permanent Fund is available at http://www.apfc.org/home/Content/aboutFund/aboutPermFund.cfm

11. You can read about the municipal securities market by visiting the Municipal Securities Rulemaking Board, available at http://emma.msrb.org/. To see an example issue for general obligation debt in the State of Tennessee, see http://emma.msrb.org/EP462971-EP361615-EP758580.pdf

12. Credit rating agencies explain that their ratings are opinions of relative credit risk and should not be considered as investment advice, indicative of security prices, or determined to be a guarantee of credit quality or future credit risk. To learn more about credit ratings and agency analytics, see Fitch https://www.fitchratings.com/jsp/general/Research.faces;jsessionid=FtrDC+nOaQwKSNlRDppt8A7u?listingName=criteriaReport, Moody's https://www.moodys.com/researchandratings, or Standard & Poor's http://www.standardandpoors.com/aboutcreditratings/

13. Available at http://www.pewstates.org/projects/stateline/headlines/info graphic-sp-state-credit-ratings-20012012–85899404785 and type "state credit ratings" into search engine.

14. See www.gasb.org

15. See www.gfoa.org

REFERENCES

Barnett, J. L., and P. M. Vidal. July 2013. *State and Local Government Finances Summary: 2011.* Available at http://www2.census.gov/govs/local/summary_ report.pdf

Denison, D. V., and R. A. Greer. 2014. "State Competition for Debt Resources." In *Sustaining the States: The Fiscal Viability of American State Governments*, edited by Marilyn M. Rubin and Katherine G. Willoughby, 85–98. Boca Raton, FL: CRC Press.

Dinan, J. 2013. "State Constitutional Developments in 2012." In *The Book of the States*, edited by Audrey Wall, 3–11.

Holcombe, R. G., and R. S. Sobel. 1997. *Growth and Variability in State Tax Revenue: An Anatomy of State Fiscal Crises.* Westport, CT: Greenwood Press.

Hou, Y., and D. L. Smith. 2006. "A Framework for Understanding State Balanced Budget Requirement Systems: Reexamining Distinctive Features and an Operational Definition." *Public Budgeting & Finance* 26 (3): 22–45.

Inman, R. P. November, 1996. "Do Balanced Budget Rules Work? US Experience and Possible Lessons for the EMU." NBER Working Paper Series, No. 5838. Available at http://www.nber.org/papers/w5838.pdf?new_window=1

Joyce, P. G. 2003. "Linking Performance and Budgeting: Opportunities in the Federal Budget Process." Washington, DC: IBM Center for the Business of Government. Available at http://www.businessofgovernment.org/sites/default/files /PerformanceandBudgeting.pdf

Kioko, S. N. 2011. "The Structure of State-Level Tax and Expenditure Limits." *Public Budgeting & Finance* 31 (2): 43–78.

Kraines, O. 1970. "The President versus Congress: The Keep Commission, 1905–1909: First Comprehensive Presidential Inquiry into Administration." *The Western Political Quarterly* 23 (1): 5–54.

Krislov, M., and D. Katz. 2008. "Taking State Constitutions Seriously." *Cornell Journal of Law and Public Policy* 17: 295–342.

Lu, Y., K. Willoughby, and S. Arnett. 2009. "Legislating Results: Examining the Legal Foundations of PBB Systems in the States." Public Performance and Management Review 33 (2): 266–287.

————. 2011. "Performance Budgeting in the American States: What's Law Got to Do with It?" State and Local Government Review 43 (2): 79–94.

Lu, Y., and K. Willoughby. 2012. "Performance Budgeting in the States: An Assessment." *IBM The Business of Government*, Fall/Winter: 71–75.

Madison, J. 2012. The Federalist Papers, Number XLV. In *The Constitution of the United States of America and Selected Writings of the Founding Fathers.* New York: Barnes & Noble. (First published 1778. Citations are to the Barnes & Noble edition.)

Montague and DeRose and Associates, LLC. 2011. "Presentation on State Debt Limits." Available at Washington State Treasurer, Debt Commission website: http://www.tre .wa.gov/documents/debtCommissionStateDebtLimits100411.pdf

National Association of State Budget Officers (NASBO). Summer, 2008. *Budget Processes in the States.* Available at http://www.nasbo.org/publications-data/budget-processes-in-the-states

National Conference of State Legislatures (NCSL). October, 2010. "NCSL Fiscal Brief: State Balanced Budget Provisions." Available at http://www.ncsl.org/documents /fiscal/StateBalancedBudgetProvisions2010.pdf

————. November/December, 1998. "A LegisBrief: Supermajority Vote Requirements to Pass the Budget." Updated October, 2008. *LegisBriefs* 6 (48). Available at http:// www.ncsl.org/research/fiscal-policy/supermajority-vote-requirements-to-pass-the-budget.aspx

Pattison, S. 2011. "Commentary on 'State Performance-Based Budgeting in Boom and Bust Year: An Analytical Framework and Survey of the States.'" *Public Administration Review* 71 (3): 389–390.

Poterba, J. April 1996. "Do Budget Rules Work?" NBER Working Paper Series, No. 5550. Available at http://www.nber.org/papers/w5550.pdf?new_window=1

Poterba, J., and K. Rueben. 1995. "The Effect of Property Tax Limits on Wage and Employment in the Local Public Sector." *American Economic Review* 85 (2): 384–389.

Samuel, P., and G. F. Segal. June 2007. "Leasing the Pennsylvania Turnpike: A Response to Critics of Gov. Rendell's Plans." Los Angeles: The Reason Foundation.

Stallmann, J. I., and S. Deller. 2011. "State Tax and Expenditure Limitations, Business Climate, and Economic Performance." *Public Budgeting & Finance* 31 (4): 109–135.

State of Georgia. 2014. The Governor's Budget Report, Fiscal Year 2014. Available at http://opb.georgia.gov/sites/opb.georgia.gov/files/related_files/document/Governors %20Budget%20Report%20FY%202014.pdf

State of Hawaii Revised Statutes. 2013. Title 5. State Financial Administration. 37. Budget Chapter 37–63 Statement of Policy, 1970. Available at http://law.justia.com/ codes/hawaii/2013/title-5/chapter-37/section-37-63

State of New Jersey. 2007. Title 52 State Government, Departments and Officers— 52:15C-8 Powers of the State Comptroller. Available at http://law.onecle.com/new-jersey/52-state-government-departments-and-officers/15c-8.html

State of Pennsylvania. 2011. Title 71, Part V. Chapter 41, §4104. Available at http:// www.legis.state.pa.us/cfdocs/legis/LI/consCheck.cfm?txtType=HTM&ttl=71&div=0 &chpt=41&sctn=4&subsctn=0

The Book of the States. July 1, 2013. State Constitutions, Table 1.1.: General Information on State Constitutions. Lexington, KY: Council of State Governments. Retrieved August 10, 2013. Available at http://knowledgecenter.csg.org/kc/content/ book-states-2013-chapter-1-state-constitutions

————. July 1, 2013. State Constitutions, Table 1.3. *Constitutional Amendment Procedure: By Initiative (Constitutional Provisions).* Lexington, KY: Council of State Governments. Retrieved August 10, 2013. Available at http://knowledgecenter.csg. org/kc/content/book-states-2013-chapter-1-state-constitutions

The Pew Charitable Trusts. 2012. "Infographic: S&P State Credit Ratings, 2001–2012." *Stateline*, July 13. Available at http://www.pewstates.org/projects/stateline/headlines/infographic-sp-state-credit-ratings-20012012–85899404785

US Federal Budget. 2012. Historical Tables, Table 15.1—Total Government Receipts in Absolute Amounts and as Percentages of GDP: 1948–2011. Retrieved September 10, 2012. Available at http://www.whitehouse.gov/omb/budget/Historicals

US Federal Budget. 2012. Historical Tables, Table 15.2—Total Government Expenditures: 1948–2011. Retrieved September 10, 2012. Available at http://www.whitehouse.gov/omb/budget/Historicals

Waisanen, B. 2010. "State Tax and Expenditure Limits—2010." National Conference of State Legislatures. Available at http://www.ncsl.org/research/fiscal-policy/state-tax-and-expenditure-limits-2010.aspx#typesoflimts

Wallis, J. J. 2000. "American Government Finance in the Long Run: 1790 to 1990." *The Journal of Economic Perspectives* 14 (1): 61–82.

Zolt, E. M. 2008–2009. "Inequality, Collective Action, and Taxing and Spending Patterns of State and Local Governments." *Tax Law Review* 62: 445.

chapter FIVE

Budget Foundations in US Local Governments

[In the United States], the state-local relationship is not one between sovereign governments. The states are by law the masters of these local governments; that is, the relationship is unitary.

—J. Richard Aronson and John L. Hilley,
Financing State and Local Governments, (4ᵗʰ ed.)

LEARNING OBJECTIVES

After reading this chapter, you should be able to

- Distinguish among types of local governments that exist in the United States

- Articulate the services and programs that different US local governments deliver

- Understand the legal foundations for local government budgeting and operations in the United States

- Describe the incorporation process of cities in the United States

- Access data about US local government charters, budgets, and finances to assess the impact of governance structure on US local government budgets

- Understand local government bankruptcy in the United States and consider state-local relationships and their impact on local government fiscal sustainability

---

The US Constitution, unlike the constitutions of some other countries, does not include anything about local government; in the United States, state governments have authority over local governments. The US Census Bureau defines a government as "an organized entity subject to public accountability, whose officials are popularly elected or are appointed by public officials, and which has sufficient discretion in the management of its affairs to distinguish it as separate from the administrative structure of any other government unit" (US Census Bureau 2014). As explained in chapter 4, subnational governments in the United States are different from those in other countries that may not have revenue-raising capabilities or even a tax base. Local governments in the United States have some degree of self-governance and fiscal capacity: some are afforded wide berth; others, not as much. There are over 90,000 US local governments of numerous types and with a wide range of discretion afforded to them. Local governments must abide by the US Constitution, federal laws, their state's constitution, state laws, as well as their own. Fiscal federalism, in particular, provides opportunities and constraints on local government taxing and spending authority, flexibility, and options.

This chapter examines the legal foundations for local government budgeting in the United States. The chapter begins with an explanation of the roles, multiplicity, and types of local governments in this country. We then introduce home rule and the requirements of incorporation for cities, and explain municipal code and the local budget ordinance. A final section regards municipal bankruptcy. The chapter ends with descriptions of two recent local government financial debacles as examples of what can occur when fiscal stress, poor planning, and, in one case, malfeasance come together. These examples also illustrate distinctive state-local relationships that affect local government budget and financial management capacities.

THE MULTIPLICITY AND RESPONSIBILITIES OF LOCAL GOVERNMENTS

Local governments have expansive responsibilities as direct service providers to their residents and visitors. On any given day, you can open (or scroll through) the daily newspaper and read about the breadth of local government operations, responsibilities, new initiatives and challenges. The following is just a sampling from the *Atlanta Journal Constitution* of December 4, 2013:

- "County Magistrate and Probate Courts have new wedding hours"
- "Gem and metal dealers ordinance hearing set"

- "City creates urban redevelopment plan"
- "City School Board to revisit 'Blue Ribbon Committee'"
- "Dementia cases pose challenge for local police"
- "City in line for federal funding for streetcar project"
- "City reels as center closing"
- "City Council OKs playground funds"
- "County educators collect a rare second pension paid by local taxes"

Even a quick scan reveals that local governments provide substantial services and programs to their residents, have significant internal management issues to address continually, and have innumerable new policies that must be considered. In the preceding list, local governments provide marriage services, economic development and urban planning, police protection and support of the elderly, business and safety regulation, recreation and child services, and transportation projects. And of course, these governments must provide salaries and benefits to their employees to do all of this work.

Primarily, local governments in the United States provide education; local expenditures for elementary and secondary education services made up 35 percent of local direct expenditures in 2008, the single largest category of direct spending by local governments. The second largest category of spending at the local level is for utilities, water, sanitation, sewer, and waste management services, which collectively account for 15 percent of total direct expenditures in 2008. In addition, local governments are chiefly responsible to their residents for public safety and fire protection services; the operation of jails; maintaining roads, sidewalks, and other such infrastructure; operating hospitals; and providing libraries, parks, and recreation programs, community development, and housing (US Census Bureau, 2012b).

To pay for all this, local governments manage a significant flow of money into their coffers. In 2008, American local governments raised over $1 trillion in total revenues from their own sources—their predominant own-source revenue is derived from the property tax, which made up 40 percent of local own source revenues in 2008. Of all tax receipts of local governments, property tax receipts represent the largest share, at 74.2 percent (Barnett and Vidal 2013). In 2012, approximately 13.7 million people were employed by US local governments; local expenditures to pay these employees reached $608 billion (US Department of Labor 2013). Local governments spent more than $1.5 trillion in 2008, evidence of fiscal federalism in play. Local governments depend upon intergovernmental funds to offer programs and develop infrastructure. Grants from federal and state governments often determine what work will be conducted and which projects will be built (note the local streetcar project mentioned in the earlier list).

There are 90,056 local governments in the United States today (US Census Bureau 2012a), a 23 percent decline in number from sixty years ago but a slight uptick (0.6 percent) from five years ago. The number of local governments varies over time for many reasons, especially in light of demographic changes and often because of the effects of economic downturns on local budgets. Certainly since the Great Recession, many local governments have attempted to or had to shift certain service responsibilities to special districts that are often created to conduct one type of activity.

Local governments are categorized by purpose; general purpose ones provide a mix of services and programs directly to residents. General purpose governments include counties (3,031), municipalities (19,519), and towns or townships (16,360). Special purpose governments (51,146) include special districts and authorities that might operate one particular activity, such as hospitals, water, sanitation, community development districts, or independent school districts (US Census Bureau 2012a).

The National League of Cities (2013) provides information on the wide range of populations of US local governments, noting that less than one percent of municipalities have populations over 300,000 while most (over 90 percent) have populations of 25,000 or less.[1] The US Census Bureau conducts a periodic survey of the number of local government in the United States, by type and state; examination of its most recent map indicates the greatest number of local governments and public school systems exist in the Northeast and into the Midwest, and among the West Coast states of Washington, Oregon, and California. The fewest local governments and school systems are found among Southern states, excluding Florida and Eastern Texas.[2]

County governments are administrative arms of the state and this tight link with the state means that they are more restricted than many cities in terms of the discretion they have regarding service delivery, programming, and financial operations. Every state is divided geographically into counties (called boroughs in Alaska and parishes in Louisiana). Counties in some states are not functional governments but demark geographic location only, such as in Connecticut, Rhode Island, and some in Massachusetts. Counties provide significant protective and social services. For example, examine the 2012 comprehensive annual financial report (CAFR) of Broward County, Florida,[3] and see this county's stated commitment to providing its residents, businesses, and visitors a comprehensive and collaborative social safety net. The CAFR indicates county investment in a new courthouse; the statement of revenues, expenditures, and changes in fund balances for governmental funds on page 17 shows the greatest expense of the county to be for public safety (including the sheriff's office). These services are in addition to maintenance of water and sewer systems, environmental protection and urban planning, recreation and cultural services, and continued development as a regional intermodal transportation network.

Cities are chartered entities—the municipal charter is a city's constitution, or "organic law" that specifies its organizational structure, powers, functions, and vital processes. The granting of charters by state legislatures or by voters is discussed later in this chapter's section about home rule. Once a charter is granted, a city is a legal corporation. Townships do not have the population requirements of cities for their creation, but do have a variety of forms—"municipal or civil, incorporated or unincorporated, the school, the judicial and congressional" (National League of Cities 2013).

A special purpose government must be authorized to exist by a state government; the state may provide authority to general purpose local governments to create special purpose ones. Special (38,266) and school (12,880) districts fall within this category of local government. Special purpose governments indicate a range of revenue-raising abilities—taxing, setting and collecting fees, borrowing or having the ability to receive and spend specific grant funds from the state or federal governments (National League of Cities, 2013). By this time, you should have a feel for the layers of governments that exist in the United States. Morton Grodzins (1984) writes about the "chaos of the American system" (3–4) by giving the example of a resident of Park Forest, Illinois, paying taxes to the eleven governments within which he resided (at the time)—inclusive of one national government, one state government, a county government, a township, several sanitary and educational districts, a forest preserve district, and a mosquito abatement district. Within how many governments do you reside?

LOCAL GOVERNMENT POWERS

As discussed, US local governments are afforded their powers by state governments. The following section explains the types of authority that can be provided by states to local governments, distinguishing tight and loose discretion that local government may be afforded by states to operate, raise revenues, and spend funds. Using Georgia as an example, the process of incorporation is explained, highlighting the intensive work necessary by interested residents in determining governance structure and the services that the new government will be responsible for. An example city charter is presented; a charter serves as a local government constitution, structuring how budgeting will be conducted and influencing the future fiscal capacity of the government.

Dillon's Rule and Home Rule

Traditionally in the United States, state legislatures have controlled the creation, governing authority, structure, financing, and functions of their local governments through constitutional or statutory law. In 1868, Judge John Forrest Dillon of Iowa issued a decision on local government authority in the United States that held to the limited powers of this level of government. Rather than allow local residents to make decisions about governance, financing, and debt for their communities, Judge Dillon ruled in *City of Clinton v. Cedar Rapids and the Missouri River Railroad* (24 Iowa 455, 1868) that local governments have the following powers:

- Those granted in express words by state government
- Those necessarily or fairly implied in or incident to the powers expressly granted by state government
- Those essential to the declared objects and purposes of the corporation, not simply convenient, but indispensable

Judge Dillon made this ruling during a period of rampant corruption and growing inefficiency in US local governments—a good example being the political machine that was Tammany Hall in New York City at the time. Judge Dillon's ruling further determined that "if there is any reasonable doubt whether a power has been conferred on a local government then the power has not been conferred." The Judge's ruling has been challenged but affirmed twice by the US Supreme Court, in 1903 and 1923.

Dillon's Rule essentially maintained that action was necessary by the state legislature for the establishment and operation of local governments. But this is a very cumbersome, time-consuming process for local community living and functioning and has the potential to consume the relatively short period of time that legislators have to deliberate about state budget and policy matters. Thus, home rule provisions have been adopted by states to provide for local government autonomy in order to avert the need for the repeated generation of locality-specific legislation. But, just as there are literally thousands of local governments in the United States, so too are there a broad range of powers that may be provided to local governments by states through home rule. Home rule may be expressed constitutionally or statutorily and may relate to local governing structure, financing, or function. Also, home rule may be made available to all cities or there may be special requirements, such as minimum population, that determine whether a city can operate under home rule.

Georgia's constitution[4] provides an example of the mix of Dillon's Rule with home rule provisions for its local governments. Article IX of the constitution stipulates the governing authority, revenue, expenditure, and debt powers and the limits of counties, municipal corporations, special authorities, and districts. The constitution specifies no more than 159 counties, and indicates boundaries and a protocol for their consolidation. It states that "the governing authority of each county shall have legislative power to adopt clearly reasonable ordinances, resolutions, or regulations relating to its property, affairs, and local government for which no provision has been made by general law and which is not inconsistent with this Constitution or any local law applicable thereto." The constitution articulates county powers preempted by state constitutional or statutory laws, including such items as the election and salaries of county governing officials, defining criminal offenses, criminal punishment, or "adopting any form of taxation beyond that authorized by law or this Constitution." Counties in Georgia are authorized by the constitution, however, "to set the salaries, maintain pensions, insurance, workers' compensation and health care benefit for employees of governing authority."

Regarding cities, the Georgia constitution provides that the state legislature can pass laws for municipal self-government and can "delegate its power so that matters pertaining to cities may be dealt with *without the necessity of action by the General Assembly*" (italics added). The constitution also confers on local governments the ability to conduct numerous services and programs, enumerated as "supplementary powers in addition to all powers possessed by or conferred upon any county, municipality, or any combination thereof," including

- Police and fire protection
- Garbage and solid waste collection and disposal
- Public health facilities and services, including hospitals, ambulance and emergency rescue services, and animal control
- Street and road construction and maintenance, including curbs, sidewalks, street lights, and devices to control the flow of traffic
- Parks, recreational areas, programs, and facilities
- Storm water and sewage collection and disposal systems
- Development, storage, treatment, purification, and distribution of water
- Public housing
- Public transportation
- Libraries, archives, and arts and sciences programs and facilities
- Terminal and dock facilities and parking facilities
- Codes, including building, housing, plumbing, and electrical codes
- Air quality control
- Pension systems and retirement benefits for elected officials and employees of the government

Special districts can be created by state law or by city or county ordinance or resolution, as long as local law does not "supersede a law enacted by the General Assembly." Special districts are afforded the ability to exist and the ability to engage fees, assessments, and taxes to pay "wholly or partially, the cost of providing specific services and to construct and maintain facilities therefore" in Georgia's constitution.

Becoming a City in Georgia

Residents of an unincorporated area in the Georgia who are interested in becoming a city must appeal to the state's General Assembly for a charter. The Georgia Municipal Association (2007) provides a model municipal charter, explaining the legal complexity of the process, given the state's multiple constitutions (the tenth is dated 1983):

One oddity of Georgia law is that the 1945 and the 1976 Georgia Constitutions permitted local constitutional amendments. These were amendments to the state constitution that were applicable to one or just a few political subdivisions of the state and voted on by the people in those areas. The 1983 Georgia Constitution prohibited the enactment of future local constitutional amendments but provided a mechanism for continuing existing ones. Thus, some municipalities may be subject to local constitutional amendments which are not published as part of the Georgia Constitution. Local governing bodies may be unaware of these laws.

A referendum by residents is not a requirement for a charter to be enacted or repealed in Georgia; however, communities interested in becoming a city must present the following to their state legislative delegation:

- Name for proposed city
- Geographic boundaries of proposed city
- Evidence of a city population of at least 200 residents and an average residential population of at least 200 persons per square mile
- Evidence that 60 percent of the area within proposed boundaries is developed for residential, commercial, industrial, institutional, governmental, or recreational purposes
- Evidence that 60 percent of the total acreage within proposed boundaries exists in lots and tracts of five acres or less

Legislation granting city charters must be certified that minimum legal requirements have been met, indicating the ability of the city to operate and be fiscally sustainable. All reporting and justification documents related to the proposed city are included with the charter as it moves through the General Assembly. A charter that is passed would include

- Provisions governing incorporation, boundaries, and powers
- Provisions governing the structure and form of the government
- Administrative organization and function
- Judicial powers and procedures
- Election procedures and regulations

- Financial procedures

- General provisions

Georgia offers three city government structures that vary in the division of power and duties between the executive and legislative branches of government. The three structures include (1) council-manager, in which the mayor is "first among equals" on the council; (2) weak mayor-council, in which the mayor has some administrative duties along with council membership, and; (3) strong mayor-council, in which the mayor acts as a traditional chief executive and head of the government vis-à-vis the legislative branch (the council). Other states may offer more choices of governing structure—for example, New Jersey provides communities a dozen options for classification.[5] Once granted, municipal charters can be amended by local act or by "home rule" charter amendment, though aspects related to form of governance, elections, and tenure of city officials can only be changed by the state legislature.

Choice of governance structure matters for local budgeting and policy implementation. Figure 5.1 presents the relationship of the US national and state governments in the federalist governance system. This schematic illustrates state sovereignty, but the divisions of power (only the national government can declare war) and certain shared powers (such as the power to tax). Also, subnational governments cannot have constitutional or statutory laws that conflict with the US Constitution and federal laws. That is, where federal legislation occupies a field, it preempts conflicting state or local legislation.

Barbara McCabe and Richard Feiock (2005) distinguish between "constitutional-level" and "substantive-level" state and municipal rules that further illustrate a nested quality of local governance (638). These scholars specify that local governance structures shape how state mandates are implemented at the local level. According to McCabe and Feiock, regarding state and local relationships, constitutional-level rules specify governance rules, form of government, decision authority, or broad parameters of local self-governance, whereas substantive rules provide for decision making surrounding a policy area, such as taxes or the environment. Their research determines that "local choice of government form influences how state-level rules impact city fiscal policy" (635). Specifically, they determine that a community's choice of governance system "may do as much—or more—to keep local tax and spending decisions in line with citizens' preferences" (650).

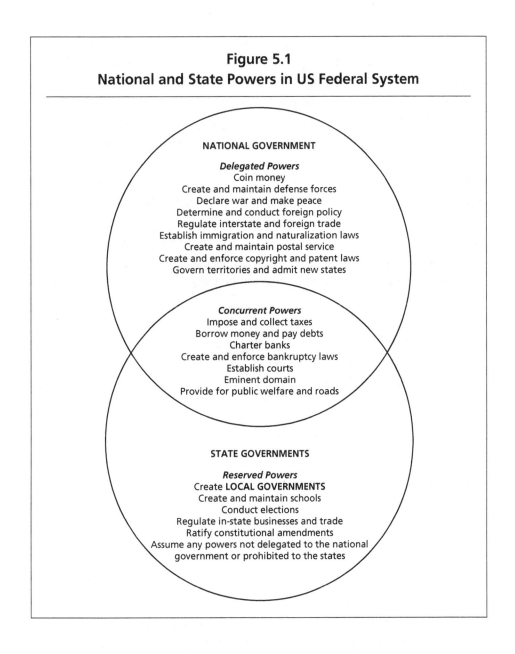

Figure 5.1
National and State Powers in US Federal System

NATIONAL GOVERNMENT

Delegated Powers
Coin money
Create and maintain defense forces
Declare war and make peace
Determine and conduct foreign policy
Regulate interstate and foreign trade
Establish immigration and naturalization laws
Create and maintain postal service
Create and enforce copyright and patent laws
Govern territories and admit new states

Concurrent Powers
Impose and collect taxes
Borrow money and pay debts
Charter banks
Create and enforce bankruptcy laws
Establish courts
Eminent domain
Provide for public welfare and roads

STATE GOVERNMENTS

Reserved Powers
Create **LOCAL GOVERNMENTS**
Create and maintain schools
Conduct elections
Regulate in-state businesses and trade
Ratify constitutional amendments
Assume any powers not delegated to the national
government or prohibited to the states

Home rule for cities in Georgia is spelled out in the Municipal Home Rule Act of 1965 which authorizes these governments' ability to make local laws and rules if they do not conflict with the state constitution, state laws, or charter provisions. Examples of types of powers provided to local governments from the 1965 Act include "to hire employees, set duties and compensation, establish departments, authorize municipal employees and agents to serve any process or summons in the city for activity in the city which violates a law or ordinance, establish retirement, merit and insurance systems for employees, contract with other governmental agencies or political subdivisions, and grant franchises to public utilities for use and occupancy of the streets" (Moore 2012, 2).

Once they are legally incorporated, Georgia cities are required to justify their active status. State law in 1995 establishes certain minimum requirements for certification as active. Another state law passed in 2005 allows newly created cities two years to comply with the requirements for active status. Active status means that (1) cities must hold at least six regular public meetings within a twelve-month period to stating that they meet minimum active standards; (2) cities qualify candidates and hold municipal elections, as required by law; and (3) cities must also provide at least three of the following services, either directly or by contract:

- Law enforcement
- Fire protection/fire safety
- Road/street maintenance/construction
- Solid waste management
- Water supply or distribution, or both
- Wastewater management
- Stormwater collection/disposal
- Electric or gas utility service
- Code enforcement (building, housing)
- Planning and zoning
- Recreational facilities

Cities must file certifications confirming active status with Georgia's Department of Community Affairs. Cities lose their charter with failure to maintain active status, "resulting in the loss of all assets, property, and legal rights as a municipal corporation and causing the dissolution of any local authority created by the former municipal corporation. If this occurs, the state empowers the county to use the assets of the municipal corporation or local authority to retire any outstanding debt" (Georgia Municipal Association 2005).

Once a city has legal status, it must develop its organizational and fiscal capacities for successful and lawful operations. Examining the charter and laws of any municipality should illustrate for you the breadth of knowledge needed by public officials, the budget and finance directors, agency heads, and government employees, generally, for such success. Figure 5.2 provides charter and code information for Atlanta, Georgia, originally incorporated in 1847, with a population of 2,500 and boundaries encompassing a one-mile radius from the railroad depot. Today, the city's boundaries cover 131.4 square miles and include a resident population of 432,427 (City of Atlanta, CAFR 2012, ii;164).

The section of Atlanta's charter illustrated in Figure 5.2 is from Subpart A of the Charter, up to Article 6, Revenue and Fund Administration. Within Article 6, Chapter 3 (Fiscal Control) has been accessed; within Chapter 3, Section 6–315 regarding fund balance policy is of interest here. Within fund balance policy, the charter stipulates that the city must "report fund balance amounts consistent with the appropriate Governmental Accounting Standards Board (GASB) guidance." Immediately, you see that the legal basis for the city to operate includes definitions and rules for budgeting and financial management and sets requirements for Atlanta's adherence to professional guidelines and standards (GASB).[6]

The charter provisions shown in Figure 5.2 for just one component of budgeting and financial management (fiscal controls) to be practiced in a city illustrate the multiple layers of laws, rules, and regulations that typically orchestrate these processes in a US municipality. It is for this reason that the Georgia Municipal Association (2005) emphasizes that "it is critical that residents understand the administrative (official reporting and record keeping) requirements that will be necessary once municipal incorporation is achieved." The Association also encourages communities seeking incorporation to consult an attorney "familiar with state laws related to local governments."

Practically speaking, although home rule may be specified by a state constitution and even traditionally interpreted as a local right in a particular state government, the actual practice of home rule by local governments may be far different. In other words, local governments may be given authority which they do not fully implement, may misinterpret, or may practice corruptly. The layers of laws, rules, and regulations applicable to local governments and the multiplicity of these strictures over time through amendment to current laws, the passage of new laws, and promulgation of new rules provide for a confusing environment within which local governments must operate. Much of the literature

Figure 5.2
Components of City of Atlanta Charter Related to
Fiscal Control and Fund Balance Policy

BILL OF RIGHTS
ARTICLE 1. - NAME, POWERS, AND BOUNDARIES
ARTICLE 2. - LEGISLATIVE
ARTICLE 3. - EXECUTIVE
ARTICLE 4. - COURTS
ARTICLE 5. - ELECTIONS, REMOVAL AND CONFLICTS OF INTEREST
ARTICLE 6. - REVENUE AND FUND ADMINISTRATION

    CHAPTER 1. - REVENUE
    CHAPTER 2. - BORROWING AND INDEBTEDNESS
    CHAPTER 3. - FISCAL CONTROL

        Section 6-301. Budget commission.
        Section 6-302. Adoption of budget.
        Section 6-303. Expenditures of excess in receipts over appropriations.
        Section 6-304. Budget amendments.
        Section 6-305. Unlawful obligations void.
        Section 6-306. Appropriations for charitable purposes.
        Section 6-307. Authority of city to contract with commissions, councils, boards, etc.
        Section 6-308. Audit.
        Section 6-309. Accounting systems.
        Section 6-310. Increase in salaries.
        Section 6-311. Evidence of justice of claims.
        Section 6-312. Financial stabilization plan.
        Section 6-313. Pension Actuarial Audit.
        Section 6-314. Pension Experience Study.
        Section 6-315. Fund balance policy.

            a. Fund balance terms.
            b. Prioritization of fund balance use.
            c. Authority to commit or assign balances.
            d. Required minimum unrestricted fund balance in the General Fund.
            e. Replenishing deficiencies in the General Fund.
            f. Actions if a surplus fund balance exists.
            g. Financial reporting requirements.

Source: See municipal charters and code available at www.municode.com; access the Code Library, the State of Georgia, City of Atlanta, for information related to charter components discussed.

about fiscal decentralization (central to subnational government financial relationships) rests on economic conceptions of local governments as the most efficient providers of public services (Oates 1972) and that citizens are mobile and can move to communities that provide the mix of services they are willing to support through taxes (Tiebout 1956). You can see here that modern local governments in the United States operate in what Elinor Ostrom (1990) has conceptualized as a nested hierarchy.

LOCAL GOVERNMENT FISCAL STRESS AND BANKRUPTCY

Hemmed in by legal responsibilities and fiscal capacities, local governments do not have many options for managing through severe fiscal stress without making difficult decisions about spending, taxes, or debt. Like the US states, local governments in dire fiscal straits cannot afford to compromise their credit rating that influences how much it costs them to borrow money. As noted in the previous chapter on the legal foundations for state budgeting, subnational governments must be mindful of the ratings of their bonded debt. Lower ratings mean higher interest rates on the borrowed funds.

Though the US federal government allows local governments to file for Chapter 9 bankruptcy if the home state makes such an allowance in law, not every state affords this option. About half of states allow their cities to file for Chapter 9; laws of other states are unclear or, in effect, ban bankruptcy filing by local governments. States may restrict bankruptcy to certain types of local governments. *Governing* (2013) provides a map of state laws on municipal bankruptcy in the United States.[7] This map shows that just over half of states (28) offer at least limited authorization to local governments to file Chapter 9 and of these states, twelve specifically provide their local governments by law the option to file for bankruptcy. In the rest of the states, there exists no authorization, laws are unclear about filing, or filing is forbidden. Of these twenty-two states, Georgia is the only one in which state law expressly prohibits local governments from filing bankruptcy.

Nonetheless, the resiliency of US local governments is evidenced by the fact that a very, very small fraction of them have filed for bankruptcy in the past. Malone (2011) quotes one municipal bankruptcy expert that "there have been only 624 municipal bankruptcies under Chapter 9 of the US Bankruptcy Code since 1937." The Pew Charitable Trusts (2013) recently analyzed state government intervention in the case of local government fiscal distress and confirms that "of the nation's 55,000 municipal governments that sell bonds, fewer than ten file for bankruptcy each year" (7). Also, of the more than 7,500 local governments with debt scored by Moody's credit rating agency, just 34 received a below investment grade. Moody's has determined that since the end of the Great Recession in June 2009, most local governments have been able to "soldier through" in spite of plummeting home values, the decline in revenues from property taxes, the limping economy, and increasing spending needs (Moody's Investors Service 2013).

In fact, most Chapter 9 bankruptcy filings in the United States today are by utilities and special districts, such as for hospitals, rural water, general improvement, and even an off-track betting corporation in New York State. Of the 38 local government bankruptcies since 2010, just eight general purpose governments (cities, towns, or counties) have filed for bankruptcy, including

- Boise County, Idaho (Dismissed)
- City of Detroit, Michigan
- City of Central Falls, Rhode Island
- City of Harrisburg, Pennsylvania (Dismissed)
- City of San Bernardino, California
- City of Stockton, California
- Jefferson County, Alabama
- Town of Mammoth Lakes, California (Dismissed)

The Pew study finds that a filing of bankruptcy by general purpose local governments tends to have "a single identifiable cause: a bad investment decision (Orange County, CA); a failed infrastructure project (Jefferson County, AL, and Harrisburg, PA); an expensive legal decision (Mammoth Lakes, CA); or escalating public pension costs (Central Falls, RI)" (The Pew Charitable Trusts 2013, 7).

In the following sections we describe the bankruptcies in Jefferson County, Alabama, and Central Falls, Rhode Island. We compare these two local government bankruptcies because they occurred in states with widely differing state-local relationships. The Pew study determined that the state-local relationship when local governments are in fiscal distress tends to be "hands off" on the part of most states. Just nineteen states have laws that allow them to intercede in municipal finances and most become involved "to protect their own financial standing and that of their other municipalities, to enhance economic growth and to maintain public safety and health" (The Pew Charitable Trusts 2013, 4). After reading about the two recent bankruptcy examples, you should have a better idea about the importance of the state-local relationship to local government fiscal sustainability in the United States.

Jefferson County, Alabama

Incurring debt (selling bonds) is a common way that local governments in the United States fund large infrastructure projects. As you can imagine, however, these offerings are complicated, involve numerous public officials, finance and budget officers, money managers and investment firms, and the courts. The process is hardly transparent. Improper management of the offering process or the funds themselves has significant consequences for the fiscal sustainability of governments, not to mention compromising the public trust. Jefferson County, Alabama, provides an example of bond mismanagement in which a lack of oversight, corruption, and substantial cost overruns culminated in the county filing for bankruptcy in November 2011, becoming the second-largest municipal bankruptcy in US history behind Detroit, Michigan (which filed Chapter 9 in July 2013, with debts totaling ~$18 million).

The Jefferson County bankruptcy example occurred in a state that has exhibited a hands-off approach to its failing local governments. Alabama is a state that operates under Dillon's Rule and counties, in particular, cannot levy taxes without state permission. In the past, Jefferson County has been an economic engine for the state, the strongest of Alabama's sixty-seven counties; the county seat, Birmingham, is the state's most populous city (The Pew Charitable Trusts 2013). In 1997, to finance an EPA-mandated replacement sewer system, Jefferson County sold bonds, tying debt repayment to future revenues to be generated by the system (Selway 2011). Originally estimated to cost $1.5 billion, poor predictions, political corruption, and lack of oversight led actual costs of the project to balloon—the county eventually incurred $3.3 billion in debt.

To assuage fears regarding repayment, the county refinanced the debt in 2002, adhering to the advice of JPMorgan Chase to transition most of the debt for the project from traditional, fixed-rate securities to variable and auction-rate ones (Denison and Gibson 2013; Selway 2011). The county refinanced the debt without direction from the county manager or that of any single financial expert, instead relying solely on the advice of JPMorgan Chase. Especially in light of the Great Recession, by 2008 the value of the sewer bonds plummeted, the credit status of Jefferson County debt spiraled to junk, and the county began to tumble into default (Howell-Moroney and Hall 2011). In March 2011, the Alabama Supreme Court declared Jefferson County's occupational tax to be unconstitutional, immediately cutting $70 million or one-third of the county's total operating revenue (Fehr 2012; Selway 2011). To forestall bankruptcy, the county then cut $120 million from its fiscal year 2012 budget, sliced services, and laid off over 1,200 employees. Nonetheless, Jefferson County filed Chapter 9 in November 2011 (Business Wire 2013; Fehr 2012; Selway 2011). The lack of financial oversight of debt issuance and its management allowed for the corruption and fraud evidenced that led to the eventual convictions of twenty-one county and bank officials (Denison and Gibson 2013; Howell-Moroney and Hall 2011).

Currently, after years of negotiations, Jefferson County is attempting to leave bankruptcy. A tentative deal has the county replacing $3.1 billion of sewer debt with a cash settlement of $1.74 billion, cash that the county plans to raise through the sale of municipal bonds tied to future sewer revenues. (Sound familiar?) Annual hikes in sewer rates will drive payback on these new bonds, and the bond sale pledges annual sewer rate hikes of 7.9 percent from 2014 to 2017 and 3.5 percent from 2018 to 2053.

Reaction to this new debt sale has been mixed, with Standard & Poor's credit rating agency classifying the bonds as "low-investment grade" quality, while both Fitch and Moody's have rated the bonds as "junk." Though some investors view the plan as an investment opportunity (as the November 2013 sale ended with the county selling all $1.7 billion in bonds offered), some financial analysts are concerned about citizen and state reaction to required annual sewer rate hikes (Business Wire 2013; Sigo 2013; Walsh 2013). Citizen litigation against the bankruptcy deal has continued. Residents argue that as sewer rates have already been increased by 300 percent, any further increases in rate hikes would be unreasonably burdensome and thereby unconstitutional under Alabama state law (Faulk 2013). This has left analysts at both Fitch and Moody's concerned over the possible conflict between Alabama state law and the rulings of the federal bankruptcy judge (Business Wire 2013; Sigo 2013, Walsh 2013).

There also remains much apprehension regarding Jefferson County's long-term fiscal health. The agreement just discussed has cut the county's debt by $1.4 billion. However, although the first ten years of debt service costs will be

$70 to $85 million a year, such costs jump to $141 million in 2024 (Whitmire 2013). Jefferson County officials have acknowledged concerns about paying an estimated $1.2 billion of federally mandated sewer costs through 2053, as well.

Analysts remain troubled about Jefferson County's inability to increase revenues, particularly given that the state legislature still has yet to support county means to replace any of the $70 million lost in annual revenue back in March, 2011 (Business Wire 2013; Sigo 2013; Whitmire 2013). Current Governor Robert Bentley has conceded that the county's financial distress warrants state attention but says the local delegation in the legislature must unite around a plan of assistance before he can effect change. Specifically, of Jefferson County's senators and representatives, the urban lawmakers support providing the county authority to raise taxes, but the suburban legislators do not, claiming that their constituents do not think that they should be responsible for bailing out a mismanaged, corrupt county government (The Pew Charitable Trusts 2013). As the Fitch report (Business Wire 2013) notes,

> Complete dependence on the state legislature for revenue enhancements is a fundamental credit risk. The ability of the state legislature to adopt measures adverse to the county's credit was amply demonstrated by the legislature's repeal of the occupational tax in 1999, with the repeal eventually affirmed by the courts in March 2011, and its failure to approve a satisfactory substitute. While county officials contend that none of their remaining revenue sources are controversial, the county will continue to be subject to arbitrary actions at the state level.

In Alabama, there is no protocol for state intervention when a local government may be approaching or reach the point of fiscal distress. More important, perhaps, is that the state does not have a tradition of this type of involvement in practice. The challenge for Jefferson County going forward is to maintain and grow its tax base and increase sewer rates, yet provide an ever-diminishing mix and level of public services.

Central Falls, Rhode Island

The Central Falls bankruptcy example occurred in a state that took aggressive action to rescue a failing local government. John Simmons (2013) describes the perilous position of Rhode Island cities, generally, following the onset of the Great Recession and given the lingering aftereffects of years of lost manufacturing statewide. He points out that after the economic downturn in 2008, assessed residential property values declined by 17 percent from FY2009 to FY2012; single-family home prices fell 30.7 percent, well over twice the national decline of 11.7 percent. State direct aid to cities (excepting educational grants) decreased by 72.6 percent during this period, though cities were still being held to state directives regarding employee salaries, benefits, and contract negotiations (Simmons 2013).

Central Falls, Rhode Island, is a very small city located to the north of Providence and Pawtucket, with a population of just under 20,000 and comprising 1.2 square miles. Approximately 25 percent of its population lives below the poverty line, twice that of the state. Coming out of the recession, the city had an estimated $6 million deficit (FY2011) that made up 35 percent of its $17 million operating budget. The city had individually negotiated benefits and widely disparate pension plans among firefighters, police officers, and municipal employees; some groups of employees had been offered early retirements—many took the offers—with lifetime health benefits for individuals and their families, in some cases. Also, during the economic downturn, local pension assets tumbled. Central Falls' outstanding liabilities for retired employee pensions and benefits stood at $80 million (FY2010) (Simmons 2013).

Rhode Island traditionally presents as a state with a higher tax burden than the national average.[8] Central Falls had the highest tax burden of all Rhode Island cities in FY2009 and among the highest for the years since (Simmons 2013). Tax burden is the ratio of the total taxes paid by an individual or business to total income, for a certain period. This measure is affected by the jurisdiction's tax structure that includes the mix of taxes imposed by the government, tax rates, exemptions, deductions, and other components. You can examine data from Rhode Island's Department of Revenue for the last several years to see how Central Falls' tax rates compare with other cities across the state. Notice that Central Falls consistently competes with North Providence for the highest personal property and other tax rates—North Providence has a population of about 32,000.[9]

In June 2010, the Rhode Island legislature passed the Fiscal Stability Act that strengthened state intervention in the case of city financial distress; the law established the steps necessary for a city to file Chapter 9 and defined state responsibilities throughout the process.[10] Prior to passage of this law, the governor determined the state's role regarding local governments in fiscal distress. When Central Falls filed for bankruptcy later that summer, the state-appointed receiver (or custodian) who had been assigned to the city stated that, "everything was done to avoid this day. Taxes have been raised to the maximum level allowable. We negotiated with . . . the police and fire unions, without success, attempting to reach voluntary concessions, and we tried in vain to persuade our retirees to accept voluntary reductions in their benefits" (Malone 2011). This was the first city bankruptcy in Rhode Island's history.

The Fiscal Stability Act is important as it brings about a new relationship between the state and local governments in Rhode Island. The Act requires the conduct of significant analysis and a declaration of fiscal stress to be provided before a city can file for bankruptcy. Also, data gathering, budgeting monitoring, and attempts to balance the city's books passes from an overseer to a budget commission and then to a receiver. The receiver has the power to declare the bankruptcy and, most significantly, "unilateral power to reject or accept any or all existing executor contracts" (Simmons 2013, Slide 8). That is, the receiver has the power "to go to court to vacate pensions, or other benefit commitments, which expanded the available options for improving [Central Falls'] finances" (Simmons 2013, Slide 9). State legislation also promised that city investors would be at the front of the line for repayment—bondholders of the city's general obligation debt would be paid first in any financial restructuring.

In the end, state monitoring of the situation continues until all requirements are met. In Rhode Island, the receiver in a bankruptcy takes on the powers of the elected officials of a local government and past and current promises of the government can be broken. In the case of Central Falls, the state "cut core pension benefits for current workers" and, coupled with tax increases and personnel cuts, these efforts support Central Falls' financial recovery (The Pew Charitable Trusts 2013, 41). In fact, the municipality was able to come out of bankruptcy after only thirteen months and "the state returned control to city officials in April 2013" (The Pew Charitable Trusts 2013, 5).

CONCLUSION

Previous chapters have introduced you to the legal foundations for budgeting in a few countries around the world and in US national and state governments. Especially after reading in chapter 4 about the great variability among state government constitutions and their budget institutions and rules, it should be clear that budgeting is as constrained, if not more so, as you move to lower levels of government. State governments, even as sovereign entities, must operate within the confines of the US Constitution, federal laws, and regulations, in addition to their own constitutions, laws, and regulations. Local governments as "creatures of the state" must operate within the confines of the US Constitution, federal laws, and regulations; their state's constitution, laws, and regulations; as well as their own charters, ordinances, resolutions, and regulations. Public budgeting and financial management, especially at the subnational levels in the United States, also take cues from professional associations, such as the GASB, which establish standards for financial and performance accounting and reporting. For example, the charter for Atlanta, Georgia, which was presented in this chapter, stipulates that the city provide financial information according to GASB financial accounting guidelines.

In this chapter, you have been exposed to the breadth of street-level services and programs delivered by local governments in the United States. You should understand how these governments are established, the different governance structures possible, and the various degrees of authority provided to them by the states. You should be able to conduct your own research about these governments in the United States—access the city charter, look up local code, find county tax rates—in order to learn about them, the responsibilities of public officials, and legal requirements for budgeting.

This chapter introduced you to two local government bankruptcies that recently occurred in the United States. These examples illustrate how fiscally stretched local governments can become as they attempt to balance their legal responsibilities and promises made to employees with the needs, desires, and expectations of their residents. The outcomes in Jefferson County and Central Falls suggest the benefits of a state protocol for intervening in local fiscal business—first to determine how far into a fiscal descent a local government may have gone, and then to support that government in generating a plan for readjusting back to fiscal stability. By now, you should have some knowledge of the eternal tug-of-war within and between governments regarding authority and discretion.

DISCUSSION QUESTIONS

1. Why might a special district or utility more likely be prone to bankruptcy than a general purpose local government?

2. How can actions by a state government assist or impair its local governments in times of fiscal stress? Explain different ways that states could take an active role as a local government nears bankruptcy?

3. In chapter 2, the budget practices of developed and developing countries were explained. Do you think the ways of characterizing countries explained in that chapter is applicable to local governments in the United States? Justify your response.

4. Distinguish between Dillon's Rule and home rule. What are the implications for local government budgeting under each rule?

5. Based on chapters 3–5, compare and contrast the roles and institutions at each level of government (federal, state, and local). Distinguish the services and programs provided by level: How do budgeting rules and authorities vary by level of government? How does this influence fiscal sustainability at each level?

NOTES

1. See the National League of Cities website, available at http://www.nlc.org/build-skills-and-networks/resources/cities-101/city-structures/number-of-municipal-governments-and-population-distribution

2. See the US Census Bureau, *2012 Census of Governments, The Many Layers of American Government*, available at http://www2.census.gov/govs/cog/2012/2012_cog_map.pdf

3. See *Broward County, Florida 2012 Comprehensive Annual Financial Report, Fiscal Year Ended September 30, 2012*. Available at https://www.broward.org/Accounting/Documents/2012CAFR.pdf

4. See the State of Georgia Constitution, available at http://sos.ga.gov/admin/files/Constitution_2013_Final_Printed.pdf

5. See the New Jersey State League of Municipalities, available at http://www.njslom.org/magart0307_p14.html

6. GASB's applicability to budgeting and financial management in subnational governments in the United States is discussed in the previous chapter.

7. See *Governing*, "Municipal Bankruptcy State Laws," 2013. Available at http://www.governing.com/gov-data/state-municipal-bankruptcy-laws-policies-map.html

8. See The Tax Foundation, "Rhode Island's State and Local Tax Burden, 1977–2010," available at http://taxfoundation.org/article/rhode-islands-state-and-local-tax-burden-1977-2010

9. See information about Rhode Island's municipal finances available at http://www.muni-info.ri.gov/finances/taxrates.php

10. Components of the law are available at http://www.muni-info.ri.gov/finances/

REFERENCES

Barnett, J. L., and P. M. Vidal. July 2013. *State and Local Government Finances Summary: 2011.* Available at http://www2.census.gov/govs/local/summary_report.pdf

Business Wire. 2013 "Fitch Expects to Rate Jefferson County, AL's Series 2013 GO Warrants BBB-Outlook Stable." Berkshire Hathaway Company, November 14. Available at http://www.businesswire.com/news/home/20131111006104/en/Fitch-Expects-Rate-Jefferson-County-ALs-Series

City of Atlanta. 2012. *CAFR, Comprehensive Annual Financial Report,* for the Year Ended June 30, 2012. Available at http://www.atlantaga.gov/modules/showdocument.aspx?documentid=6532

City of Clinton v. Cedar Rapids & Missouri River R. R. Co., 24 Iowa 455. (1868).

Denison, D. V., and J. B. Gibson. 2013. "A Tale of Market Risk, False Hope, and Corruption: The Impact of Adjustable Rate Debt On The Jefferson County, Alabama Sewer Authority." *Journal of Public Budgeting, Accounting & Financial Management* 25 (2): 311–345.

Faulk, K. 2013. "Birmingham Residents Object to Jefferson County's Bankruptcy Exit Plan." *The Birmingham News,* Alabama Media Group, November 20. Available at http://blog.al.com/spotnews/2013/11/birmingham_residents_object_to.html

Fehr, S. 2012. "Alabama's Largest County Faces Bankruptcy Without State Help." *Stateline,* August 22. The Pew Charitable Trusts. Accessed on November 20, 2013. Available at http://www.pewstates.org/projects/stateline/headlines/alabamas-largest-county-faces-bankruptcy-without-state-help-85899412766

Georgia Municipal Association. August 11, 2005. "Municipal Incorporation: Requirements under Georgia Law." Atlanta: Georgia Municipal Association. Available at http://www.gmanet.com/MDR.aspx?CNID=20732

————. 2007. "Georgia Model Municipal Charter," 4th ed. Atlanta: Georgia Municipal Association.

Grodzins, M. 1984. *The American System: A New View of Government in the United States.* Transaction Edition.

Howell-Moroney, M. E., and J. L. Hall. 2011. "Waste in the Sewer: The Collapse of Accountability and Transparency in Public Finance in Jefferson County, Alabama." *Public Administration Review* 71 (2): 232–242.

Hudson, B. January 6, 2011. "Amending Municipal Charter Amendments by Legislative Action and Home Rule." Atlanta: Georgia Municipal Association.

Malone, S. 2011. "Rhode Island's Central Falls Files for Bankruptcy." *Reuters,* August 1. Available at http://www.reuters.com/article/2011/08/01/us-rhodeisland-centralfalls-idUSTRE7703ID20110801

McCabe, B. C., and R. C. Feiock. "Nested Levels of Institutions: State Rules and City Property Taxes." *Urban Affairs Review,* 2005, 40 (5), 634–654.

Moody's Investors Service. 2013. "Moody's: Detroit Bankruptcy May Change How Other Distressed Cities Approach Obligations," *Global Credit Research,* July 26. Available at https://www.moodys.com/research/Moodys-Detroit-bankruptcy-may-change-how-other-distressed-cities-approach-PR_278692

Moore, S. 2012. "Part One: Structure of Municipal Government—Municipalities: Sources and Limits of Powers." In *Handbook for Georgia Mayors and Councilmembers,* 5th ed., 1–12. Available at http://www.gmanet.com/Assets/Pdf/handbook/handbook_complete.pdf

National League of Cities. 2013. "Number of Municipal Governments & Population Distribution." Available at http://www.nlc.org/build-skills-and-networks/resources/cities-101/city-structures/number-of-municipal-governments-and-population-distribution

Oates, W. E. 1972. *Fiscal Federalism.* New York: Harcourt, Brace, Jovanovich.

Ostrom, E. 1990. *Governing the Commons.* Cambridge, UK: Cambridge University Press.

Selway, W. 2011. "Jefferson County's Journey from Sewer-Bond Scandal to Settlement: Timeline." *Bloomberg.com,* September 16. Accessed November 12, 2013. Available at http://www.bloomberg.com/news/2011-09-16/jefferson-county-alabama-s-path-from-scandal-to-debt-settlement-timeline.html

Sigo, S. 2013. "Moody's: Jefferson County's Sewer Deal Should Be Junk." The Bond Buyer. Source Media, November 13. Available at http://www.bondbuyer.com/issues/122_219/moodys-jefferson-countys-sewer-deal-should-be-junk-1057335-1.html

Simmons, J. 2013. "Rhode Island's State Intervention and Distressed Communities," of the Rhode Island Public Expenditure Council, October 3. PowerPoint Presentation at the annual conference of the Association for Budgeting and Financial Management, Washington, DC. Available at http://www.ripec.org/pdfs/2013-ABFM-Presentation.pdf

The Pew Charitable Trusts. July 2013. "The State Role in Local Government Financial Distress." Available at http://www.pewtrusts.org/en/research-and-analysis/reports/2013/07/23/the-state-role-in-local-government-financial-distress

Tiebout, C. M. 1956. "A Pure Theory of Local Expenditure." *Journal of Political Economy* 64 (5): 416–424.

US Census Bureau. 2012a. *Local Governments by Type and State.* Available at http://www2.census.gov/govs/cog/2012/formatted_prelim_counts_23jul2012_2.pdf

US Census Bureau. 2012b. *2012 Statistical Abstract, Table 436. State and Local Governments—Revenue and Expenditures by Function, 2007 and 2008.* Available at http://www.census.gov/compendia/statab/cats/state_local_govt_finances_employment/state_and_local_government_finances.html

US Census Bureau. 2014. *Lists & Structure of Governments, Population of Interest.* Accessed on January 3, 2014. Available at http://www.census.gov/govs/go/population_of_interest.html

US Department of Labor. 2013. "Quarterly Census of Employment and Wages." Bureau of Labor Statistics. QCEW Industry Tables. Available at http://www.bls.gov/cew/cewind.htm#year=2012&qtr=A&own=3&ind=10&size=0

Walsh, M. W. 2013. "A Municipal Bankruptcy May Create a Template and Comments." *The New York Times: DealBook.* The New York Times Company, November 19. Available at http://dealbook.nytimes.com/2013/11/19/a-municipal-bankruptcy-may-create-a-template/

Whitmire, K. 2013. "Jefferson County Bankruptcy: 2024, the Year the County Hits the Wall, Again (Analysis and Video)." *The Birmingham News*, Alabama Media Group, November 1. Accessed November 20, 2013. Available at http://blog.al.com/spotnews/2013/11/jefferson_county_bankruptcy_20.html

Executive Leadership and the Budget Agenda

Guiding the national economy in the context of political accountability involves shaping policy so that it serves both to foster the growth of material productivity and to spread the opportunity and legitimacy that nourishes democratic participation. Timing and the good fortune of favorable events also come into it, of course; no president is above blaming his predecessor or market transactions.

—M. Stephen Weatherford, 2009

LEARNING OBJECTIVES

After reading this chapter, you should be able to

- Describe the components of an executive budget process
- Investigate the budget powers afforded to chief executives in various governments
- Understand public leadership and budget and policy agenda setting by government chief executives
- Find and analyze data about public chief executives and their leadership success

---

This chapter introduces you to the executive role in generating public budgets, the components of an executive budget process, and concepts of public leadership. The chapter begins by distinguishing presidential and parliamentary systems, followed by an overview of the stages of the budgetary process and the importance of executive development of a budget plan and strategy for government operations. The next section concentrates on what governmental leaders discuss in their speeches and budget messages. What these leaders talk about is important for guiding government actions and, from a budgetary perspective, future public investment. The centrality of party power and budget messages by government officials in several countries are discussed. Executive leadership and budgeting in the US federal government is described and polling data about presidential success is presented. The confluence of circumstances surrounding the Bill Clinton and George W. Bush administrations illustrate how the external environment works in conjunction with a chief executive to further steer a government. Budget and policy agenda setting by US state governors and the mayor of a large US city are presented as well to illustrate the distinctive budgetary foci of chief executives at these levels of government.

PRESIDENTIAL VERSUS PARLIAMENTARY SYSTEMS

The distinction between presidential and parliamentary political systems is important for understanding how budgeting is accomplished by the governments discussed here and for others that you may be interested in studying. In parliamentary or Westminster systems, on the one hand, there is a melding of executive and legislative responsibilities. Generally, one party controls both branches of government and executive agency ministers (cabinet secretaries or department heads) are also members of parliament. The head of state in a parliamentary government has the discretion to dissolve the legislature and call for elections, but it is usually the prime minister who is responsible for setting forth an agenda for the country. The prime minister generally works in committees on crafting the budget that will be submitted to the parliament for approval. The Secretary of the Treasury or the Minister of Finance might present the budget to the parliament. Parliamentary approval of the executive budget is often pro forma in that there is little change from the submitted recommendation to the appropriation bill or bills that are passed by the legislature.

On the other hand, presidential systems have a chief executive that develops and presents a budget to the legislature; the legislature may develop its own budget or consider the executive recommendation when determining appropriations. Of the countries of studied here, Brazil, Guatemala, and the United States have presidential systems in which the president is head of state and the government (responsible for international relationships, national defense, and domestic policy as well as management of the executive branch). Tanzania has a semipresidential system. The president is head of state and part of the parliament (National Assembly).[1] According to the Tanzanian Constitution, the president appoints a prime minister who must be a member of parliament as well as a member of the majority party of the Assembly. The prime minister is confirmed by a majority of the National Assembly or, if no majority political party exists in parliament, the president can appoint someone who "appears to have the support of the majority of the Members of Parliament." The constitution assigns the prime minister "authority over the control, supervision and execution of the day-to-day functions and affairs" of the Tanzanian government, as "Leader of Government business in the National Assembly" and the duty "to perform or cause to be performed any matter or matters which the President directs to be done."

Tanzania's governance system is quite different from the presidential system in the United States. Nicolas van de Walle (1999) categorizes Tanzania as a nondemocratic government in the 1990s and explains that the democratization efforts in African countries during this period introduced people to concepts of individual and political rights and brought multiparty politics into regime governments. Even though there has been progress in Africa in opening up government to public input, much needs to be done to strengthen participation, improve and expand public program operations, and advance economic development across the continent. In a study of twenty-nine African countries, comparing newly democratic regimes with nondemocratic ones,[2] van de Walle (1999) determines that public participation and representation have not improved with democratization. Specifically, local mobilization efforts are hindered by fragmentation; interest groups are often broken up along "ethnoregional lines" (van de Walle 1999, 27). Also, he finds that in these countries, "executive dominance of policymaking process remains patent. Not a single country has moved from a presidential to a parliamentary form of government as a result of democratization" (28). Long-standing problems in countries like Tanzania include a dysfunctional civil service, a history of foreign aid that has supported specific regimes or imposed fiscal and economic policies in conflict with governance and public management capacities, and the fact that national economic advancement is so closely tied to climate and agriculture. "It is useful to remind ourselves that the biggest single determinant of economic growth in most of low income Africa remains the level of annual rainfall" (37).

Different from presidential or semipresidential structures, parliamentary republics have a prime minister who is head of government and leader of the legislature. In these governments, the president is largely a symbolic figure and, as noted above, the executive budget message often comes from the prime minister, a deputy prime minister, or the cabinet-level finance minister. Of the governments examined here, India and Italy have parliamentary republics. Australia, as a federated constitutional monarchy, has a head of state who serves as proxy for the Queen (governor-general) and a prime minister who is head of government. All are members of the parliament. According to the Australian Constitution, "the legislative power of the Commonwealth shall be vested in a Federal Parliament, which shall consist of the Queen, a Senate, and a House of Representatives . . . a Governor-General appointed by the Queen shall be Her Majesty's representative."

STRATEGIC PLANNING AND THE BUDGET PROCESS

High-quality planning provides one path toward goal clarification (Chun and Rainey 2005). The strategic plan sets this path and advanced budgetary systems begin with such a plan. A results-oriented process requires defining the performance to be measured, whereas performance measurement developed and examined along the way provides the feedback that keeps the strategic plan on target. The primary component of an executive budget process is the preparation of the budget plan by a chief executive. The chief executive consolidates a plan for executive branch agencies to carry out the work of government. A chief executive can push agencies to conform to his or her budget and policy agenda by requiring agencies to develop budget requests that include information about how their goals and objectives feed into the overall, government-wide strategic plan. In a previous chapter about the legal foundations for budgeting in state governments, you learned that many US states have laws that specify the conduct of strategic planning; include language linking budgets with strategic plans, performance measures, or both; and require performance reporting that compares actual performance with targets.

The stages of the budget process—(1) agency budget development and executive budget recommendation; (2) legislative deliberation and passage of appropriations; (3) budget execution and monitoring; and (4) budget evaluation and financial audit—indicate the first stage as pivotal for the executive to have an impact on the direction of government. A chief executive, in developing a budget and policy plan, clarifies his or her goals for departments and agencies as they prepare their budget requests. The greater the focus of the plan and the more comprehensive it is in terms of providing a government-wide roadmap, the less ambiguity will exist about future direction (Bryson 2004). The following section examines public leadership generally and then describes budget and policy agenda setting on the part of chief executives, concentrating on executive leadership at different levels of government in the United States.

PUBLIC LEADERSHIP: GENERATING A BUDGET PLAN

A leader is "one who creates or strives to create change, large or small" and public leadership regards "the domain of individuals and institutions dedicated to governance and public policy" (Kellerman and Webster 2001, 487). Public leadership literature has evolved mostly from the disciplines of political science and psychology, producing much research about the relationships of power among individuals and groups and the budget rules and institutions that structure those relationships. Barbara Kellerman and Scott Webster (2001) explain that understanding leadership through "one disciplinary lens does not suffice" (508), as the concept is complex.

It is hard to pin down the characteristics of a good public leader without understanding the context within which the leader operates, the rules and institutions regarding executive responsibilities, and the distinctive personality of the leader in question. In the political arena, leadership potential springs from the ability to initiate legislation (develop policy and make laws), set the agenda (strategic vision for future action), and steer the agenda through execution. In many governments, though, the ability to initiate law is strictly legislative. In the United States, for example, the president cannot initiate legislation but must work through representatives and senators. The president can, however, set an agenda for national advancement and a primary method of doing so is by providing the state of the union address and submitting a national budget to Congress.

EXECUTIVE LEADERSHIP IN PARLIAMENTARY SYSTEMS

Leadership and budgetary influence varies depending upon governmental systems, how power may be dispersed, and the centrality of the budget message. Differences between presidential and parliamentary systems were described earlier. José Antonio Cheibub (2006) explains that presidential systems work better than parliamentary ones in fostering budget balance because voters are more inclined to hold president as chiefly responsible for the economy. Policy responsibility is more opaque in parliamentary systems and blame assignment is murkier, thus "presidents, more than prime ministers, have an incentive to keep budgets under control" (Cheibub 2006, 365).

Parliamentary systems meld some legislative and executive powers. The head of state in a parliamentary government has the discretion to dissolve the legislature and call for elections, but it is usually the prime minister who is responsible for setting forth an agenda for the country. The prime minister generally works in committees on crafting the budget that will be submitted to the parliament for approval. Thus, members of parliament have been included in budget development.

Political power is diffused in governments that have a prime minister who provides the policy lead rather than the head of state—be it a president or governor-general. Italy has had five presidents since 1978 and sixteen different prime ministers, representing half a dozen different parties during the period. Tanzania has had four presidents since 1964 (all representing the Party of the Revolution) and nine different prime ministers. Since 1996, Australia has had four governor-generals and five different prime ministers (as in Italy, some have served several different terms for more than one governor-general). Parliamentary turnover in this country is frequent (every two to three years), which further disrupts party hold and thus budget and policy focus. In Australia, the budget message is provided by the Deputy Prime Minister and Treasurer. In this year's message on May 14, 2013, Deputy PM and Treasurer Wayne Swan (2013) discussed the budget and policy considerations of the labor party that he represents, opening by admitting to a deficit of $18 billion,

> Because of our deep commitment to jobs and growth and due to a savage hit to tax receipts . . . The alternative, cutting to the bone, puts Australian jobs and our economy at risk, something this Labor government will never accept.

Since 1992, India has had five presidents and five different prime ministers. In this case, Manmohan Singh, a member of the (Indian National) Congress Party, has served as prime minister since 2004, though just recently he stated that he will not seek another term when elections are held in summer 2014. Jos Mooij and S. Mahendra Dev (2004) discuss poverty and social priorities of the Indian central government during the 1990s by studying the budget speeches of the central government's finance ministers from 1990 to 2002. Mooij and Dev (2004) explain as follows:

> Budget speeches are, of course, political documents and their content cannot be taken at face value. Nevertheless, they present and justify particular allocation decisions and policies and reveal the way of thinking underlying them. The fact that these allocations can later be delayed or withdrawn altogether means that one should not give too much weight to budget decisions and budget speeches. These speeches do illustrate, however, how governments, or rather Finance Ministries, would like to present themselves to the outside world, including international agencies/policy-makers and economists. (100)

These scholars determine that conceptualizations of the poor and poverty alleviation by the government morphed throughout the decade, from consideration of economic reforms as poverty alleviation to a broadening of the plight of the poor and the road out as a multidimensional effort (necessitating government investment in health and education programs, clean water, nutritious food, roads, housing, and the empowerment of women). In terms of the frequency of words used in budget speeches during the period of study, Mooij and Dev (2004) find that poverty, the poor, and employment are mainstays; human development, self-help, macro-credit/finance, and empowerment references jump in the second half of the twelve-year span, whereas considerations of inequality and distribution of income drop out totally by 1997. Following their analysis of government spending for the same period, these scholars conclude that the focus of budget speeches has contributed to the expenditure shift from income redistribution to human development—a shift that these scholars deem unhelpful in making progress on true poverty alleviation in the country. The budget speech of then current Minister of Finance, Palaniappan Chidambaram, made in February, 2013, seems to continue the focus on advancing human development for poverty alleviation. According to Chidambaram (2013):

> We are a developing country. The link between policy and welfare can be expressed in a few words: opportunities, education, skills, jobs and incomes. Every mother understands this. Every young man and woman understands this. My budget for 2013–14 has before it one overarching goal: to create opportunities for our youth to acquire education and skills that will get them decent jobs or self-employment that will bring them adequate incomes that will enable them to live with their families in a safe and secure environment.

US PRESIDENTIAL LEADERSHIP AND BUDGETING

M. Stephen Weatherford (2009) studies presidential economic agenda setting and determines that presidents naturally set out to make a mark for themselves. However, to keep the nation on an even keel economically, a president "needs to have a clear idea of his own goals, and enough economic knowledge, curiosity, and self-confidence to seek constructive diversity in his advisors, and then to engage them in the give-and-take of genuine deliberation" (Weatherford 2009, 551). Similarly, Roy Meyers (1996) discusses the importance of understanding the goals of the decision makers in a budgetary process in order to comprehend the strategies and tactics these individuals use when making budget decisions. In dollar terms, a study of aggregate federal outlays in the forty-eight continental states from 1982 to 2000 determined that US presidents matter significantly in federal budget outcomes (Larcinese, Rizzo, and Testa 2005). Presidents are tactical in directing money to specific states, not only for fiscal policy reasons (stabilization, allocation, and distribution) but also for political reasons. Presidents use budget allocations to enhance reelections, to maximize chances of winning elections, and to reward party members and the legislative districts of like-minded, supportive representatives and senators. But the outcome of all this strategy is distinctive and monetary. According to Valentino Larcinese, Leonzio Rizzo, and Cecilia Testa (2005), "states that ideologically lean towards the president, i.e. states with a high share of presidential votes or with a governor belonging to the party of the president, tend to be rewarded with more funds . . . and Congress members opposing the president bring less funds to their states" (8). According to Philip Joyce and Roy Meyers (2001) "the president is more than the political equal of the Congress" (15) in budgetary matters, given the veto power and bully pulpit of the position.

George Edwards' research (2009) about strategic leadership of the president turns traditional conceptions of American presidential influence, if not upside down, at least onto one side. He distinguishes between presidential discretionary authority and the powers provided by the Constitution and federal code with the ability to persuade others to support an agenda. Think about when President George W. Bush, in defending Donald Rumsfeld as his secretary of defense, claimed, "I am the decider and I decide what is best." US presidents can choose their cabinet officers, though these choices are reviewed and approved by the Senate. President Bush did have many decisions that he was responsible for making as the nation's chief executive officer. But he also needed the ability to draw the public together in support of his budget and policy agenda, if he was going to be successful. In his case, the 9/11 terrorist attacks on the Twin Towers in New York City and the Pentagon presented a direction for him and he was able to secure public support for the defense initiative early in his first term. In his address to Congress on September 20, 2001, President Bush set forth his vision for combating a "War on Terror"[3]

> On September the 11th, enemies of freedom committed an act of war against our country . . . Al Qaeda is to terror what the Mafia is to crime. But its goal is not making money; its goal is remaking the world and imposing its radical beliefs on people everywhere. The terrorists' directive commands them to kill Christians and Jews, to kill all Americans and make no distinctions among military and civilians . . .
>
> Our war on terror begins with al Qaeda, but it does not end there. It will not end until every terrorist group of global reach has been found, stopped and defeated . . . tonight I announce the creation of a Cabinet-level position reporting directly to me, the Office of Homeland Security. Tom Ridge . . . will lead, oversee and coordinate a comprehensive national strategy to safeguard our country against terrorism and respond to any attacks that may come.

In this speech, President Bush defined the problem, provided an assessment of its breadth and frightening consequences, and directly (and almost immediately) affected future budgets. Soon after, William Newmann (2002) discussed the possible ways to reorganize the federal government to include these home-land security activities, suggesting that the creation of one department to conduct all the work "would take years to plan, even longer to implement, and lead to bureaucratic infighting the likes no one has ever seen" (130). In fact, the fiscal year 2013 budget for the US Department of Homeland Security—just about a decade after its creation—is $59 billion in total budget authority, $48.7 billion in gross discretionary funding, and $39.5 billion in net discretionary funding. The number of employees in the department in the fiscal year 2013 budget in brief (including military reserve and auxiliary personnel) is 232,129![4] This example illustrates the complexity of the concept of public leadership suggested earlier by Kellerman and Webster as well as the window of opportunity for policymaking conceived by John Kingdon (1995) that was introduced in the first chapter of this book. Public leadership is a function of individual characteristics exposed to outside circumstances and affected by timing—these components can come together and effect change that has lasting impact on public budgets.

George W. Bush's approval ratings jumped from 51 percent the week of 9/11 to 85 percent by September 14, 2001. In an examination of polling data and comparing presidential budget policy with presidential approval ratings, Nooree Lee (2008) finds that the data related to this president "most strongly supports the notion of a relationship between presidential approval rating and budget policy approval rating" (21). But she clarifies that the very high and low ratings fluctuations realized by George W. Bush may cloud results. That is, public approval of President Bush in handling his job stayed above 80 percent for more than four months following 9/11, before dropping to 76 percent on March 4, 2002. But after October 6, 2006, President Bush's approval ratings never peaked above 38 percent again.[5]

Edwards (2009) argues and presents data illustrating the very real and powerful role that presidents have in setting an agenda for the nation, which in turn influences the fiscal, economic, and social path of the country. He describes presidential leadership in terms of the chief executive as director or facilitator. These kinds of roles are discussed by others in a budgetary context and relate to theoretical perspectives about the budget and policy process as expounded by Kingdon (1995), Aaron Wildavsky (1984), Irene Rubin (2000), and Kurt Thurmaier and Katherine Willoughby (2001). That is, successful presidential leadership requires framing policy choices to coincide well with the public mood, increasing the salience of proposals to the public that then pressures

Congress to go along, clarifying how budget and policy initiatives agree with public sentiment, currying support (building a clientele) for the initiative, and effectively timing its presentation (Edwards 2009). According to Edwards, "skilled presidents who understand the nature of public opinion may be able to use it as a resource to further their goals. At the core of this strategy is choosing the issues they emphasize and the manner in which they present their policy initiatives" (61). He highlights President Dwight Eisenhower's references to national defense to promote education and highway spending, President Lyndon Johnson's war on poverty, President Richard Nixon's general revenue sharing, and President Ronald Reagan's revenue-neutral tax policy initiative as all representative of adroit application of these presidential leadership principles.

Edwards points out, however, that presidents may not be as powerful or persuasive as has been thought. He debunks long-standing, even mythical ascriptions of the enduring legacies of Presidents Abraham Lincoln, Franklin D. Roosevelt, and Ronald Reagan. Certainly, each of these presidents exhibited exceptional communication skills—each faced obstacles regarding their policy choices that were not fully or easily realized, in particular, Lincoln on equality, Roosevelt regarding the war effort, and Reagan on Central America and defense spending. Similarly, President Richard Nixon sought public support to impound spending already approved by Congress, framing the issue as necessary budget discipline. But "it appears that even just a few months after his landslide reelection victory, Americans were either deeply divided or, at best, merely ambivalent on the issue of impoundment. The sweeping support Nixon sought for his contentious use of impoundment was not forthcoming" (Lee 2008, 21). Interestingly, more than two decades later, the presidential campaign would be all about federal budget deficits.

Joyce and Meyers (2001) analyze budgeting during President Bill Clinton's administration, discussing the president's success in terms of macro- and micro-budgetary policy, presidential-congressional relations, and budgeting within the executive branch. The president experienced some early success in his new administration with passage of the Omnibus Budget Reconciliation Act of 1993, which included tax increases and extended the spending cap and PAYGO provisions of the 1990 Budget Enforcement Act. By 1994, however, Congress was majority Republican so that for the rest of his first and second terms, President Clinton was managing in a split party government. Joyce and Meyers (2001) explain that President Clinton's attempt at health care reform probably suffered from putting his wife in charge, the plan's complexity, media attention on its strategic development, and because of reports by the Congressional Budget Office (CBO) of its probable and projected costs.

In fact, the disagreements between the president and Congress resulted in two government shutdowns—one in November, 1995 for a week and another from December 1995 to January 1996 that lasted three weeks, before the fiscal year 1996 budget was agreed upon. In 1996, President Clinton more easily won a second term and the next year, the Balanced Budget Act passed. By fiscal year 1998, the federal budget realized a unified budget surplus of $69 billion—its first since 1969. Joyce and Meyers (2001) explain that in spite of budget surpluses, Congress held to the spending caps established in law. This led to what are today understood as "budget gimmicks" or "smoke and mirrors" accounting, such as declaring certain spending to be "emergency spending" even if it is not, or "advance appropriations" when supposedly current spending is unavailable until a future year, payment shifts from one fiscal year to the next, and "directed scoring that informs CBO that a particular bill costs less than the CBO thinks it does" (Joyce and Meyers 2001, 8).

According to Richard Conley (2001), President Clinton's "success rate on floor votes from 1995–2000 was among the lowest for presidents who have faced divided government in the post-War era according to the Congressional Quarterly Almanac's yearly tabulations" (3). While he was not able to advance his preferred agenda during this period, Clinton was able to "influence the policy process and policy outcomes, either by halting the Republican agenda with applied vetoes, or redefining available solutions with implied vetoes—threats—as a means of bringing policy outcomes closer to his own preferences" (4).

Joyce and Meyers (2001) highlight the confluence of circumstances surrounding the federal budget environment that fostered multiple year surpluses (from 1998 to 2001). Previous law (1990 BEA), the strong economy, higher incomes yielding increased federal tax receipts, welfare reforms supporting stronger labor flexibility, deregulation, tax simplification, the end of the Cold War, depressed defense spending, low energy prices, and even luck are all included as contributing factors. These scholars also emphasize that trade liberalization and the Federal Reserve's management of monetary policy contributed to the federal government's positive balance sheet. Of micro-budgetary changes arising during the Clinton administration, net interest on debt and defense discretionary spending declined while spending for transportation, health research and training, and criminal justice programs increased, and spending for income security stabilized. President Clinton had a Republican Congress and impeachment proceedings also pressuring his influence.

Alternatively, Joyce and Meyers (2001) point to the president's strong budget support from the Office of Management and Budget (OMB) that was led by seasoned officials with high credibility throughout both his terms. (Recent OMB director, Sylvia Mathews Burwell, was deputy director of OMB, among other federal positions, during the Clinton Administration.) Clinton also initiated performance management and budgeting reforms through the work of the National Performance Review or National Partnership for Reinventing Government (NPR) and with passage of the Government Performance and Results Act (1993). Finally, a handful of laws passed during the Clinton Administration contributed to reforms of federal financial management practices, including amendments to the Chief Financial Officers Act (1990), the Government Management Reform Act (1994), the Federal Financial Management Improvement Act (1996), the Federal Acquisition Streamlining Act (1994), and the Information Technology Management Reform Act (1996) (Joyce and Meyers 2001).

PRESIDENTIAL JOB PERFORMANCE

Table 6.1 presents public approval ratings of the job performance for the last six presidents produced by the Gallup Poll.[6] Trends indicate the overall trajectory of the polling numbers for each president and data is provided on the approval ratings realized in the first and last polls conducted for each president, and the average approval rating for all polls conducted for each president. Use caution when considering ratings averages, given the very wide disparity in the number of polls conducted for individual presidents. Monthly and weekly polls give way to almost daily ones in the case of President Barack Obama; the last poll of this president in this table is dated December 29, 2013. Still, it is interesting to consider public views about presidential job performance. Seemingly, Presidents Jimmy Carter and Obama have never realized any uptick in ratings. While President Reagan's ratings are higher at the end of his administration than at the start, he does not have smooth sailing either. President George H. W. Bush evidenced a big dip in ratings—no doubt resulting from the eight-month recession that lasted from July 1990 to March 1991. Still, this president recoups to end a bit higher than he began in the public's view. His son, George W. Bush, reaped

Table 6.1
Presidential Approval Ratings, Trends, First and Last Poll Scores and Averages

President	Trend	First and Last Poll Approval Rating	Average Approval Rating (# of polls conducted)
Carter		66% and 34%	46.1% (91)
Reagan		51% and 63%	52.6% (148)
Bush I		51% and 56%	60.1% (158)
Clinton		58% and 66%	55.6% (228)
Bush II		57% and 34%	51.0% (270)
Obama		68% and 44%	48.5% (1,722)

Source: The American Presidency Project, available at http://www.presidency.ucsb.edu/data/popularity .php?pres=44&sort=time&direct=DESC&Submit=DISPLAYData from the Gallup Poll and compiled by Gerhard Peters, based on the question, "Do you approve or disapprove of the way [first & last name] is handling his job as President?" The number of polls conducted throughout each president's administration varies; last poll included for President Barack Obama is dated 12/29/2013.

the benefits of a surge in public approval following 9/11 (which contributes to his overall average of 51 percent), but soon makes a precipitous, continuous fall in the polls after public fears wane. In spite of the budget wars and difficulties of President Clinton across his two terms as presented by Joyce and Meyers (2001), he is the only president to have ratings that maintain a positive trajectory.

The Siena Research Institute (2010) has employed another way of quantifying leadership success by conducting a periodic survey of scholars and experts on the US presidency and developing rankings of American presidents on a number of characteristics.[7] The survey asked respondents to rank presidents according to personal attributes (such as imagination and intelligence), abilities (such as leadership and communication), and areas of accomplishment (related to the economy and working with Congress, for example). Consistently, President Franklin D. Roosevelt has been rated as the top chief executive in this survey. The next highly ranked presidents include Theodore Roosevelt, Abraham Lincoln, George Washington, and Thomas Jefferson. In 2010, results rank Teddy Roosevelt highest on personal attributes, Abraham Lincoln highest on abilities, and Franklin Roosevelt highest regarding accomplishments. This latest survey ranks George W. Bush 39 of 43 presidents, rating him "especially poorly in handling the economy, communication, ability to compromise, foreign policy accomplishments and intelligence" (2). Bill Clinton ranks 13 overall, though his rankings on integrity and ability to avoid crucial mistakes are among the lowest of all presidents. Jimmy Carter (32 overall) is highly ranked on integrity, and 13 on intelligence, but is placed 40 for his handling of the economy. President Obama's overall ranking is 15, Reagan's is 18, and George H. W. Bush is ranked 22 of 43.

STATE EXECUTIVE LEADERSHIP AND BUDGETING

Studying state-level public leadership in the United States is interesting given the wide range of budget powers afforded to governors across states, as well as the distinctive balance of powers across branches of these governments (see Clynch and Lauth 1991 and 2006). Governors can be distinguished by their use of a number of budgetary powers, which vary from state to state (Thurmaier and Willoughby 2001). Most governors appoint their budget office directors and in more than half (27), the state budget director is a member of the cabinet (NASBO 2008). In ten states, the budget office is within the office of the governor (just as the OMB is within the Executive Office of the President); in ten others, this office is freestanding and the rest are within a department of finance, management, or administration. In many states, the governor is solely responsible for generating the revenue estimate for the upcoming fiscal year—this provides the foundation for determining appropriations (remember from chapter 4 that some type of budget balance is required in virtually all states). The National Association of State Budget Officers (NASBO 2008), in their periodic survey of these offices, has determined that 24 states allow the governor to reorganize departments without legislative approval, 30 can spend unanticipated funds without such approval, 38 can reduce the enacted budget without approval and 32 can place restrictions on budget reductions without consent from the legislature. All states provide their chief executives with some type of veto power;

many offer different types of veto authority, including line item (44), item veto of appropriations (41), item veto of selected words (15), and item veto to change the meaning of words (4) (NASBO 2008).

Irene Rubin and Roy Meyers (2012) explain that though most states conduct some type of executive budgeting, the budget powers of governors can be diluted. For example, if agencies are able to submit their budget requests to the legislature at the same time that they submit them to the governor, (1) the legislature has more time to analyze and react to executive branch budget requests and (2) agencies can conduct an end run around the governor if their legislative proposal differs from the one made to the governor. These scholars studied the effects of budget rules and institutions in three states with historically strong executive budgeting systems—Illinois, Maryland, and New York. In spite of these states' strong executive systems, Rubin and Meyers (2012) describe dysfunctional budgeting in Illinois (corruption) and New York (extremely closed and lacking transparency). They determine that increasing executive strength will not help states to solve their budget problems because "empowering governors works only when the individuals elected as governors are responsible leaders" (18). The following section analyzes budget leadership of US state government chief executives considering their most significant budget and policy statement—their annual state of state addresses.

Governors as Budget and Policy Leaders

Larry Sabato (1983) describes a new breed of American state governors that emerged in the twentieth century. Far from the compliant executives afforded few powers evidenced in the 1800s, state government chief executives in the 1900s became significant public policy leaders, given strength through enhanced formal powers, state reorganizations, evolving relationships with state legislatures, changing intergovernmental relationships, and a stronger collective voice professionally—for example, via the National Governors Association (Beyle 1988). By 2013, Rosenthal (2013) indicates that the American governor is viewed by many as "the best job in politics," (8) even better than the presidency of the United States. Many consider that governors, more so than the president or local chief executives, are able to conceptualize what they want to accomplish, generate a strategy, implement their plans, and have an impact. As Rosenthal (2013) points out, "governors are where the action is . . . they are able to get things done" (8).

Following an election, no matter how close the vote, the governor provides a single voice for the state. Whereas state legislators are beholden to the constituents of their district only, the governor's constituency is the entire state. Policy leadership of the state is naturally centered with the governor and advanced through the budget process. Compared with the president of the United States, governors are able to exert tremendous force in terms of the budget. Many states have budgeting systems in which the governor is chiefly responsible for setting the revenue estimate, has strong policy-oriented staff for developing the budget, robust budget powers vis-à-vis the legislature, and then chief responsibility for managing money flow throughout the fiscal year (Thurmaier and Willoughby 2001). Many governors have strong veto powers that can be leveraged to pursue their budget and policy visions. Although a tremendous constraint on governors, state requirements for budget balance contribute to their strong budget and policy role vis-à-vis the legislature. A survey of American governors by Rosenthal (2013) shows that most consider that "the budget is the most important thing governors do" (95). According to Dall Forsythe and Donald Boyd (2012) "success in budgeting marks a governor as a strong leader, whereas failure in budgeting makes a governor look weak and ineffectual" (1–2). Because the budget serves as the governor's strongest policy tool, gubernatorial state of the state speeches are vital in generating momentum to advance their budget initiatives.

Today's governors may be more prepared than ever before to be budget and policy leaders—they indicate being schooled in more than just politics. For example, the class of 2013 governors is very well educated: 48 of 50 have a bachelor's degree, 8 have master's degrees, 25 have a law degree, one has a doctorate in American Studies, and another a medical degree. Obviously, many have multiple degrees. The most popular universities include Yale and Brown, with 3 graduates each, and there is one Rhodes Scholar in the bunch. The average age of the current class is 58.5 years and thus many governors bring to the job a wealth of work experiences spanning the public, private, and nonprofit sectors. More than half have a career background in the private or nonprofit sectors. Twenty-nine indicate having spent some time in the private practice of business, law, or medicine; several have farming or ranching experience (one governor lists blacksmithing as a previous occupation); a few others have headed up or been members of foundations or think tanks; and some are published authors or have worked in television or radio. The next most popular preparation for state executive leadership is service in the state legislature—half of governors (25) indicate having served as a state representative or senator or both. Eighteen governors have management experience given their past roles as state attorney general, treasurer, auditor, or as head of some other state agency; a dozen governors have served previously as their state's lieutenant governor. Five list careers as educators (teacher, university instructor, or head of a state university system). Collectively, 29 governors have some federal government work experience—10 as federal judges or attorneys, 10 as members of the US Congress, and 9 with service in the military. Finally, 17 governors have local government work experience, 9 on city councils or county commissions, and 8 as local chief executives. Today's governors include the past mayors of Baltimore, Maryland; Charlotte, North Carolina; Denver, Colorado; Knoxville, Tennessee; Oakland, California; Stamford, Connecticut; Warwick, Rhode Island; and Waterville, Maine.

Gubernatorial Agenda Setting: The Budget Message

Daniel DiLeo and James Lech (1998) have referred to the annual or biennial addresses of governors as the primary means of communicating an executive agenda to the public. In these addresses, governors alert citizens and legislators (among others) of their interests and foci in the coming fiscal year. Also, these public talks "provide the best insight available into [gubernatorial] preferences, values and ideology" (Coffey 2005, 90). Laura van Assendelft (1997) concurs that governors pursue major policy issues "consistent with their political phi-losophies" (221). Eric Herzik (1983) determines that the gubernatorial concerns that surface in these messages can be characterized as cyclical, perennial, or temporal—governors express their considerations of issues in which their interest might ebb and flow (such as tax reduction or government performance), those they consider rather consistently over time (like education or transportation), and those that might generate a spike in their interest (like a natural disaster or ethics reform).

DiLeo and Lech (1998) replicated Herzik's analysis of gubernatorial addresses in the 1970s and 1980s by examining state of state addresses in the 1990s for eight consecutive years, determining that governors' interests in various agenda items vary over time and are influenced by a number of factors, not just by type of policy issue. That is, context matters. This squares with the work of John Kingdon (1995) which describes the visible and hidden clusters of actors that influence the public policy process. Richard Herrara and Karen Shafer (2012) study the influences of horizontal and vertical diffusion on governors' policy pursuits and consider that gubernatorial gender and political party might also interact with diffusion in effecting a governor's policy emphases. They find that policies, as defined by Herzik (1983), perform differently across time—that is, "economic policy, a cyclical issue, appears to behave more like a perennial one from 1991 through 2012 . . . The perennial issues of health policy, education, and social welfare show considerable variation with regard to attention as a priority" (Herrara and Shafer 2012, 24). These scholars find that gubernatorial agenda setting is dynamic—specifically, that vertical influence goes both ways.

Van Assendelft (1997) examines gubernatorial agenda setting through analysis of the state of state addresses of just four governors. She determines that although partisan divisions in states do not affect the number of issues or specifics addressed by governors as represented in their state of state addresses, these chief executives "develop different strategies of agenda setting" (1997, 211) depending upon their political capital. Gubernatorial agenda setting is affected by an "interaction between personal and political factors" (215). Those in unified governments with support from their legislature are more likely than those in divided government to focus on controversial issues. "Governors working in divided government have less flexibility in the kinds of issues they can pursue [successfully]" (214). Her results about gubernatorial agenda setting differ from findings related to presidential agenda setting—unlike presidential influence that declines over time (lame duck), van Assendelft (1997) finds that gubernatorial influence gains strength over time.

One component that affects a governor's policy strength regards communication strategy. Certainly, today's governors and their staffs must be media wizards to effectively disseminate their message to all stakeholders. And, as explained earlier, the annual state of state address may just be a governor's most important tool for advancing his or her budget strength and policy initiatives. Current state of state speeches are available in print and online. Electronic versions (and often archived speeches) are provided on gubernatorial websites as well as through several professional associations such as the National Governors Association and the Council of State Governments. Many governors' websites also provide live feed of their speeches, or links to videos, along with "stay connected" social media options. Maryland Governor Martin O'Malley catches the spirit of the contemporary governor as a research and technology wizard, perfectly capable of presenting his comprehensive and complex budget and policy initiatives to his state in a number of different formats. Every year he posts his address, complete with footnotes, on the Maryland governor's website, which includes links to a video of the speech and a downloadable PDF (see the Office of Governor Martin O'Malley at http://www.gov.state.md.us/). Governor O'Malley's 2014 state of state message is fourteen pages long, single-spaced, with a hundred footnotes, which include websites that can be accessed directly from the document (the 2014 State of the State Address is available at http://www.governor.maryland. gov/blog/?p=9788). His website also offers access to an extensive list of social media for the state that includes Facebook, Twitter, RSS feed, Podcast, Pinterest, and Flickr, among others.

State of State Addresses Before, During, and After the Great Recession

As the discussion of Governor O'Malley illustrates, modern governors are able to speak knowledgeably about a wide range of budget and policy issues and often they do. Nonetheless, the context and personal characteristics dictate what the speech is about, how many budget and policy initiatives may be introduced, and how thoroughly each may be discussed.[8] A notable example was in 2011, when Arizona Governor Jan Brewer, in her January 10 address to the legislature and state citizens, spoke only of the shooting of US Representative Gabrielle Giffords and others in Tucson on January 8, 2011. Governor Brewer explained, "I had intended to deliver a State of the State address to you today—remarks that outline an exciting and solid plan for job creation, education, and tax reform and I will deliver that plan to you. But not now. Not today." On the other hand, those who study and listen to these speeches consistently have come to expect that governors tend to focus on a handful issues likely to include any crisis of the day, core state functions, and then specific initiatives that might fall outside of these topics—issues that fall into Herzik's characterizations as cyclical, perennial and/ or temporal.

Table 6.2 presents fifteen issues expressed by governors in their annual speeches as priorities in the following fiscal year. This is by no means a complete list of all issues addressed by governors every year, but it does include those that fall into Herzik's categorizations (1983), though as pointed out by Herrara and Shafer (2012), these may change categories across time.

What is evident from the table is that prior to the official start of the Great Recession (December 2007), at least two-thirds of governors addressed eight issues important to them for the next fiscal year. By the end of the Great

Table 6.2

Issues Expressed by Governors as Priority in Next Fiscal Year in State of State Addresses, 2007–2012

Issue expressed by governor	2007 N=43	2008 N=42	2009 N=44	2010 N=42	2011 N=47	2012 N=43
	Percentage of governors mentioning issue					
Education	100.0	90.5	86.4	90.5	93.6	95.3
Economic Development/Jobs	79.5	81.0	79.5	88.1	87.2	90.7
Tax/Revenue Initiative	84.1	59.5	65.9	83.3	70.2	81.4
Natural Resources/Energy	84.1	71.4	79.5	73.8	44.7	65.1
Surplus/Deficit/Rainy Day Funds/Reserves	70.5	54.8	45.5	78.6	34.0	60.5
Health Care	86.4	83.3	79.5	57.1	72.3	55.8
Safety/Corrections	75.0	59.5	50.0	54.8	38.3	55.8
Performance/Accountability	72.7	42.9	52.3	73.8	83.0	55.8
Transportation/Roads/Bridges	52.3	59.5	65.9	50.0	46.8	48.8
Pensions/OPEBs	36.4	21.4	18.2	19.0	36.2	32.6
Local Government	52.3	35.7	20.5	11.9	17.0	25.6
Transparency	20.5	14.3	31.8	14.3	2.1	25.6
Borders/Illegal Immigrants	11.4	16.7	6.8	4.8	8.5	11.6
Ethics Reform	13.6	11.9	15.9	26.2	8.5	7.0
Debt Reduction	13.6	9.5	4.5	0.0	8.5	7.0
Number of issues considered by at least two-thirds of governors	**8**	**4**	**6**	**6**	**5**	**3**

Source: This table is reproduced from "The State of the State Addresses: The New Normal Fosters Gubernatorial Funnel Vision" by Katherine G. Willoughby in The Book of the States, Vol. 43, edited by Audrey S. Wall (Lexington, KY: Council of State Governments, 2012), 193–202.

Recession (June 2009), the number of issues considered in annual messages declines to six, and three years after the official end of the recession, two-thirds of governors are focusing on just three issues that include education, jobs, and taxes.

The Impact of Party on Gubernatorial Agenda

This section provides some assessment of how politics relates to agenda setting on the part of US state governors. First we consider how the party of the governor affects his or her consideration of the state budget plan; that is, are the concerns of governors different depending upon party? Next, we assess gubernatorial agendas based upon party split between the executive and legislature. Results indicate that politics influences these executive plans, but in nuanced ways.

The Governor's Party   Daniel Coffey (2005) recognizes that "gubernatorial ideology is multidimensional" (97), meaning that when push comes to shove, it is difficult to label a Democratic governor as liberal or a Republican as conservative on *all* issues. Table 6.3 breaks down the issues considered important going forward by governors during and after the Great Recession and accounting for the political party of the governor. Considering only the differences across the parties of 10 percent or greater, in the period just before and during the recession, Democratic governors are more likely than the Republicans to discuss natural resources and energy, safety and corrections; Republican governors are more likely than the Democrats to discuss budget balance issues of surplus, deficit, reserve, and rainy day funds.

Examining the content of governors' remarks surrounding these issues helps to determine if there are any substantive (partisan or policy) differences. Regarding the category of corrections and public safety, which shows the widest spread across governors by party during the recession, there are a number of considerations addressed by both Democratic and Republican governors. Governors in both parties discussed the scourge of methamphetamines, the need for more money for enhanced or expanded state drug courts, and the necessity for treatment facilities and programs for offenders with substance abuse problems. They also considered ways to combat domestic violence, substance abuse, identity theft, and sex offenders; governors of both parties called for tougher penalties for those convicted of sex crimes (especially against children) or repeat offenders of domestic violence or stalking. Governors of both parties discussed improving

Table 6.3
Percent of Governors Mentioning an Issue as Priority for Next Fiscal Year, Before and After the Great Recession and by Governor's Party

Issue Mentioned by Governor as Priority for Next Fiscal Year	Recession 2007–2009		After Recession 2010–2012	
	Governor's Party			
	Democrat *n*=71	Republican *n*=54	Democrat *n*=56	Republican *n*=73
Education	90.1	92.6	94.6	91.8
Health Care	84.5	75.9	73.2	52.1
Natural Resources/ Energy	80.3	70.4	67.9	58.9
Economic Development	76.1	72.2	89.3	87.7
Safety/Corrections	70.4	44.4	53.6	46.6
Tax/Revenue Initiative	66.2	74.1	78.6	79.5
Transportation	56.3	53.7	53.6	43.8
Performance/ Accountability	54.9	48.1	71.4	71.2
Surplus/Deficit/Rainy Day/Reserves	42.3	59.3	50.0	61.6
Transparency	33.8	35.2	16.1	12.3
Local Government	22.5	14.8	14.3	19.2
Pensions/OPEB	15.5	22.2	33.9	24.7
Ethics Reform	11.3	16.7	19.6	9.6
Borders/Immigration	9.9	9.3	3.6	12.3
Debt Reduction	5.6	5.6	5.4	5.5

Source: Raw data collected from governors' state of state addresses. See also Audrey S. Wall (ed.), *The Book of the States* (Lexington, KY: Council of State Governments), for the years 2007–2012.

law enforcement communications and expanding correctional facilities via renovations and new construction. A Democratic governor suggested shutting down in-state prisons and coordinating with neighboring states to develop a 2,000- to 3,000-bed regional facility that would reduce state operating costs but provide new jobs. Democratic and Republican governors called for more boots on the ground in terms of troopers and corrections officers, improvements to highway safety, increased efforts to combat drunk drivers and speeders, and upgrades of state labs to speed processing of crime data and samples and to expand DNA fingerprinting to solve crimes more quickly.

There were some marked differences, however, in approaches to public safety policies that may reflect partisan persuasion. Only Democratic governors discussed advancing citizen safety by improving the salaries of corrections personnel, adequately funding corrections to advance public safety and upholding general union agreements for corrections personnel that require pay increases. Other Democratic chief executives emphasized the need to protect corrections personnel positions or suggested reorganizations that would strengthen coordination of corrections with local officials to enhance public safety. One Democratic governor called for a drug test requirement for all state employees. Some discussed relief valves to prison overcrowding, with one suggesting a smart sentence strategy that would allow the head of the state's Department of Corrections to release inmates convicted of nonviolent crimes up to ninety days before the end of their term, instead of thirty days for good behavior. Another mentioned lowering prison populations by reducing the number of offenders sent back to prison every year for violating technicalities of their parole. One governor proposed that the state enter into an agreement with the US Immigration Services to speed deportations to help reduce the number of inmates in state prisons; another suggested the expanded use of electronic monitoring and home confinement for nonviolent traffic offenders; and one noted that closing prison facilities would reduce the corrections budget.

Other agenda items related to public safety and corrections mentioned by Democratic but not Republican governors included catching human smugglers (broadening human trafficking laws to crack down on those smuggling people across borders); tackling nursing home abuses; reducing gang violence and recruitment into gangs; eradicating gun violence (by maintaining a central database of mentally ill and dangerous persons, requiring instant background check at gun shows, and limiting illegal access to guns); banning cockfighting; enhancing the regulation of mines and mining safety; improving child and school safety generally and addressing bullying (protecting children by fingerprinting every fourth grader in the state); and better monitoring of foster care programs. Other topics included strategic deployment of troopers to the greatest pockets of violence and the expanded use of modern GPS technology to track high-risk young offenders in the most violence-plagued neighborhoods. Finally, one governor suggested that safety in communities could be improved by tearing down abandoned buildings.

Republican governors presented a few ideas that were not brought up by any of their Democratic counterparts, too. At least one Republican governor discussed enhancing self-protection strategies while another discussed a virtual prison program to reduce prison populations. No Republican governor in this group discussed gun control.

Of the issues with the widest spread of interest between Democratic and Republican governors before and during the recession, only that related to surplus/deficit/rainy day/reserve funds carries over similarly in spread after the recession. Safety and corrections falls in interest among Democrats and increases only slightly among Republicans; the wide disparity dissipates following the recession. The gulf in interest related to natural resources and energy between Democrat and Republican governors is just slightly diminished after the recession. The widest gulf in terms of interest by governors of the two parties following the recession regards health care.

Unified or Divided State Government   Table 6.4 breaks down the issues considered important going forward by governors during and after the Great Recession and accounting for political party divide in the state. Considering only the differences between unified and divided governments of 10 percent or more, in the period just before and during the recession, governors in unified states (governor's party is the same as the majority party of the legislature) are more likely than those in divided ones to push their ideas related to safety and corrections; governors in divided states are more likely than those in unified ones to relay their interests regarding economic development and transparency. Thinking back to van Assendelft's conclusions related to state party divide and gubernatorial use of political capital to pursue specific policy issues, results here might indicate that governors in unified states are more confident in pursuing policies for which they already have the backing of their legislature (gun control in Democratic states, and the individual right to bear arms in Republican states). Those in divided states must test the waters or gauge the public mood in their efforts to secure external capital for their initiatives.

This examination of governors and their agendas just before, during, and after the Great Recession assesses their interests, the specifics of their budget

Table 6.4
Percent of Governors Mentioning an Issue as Priority for Next Fiscal Year, Before and After the Great Recession and by State Party Split

Issue Mentioned by Governor as Priority for Next Fiscal Year	Recession 2007–2009		After Recession 2010–2012*	
	Party Split across Branches			
	Unified n=57	Divided n=65	Unified n=77	Divided n=51
Education	89.5	92.3	92.2	96.1
Health Care	84.2	78.5	62.3	60.8
Natural Resources/ Energy	82.5	73.8	62.3	64.7
Safety/Corrections	70.2	52.3	49.4	49.0
Tax/Revenue Initiative	70.2	67.7	75.3	84.3
Economic Development	68.4	81.5	88.3	88.2
Transportation	57.9	55.4	54.5	41.2
Performance/ Accountability	50.9	53.8	71.4	72.5
Surplus/Deficit/ Rainy Day/Reserves	47.4	49.2	54.5	64.7
Transparency	29.8	40.0	14.3	15.7
Pensions/OPEB	21.1	16.9	33.8	25.5
Ethics Reform	19.3	9.2	9.1	21.6
Local Government	19.3	20.0	16.9	21.6
Borders/Immigration	10.5	7.7	9.1	7.8
Debt Reduction	5.3	6.2	7.8	2.0

Source: Raw data collected from governors' state of state addresses. See also Audrey S. Wall (Ed.), *The Book of the States* (Lexington, KY: Council of State Governments), for the years 2007–2012.

*Data does not include the State of Nebraska in any year, given its unicameral legislature. Assigns the State of Rhode Island "split" status for the years 2010 to 2012; 2010 when Governor Don Carcieri (R) faced a Democratic legislature and 2011 and 2012 when Governor Lincoln Chafee (I) faced a Democratic legislature.

and policy initiatives, and consideration of the factors that might affect their foci at any given time. Results indicate that the single most significant economic downturn in the United States since the Great Depression resulted in governors whittling down their budget and policy agendas significantly by 2012 to include (1) the most important and consistent core function of states, education; (2) a function that has become perennial to states within the last 30 years, economic development (jobs); and (3) a cyclical issue of import, taxes. More generally, education, economic development, taxes, government performance, budget balance, and pensions gained steam in terms of interest by governors in the three years following the Great Recession. Policies related to health care, natural resources and energy, safety and corrections, transportation, and transparency lost ground in this period.

Temporal issues such as local government, immigration, ethics reform, and debt reduction are of less interest to governors and remain so throughout the period of study. As fiscal resources have dried up and remained stagnant, governors have focused on traditional state functions, developing and presenting very specific, often multipronged methods of service delivery in their addresses. Though holding to a "no new taxes" mantra in the aftermath of the Great Recession, many governors have pressed for new or increased state fees and charges or earmarked revenues; they have suggested improving their chances in the competition for federal dollars, or called for further stretching the federal funding they now receive. Some have called for increased bonding or providing their local governments the ability to generate more in own-source revenues. After the Great Recession, governors also indicate increasing concern with fiscal stewardship (balance and pensions) and accountability (government performance).

There are differences within issues of interest to governors, depending upon party. Democratic governors, for example, were much more likely than the Republicans to discuss their initiatives related to safety and corrections in their addresses (during and after the recession, but especially during the downturn). Examination of governors' comments related to this policy area indicates that Democratic governors were more likely to support gun control, whereas no Republican governor discussed such policy. Democratic governors were more likely to bring up management strategies—personnel concerns and protections—to solve public safety problems.

There seem to be some interactive effects of the recession on gubernatorial agenda setting as certain issues fall off the radar while others gain momentum over time. Following the recession, safety and corrections and transparency are considered equally by governors in unified and divided states but by a lesser percentage of governors in both circumstances. Transportation is less important to governors in both circumstances after the recession, though a greater gap in interest exists across unified and divided states in the years 2010 to 2012. On the other hand, perennial issues such as economic development, a strong concern for governors (especially in divided states) before and during the recession, gain strength in interest by governors in both circumstances—second only to education in interest as expressed in addresses from 2010 to 2012. Undoubtedly, the very slow economic upturn since the recession has focused governors on state (and regional) recovery efforts.

This analysis has exposed you to nearly all the state of the state speeches by US state governors for six consecutive years, and regards gubernatorial agenda setting and budget interests during and after the second most significant economic downturn experienced in the United States. Past work has developed ways of categorizing and quantifying gubernatorial budget and policy interests and the factors regarding these interests. The above analysis finds that policy issues addressed by governors do fall into said categories (perennial, cyclical, temporal), issues crossover categories over time (perennial crossover to temporal and back), and issues can present in gradations or turn into different categories (perennial issues that readjust and issues that present as a mix of categories over time). Also, results suggest that working in a split party state, in conjunction with the economic downturn, may be related to gubernatorial policy pursuits. Finally, examination of the specific initiatives of governors in their addresses for the study period finds that most governors consistently provide very thoughtful, complex, and comprehensive ideas about how to keep states functioning and to improve operations going forward. In some ways, perhaps, fiscal stress, or being pushed to the wall, seems to challenge governors to get things done.

US LOCAL LEADERSHIP

In *The Politics of Public Budgeting: Getting and Spending, Borrowing and Balancing*, Irene Rubin (2000) discusses a new DeKalb, Illinois mayor's response to negative media reports of coming into office and "messing up" the good system created by the past mayor. The new mayor promptly clarified the budget situation he faced upon entering the chief executive's chair, methodically addressing every charge: the fund balance really needed boosting; past hiring in preparation for new development that never materialized required reassessment; tax increases were necessary to accommodate state mandates, honor inter-local agreements, and for directed spending; and the fee structure actually compared well with DeKalb's competitors. Rubin discusses this story and its lessons, including the often "muddled communication" among public officials, voters, residents, and the media. This example also illustrates a public executive with good leadership skills responding quickly and clearly to criticisms, providing transparency, and giving a rational response with little hysteria. According to Rubin (2000), to be successful, "public officials need not only to do the right thing for the community and follow the public will, as best they understand what that is, but also to figure out a way to explain and justify their choices" (8–10).

As Rubin explains later in the book, "executive budgetary leadership and powers are not uniform across local governments" (96) in the United States. The International City/County Management Association (ICMA 2008) defines local forms of government in the United States accordingly:

- **Mayor-Council.** This form has a separately elected mayor and council; the mayor is head of the government with powers that may be ceremonial and weak or expansive and strong in terms of developing and directing policy. According to the ICMA (2008), the mayor's "duties and powers generally include: hiring and firing department heads, preparation and administration of the budget, and veto power (which may be overridden) over acts of the council." The council is responsible for adopting policies and budgets, passing ordinances and resolutions, and auditing government performance. Some cities engage an administrator who manages the city day to day so that the chief executive can engage in a stronger policy role.

- **Council Manager.** A council is elected by voters, with a manager hired to administer policies, develop the budget, manage operations, and oversee personnel. A mayor or council president heads the council and may be elected by the council or the voters; council elections are usually nonpartisan. "The mayor and council, as a collegial body, are responsible for setting policy, approving the budget, and determining the tax rate" (ICMA 2008). A mayor in this governance structure is the political head of the government, though budget duties rest with the manager.

- **Commission.** A board or commission is elected by voters and operates as both the legislature and executive of the government. The board collectively serves as head of government and is responsible for (1) adopting policies and budgets and (2) passing local laws and regulations. Most of these governments have separately elected department heads, as well, such as the county clerk or the sheriff. Although this is the oldest form of local government in the United States, it has lost ground—less than half of US counties use this form of government today. About 34 percent of counties use a commission-manager form of government (like council-manager), and 21 percent use an elected executive form of government (Stirgus, 2013).

- **Representative Town Meeting.** Voters choose representatives who are the only ones able to vote on issues that come before the town, though the public can participate in local governance by attending meetings and determining policy and budget issues to be voted on.

- **Town Meeting.** This form offers direct democracy, as all qualified voters participate in town governance, electing a board (of selectmen) but also voting on policy. Selectmen carry out policy determined by voters. Sometimes a manager is employed to run the town's day-to-day operations. This form of government is usually found in very small towns.

As discussed in chapter 5, there are many hybrid governance structures among the thousands of local governments in the United States. In DeKalb County, Georgia, for example, there is an elected commission *and* a chief executive officer (CEO) elected by voters. This CEO is very powerful—"while commissioners approve some contracts and the annual budget, the CEO can change purchasing policy without the approval of commissioners" (Stirgus 2013, B8). The power of the CEO in this county is unusual. The governance structure has been hotly debated in the past year given extortion charges against the CEO, who has since stepped down. On the other hand, hiring professional administrators is a growing trend in local governments because of the growing complexity of government operations. According to Jim Phillips, a spokesman for the National Association of Counties, "as things get more complicated and counties have more services to provide, they move to an administrator instead of an elected board" (Stirgus 2013, B8).

What follows is an examination of public leadership in a large US city in the South that engages a strong mayor-council governance structure. The effort here is to provide the reader with a comparison of chief executives and their budget and policy agendas at the various levels of government in the United States. As you read about this local chief executive, consider his agenda and how his focus is similar and varies with those at the state and national levels of government. Consider the responsibilities of these different governments, as determined in their legal foundations, and how this affects the focus of each public leader.

LEADERSHIP IN A STRONG MAYOR CITY GOVERNMENT

The City of Atlanta (incorporated in 1847) is the capital of Georgia. Encompassing about 132 square miles, the US Census Bureau 2008 population of the city is listed at more than half a million residents (533,016); the population of the metropolitan area where it sits exceeds five million people. Atlanta's population during weekdays easily swells to over a million. "The City of Atlanta differs from its larger metropolitan region in that it has a higher minority population (62 percent versus 42 percent), lower median household income ($47,464 versus $59,882), and twice the crime rate (1,389 versus 501 violent crimes per 100,000 residents)" (Searcy and Willoughby 2011, 13). The city has been able to fight crime effectively, decreased rates of violent and property crimes in the last decade have helped to entice new people and businesses to settle within its borders, and home values have improved and unemployment has declined. Atlanta's population grew by 26.2 percent from 2000 to 2008, compared with an 8 percent increase nationwide.

Chapter 5 examined part of Atlanta's charter related to fiscal control and fund balance policy. Figure 6.1 presents Atlanta's charter with information about mayoral duties and powers. These powers and duties include such activities as the execution and enforcement of laws, management and supervision of city work, development and presentation of policy, budget development and submission, voting on local laws, convening meetings, conducting research, analyzing systems and performance, developing management standards, advisement, city representation and public relations, reorganization, and purchasing. The term of office for Atlanta's mayor is four years, with a two-term limit. The mayor has a line-item veto power. There are fifteen council members and one council president; twelve members are elected by district and three are selected at large. These elections are nonpartisan.

Figure 6.1
Components of City of Atlanta Charter Related
to Governance and Mayoral Powers

BILL OF RIGHTS

ARTICLE 1. – NAME, POWERS, AND BOUNDARIES

ARTICLE 2. – LEGISLATIVE

ARTICLE 3. – EXECUTIVE

Chapter 1. The Mayor

Section 3-104. Powers and duties.

*Execute and enforce laws

*Supervise administration of departments and delegate such to COO

*Annually present policy to council of Atlanta's physical, economic and social aspects, goals and objectives, and recommendations, policies, plans, programs and priorities to attain them

*Submit annual budget to council

*Approve or veto proposed ordinances and resolutions

*Convene special meetings of council, upon discretion

*Conduct studies, investigations and reports to council about department operations

*Prescribe, require, publish and implement standards of management and operating practices and procedures for city agencies or delegate such responsibilities to COO

*Advise council and make recommendations about city financial condition, future needs and general welfare

*When authorized by council, negotiate deeds, bonds, contracts, and other instruments and documents on behalf of Atlanta and execute same after final approval by council

*Represent Atlanta in intergovernmental relations, promote and improve the government, encourage city growth, promote and develop prosperity and social well-being of its people

*Initiate administrative reorganization of city government, as desired

*Perform all duties authorized by law

*Purchase supplies, material, equipment and personal property provided the purchase amount does not exceed $100,000.00, as conform with city provisions

*Annually prepare plan for increasing efficiency of city services based on findings and recommendations of citizen's service planning review commission

Source: See municipal charters and code available at www.municode.com; access the Code Library, the State of Georgia, City of Atlanta for information related to charter components above.

In Georgia, local governments must balance their budgets, use a state mandated uniform chart of accounts, and participate in an annual fiscal survey conducted by the Georgia Department of Community Affairs (Searcy and Willoughby 2011). The city's primary own-source revenue is the property tax; Atlanta provides most, if not all, of the services allowed by law as listed in chapter 5—police and fire protection, roads and other capital projects, land use, planning and regulation, water, solid waste collection and disposal, recreational and cultural programs, and transportation services. The city has a separate public school district; Atlanta Hartsfield-Jackson International Airport has been labeled the busiest airport in the world.[9] Atlanta sits in the middle of Fulton County, with a small portion of city boundaries within DeKalb County.

Atlanta's mayor has strong budget powers as part of the city's budget commission that develops revenue estimates and given responsibility for presenting a budget to the city council. The mayor oversees the work of a chief operating officer (COO) as well as a chief of staff. The city's chief financial officer (CFO) serves the mayor and council. The city's fiscal year runs from July 1 to June 30.

Cynthia Searcy and Katherine Willoughby (2011) discuss more than a half a dozen past problems associated with Atlanta's budget, including

- The daily traffic of workers into Atlanta takes a toll on city services and infrastructure.
- A large number of nonprofit and government properties in the city are exempt from the city's property tax.
- Atlanta has created numerous tax allocation districts (TADs) that incentivize economic development by providing tax exemptions to developers.
- Atlanta has been under federal and state court orders regarding its sewer and water systems that have required substantial service rate increases on residents.
- Atlanta's pension obligations ballooned from 2000 to 2010, with payouts reaching 20 percent of the city's general fund budget by 2010.
- Atlanta has experienced high turnover in key positions; by 2011, the city had five different CFOs within eight years.

Shirley Franklin was mayor of Atlanta prior to current Mayor Kasim Reed. Mayor Franklin spent much of her two terms pulling the city out from under a blanket of corruption and poor finances that characterized the administration of her predecessor, Bill Campbell, who went to prison for tax evasion in 2006. Searcy and Willoughby (2011) explain that the history of budget gaps, no reserves, and poor, if not unlawful, financial management practices necessitated immediate action on her part. For example, an interim CFO under Franklin in her first term determined that a number of felons were employed in his department—one in accounts payable had been convicted for embezzlement! All of these factors culminated in the March, 2009 downgrade of Atlanta's credit from AA– to A by Standard & Poor's.

Mayor Reed, previously a Georgia state legislator, won a close race against former city council member Mary Norwood in November 2009 and came into office in January 2010. In his first state of the city address, Reed[10] discussed the successful leader—that is, great leaders do not give people what they *say* they want, but what they *really* want, "genuine leadership in a time of crisis." This harkens back to the work of Cheibub (2006), which opens this chapter, regarding voter assignment of policy responsibility and presidential incentives to control budgets. According to Cheibub (2006), "even if voters do not value low budget deficits, governments [i.e. their chief executives] know that they are an element in generating what voters care about: low inflation" (363). In this case, the stated priorities of the new mayor included hiring more police, reducing crime, cracking down on panhandlers, improving efficiency in trash and recycling collections, pension reform, reenergizing after-school and recreational programs for children and youth, economic development, and arts and even cultural enhancements. Regarding panhandling, Reed explained, "We need a law that protects our residents and visitors from those who would take advantage of their kindness by aggressively soliciting money for a living."

Examining the mayor's 2014 proposed budget[11] indicates his making good on some of the promises that have budgetary implications. He explains that

- The police force has increased by 525 recruits, and has reached the goal number of 2,000 officers.

- The city's fund balance stands at over $100 million at the end of fiscal year 2012.

- City recreation centers have been reopened.

- Core services, including fire-rescue response times and sanitation operations, have been improved.

- The city pensions have been renegotiated and reformed.

The CFO of Atlanta also noted in this budget proposal that the city has engaged advanced revenue forecasting technology and is working with a state university to improve its estimates. The city is also investigating a new capital projects model that will enhance the validity and reliability of capital planning and cost estimation. Concerning panhandling—a primary agenda item of the mayor's upon entering office—the city council passed an ordinance in October, 2012 that was a compromise on an earlier law vetoed by the mayor because he claimed it would not solve the problem. The new ordinance cracks down on panhandlers, has lighter minimum penalties, but bans "panhandlers from continuing to ask for money after they have been told no" (McWilliams 2012).

Reed won a landslide reelection as Atlanta's mayor in November, 2013. In summing up his leadership over the past year, Leslie (2013) points to several successes—the mayor negotiated for Atlanta's NFL team, the Falcons, to stay in the city and build a new $1.2 billion arena. The mayor pushed for state law to be able to issue $200 million in bonds to contribute to building the stadium; the bonds are collateralized against city hotel-motel tax receipts. The old stadium will be torn down and a new one built in a nearby location that was Reed's first choice. Reed has framed this deal as economic development and neighborhood redevelopment, offering that new construction and the resulting business will also build up the poor neighborhoods and communities that surround the project. Reed has also pushed economic development by lobbying for expansion of the Savannah Port, symbolically appearing with Vice President Joe Biden during his visit to review the project. The mayor has been successful in pulling federal funds into the city as well—for the Atlanta Beltline (a redevelopment, mixed use, residential, retail, leisure project that surrounds the city) and for various transportation projects (streetcars)—and has extended the city's ability to compete for funds as a US Federal Transportation Agency grant designee (Leslie 2013).

The mayor's losses have included the fiscal and personal capital that he sunk in a number of recent local elections in which candidates of his choice lost their current seats or failed to bump out an incumbent (Leslie 2013). (In one race for city council, the woman that Reed barely beat in his first race for mayor won against Reed's choice.) Also, at the same time that Reed was brokering the deal with the Falcons, negotiations were ongoing with the Atlanta Braves, the city's signature MLB team. In light of the $200 million bonding deal for the Falcons, the Braves felt slighted when Reed determined their demands too expensive for the city. The Braves blindsided the mayor by bolting to an adjacent government, Cobb County, and accepting a $672 million deal to build a new stadium and develop surrounding property there. In other negotiations with its home county, Fulton, Atlanta lost part of its annual take ($96 million) from local option sales tax receipts that are divvied up among the fourteen cities in the county (Leslie 2013).

CONCLUSION

This chapter has introduced executive budgeting and leadership—highlighting the means and content of chief executives' communication with the public about their budget and policy agendas. In addition to budget rules and institutions, government leaders have avenues to influence the road taken by their governments through the bully pulpit, by their speeches and, more directly, their budget messages. Centrality of message delivery matters as well as the circumstances surrounding such delivery. You have been exposed to budget and policy agendas of executive government leaders in governments at the national, state, and local levels that illustrate distinctive interests—the national policy issues considered and aired by presidents, the specific functions and programming interests of governors, and the street-level, service delivery concerns of local chief executives. You should also have an appreciation for ways that public leadership has been measured, by coding the content of speeches, by polling the public (job approval ratings), by surveying experts (ranking certain defined abilities), and by tabulating the numbers themselves (number of government employees, funding levels, spending amounts by category or function). An executive budget process is one in which the chief executive is a centralizing force—with help, he or she develops the budget plan for government and then uses the office to project this plan forward by communicating about his or her agenda. The mix of revenues and expenditures that make up a public budget are influenced by the government's chief executive and this mix is reflected, in part, by past and present leadership.

DISCUSSION QUESTIONS

1. Define an executive budget process and why such a process might enhance or challenge a government budget.

2. The US president, state governors, and city mayors use their "state of the government" addresses to outline budget and policy proposals and garner support for their agendas. How do you think the rise of technology and mass media has changed this process for public leaders? Specifically, do you think it has made it easier or harder for them to communication about their agendas and to garner support for them? Justify your response.

3. Presidential popularity and budget agenda success seem to go hand-in-hand. Does this mean that public budgeting is nothing more than "politics as usual"? Explain your response.

4. Some scholars argue that governors are more likely to accomplish policy and budget objectives than a president. Why might this be the case?

5. When you think of a "good" public leader, who comes to mind and why? What characteristics or accomplishments define quality of public leadership for you?

6. Budget speeches can reveal how leaders conceptualize an issue. For example, poverty may be described in economic or moral terms by public leaders as they propose poverty-alleviation programs. Discuss how language

has changed regarding public budgeting issues in the United States. Specifically, do public leaders use different language today, as compared to the past, when discussing education, criminal justice, health, poverty, and the environment? What are the implications for government budgets with differing interpretations of these issues?

NOTES

1. The Tanzanian Constitution determines that "there shall be a Parliament of the United Republic which shall consist of two parts, the President and the National Assembly."

2. Full transition "democratic" governments indicate elected changes in administration/governance without conflict. That is, transition election is free and fair and the loser publically accepts election results. Van de Walle (1999) emphasizes that sharp distinction across the countries in his study was difficult. "Most of the nondemocratic states can legitimately claim some significant political liberalization, while even the most successful transitions have been marred by setbacks and evidence of shaky consolidation" (van de Walle 1999, 24).

3. See the transcript of President George W. Bush's address to a joint session of Congress on Thursday night, September 20, 2001, available at http://edition.cnn.com/2001/US/09/20/gen.bush.transcript/

4. See the US Department of Homeland Security, Budget in Brief, available at http://www.dhs.gov/xlibrary/assets/mgmt/dhs-budget-in-brief-fy2013.pdf and to view the current organization of the US Department of Homeland Security, see http://www.dhs.gov/xlibrary/assets/dhs-orgchart.pdf

5. See The American Presidency Project, available at http://www.presidency.ucsb.edu/data/popularity.php?pres=&sort=time&direct=DESC&Submit=DISPLAY and customize display for George W. Bush.

6. Polling data is also available directly from Gallup, at http://www.gallup.com/home.aspx?ref=b or from the Roper Center, at http://www.ropercenter.uconn.edu/

7. See survey results, available at https://www2.siena.edu/pages/3390.asp?qs=ir and accessing July 1, 2010 independent research.

8. State of state addresses for American governors have been analyzed by the author and a team of graduate students for the last decade; the addresses and content analyses considered here are those for the years 2007 to 2012. To conduct a content analysis of state of state addresses, a topic was considered addressed and part of the chief executive's budget and policy agenda if the governor specifically discussed the issue as relevant to state operations or the budget *going forward*. The governor needed to relay that the function, activity, or issue was an important item in next fiscal year's budget and policy direction. Just mentioning a state function or policy area, such as health care, in a speech did not classify the issue as an agenda item addressed by a governor. Further, a review by a governor of his or her past accomplishments regarding any particular issue area did not count in the content analysis. If a governor indicates a specific issue as part of his or her agenda going forward, the issue was coded "1," and if not mentioned so, the issue was coded as "0" in an Excel spreadsheet. The details provided by any governor regarding an agenda item or issue were recorded using the "Comment" feature of Excel. Therefore, for the years 2007 to 2012, governors' state of state speeches are coded, using 1 or 0 to indicate that an issue is a gubernatorial agenda item going forward, and using the "Comment" feature to record governors' particular initiatives regarding any given agenda item. Detailed analyses of these state of state addresses by year are available from current and back issues of *The Book of the States*, produced by the Council of State Governments at http://knowledgecenter .csg.org/drupal/view-content-type/1219

9. See World Top 30 Airports at http://www.world-airport-codes.com/world -top-30-airports.html

10. Available at http://www.atlantaga.gov/index.aspx?page=24

11. City of Atlanta, Fiscal Year 2014 Proposed Budget, available at http://www .atlantaga.gov/modules/showdocument.aspx?documentid=8625

REFERENCES

Beyle, T. L. 1988. "The Governor as Innovator in the Federal System. *Publius* 18 (3): 131–152.

Bryson, J. 2004. *Strategic Planning for Public and Non-Profit Organizations*, 3rd ed. San Francisco: Jossey-Bass.

Cheibub, J. A. 2006. "Presidentialism, Electoral Identifiability, and Budget Balances in Democratic Systems." *American Political Science Review* 100 (3): 353–368.

Chidambaram, P. 2013. "Budget 2013–2014." Government of India, February 28. Available at http://indiabudget.nic.in/ub2013-14/bs/bs.pdf

Chun, Y. H., and H. G. Rainey. 2005. "Goal Ambiguity and Organizational Performance in Federal Agencies." *Journal of Public Administration Research and Theory* 15 (4): 529–557.

Clynch, E. J., and T. P. Lauth. 1991. *Governors, Legislatures, and Budgets*. New York: Greenwood Press.

_____. 2006. *Budgeting in the States: Institutions, Process, and Politics*, New York: Praeger.

Coffey, D. 2005. "Measuring Gubernatorial Ideology: A Content Analysis of State of the State Speeches." *State Politics & Policy Quarterly* 5 (1): 88–103.

Conley, R. S. 2001. "President Clinton and the Republican Congress, 1995–2000: Political and Policy Dimensions of Veto Politics in Divided Government." Paper presented at annual conference of the American Political Science Association, San Francisco, California, August 30–September 2.

DiLeo, D., and J. C. Lech. 1998. "Governors' Issues: A Typology Revisited." *Comparative State Politics* 19 (6): 9–20.

Edwards, G. C., III. 2009. *The Strategic President: Persuasion and Opportunity in Presidential Leadership*. Princeton, NJ: Princeton University Press.

Forsythe, D. W., and D. J. Boyd. 2012. *Memos to the Governor: An Introduction to State Budgeting*, 3rd ed. Washington, DC: Georgetown University Press.

Herrera, R., and K. Shafer. 2012. "Governors Policy Agendas Over the Long Haul: State Priorities in a National Context." APSA 2012 Annual Meeting Paper. Available at http://papers.ssrn.com/sol3/papers.cfm?abstract_id=2104951

Herzik, E. B. 1983. "Governors and Issues: A Typology of Concerns." *State Government* 54: 58–64.

International City/County Management Association (ICMA). 2008. Forms of Local Government Structure. Reference # 106142. Available at http://icma.org/en/icma/knowledge_network/documents/kn/Document/9135/Forms_of_Local_Government_Structure

Joyce, P. G., and R. T. Meyers. 2001. "Budgeting during the Clinton Presidency. *Public Budgeting & Finance* 21 (1): 1–21.

Kellerman, B., and S. W. Webster. 2001. "The Recent Literature on Public Leadership Reviewed and Considered." *The Leadership Quarterly* 12: 485–514.

Kingdon, J. W. 1995 / *Agendas, Alternatives, and Public Policies*, 2nd ed. New York: HarperCollins.

Larcinese, V., L. Rizzo, and C. Testa. June 2005. "Allocating the US Federal Budget to the States: The Impact of the President." *Political Economy and Public Policy Series* 3. London: London School of Economics and Political Science.

Lee, N. 2008. "Congressional Budget and Impoundment Control Act of 1974, Reconsidered." Federal Budget Policy Seminar, Harvard Law School, April 29, Briefing Paper No. 34.

Leslie, K. 2013. "2013's Highs and Lows for Atlanta's Mayor." *Atlanta Journal-Constitution*, December 30, Section B, 1 and 3.

McWilliams, J. 2012. "Atlanta City Council Passes New Anti-Panhandling Law." *Atlanta Journal-Constitution*, October 2. Available at http://www.ajc.com/news/news/local/atlanta-city-council-passes-new-anti-panhandling-l/nSRpM/

Meyers, R. T. 1996. *Strategic Budgeting.* Ann Arbor: University of Michigan Press.

Mooij, J., and S. M. Dev. 2004. "Social Sector Priorities: An Analysis of Budgets and Expenditure in India in the 1990s." *Development Policy Review* 22 (1): 97–120.

National Association of State Budget Officers (NASBO). Summer 2008. "*Budget Processes in the States.*" Washington, DC. Available at https://www.nasbo.org/sites/default/files/BP_2008.pdf

Newmann, W. W. 2002. "Reorganizing for National Security and Homeland Security." *Public Administrative Review* 62 (s1): 126–137.

Rosenthal, A. 2013. *The Best Job in Politics: Exploring How Governors Succeed as Policy Leaders.* Washington, DC: Sage/CQ Press.

Rubin, I. 2000. *The Politics of Public Budgeting: Getting and Spending, Borrowing and Balancing*, 4th ed. New York: Chatham House Press.

Rubin, I. S., and R. T. Meyers. 2012. "Political Institutions for Sustainable State Budgets." Paper presented at annual conference of the Association for Budgeting and Financial Management, New York, NY. October 11–13.

Sabato, L. 1983. *Goodbye to Good-Time Charlie*, 2nd ed. Washington, DC: CQ Press.

Searcy, Cynthia, and Katherine Willoughby. 2001. "The Great Recession's Impact: The City of Atlanta's Budget." *Municipal Finance Review* 32 (1): 11–32.

Siena Research Institute. July 1, 2010. "American Presidents: Greatest and Worst." Available at https://www2.siena.edu/pages/3390.asp?qs=ir

Stirgus, E. 2013. "Commission Form Statement Is True." *Atlanta Journal Constitution*, December 31, Metro Section, B1 and B8.

Swan, W. 2013. "Budget Speech 2013–2014." *Australian Government*, May 14. Available at http://www.budget.gov.au/2013-14/content/speech/html/speech.htm

Thurmaier, K., and K. G. Willoughby. 2001. *Policy and Politics in State Budgeting.* New York: M.E. Sharpe.

Van de Walle, N. 1999. "Economic Reform in Democratizing Africa." *Comparative Politics* 32 (1): 21–41.

Van Assendelft, L. A. 1997. *Governors, Agenda Setting, and Divided Government.* Lanham, MD: University Press of America.

Weatherford, M. S. 2009. "Comparing Presidents' Economic Policy Leadership." *Perspectives on Politics* 7 (3): 537–560.

Wildavsky, A. B. 1984. *The Politics of the Budgetary Process*, 4th ed. Boston: Little Brown.

Budget Powers of the Legislative Branch

Determining the allocation of resources among competing claims was critical to establishing the legitimacy and authority of the legislature as an institution competing with the monarchy.

—Paul Posner and Chung-Keun Park,
Role of the Legislature in the Budget Process: Recent Trends and Innovations

---

LEARNING OBJECTIVES

After reading this chapter, you should be able to

- Distinguish between presidential and parliamentary systems of government
- Measure the budget powers of legislatures
- Compare the budget powers and processes of legislatures by governance structure and level of government
- Understand reforms governments engage to balance budget powers across different branches of government
- Find and analyze budget institutional and process data about governments of interest

---

L egislative bodies, as representative institutions, serve as the fundamental connection of people with their government. Well-working governmental systems have legislatures that establish policy (make laws), determine the means for accomplishing policy goals (produce budgets), and conduct oversight of policy execution (evaluate spending). The "power of the purse" (the means for accomplishing policy goals) is a constitutionally established responsibility of parliaments and legislatures in governments around the world and the most important feature of a governmental system. The power of the purse is the ability to generate revenues, decide on taxes, and determine how and where public funds will be spent. The ability of legislatures to make laws and budgets and evaluate spending arises not just from constitutions and code, but also from the evolution of institutional organizational arrangements, procedural systems and rules, technical and research support, and the influences of culture and tradition. These factors and the state of modern legislative budgeting are discussed in this chapter.

The opening section explains factors that influence legislative budget power and how legislative power has been quantified in past research. Then, we compare budget-making capabilities of legislatures, with a focus on two countries of different governance structures; in addition, we describe congressional budgeting in the United States. The following section examines budgeting strength in US state legislatures, touching on three governments of diverse budget power arrangements. This chapter illustrates that legislatures may have strong budget-making powers and thus have the potential to influence significantly the lives of the people that they represent. On the other hand, legislatures do not necessarily engage every budget power that has been provided to them, may not engage powers well, or may have delegated budget powers to their executive branch so that, over time, their actual influence becomes diluted (Santiso 2004).

MEASURING LEGISLATIVE POWERS IN THE BUDGETARY PROCESS

Paul Posner and Chung-Keun Park (2007) discuss the shifting of legislatures in governments around the world during the twentieth century to reassert their powers in order to deal with multifaceted, difficult budget problems. These scholars discuss that such changes have come about because of

1. Significant fiscal imbalances that governments have experienced

2. Political party fractures in some governments that weaken executive attempts to rally the public around national fiscal policies

3. Democratization efforts in governments to effect greater representation in legislatures

4. Accountability reforms worldwide that press for more and better information for decision making

5. Legislative advancements of technical and research support to equate with that already provided to the executive

Posner and Park point out that party systems and political party splits have an impact on legislative abilities in determining the public budget. In particular, multiple parties or a weaker two-party system in which legislators are more likely to be concerned with local constituencies rather than the party line can strengthen the legislature vis-à-vis the executive in budget making. There is an incentive for multiparty or coalition governments to secure early agreement on the budget, rather than let deliberations dissolve into fragmented squabbles. In weaker two-party systems or multiparty systems, the chief executive does not have strong party allegiance to depend upon when seeking agreement on the budget.

Institutional aspects that influence legislative budget powers include overall structure and internal organization. Bicameral and full-time legislatures, as opposed to unicameral, part-time ones, enhance the power of legislatures in the budget process. Longer terms of office and the ability to serve multiple terms as a legislator on committees are factors favoring a stronger role of the legislature in budgeting. Legislative committee structures and budgeting protocols have evolved to account for increasing budget complexity. The existence of centralizing committees such as a finance or budget committees can positively affect legislative budget power. Committees with the responsibility for developing an overall budget framework set a path for appropriation and other standing committee deliberations regarding their separate portions of the budget. This framework provides cohesiveness to the legislative budgeting process (Posner and Park 2007). The hope is that budget committees, having an aggregate perspective of taxing and spending, provide a balanced, fiscally disciplined approach to budget making for all other committees (Forestiere and Pelizzo 2008).

Legislative powers can range in influence depending on their ability to formulate their own budget and to change or reject the executive budget. Presidential systems generally allow their legislatures generous powers to reject or amend the executive budget, though executives usually maintain some veto powers (Krafchik and Wehner 1998). Parliamentary systems are more likely to have some restricted legislative powers of amendment to the executive budget, perhaps limiting tax changes, banning spending increases, or requiring that any changes be revenue neutral.

A primary power of chief executives in the public budgeting process is the ability to submit a budget that includes an overarching framework for revenue generation and spending in both the short term (next fiscal year) and medium term (three to five years hence). Legislative budget powers are further influenced by the ability of this branch to review, approve, or change this framework. Posner and Park (2007) find that in most OECD countries, the executive presents to the legislature an overarching fiscal policy framework with spending ceilings that limit legislative budget formulation; however, 30 percent of responding OECD countries claim that their legislatures vote on spending totals before determining individual appropriations. Half of these countries specify that their legislatures review tax expenditures when developing the budget.[1] This same survey finds that the legislature is not constrained in amending the budget in 60 percent of OECD countries. Still, just over half of these countries indicate that a vote by the legislature to change the executive budget is interpreted as a vote of no confidence.

The amount of time afforded to legislative debate about the budget influences the power of this branch as compared with the executive. Obviously, more time can provide for more substantive assessment of individual budget components as well as considered amendments to the executive budget. Most countries provide their legislature several months for budget analysis, deliberation, and passage. The timing of receiving relevant information, compared with when it is provided to the executive, also contributes to the budget powers of a legislature.

Budget formats and appropriation account structures affect legislative budget powers. Comprehensive budgets that account for all government spending afford greater influence of legislatures in budgetary deliberations than do government budgets in which significant spending is in the form of earmarks, trusts, or entitlements that account for directed, restricted, or automatic expenditures (Posner and Park 2007). Agency flexibility and discretion related to money management hinges on budget format and account structure as well. Generally, legislatures allow agencies to spend money only as specifically appropriated and chief executives are usually hindered from impounding or deferring appropriated funds without legislative approval. Objects of expenditure appropriations specify in detail the amounts of money that can be spent by line item, thus affording more control to the legislature. Program budgets in which appropriations are provided by program rather than line item are more empowering to the executive—that is, agencies have some greater discretion in managing money across categories of spending within programs than a line-item format would normally allow. Legislatures can provide agencies with greater or lesser discretion in the movement of money across objects, programs, and even appropriations, as well as the ability to carry over unspent funds, or not, into future fiscal years. Budget systems that afford greater control of spending to the legislature usually mean more restrictive spending abilities for the executive (Posner and Park 2007).

Provisions to account for executive agency spending if the budget is not passed by the start of the fiscal year relate to legislative budget powers. Laws may be in place stipulating that the executive budget or previous year's budget take effect if the budget is not passed in time. William Dorotinsky (2008), current acting director of Governance and Public Sector Management Practice at the World Bank and an expert on global public budgeting and financial management, accessed a 2003 World Bank-OECD survey,[2] finding that 41 percent of responding countries have provisions for their legislatures to adopt last year's approved budget if a new budget is not passed in time. Governments also differ according to whether the legislature must act to allow agencies to continue to spend money and operate should the budget not be passed on time. Dorotinsky finds that 26 percent of countries require their legislature to make special provisions to keep government open. "Roughly 40 percent of OECD countries require legislative action to continue spending in the event of no approved budget, whereas *none* of the non-OECD countries reported required legislative action" (Dorotinsky 2008, 112). Almost a fifth (19 percent) of OECD countries in this study indicate having other or no provisions regarding what happens if the budget is not passed on time.

Posner and Park (2007) explain legislative budget powers in terms of ex ante and ex post roles. Ex ante roles include all those related to budget development up to legislative passage of appropriation bills. Ex post duties relate to legislative oversight of budget execution, programming, and spent funds—essentially the work of the legislature after the budget has been approved. Legislatures conduct studies of agency spending and program reviews; chief executives and agencies have responsibilities to report on the financial and sometimes performance costs and results of spending throughout each fiscal year and at its conclusion. There are numerous ways that legislatures conduct such oversight, including through questioning of executive officials, committee hearings and special inquiries, by hearings in plenary sitting, and via an ombudsman. Upon the request of legislators, modern external audit offices (usually an arm of the legislature) conduct formal financial and performance audits of agencies as well as program evaluations and special studies. Many of these offices have extended their work to include return on investment audits and program reviews. Unfortunately, it is not unusual for the audit work of these offices to uncover corruption that then is investigated and prosecuted through the government's courts.

The quality and timeliness of information that is available to legislatures has an impact on the budget powers of this branch of government (Santiso 2004). For example, prebudget reports that provide information about government budget and policy priorities, and about aggregate estimates of revenues, expenditures, surplus or deficit, and debt are important for orienting legislators to future budget discussions, deliberations, and relevant trade-offs that will have to be considered. Warren Krafchik and Joachim Wehner (1998) find that more countries with presidential systems, as compared to those with parliamentary systems, release these kinds of reports prior to executive budget submission to the legislature, allowing for a "first look" at budget constraints and priorities.

The research and technical support available to legislatures can provide these bodies the information vital to the conduct of budget work. Barry Anderson (2009) explains the need for legislators to have input, such as the prebudget reports discussed earlier, that simplifies complex information and makes it understandable. If truly independent, a legislative budget office serves the entire body and not just individual members; output should be both objective and nonpartisan in orientation. Such output can include economic forecasts, cost and baseline estimates, medium- and long-term analyses, technical and policy briefs, analyses of policy proposals, options for revenue enhancements and expenditures, and technical and policy briefs—all of which can promote transparency, enhance credibility, and spur accountability of the budget process (Anderson 2009). Anderson examines staffing and the research that is conducted in the US Congressional Budget Office, California's Legislative Analyst's Office and the Independent Budget Office of the City of New York and finds that the overwhelming majority of work in these offices regards budgetary analysis.

Ian Lienert (2005) developed an index of legislative budget powers that brings together several of the concepts just discussed. These measures quantify the abilities of a legislature to develop and change the executive budget, the time afforded for deliberation about the budget, research, and technical support available to the legislature, and the ability of the executive to make budget changes during execution. The five variables used in Lienert's index include legislative approval of medium-term spending constraints (ex ante, or before the budget has been determined), legislative budget amendment powers, the time available for the legislature to discuss and approve the budget, legislative research and staff support, and restrictions on executive flexibility of budget management and change during execution. More recently, Joachim Wehner (2008) finds fault with Lienert's index. He points out that in the countries studied by Lienert, "only one out of 28 legislatures formally passes a law on the medium-term strategy," (80) and this lack of variation along with poor justification for variable weighting, "calls into question the usefulness of [the index] as a comparative indicator" (80).

Table 7.1 presents the Wehner (2008) index to measure the legislative powers of the purse.[3]

Wehner (2008) claims his measure of legislative budgetary power is more comprehensive and robust than Lienert's. He points out that his index includes legislative budget powers ex ante and ex post to budget approval, inclusive of timing for legislative deliberation, ability of the legislature to react to the executive budget, impact of not passing the budget on time, legislative oversight capabilities during the execution *and* audit phases of the budget process, and committee structure and protocol. He runs several tests of the robustness of his index, determining that an index resulting from a simple additive score of all measures equates well with one that incorporates the two subindices (restrictions on executive flexibility and legislative committee involvement).

Wehner's findings (2008) result in Australia landing in the lowest quartile regarding legislative budget institutions (and thus, legislative budget powers) and Italy in the second lowest quartile. The United States is in the highest quartile, with the highest index of legislative budgeting power of all countries included in this study. "The U.S. Congress has an index score that is more than three times as great as those for the bottom nine cases, predominantly Westminster-type systems. Even allowing for U.S. exceptionalism, the top-quartile legislatures score twice as high on this index as the bottom quartile" (Wehner 2008, 91). Essentially, these findings confirm the US Congress as the most influential legislative policymaking

Table 7.1
Variables Comprising Wehner (2008)
Measure of Legislative Budgetary Power

Variable	Coding[a] (score) Variable Value
Time prior to start of fiscal year that executive submits budget to legislature	(0) Up to two months
	(3.3) Between two to four months
	(6.7) Between four to six months
	(10) More than six months
Legislative amendatory powers	(0) Legislature may only accept or reject budget, as tabled
	(3.3) Legislature may cut existing items only
	(6.7) Legislature may shift funds as long as specified aggregate constraint is met
	(10) Legislature has unfettered amendatory powers
If legislature does not pass a budget by the start of the fiscal year	(0) Executive budget approved and implemented
	(3.3) "Vote on account" conducted[b]
	(6.7) Last year's budget approved and implemented
	(10) No spending approved and implemented; government shutdown possible
Restrictions on executive flexibility to during budget execution	*Sum of the following:*
	(3.3) Appropriations cannot be reallocated across programs without legislative approval
	(3.3) Executive may not withhold funds "appropriated, but not available" without legislative approval
	(3.3) Central reserve funds are not available to meet unforeseen expenditures
Legislative committee (1) involvement in budget approval and/or (2) legislative committees circulate and discuss audit results	*Sum of the following:*[c]
	(3.3) Budget or finance committees conduct (1)
	(3.3) Sectoral, departmental, or standing committees conduct (1)
	(3.3) Ex post audit committee conducts (2)

Variable	Coding[a] (score) Variable Value
Legislative budget research capacity	(0) No budget research capacity
	(2.5) Budget office with up to 10 professional staff
	(5.0) Budget office with 11 to 25 professional staff
	(7.5) Budget Office with 26 to 50 professional staff
	(10) Budget Office with more than 50 professional staff[d]

Source: Wehner, J. 2008. "Assessing the Power of the Purse: An Index of Legislative Budget Institutions." In *Legislative Oversight and Budgeting: A World Perspective*, edited by Rick Stapenhurst, Riccardo Pelizzo, David M. Olson, and Lisa von Trapp. Washington, DC: World Bank. https://openknowledge. worldbank.org/handle/10986/6547 License: Creative Commons Attribution CC BY 3.0, 79–97.

[a]Variables coded on a scale from 0 to 10; 0 indicates least favorable or powerful to legislature and 10 as most favorable or powerful to legislature; maximum possible score of 10 is divided by levels of power according to each variable.

[b]"Vote on account" relates to the practice by some parliaments to approve interim spending if the budget is not passed on time.

[c]Wehner (2008) clarifies measurement of this variable, explaining that "Involvement of sectoral committees gets a score of 3.3 only if they have actual authority over departmental budgets, but not if they are merely consulted or submit nonbinding recommendations while a finance or budget committee retains full authority. Also, if a legislature uses an audit subcommittee of the budget committee for parliamentary audit, it receives half the available score for this item (1.7)" (85).

[d]US Congressional Budget Office is the only office in this category, with about 230 staff at the time of the study.

body of the countries studied here and, undoubtedly, one of the most influential such bodies in the world. The separation of powers enumerated in the US Constitution present a marked difference in the detail of expressed legislative versus executive budget powers. Those for the legislative branch are found in Article I, sections 1–10, whereas those regarding executive powers in Article II comprise just four sections. Powers of the president have to do with acting as commander in chief of the military, making treaties (with Senate concurrence), and nominating and appointing various federal officials. In addition, there is a requirement that the president periodically "give to the Congress Information of the State of the Union" (there is no stipulation that this be provided in a speech). The final section of Article II stipulates removal of the president, vice president, and all civil officers of the United States "on impeachment for, and conviction of, treason, bribery or other high crimes and misdemeanors." In fact, there is nothing in the US Constitution about executive budget powers or execution.

LEGISLATIVE BUDGETING IN SELECT GOVERNMENTS

The following section explains legislative budgeting in Australia, which has a parliamentary system of governance; in Brazil, which has a presidential, multiparty system; and in the United States, which has a presidential, two-party system. Each presents a distinctive legislative budget process. Then we will consider three US state governments that are representative of different budget power balance across executive and legislative branches. Texas has a budget system that rests most power with the legislature; New York has a strong executive budget process; and Georgia's budget powers are balanced across the branches. Though it is unclear that such power differences significantly affect budget outcomes in these governments, these states certainly differ in their populations, budget size, and fiscal capacities. Also, of these three states, Georgia has the highest credit rating from Standard & Poor's (AAA) and New York's is the weakest of the three (AA). Texas has a credit rating that falls between the two (AA+).

Australia

There have been significant reforms to the Australian budget process over many years and across changes in governments. The Labor and Conservative Coalition parties have both contributed to these reforms that have embraced New Public Management principles,[4] advanced transparency, and improved accountability (Blöndal et al. 2008). On the other hand, Australia's parliamentary budget powers have changed little, though the legislative budget process is open to more and better information (Schick 2002). The House can modify the government budget but rarely does, given that the government and the House are of the majority party. The House initiates tax and appropriations bills; the Senate cannot amend these bills, but can refuse to pass them unless amended by the House according to Senate desires.

Australia's fiscal year is July 1 to June 30. Budget development begins ten months prior to the start of the fiscal year. Prior to budget review, the Parliament examines the government's Fiscal Strategy Statement and can debate and assess the government's macro fiscal policies and current and future economic performance. The government submits the budget to Parliament on "Budget Night" in May before the start of the fiscal year. The Treasurer presents budget details on this evening and the Opposition leader will follow up with a response a few days later. The budget is presented to Parliament on accrual and cash bases, though members deliberate about the budget on a cash basis. Appropriations are made on an accrual basis, and this basis of accounting is used for budget execution and reporting. Once submitted, Parliament then has about six weeks to examine and pass the budget. Before the mid-1990s, Parliament passed a budget after the start of the fiscal year necessitating that government run on interim funding (last year's budget) for several months until passage of the budget (Blöndal et al. 2008).

General debate about the budget occurs in the House (plenary session) and regards macro policy issues rather than budget detail. There is no central-izing budget committee in the House that provides budget review.[5] A parallel plenary session (termed the Main Committee) conducts a review of the bud-get during this period as well. A vote to approve the budget in principle by the Main Committee leads to detailed consideration of it and amendments can be made. Senate committees are examining the budget during this period as well. Eight specialized committees in the Senate analyze the budget by portfolio; the Economics Committee assesses the overall fiscal policy framework inherent in the budget. Hearings with ministry officials help the Senate to screen the budget. These committees have their own staff and are able to access independent par-liamentary research support as well. These committees report to the full Senate about their findings and concerns (Blöndal et al. 2008). Members of Parliament can only vote to reject or reduce an expenditure proposed by the government; members cannot propose spending or reallocate funds across appropriations.

Government introduces three appropriation bills each year: Appropriation Bill 1 (AB1) for continuing spending for present policies (Senate cannot amend); Appropriation Bill 2 (AB2) for spending related to new policies, capital spend-ing, and grants to states) (Senate can amend); and a third bill includes con-tinuing and new spending for Parliament "subject to Senate amendment and therefore contained in the separate Appropriation (Parliamentary Departments) Bill" (Blöndal et al. 2008, 32–33). There are other budget changes incorpo-rated into legislative decision making; in 2008, these appropriations equaled nearly 5 percent of the original budget appropriations. Another type of appro-priation, supplementary additional estimates, may also be introduced at this time. Eventually, the budget as considered in the House is sent to the Senate, where passage is a formality.[6] The governor-general then assents to the budget. The Australian Parliament usually passes the government budget—amendments offered generally arise from opposition Senators, who must disseminate an amendment request; in any case, most of these fail. Just 20 percent of total spending is approved by the Australian Parliament annually, with legislative consideration focused on the 80 percent "special" or permanent legislation which Parliament can amend or reject (Blöndal et al. 2008).

The Joint Committee of Public Accounts and Audits (JCPAA), a mix of senators and representatives including some of the Opposition party, is appointed at the start of each Parliament. This committee conducts evaluations of Commonwealth agencies and can secure budget, expenditure, and other data from these agencies; these evaluations are used "to account for the lawfulness, efficiency and effectiveness with which they use public monies."[7] The JCPAA assesses the financial and performance audits of the Auditor-General and can conduct hearings about these and other evaluations the JCPAA conducts. This committee has research support in the form of a secretary and approximately ten staff members (Blöndal et al. 2008).

Oversight by the Parliament is conducted through the Australian National Audit Office (ANAO). The Auditor-General directs this office, is appointed to a ten-year term by the Governor-General after having been recommended by the Prime Minister, and must be approved by the Parliament. This office provides independent research, evaluation and audit support to the Parliament, conducting mostly financial and performance audits (Blöndal et al. 2008).

Australia's members of Parliament have access to a significant amount of budget and financial information, though such information does not necessarily play into their consideration of government budgets. The eight Senate committees that review the budget each have a small research staff (about four or five people); these committees can also access research support through the relatively new, Parliamentary Budget Office (PBO). The PBO was established in 2012 to provide independent, nonpartisan analytical support about the budget, fiscal policy, and proposed legislation to the Parliament.[8]

Brazil

Brazil has a presidential, multiparty system of government. There are numerous different parties represented in the National Congress and many party configurations possible in the executive cabinet. Politics in the country is explained as particularistic—legislative members are more interested in special interests than national ones. A president can bring ministers from other parties into the government to strengthen his or her congressional alliances but does not have to form a coalition government to shore power (Hallerberg and Marier 2004).

Brazil's fiscal year is January 1 to December 31. A new president must submit a Plano Pluri-Annual (PPA), a multiyear plan that maps over four years administration priorities and the means to reach budget goals, to the congress by August 31 and this must be approved before the end of the fiscal year (December 31). A PPA begins one year after the election of a new president and ends one year after the election of a new president, advancing continuity across administrations. A typical budget year is marked by the preparation of a Law of Budget Directives (Lei de Diretrizes Orcamentarias or LDO) by the executive branch, submitted to the congress by April 15, to be approved by the legislature by June 30. The LDO prioritizes goals of the PPA and provides how the budget will be carried out in the coming year, linking the PPA with final budget law. After legislative approval of the LDO, the directive is signed into law by the president. A formalized budget proposal that updates estimates and incorporates revised agency spending plans is submitted to the congress by August 31 (Martell 2011).

The National Congress can amend the budget, but annual budget guidelines and multiyear plans restrict member and committee ability to increase total spending or change salaries, debt service, or constitutional transfers. The legislature is allowed to increase expenditures to account for executive errors and omissions that could be defined as underestimated revenues or overestimated expenditures. A Joint Budget Commissions (CMO) discerns which amendments to carry forward, analyzes them, holds hearings, and votes on them. A revised budget is presented to the National Congress floor for a vote which, once approved, is signed by the president and becomes law (Lei do Orcamento Anual or LOA) (Martell 2011).

Each chamber of the National Congress has research and advisory support that provides technical and analytical research, budget and plan drafts, and general research assistance and informational support upon request. These units can work at cross purposes, however, and there is some suspicion between the offices (Tollini 2009).

Brazil's budget process can be characterized as patronage politics. Helio Tollini (2009) considers that the number, types, and monetary value of amendments to the proposed budget and the parochial interests of members of congress compromises national policy direction; many projects funded nationally should be funded at the state or local levels. Though members of the National Congress can and do inject numerous individual spending initiatives into the budget, the president has the ability to negotiate which projects will be funded

(Blöndal, Goretti, and Kristensen 2003). Still, Peter Kingstone (2003) explains that in spite of this somewhat chaotic governance system, Brazil is capable of developing successful public policy. He provides the example of privatization of and improvements to telecommunications in Brazil that were realized thanks to cooperation and strong leadership in the National Congress, and because of the focused role of an executive agency minister who had the backing of the president and was able to successfully frame debate for such reform. Resulting policy underscored competition, equity, and efficiency, engaging performance contracts with providers—telephone lines doubled from 1996 to 2000 and connection charges dropped from over $1,000 in 1996 to just over $27 in 2000. According to Kingstone, successful policy in this case was instigated by the president, but did not gain traction until leadership within the National Congress took hold.

Other factors that influenced the success of this privatization effort include that debate within the congress was limited and even so, members "lacked the technical knowledge to debate alternatives effectively" (Kingstone 2003, 31). Mark Hallerberg and Patrik Marier (2004) consider that Brazil would solve some of its many budget problems by moving from an open-list to a closed-list representative system.[9] They claim that this change would work well with the Fiscal Responsibility Law of 2000 that limits spending at all levels of government and imposes the medium-term budget framework.

United States

The United States has a presidential, two-party system of government. Different from the legislatures of the countries studied thus far, the US Congress has no restrictions regarding its powers to change the president's budget. Congress develops its own budget and often the president's budget is deemed "dead on arrival." As noted several times throughout this book, the US Constitution has delineated specific responsibilities to the Congress regarding securing revenues and passing appropriation bills. Also, in chapter 3, you learned of several significant laws passed by the Congress that affect this body's budget powers. Notably, the 1921 Budget Act created an executive budget system, centralizing budget development with the president, creating an executive budget office, and a national auditing office as an arm of Congress. Then, for much of the next forty years, budgeting at the federal level of government in the United States could be characterized as incremental, with the greatest determining factor of the size and content of a budget being the previous year's budget. That is, most of the budget in any given year (barring periods of international conflict or economic down-turn) was the product of past decisions and annual budgetary decision making concentrated on increases or decreases at the margin, rather than decisions about the base. Policymakers did not consider the full range of budget options, but made successive limited comparisons with conflicts of interest downplayed and consensus building at a premium. Congressional decision making was characterized as conservative coalition building. The long-serving House Speaker during this period, Sam Rayburn, would advise new members, "If you want to get along—go along."

But as explained previously, by the early 1970s, Congress was increasingly frustrated with the president and was considering how to boost its credibility and power in the budgeting process. Factors leading up to the Congressional Budget and Impoundment Control Act of 1974 (the Congressional Budget Act or CBA) included the changing nature of federal expenditures from regular, annual appropriations to entitlement spending, the ongoing conflict in Vietnam, and President Nixon's impoundment of funds that Congress had already approved for specific spending. By 1974, Social Security was about forty years old and President Lyndon Johnson's Great Society programs had added numerous domestic programming and significant funding to combat poverty and joblessness. Medicare and Medicaid programs were established in 1965. The make-up of Congress and its committee structure were changing. Members of Congress were less likely to heed the "go along to get along" advice, with many seeking to make an impact quickly rather than sit on the sidelines. The 1970s has been characterized as period of "liberal activism" for Congress. Loch Johnson discusses the implications of new structures to conduct national security investigations by Congress in the 1970s in an interview with Timothy Lee (2013) of *The Washington Post.*[10] Johnson explains certain changes going on at the time:

> The Church Committee led to the founding of Senate Select Committee on Intelligence (SSCI) and the House Permanent Select Committee on Intelligence (HPSCI). That made oversight as different as night and day. Before, very few hearings and minimal oversight. After the Church Committee, you had two robust committees with sizable staffs of lawyers and others. It really was a dramatic change.
>
> I think SSCI and HPSCI have been serious about their budget reviews, quick to react to allegations of scandal. One of the things we

did was to put term limits on committee members to avoid coopta-
tion. People are beginning to believe that was a mistake because it
takes so long to become an expert. The Senate has gotten rid of that
idea. The House still has it.

The CBA empowered Congress in a number of ways—by creating Budget
Committees, concurrent budget resolutions and reconciliation, the Congressional
Budget Office, and by tightening up on the ability of the president to impound
funds. The complex committee structure changed. The Budget Committees centralized the previously fragmented process by providing an aggregate budget
framework that presents multiyear targets (totals) for revenues, expenditures,
deficit/surplus, and debt. Other committees were now to consider revenues and
expenditures within this framework. Appropriations Committees consider discretionary spending in separate functional areas; standing committees consider
entitlements and revenue legislation (Posner and Parks 2007).

The CBA originally established two budget resolutions, though today the
Congress attempts to pass one by April 15 in preparation for the budget that
should start on October 1. This resolution is an overarching plan, not budget
law. According to Bill Heniff and Justin Murray (2012) "revenue and spending
policies are not binding, but totals and committee spending allocations can be
enforced through points of order and reconciliation" (1). Congress has adopted
one budget resolution in each of the last thirty-one years and resolutions now
include a five-year time frame. Congress is likely to include budget reconciliation directives in the resolution which most often leads to enactment of such
measures. Both chambers of Congress have considered and adopted amendments to the resolution although the House has considered many fewer than the
Senate (Heniff and Murray 2012).

The 1980s then ushered in an era of fiscal restraint on the part of Congress.
Deficits seemed out of control and the Gramm-Rudman-Hollings or Balanced
Budget and Emergency Deficit Control Act of 1985 (GRH) established rules for
Congress to close budget gaps. The sequester procedure imposes a type of automatic trigger in case Congress cannot discipline itself. But a constitutional challenge regarding who can impose the trigger—originally the Comptroller General
of the Government Accountability Office (GAO) must bow to the Director of
the Office of Management and Budget (OMB)—and the inadequate coverage
afforded by the sequester kept Congress from reaching a zero deficit as planned

by 1990. The Omnibus Budget Reconciliation Act (Budget Enforcement Act) of that same year reoriented congressional focus from deficit reduction to limiting spending through PAYGO. Congressional PAYGO rules require certain spending increases (entitlements) to be balanced against cuts in, for example, spending or revenue (tax) increases for a zero-sum gain; PAYGO expired in 2002, but Senate rules still constrain decision making.

The United States timeframe for legislative deliberation about the budget is about eight months. The president submits the budget to Congress in February for the fiscal year starting October 1. (The fiscal year is October 1 to September 30.) In the United States, without legislatively approved appropriation bills signed by the president, executive agencies cannot spend money and continue their operations. Until appropriation bills are passed and signed, Congress and the president must approve continuing resolutions to keep agencies running, otherwise, some degree of government shutdown will occur. As noted in an earlier chapter, the United States has endured eighteen government shutdowns—the most recent in October, 2013, for sixteen days when Congress and the president could not pass a budget or continuing resolutions. A two-year budget deal was eventually approved by Congress and signed by the president in December, 2013, and then a budget deal to finance the government through September, 2014 was approved in January, 2014.

The amount, variety, and credibility of the information and data provided to members of Congress are substantial. The US Congressional Budget Office[11] (CBO) is an example of an independent, nonpartisan, objective research institution that has strengthened legislative budget making since its inception. This office was created by the 1974 CBA, fifty-three years after the birth of the executive budget office (originally the Bureau of the Budget, now the Office of Management and Budget or OMB). The CBO is recognized for its economic, cost, and budgetary estimates; cost estimates make projections about federal revenues and spending given the implementation of proposed legislation. Dynamic scoring, or accounting for macroeconomic effects of proposed legislation, is normally not incorporated into models of these cost estimates, but may be applied to major pieces of legislation and for long-term perspectives. The CBO provides scorekeeping of legislation against specific budget targets throughout the budget process, to keep members on track.

Initial legislation creating the CBO did not detail its management or orientation and, since it was created, the director of the unit has significantly influenced office direction and credibility. The CBO director is selected for a four-year term jointly by the Speaker of the House and the President Pro Tempore of the Senate upon recommendation of the Budget Committees of both chambers. The director is responsible for hiring; the more than two hundred staff members are selected without regard to political party affiliation. Philip Joyce (2011) has written an in-depth history of the creation, leadership, policy, and research focus of this office. He explains that the perspectives of early directors—especially that of the founding and longest-serving director, Alice M. Rivlin—were pivotal in the office evolving into the highly credible, nonpartisan, objective, and independent research office that it is today. Joyce (2010) states, "it is unquestionable that CBO analyses have a powerful effect on both the drafting of and the prospects for legislation" (3).

As noted earlier, the Budget Act of 1921 created the US General Accounting Office[12] (now known as the Government Accountability Office, or GAO), which is an independent audit and research arm of Congress. The comptroller general or director of the GAO is appointed by the president with the advice and consent of the Senate. A commission made up of the House and Senate members provides a list of possible candidates to the president for consideration. The comptroller general serves a fifteen-year nonrenewable term. Presently, the GAO has 2,869 employees and a budget of almost $520 million. The GAO conducts legally stipulated studies, evaluations, and audits as well as research work at the behest of Congress. The office prepares traditional financial audits, investigatory studies, reports, and testimony about government performance, programs, and policies; policy analyses and research about policy issues, legal decisions and opinions. This office, too, has high credibility and contributes significantly to knowledge building among members of Congress.

US State Governments

Carolyn Bourdeaux (2006, 2007, 2008a, 2008b) has studied state legislatures and the budgeting processes in these governments extensively. Her work highlights the push and pull of state legislatures and governors in budget wars. She points out that early reforms in states emphasized executive budgeting and empowered chief executives vis-à-vis legislatures in budget development and by articulating executive budget management duties and powers. Somewhat similar to the US Congress and its efforts to regain budget powers in the early 1970s, American state legislatures also mounted efforts through the twentieth century to pull back or generate power to be able to develop, analyze, and oversee state budgets. Philip Joyce (2005) has found in his research about state legislatures that powerful ones exercise more rather than less fiscal responsibility. Certainly, US states differ in the degree of power that their legislatures have in state budget processes. The following three state governments are reviewed because they have systems of governance that provide for very different legislative-executive budgeting relationships—strongly legislative (Texas), balanced (Georgia), and strongly executive (New York).

Texas This state government has a strong legislative budget process compared to other states. The governor's budget powers include the line-item veto of appropriations bills, appointment of the state budget director, and a small executive budget office (Office of Budget, Planning, and Policy) located in the governor's office. There is no limit on the number of four-year terms a governor can serve. In Texas, the revenue estimate arises from the comptroller's office. Of the six budget powers afforded to governors listed by the National Association for State Budget Officers in their publication *Budgetary Processes in the States* (2008), the Texas governor has four—the chief executive gives agencies funding level requests targets, can spend unanticipated funds, reduce the enacted budget, and restrict budget reductions without legislative approval. A Council of State Governments *Book of the States* (2012) survey indicates that the governor shares responsibility with the legislature for budget making. The governor is one of five state officials constitutionally or statutorily elected state by the public.

Texas conducts biennial budgeting and consistently passes its budget on time, in spite of the relatively short 140-day legislative sessions held once every two years. Special sessions may be called by the governor between biennia and these are limited to 30 days. The fiscal year begins September 1 and ends August 31. In its survey of management practices in the fifty states, the Government Performance Project[13] (GPP) (*Governing* 2008) graded Texas as strong in managing information, strategic direction, budgeting for performance (using performance information for budgetary decision making), performance auditing, and its online presence.

Texas has a ~$100 billion budget (one year), made up of about $65 billion in state funds and $35 billion in federal funds. The state's debt receives an AA+ rating from Standard & Poor's. Texas law requires the legislature to pass and the governor to sign a balanced budget; the state cannot carry over a deficit across fiscal years. Texas has an Economic Stabilization Fund that cannot exceed

10 percent of general revenue funds (excluding interest and investment income) in the previous biennium. Use of funds requires three-fifths vote of each legislative chamber to patch deficits after budget adoption; other appropriations made from this fund require a two-thirds vote.

The state's constitution limits general obligation (GO) debt to an aggregate maximum debt service not to exceed 5 percent of average general fund revenue in three preceding years, though debt retired from a dedicated revenue source is not so limited. GO debt is incurred by constitutional amendment. A state bond review board helps to plan targets and caps related to debt issuance.

The Legislative Budget Board[14] (LBB), the legislature's budget office, serves an influential role throughout the budget process—responsible for review and analysis of agency budget requests; feeding the legislature information during budget deliberation to budget passage, during budget execution; and for the conduct of financial, performance, and program audits and evaluations. The LBB was created in 1949 to provide an avenue for the continuous review of state spending, given growing concern about the state's increasing expenditures. The law stipulates that every state agency submit its budget request to the LBB for assessment. Since 1949, laws have been passed that further increase the powers and responsibilities of the LBB, particularly regarding the development of analytical reports, performance audits, and fiscal notes.

Texas operates under an expenditure restriction that limits appropriations to estimated personal income growth—appropriations in excess of anticipated revenue must be voted on and passed by four-fifths of the legislature. The Texas legislature must approve any spending or transfer of funds by a state agency in excess of the agency's current authorization. During budget execution, both the governor and the LBB can ban a state agency from spending all or part of its appropriation, can transfer appropriations among state agencies, and can repurpose an appropriation. Proposals of the LBB must be approved or amended by the governor and proposals by the governor must be approved or amended by the LBB.

Texas has been at the forefront of budget reform, engaging components of zero-based, program and performance budgeting in the past. The state's foray into strategic planning has been a stepped one, beginning in 1991 and requiring agencies and the university system to develop multiyear strategic planning processes; reforms since then have layered on performance budgeting components such as linking appropriations to agency goals, strategies, performance targets, and outcomes. The LBB has undergone several reorganizations and now per-forms significant central clearance in a number of areas and including for the approval of information resource strategic plans, quality assurance reviews of such projects, and oversight of these resources in state agencies. According to *Governing* (2008) that reported on the GPP's survey and ranking of state man-agement capacities, "the state's budget process leaves legislators with the tools they need to focus on performance" (87).

Georgia   Georgia's budget process balances power between the legislative and executive branches of government. The governor has fairly strong budget pow-ers, given the line-item veto of appropriations bills, sole responsibility for set-ting the revenue estimate, appointment of the state budget director, and a small to mid-sized executive budget office located within the governor's office. The governor has a consecutive two-term limit and then must sit out a term if seek-ing office again; terms are four years each. Of the six budget powers afforded to governors listed by the National Association for State Budget Officers in their publication *Budgetary Processes in the States* (2008), Georgia's governor has all of them—the chief executive gives agencies funding level request targets; agency requests are published in the executive budget; and the governor can reorganize departments, spend unanticipated funds, reduce the enacted budget, and restrict budget reductions without legislative approval. The governor is constitutionally elected statewide yet his powers are diluted a bit given that seven other executive officials are constitutionally elected by the public state-wide, too.

The history of budgeting in the state of Georgia can be characterized as fis-cally conservative. The state consistently passes its budget on time, prior to the start of the fiscal year that begins July 1and ends June 30. The legislature meets annually for forty days. In its survey of management practices in the fifty states, the GPP (*Governing* 2008) graded Georgia's budget process (results-oriented and passing the budget on time) and structural balance (equating ongoing rev-enues with ongoing expenditures) as strong. Other components of management in which Georgia scored well include contracting and procurement, managing the workforce, and performance. These scores are indicative of then Governor Sonny Perdue's engagement of New Public Management principles to improve customer service in the state and an overhaul of state pay and benefits at the time (*Governing* 2008). The GPP noted that performance efforts in the state have generally been developed and applied in the executive branch, though the legislature has been much slower in applying measurement for budgetary decision making.

The Georgia General Assembly created a legislative budget office in 1969. This office was originally supposed to supply fiscal and budget analytical support to both chambers, but over time it became chiefly associated with the House; thus, the Senate appropriations committee would seek analytical support from the governor's Office of Planning and Budget. In 2003, political party divisiveness in the General Assembly led to the establishment of a Senate Budget Office, which has since been renamed the Senate Budget and Evaluation Office. The Legislative Budget Office has undergone a name change as well, to the House Budget and Research Office (Lauth 2006, 36). Each office provides fiscal, budget, and policy analysis to its home chamber.[15]

In Georgia, the governor has constitutional authority to set the revenue estimate, serving as a check on the legislative power to appropriate funds. In the development of the revenue estimate used for budget purposes, the governor relies on input from the state economist; the revenue estimate is generated in the Office of the Governor. The governor has historically chosen the low end of revenues in a range provided with low, medium, and high revenue estimates.

Georgia has a ~$40 billion budget, about equal parts state own-source and federal funding. The state's debt receives the highest rating from Standard & Poor's, AAA (the state has a "triple, triple" having the highest possible score from all three credit rating agencies). Georgia law requires the governor to submit and the legislature to pass a balanced budget and the state cannot carry over a deficit across fiscal years. Specifically, OCGA §45–12–76 stipulates that the General Assembly cannot make appropriations exceeding the previous year's total expected surplus together with total estimated net treasury receipts from existing revenue sources. At the end of the fiscal year, should a budget gap exist, the state can tap reserves or withhold expenditures to secure balance. Georgia's budget stabilization fund, the Revenue Shortfall Reserve, can be used to close budget gaps in the current year; the reserve's limit is 10 percent of prior year net revenue. Georgia law limits the level of debt service payments obligated by the state; annual debt service for any year cannot exceed 10 percent of prior year's receipts. General obligation debt is limited to twenty-five years by the state constitution.

New York New York's budget process is an example of a state with a strong executive budgeting process—so much so that the legislature has been described in the past as the most dysfunctional in the United States (Forsythe and Boyd 2006). The governor has strong budget powers given a line-item veto on all bills, initial preparation of the revenue estimate by the Division of the Budget, appointment of the cabinet-level state budget director, and a large, freestanding executive budget office (Division of the Budget). There is no limit on the number of four-year terms a governor can serve. Of the six budget powers afforded to governors listed by the National Association for State Budget Officers in their publication *Budgetary Processes in the States* (2008), New York's governor has four—the chief executive gives agencies funding level request targets, can spend unanticipated funds, reduce the enacted budget, and restrict budget reductions without legislative approval. The Council of State Governments *Book of the States* (2012) survey indicates that the governor shares responsibility with the legislature for budget making. The governor is one of five state officials constitutionally elected by the public.

The history of budgeting in the state of New York can be characterized as politically charged, opaque, and fiscally unstable. As of 2013, the state received kudos for passing its budget on time for the last three years (Clark 2013)—no small feat given a past that includes over two decades of missed budget deadlines! New York's legislature meets annually and is not limited in establishing meeting days. Its fiscal year runs from April 1 to March 31. In its survey of management practices in the fifty states, the GPP (*Governing* 2008) graded New York as weak in budget management, particularly related to the maintenance of a long-term perspective (revenue forecasting and expenditure estimating), budget process (results-oriented and passing the budget on time) and structural balance (equating ongoing revenues with ongoing expenditures).

New York's revenue estimating process allows an independent estimate to be set by the state's comptroller if consensus is not reached. An initial revenue forecast is developed by the Division of the Budget and submitted to the legislature with the governor's budget recommendation. State law requires the executive and legislature to convene a consensus economic and revenue forecast conference and to issue a consensus report on tax, lottery, and miscellaneous receipts by March 1. If agreement is not reached, the comptroller issues a binding revenue forecast[16] by March 5.

Budgetary reforms in New York initiated in 2007 included

- Statutory requirement for general fund balance
- Increased multiyear financial planning from three to four years

- Enhanced rainy day reserve
- Accelerated timing of consensus revenue forecast and comptroller given authority to set revenue estimate, if needed
- Required conference committees
- Required budget summary documents for legislators
- Prohibited use of certain lump sum appropriations
- Created a "quick-start" process for future budget deliberations

Citizens Union of the City of New York posted a checklist[17] with their assessment of these reforms, declaring in April, 2012 regarding the budget adoption cycle ending March, 2012 that

- While no messages of necessity were used for budget bills in 2012, major pieces of legislation with large fiscal impacts were passed with such messages prior to adoption of the budget, including pension legislation in March 2012 and income tax overhaul in December 2011.
- Reforms left unfulfilled included missing the deadline for the "quick-start" budget negotiations in November 2011, exempting certain lump-sum appropriations from itemization in joint resolutions of the Senate and Assembly, and lack of fiscal impact statements for certain budget bills in both houses prior to votes.
- There was no movement to improve the budget process, such as incorporating performance measurement, requiring the use of Generally Accepted Accounting Principles (GAAP), and the creation of an independent legislative budget office.[18]
- The state budget continues to lack adequate transparency, with budget documents hard to decipher for the general public, and no release of budget data in user-friendly formats such as spreadsheets to allow for independent analysis.
- While no new state funds have been provided for member items for the last few years, discretionary funds continue to be available and the legislature proposed redirecting funds to new organizations through leftover monies in the Community Projects Fund. The Governor has since vetoed this funding to new organizations. Additionally, other funds have been treated like member items such as the "bullet aid" for school districts, and have largely lacked needed public scrutiny.

New York has a ~$136 billion budget, of which approximately $91 billion is state operating funds. The state's credit rating has been downgraded in the past, though its most recent rating from Standard & Poor's is AA. New York has a constitutional requirement that the governor must submit a balanced budget to the legislature. The state has a Tax Stabilization Reserve Fund which can reach 2 percent of general fund spending and can be used when a deficit is incurred, in economic downturns, for temporary loans, or in periods of crisis or natural disaster. The state's rainy day fund can reach 3 percent of general fund spending and these funds can be used in periods of natural disaster, crisis, or catastrophe (NASBO 2008). General obligation bonds can only be issued by the state of New York via voter approval and must be retired within forty years of issuance. Law in 2000 placed a ceiling on debt outstanding at 4 percent of personal income for all debt issues after April 1, 2000, with a decade long phase-in process. New debt issues are capped at 5 percent of all fund receipts and this is phased in over thirteen years. Authority-issued debt is limited to a total of less than 4 percent of state personal income. This limit has often been skirted in the past; new debt must utilize level debt service for projects' useful lives, and be retired within thirty years.

It is interesting to gather financial information about the three states discussed and make a few comparisons. Table 7.2 compiles data from the US Department of Commerce, Census Bureau regarding State and Local Government Finance. Examining this information for fiscal year 2011, distinctions are evidenced. Texas has the largest population of these states with +25.6 million residents, New York comes in second with almost 20 million residents, and Georgia trails with just under 10 million residents. Examining per capita revenues and expenditures shows that New York, the state with a strong executive budgeting process, has per capita general revenues double those of Georgia, and a bit less so compared to Texas. New York's heavy reliance on the income tax is most evident. Considering per capita expenditures, there are distinctions across these governments as well, with greater per capita spending in New York compared to the other states in education and welfare, though spending per capita for police protection and corrections are more similar across the states. New York spends about half that of Georgia for natural resources but about three times more for governmental administration. New York's spending for interest on general debt may reflect this state's heavier reliance on borrowing in the past. What conclusions might you draw from this information and given what you know about legislative and executive budget powers in these states?

Table 7.2
State Government Finances, 2011 ($ Per Capita)

	United States	Georgia	New York	Texas
Population	311,582,564	9,810,181	19,502,728	25,640,909
Total Revenue	$7,261.34	$5,330.66	$10,539.37	$5,197.40
General Revenue	5,309.39	3,788.70	7,631.79	4,178.78
Intergovernmental Revenue	1,903.18	1,556.19	3,086.75	1,671.50
Taxes	2,439.99	1,631.29	3,483.88	1,682.71
General Sales	757.23	517.91	593.82	849.96
Selective Sales	423.02	206.71	553.10	468.18
License Taxes	165.53	48.63	94.02	260.13
Individual Income Tax	832.23	780.70	1,856.62	
Corporate Income Tax	132.82	68.34	205.90	
Other Taxes	129.16	9.00	180.42	104.43
Current Charges	581.23	399.88	472.02	485.24
Misc. General Revenue	384.99	201.34	589.14	339.33
Utility Revenue	46.67	1.00	409.72	
Liquor Stores Revenue	21.63			
Insurance Trust Revenue[a]	1,883.65	1,540.96	2,497.85	1,018.62
Total Expenditure	6,432.89	4,561.62	9,435.05	4,914.23
Intergovernmental Expenditure	1,594.30	1,080.52	3,061.00	1,156.97
Direct Expenditure	4,838.59	3,481.10	6,374.05	3,757.26
Current Operation	3,153.06	2,264.02	4,145.16	2,655.46
Capital Outlay	371.74	269.05	600.19	279.13
Insurance Benefits and Repayments	1,028.74	743.72	1,271.77	678.83
Assistance and Subsidies	127.99	134.15	78.78	88.30
Interest on Debt	157.06	70.16	278.15	55.54
Exhibit: Salaries and Wages	808.95	569.71	912.24	630.99
General Expenditure	5,311.21	3,813.43	7,490.13	4,235.40
Direct Expenditure	3,716.91	2,732.91	4,429.12	3,078.43

	United States	Georgia	New York	Texas
General Expenditure, by Function				
Education	1,901.09	1,776.64	2,318.58	1,903.57
Public Welfare	1,591.86	1,056.75	2,621.77	1,219.51
Hospitals	211.45	85.47	313.48	163.66
Health	192.53	118.17	452.67	106.56
Highways	350.89	167.26	250.24	255.77
Police Protection	45.73	30.38	48.89	34.43
Correction	157.80	149.03	153.60	146.82
Natural Resources	70.57	57.03	25.95	36.07
Parks and Recreation	18.49	19.91	26.83	7.78
Governmental Administration	171.16	82.58	292.24	79.52
Interest on General Debt	150.31	70.16	211.04	55.54
Other and Unallocable	449.33	200.05	774.85	226.16
Utility Expenditure	75.58	4.47	673.16	
Liquor Stores Expenditure	17.35			
Insurance Trust Expenditure	1,028.74	743.72	1,271.77	678.83
Debt at End of Fiscal Year	3,635.68	1,366.19	6,918.44	1,502.69
Cash and Security Holdings	11,757.32	7,859.57	16,265.03	10,458.55

Source: US Census Bureau. *2011 Annual Survey of State Government Finances.* Summary Table for 2011 available at http://www.census.gov/govs/state/historical_data_2011.html Data users who create their own estimates using data from this report should cite the US Census Bureau as the source of the original data only. The data in this table are based on information from public records and contain no confidential data. Although the data in this table come from a census of governmental units and are not subject to sampling error, the census results do contain nonsampling error. Additional information on nonsampling error, response rates, and definitions may be found at http://www2.census.gov/govs/state/11_methodology.pdf (created: December 6, 2012; last revised: August 22, 2013)

[a]Within insurance trust revenue, net earnings of state retirement systems is a calculated statistic (the item code in the data file is X08), and thus can be positive or negative. Net earnings equal the sum of earnings on investments plus gains on investments minus losses on investments. The change made in 2002 for asset valuation from book to market value in accordance with Statement 34 of the Governmental Accounting Standards Board is reflected in the calculated statistics.

LEGISLATIVE REFORM

Patrick Fisher (1999) discusses the problems with congressional budgeting in the United States; the most important problem he notes is that Congress cannot produce a balanced budget. He explains that the US representative democracy produces contradictory forces. Voters want low taxes *and* government services, programs, and benefits; members of Congress, seeking reelection, provide particularistic benefits that compromise the collective good. Certainly, legislative budgeting entails balancing the particularistic priorities of individual legislators with the universalistic, public priorities of deliberative, representative bodies (Schick 2002). Carolyn Forestiere and Riccardo Pelizzo (2008) claim that rules and institutions constrain legislative budgeting, but so does politics. Based on their assessment of the current state of legislative budgeting, Posner and Park (2007, 24–25) provide a list of reforms to improve public budgeting, which include

- Budgets should be comprehensive and include every commitment of the government.
- Budget processes should require regular assessment of automatic spending such as entitlements as well as tax expenditures; assessments should be projected in the long-term (multiple years) and account for significant changes such as population aging.
- Budget processes should provide for shared information across executive and legislative budget research and analytical offices. "Where possible and politically appropriate, the executive should consult with legislative officials prior to the budget's release as a way of encouraging earlier political agreement and identifying political fallout" (Posner and Park 2007, 24).
- Legislatures should continue to develop and use budgetary targets to structure their deliberations and negotiations.
- Legislatures should continue to improve their institutional capacities to analyze budgets against assumptions as well as the abilities of individual legislators to understand and use such analysis when deciding about budgets.
- Legislatures should continue to promote their oversight powers and press for increasing agency reporting requirements about executive activities and spending.

Stapenhurst (2008) comments that it will take political will and time to strengthen legislatures and improve governance. It will be difficult for legislators to consider changing in their own institutions (and changing their own ways). Incentive for the public to push for change is equally weighty—voters want government programs, services, and support but they shy away from the responsibility and necessity of funding the full costs of such work.

CONCLUSION

After reading this chapter, you should have an idea of the ways that legislatures are empowered in the public budgeting process, the various measures of legislative budget power, and how to analyze budget laws, processes, and rules in order to make comparisons between executive and legislative branches of government regarding their budget-making capabilities. Legislative budget powers and processes have been described in different types of governments—in one national government with a parliamentary structure, two presidential structures (one a multiparty and the other a two-party system), and in three subnational governments. The next chapter will immerse you in budgeting in and by the judiciary. Thus far, you have been exposed to many executive and legislative budget perspectives and powers. Nonetheless, you may be surprised to find that the judicial branch is (or in some systems, has the potential to be) equally powerful in the budgetary process.

DISCUSSION QUESTIONS

1. Discuss the strengths and weaknesses of Lienert's and Wehner's legislative budget power indices. Are there components of each index that you find particularly compelling as a measure of legislative budget power?

2. Discuss the differences in legislative budget power between presidential and parliamentary systems of government.

3. Which branch—the executive or legislative—do you think should hold more power over the purse? Does your view change when you consider national governments versus subnational governments (e.g., states)?

4. How do the three countries discussed in detail (Australia, Brazil, and the United States) differ in the capacity of their legislative budget offices? How does this reflect the budget power of the legislature overall?

5. Review Posner and Park's list of suggested reforms. What challenges is each reform aimed at addressing?

NOTES

1. Tax expenditures equate with foregone revenue of a government. By virtue of a policy decision not to create or increase a certain tax, for example, a government has lost the potential revenue that the tax receipts could have produced.

2. Dorotinsky accessed the 2003 World Bank-Organization for Economic Cooperation and Development (OECD) Survey on Budget Practices and Procedures that included responses from twenty-seven OECD countries and fourteen others, as well as data from the Center for Budget and Policy Priorities' International Budget Project Open Budget Survey for this research. A more recent World Bank-OECD survey of international budgeting practices is available. Some results from the survey are discussed in chapter 10 and cited in footnote 11 of that chapter.

3. Ibid.

4. The precepts of New Public Management include a catalytic role of government as "steering" rather than "rowing"; a government that anticipates problems to prevent them; government that empowers citizens to solve their own problems; where government performance is cost-effective; a government that emphasizes goals, not rules; a customer-oriented, customer-driven government that offers choice; a competitive government; a government that focuses on earning and saving, not spending money; and a government in which authority is decentralized and participatory management is engaged (Osborne and Gaebler 1992).

5. See http://www.aph.gov.au/Parliamentary_Business/Committees/House_of _Representatives_Committees?url=comm_list.htm#standing

6. Political crisis occurred in Australia in 1975 when the Opposition in the Senate did not approve two appropriation bills. The Governor-General ended up dismissing the Prime Minister and replacing him with the Opposition leader until new elections were held (Blöndal et al. 2008).

7. See http://www.aph.gov.au/parliamentary_business/committees/house_ of_representatives_committees?url=jcpaa/index.htm

8. Worldwide there has been exponential growth in the creation of parliamentary budget offices, reflecting growing political fragmentation of governments as well as good governance reforms to strengthen the

budget powers of parliaments (Straussman and Renoni 2009). A listing of duties of the Parliamentary Budget Office can be found at http://www.aph.gov.au/About_Parliament/Parliamentary_Departments/Parliamentary_Budget_Office/role

9. A plurality representative system is one in which voters cast ballots for their choice and the winning candidate is the one who receives the most votes. If more than two candidates run for a position, the percentage required to win may be lower than >50 percent. Proportional representative systems include closed-list systems in which voters vote for party only, with the share of votes a party receives determining how many of the candidates on the party list win office. Open systems are similar, though voters choose the order of candidates on the party's list (Hallerberg and Marier 2004).

10. See http://www.washingtonpost.com/blogs/wonkblog/wp/2013/06/27/in-the-1970s-congress-investigated-intelligence-abuses-time-to-do-it-again/

11. See www.cbo.gov

12. Ibid.

13. The Government Performance Project (GPP) was a multi-year assessment of public management capacity funded by the Pew Charitable Trusts. Using a criteria-based approach, the GPP graded the management capacity of the 50 states in 1998, 2001, 2005, and 2008. State grades were published by *Governing* magazine in the early months following the years in which data was collected and grades assigned. The GPP used teams of academics and journalists to collect and analyze quantitative and qualitative data about the states in several management areas, using these data and analyses to assign grades to the states. Data sources that underpin the grades include: (1) interviews conducted by the journalists; (2) research provided by university faculty; and (3) a hardcopy (and later electronic) survey of state officials, administrators, staff, and managers. The criteria measured in each management area—Information, Infrastructure, Money and People—were determined through identification of best practices and consensus among team members as to how to measure such practices. More information about this research is available at http://www.pewstates.org/projects/government-performance-project-328600

14. See http://www.lbb.state.tx.us/

15. For information about Georgia's House Budget and Research Office, see http://www.house.ga.gov/budget/en-US/default.aspx For information about Georgia's Senate Budget and Evaluation Office, see http://www.senate.ga.gov/sbeo/en-US/Home.aspx

16. See http://www.budget.ny.gov/pubs/supporting/ConsensusForecastReport.pdf

17. See http://www.citizensunion.org/www/cu/site/hosting/Reports/CU_Budget ReformReportCard_April2012.pdf

18. Weakness in addressing budget analysis support to the legislature is evidenced in Assembly's efforts to create a nonpartisan legislative budget office; see http://open.nysenate.gov/legislation/bill/A79-2013

REFERENCES

Anderson, B. 2009. "The Changing Role of Parliament in the Budget Process." *OECD Journal on* Budgeting 1: 1–11.

Blöndal, J. R., D. Bergvall, I. Hawkesworth, and R. Deighton-Smith. 2008. "Budgeting in Australia." *OECD Journal on Budgeting* 8 (2): 1–64.

Blöndal, J. R., C. C Goretti, and J. K. Kristensen. 2003. "Budgeting in Brazil." Conference paper, OECD Senior Budget Officials, June 3–4, Annual Meeting, Rome, Italy.

Bourdeaux, C. 2008a. "Integrating Performance Information into Legislative Budget Processes." *Public Performance & Management Review* 31 (4): 547–569.

Bourdeaux, C. 2008b. "Dimensions of Legislative Budgetary Control." Conference paper, *Midwestern Political Science Association*, Annual Meeting, 1–26.

Bourdeaux, C. 2007. "Legislative Responsibility for State Budget Problems." Conference paper, *Midwestern Political Science Association*, Annual Meeting, 1–26.

Bourdeaux, C. 2006. "Do Legislatures Matter in Budgetary Reform?" *Public Budgeting & Finance* 26 (1): 120–142.

Citizens Union of the City of New York. April 2012. *New York State Budget Reform Report Card: 2012 An Improvement But Still an Incomplete.* http://www.citizensunion.org/www/cu/site/hosting/Reports/CU_BudgetReformReportCard_April2012.pdf, 2.

Clark, C. 2013. "New York State Passes Budget on Time Third Year in a Row." *Reuters*, March 29. Available at http://www.reuters.com/article/2013/03/29/us-state-budget-new-york-idUSBRE92S09D20130329

Council of State Governments. 2012. *The Book of the States,* Table 4.10: Selected State Administrative Officials: Methods of Selection, 231–236. Lexington, KY: The Council of State Governments.

Council of State Governments, *The Book of the States*, Table 4.4: The Governors: Powers, 219–220. Lexington, KY: The Council of State Governments.

Dorotinsky, W. 2008. "A Note on What Happens if No Budget is Passed Before the Fiscal Year Begins." In *Legislative Oversight and Budgeting: A World Perspective*, edited by R. Stapenhurst, R. Pelizzo, D. M. Olson and L. von Trapp, 111–115. WBI Development Studies, 45627. Washington, DC: The World Bank.

Fisher, P. 1999. "Political Explanations for the Difficulties in Congressional Budgeting." *Social Science Journal* 36 (1): 149–160.

Forestiere, C., and R. Pelizzo. 2008. "Dynamics in Legislative Budgeting in Italy: 1982–2001." *Journal of Legislative Studies,* 14 (3): 279–296.

Forsythe, D. W., and D. F. Boyd. 2006. "New York: The Growth, Waning, and Resurgence of Executive Power." In *Budgeting in the States: Institutions, Processes, and Politics*, edited by E. J. Clynch and T. P. Lauth, 55–78. Westport, CT: Praeger.

Governing. March 2008. *Measuring Performance: The State Management Report Card for 2008*. Governing.com.

Hallerberg, M., and P. Marier. 2004. "Executive Authority, the Personal Vote, and Budget Discipline in Latin American and Caribbean Countries." *American Journal of Political Science* 48 (3): 571–587.

Heniff, Jr., B., and J. Murray. 2012. "Congressional Budget Resolutions: Historical Information." RL30297, March 13. Washington, DC: Congressional Research Service. Available at http://www.senate.gov/CRSReports/crs-publish.cfm?pid='0E%2C*PLS2%23%20%20%20%0A

Joyce, P. G. 2005. "Linking Performance and Budgeting under the Separation of Powers: The Three Greatest Obstacles Created by Independent Legislatures." International Monetary Fund seminar, December 5–7.

———. 2011. *The Congressional Budget Office: Honest Numbers, Power and Policymaking*. Washington, DC: Georgetown University Press.

Kingstone, P. R. 2003. "Privatizing Telebrás: Brazilian Political Institutions and Policy Performance." *Comparative Politics* 3 (1): 21–40.

Krafchik, W., and J. Wehner. 1998. "The Role of Parliament in the Budgetary Process." *South African Journal of Economics* 66 (4): 242–255.

Lauth, T. P. 2006. "Georgia: Shared Power and Fiscal Conservatism." In *Budgeting in the States: Institutions, Processes, and Politics*, edited by E. J. Clynch and T. P. Lauth, 33–54. Westport, CT: Praeger.

Lee, T. B. 2013. "In the 1970s, Congress Investigated Intelligence Abuses. Time to Do It Again?" *The Washington Post*, June 27. Available at http://www.washingtonpost.com/blogs/wonkblog/wp/2013/06/27/in-the-1970s-congress-investigated-intelligence-abuses-time-to-do-it-again/

Lienert, I. 2005. "Who Controls the Budget: The Legislature or the Executive?" Working Paper WP, 115. Washington, DC: IMF.

Martell, C. R. 2011. "Budgeting in Brazil Under the Law of Fiscal Responsibility." In *Comparative Public Budgeting: A Global Perspective*, edited by C. E. Menifield, 353–368. Sudbury, MA: Jones and Bartlett Learning.

National Association for State Budget Officers (NASBO). Summer 2008. *Budgetary Processes in the States.* Washington, DC. Available at http://www.nasbo.org/publications-data/budget-processes-in-the-states

Osborne, D. E., and T. Gaebler. 1992. *Reinventing Government: How the Entrepreneurial Spirit Is Transforming the Public Sector.* Reading, MA: Addison-Wesley.

Pelizzo, R. 2008 "Oversight and Democracy Reconsidered." In *Legislative Oversight and Budgeting: A World Perspective*, edited by R. Stapenhurst, R. Pelizzo, D. M. Olson, and L. von Trapp, 29–47. WBI Development Studies, 45627. Washington, DC: The World Bank.

Posner, P., and Park, C-K. 2007. "Role of the Legislature in the Budget Process: Recent Trends and Innovations." *OECD Journal on Budgeting* 7 (3): 77–102.

Santiso, C. 2004. "Legislatures and Budget Oversight in Latin America: Strengthening Public Finance Accountability in Emerging Economies." *OECD Journal on Budgeting* 4 (2): 47–76.

Schick, A. 2002. "Can National Legislatures Regain an Effective Voice in Budget Policy?" *OECD Journal on Budgeting* 1 (3): 15–42.

Stapenhurst, R. 2008. "The Legislature and the Budget." In *Legislative Oversight and Budgeting: A World Perspective*, edited by R. Stapenhurst, R. Pelizzo, D. M. Olson and L. von Trapp, 48–65. WBI Development Studies, 45627. Washington, DC: The World Bank.

Straussman, J. D., and Renoni, A. 2009. "Establishing a Parliamentary Budget Office as an Element of Good Governance." *Comparative Assessment of Parliaments (CAP) Note Series* (September). Center for International Development, Rockefeller College, University at Albany, SUNY. Available at http://www.cid.suny.edu/capnotes1/Straussman-Renoni%20CAP%20Note.pdf

Tollini, H. 2009. "Reforming the Budget Formulation Process in the Brazilian Congress." *OECD Journal on Budgeting* 9 (1): 1–29.

Wehner, J. 2008. "Assessing the Power of the Purse: An Index of Legislative Budget Institutions." In *Legislative Oversight and Budgeting: A World Perspective*, edited by R. Stapenhurst, R. Pelizzo, D. M. Olson, and L. von Trapp, 79–97. WBI Development Studies, 45627. Washington, DC: The World Bank.

chapter EIGHT

Public Budgeting and the Courts

Judicial Influence on Economies and Budgets

I would like to choose a fresher topic, but duty calls. The budget remains the single most important issue facing the courts.

—Chief Justice John Roberts, United States Supreme Court, 2013

LEARNING OBJECTIVES

After reading this chapter, you should be able to

- Define an independent and impartial judiciary

- Understand the relationship between an independent judiciary and the economy

- Explain the expanded role of the modern judiciary vis-à-vis public policies and budgets

- Distinguish the structure and functioning of the judiciary according to civil versus common law models

- Articulate the budget strategies used by the judiciary to secure funding

- Explain the various ways that judges, court staff, and court systems become susceptible to corruption

---

Previous chapters have described the budget powers and activities of the legislative and executive branches of government. Thus far, you have been introduced to the concept of public leadership and how chief executives press their budget and policy agendas to guide government action. We have also described distinctions of presidential and parliamentary systems and compared the budget-making capabilities of legislatures among various governments.

This chapter examines the third leg of government—the judiciary. The importance of an independent judiciary to a well-functioning government and for a well-working economy is explained. We will explore how judiciaries influence public policy and budgets via the expanding role of this branch of government. Further, we will describe the budget strategies of court systems and examine in depth the vulnerability of judges and court systems to corruption. The chapter ends with a focus on corruption susceptibility of court systems in India and Guatemala, after having discussed system components and such vulnerability in United States courts.

THE JUDICIARY AND THE ECONOMY

The judicial branch may be the least visible and least understood of the three branches of government. The checks and balances of democratic governance are provided by a legislature that makes laws, an executive that implements laws, and a judiciary that interprets laws. A well-functioning judicial branch is independent and provides a fair and impartial system of recourse by which civil liberties and rights are protected. Independence means that courts and judges are separated from the political influences of the other branches of government, from lobbying interests, and from the public, generally. The courts should resolve legal disputes through unbiased and competent hearings and judicial review by a judge, a panel of judges, or by a jury of peers, based on an assessment of the facts of the case and consideration of relevant law.

The judiciary influences economies and budgets in several ways. Lars Feld and Stefan Voigt (2003) measure de jure (established in law) and de facto (as practiced) judicial independence in seventy-one countries across eighteen years and compare these measures to national economic productivity. They find that judicial independence as prescribed in law does not necessarily correspond with judicial independence as practiced. For example, many developing countries have expressed the foundations for judicial independence clearly in their constitutions, but have not realized such independence in practice. Equally important, Feld and Voigt (2003) find among fifty-seven countries that "while de jure judicial independence does not have a clear impact on economic growth, de facto judicial independence positively influences real GDP growth per capita. . .Only the constitutional specification of the court's procedures as one aspect of de jure judicial independence proves to be significant and positive" (23). Transparency International conducts periodic surveys of government corruption and in 2007, focused on the judiciary in countries around the world. Findings from this survey indicate

> a correlation between levels of judicial corruption and levels of economic growth since the expectation that contracts will be honoured and disputes resolved fairly is vital to investors, and underpins sound business development and growth. An independent and impartial judiciary has important consequences for trade, investment and financial markets. (Transparency International 2007, Executive Summary)

COURTS AND PUBLIC POLICY

Judicial decisions have had an impact on public spending and programming in many public policy areas, including education, corrections, banking and finance, housing, transportation, health care, and services for the mentally handicapped and disabled. The judiciary has a legitimate role in ensuring that government actions are in compliance with the law (either statutory or constitutional) and it carries this out by interpreting law, especially when laws are vague. Thus, court decisions do and will continue to have budgetary impacts. Courts make decisions influencing taxes and public debt, as well as the responsibilities of various budget and policy actors. The judiciary is not necessarily proactive in seeking to be involved in determining budgets, though influencing budgets does happen by virtue of the branch conducting its job. It is important to understand that the orientation of the judiciary regards (or should regard) the law and not finances. That is, the courts approach problems from a legal and not fiscal perspective.

David Rosenbloom (1987) determines that the expansion of the administrative state has contributed to a new partnership with the judiciary as the senior associate. The judiciary can influence, change, and require bureaucratic institutions and processes through its decisions and by decree. Also, an increasingly litigious society has pushed clients of government programs as well as government employees to flock to the courts to seek redress about individual and property rights and contractual relationships. Government agency immunity from civil litigation has changed from full to qualified, increasing the liability of public agency operations and budgets (Rosenbloom 1987). The entrenchment of public entitlements and programming, and a new public management focus on entrepreneurial government adds to judicial influence on policy as well. In particular, the provision of public services and programs through privatization or outsourcing opens up a significant amount of government operations (contracts) to judicial review. Rosenbloom explains that the distinctive legal perspective of the courts conflicts with management-based values related to government agencies and operations—for example, that courts do not (or should not) make decisions based on costs. He discusses possible future scenarios related to this new partnership as coping, converging, judicial withdrawal, or the further expansion of individual liberties and the attendant obligations of government to create environments that will enhance individual control and freedom.

Courts and Health Care

Perhaps the most visible example today of how the courts influence public policy and budgets is reflected in the US Supreme Court decision in *National Federation of Independent Business v. Sebelius* (NFIB, 132 S. Ct. 2566, 2012). This case relates to the constitutional challenges brought by states and others regarding the individual mandate and Medicaid expansion included in the Patient Protection and Affordable Care Act of 2010 (ACA), explained, in part, in chapter 3. Lynn Baker (2013) asks the question:

> How can the courts distinguish and invalidate those conditional offers of federal funds to the States that threaten to render meaningless the Tenth Amendment and its notion of a federal government of limited powers, while at the same time affording Congress a power to spend for the general welfare that is greater than its power to directly regulate the States? (72)

Components of the ACA include a mandate that every individual must have health insurance and state governments must expand Medicaid coverage among a greater number of individuals, with federal funding to the states to cover "some, but arguably not all" of the costs associated with greater coverage

(Baker 2013, 72). Baker explains an earlier decision of the Court (*South Dakota v. Dole* in 1987) that placed limits on federal spending power, holding this spending to five tests:

- Congress must spend "in pursuit of 'the general welfare'"
- Congress cannot spend to induce states to engage in unconstitutional activities
- Congressional notice about spending to states must be clear so that states make informed choice about accepting federal money
- Spending must be germane to federal interests in national projects or programs
- Conditional offers of federal funds cannot be so coercive as to make the acceptance of funds by states compulsory (74–77).

The Medicaid provision of the ACA did offer funds to states to expand Medicaid, yet if states chose not to accept the funds, all federal funding for Medicaid would be withdrawn. The Supreme Court in its opinions determined that this provision conflicted with two provisions from precedent about federal spending: (1) clear notice by the federal government about the funding so that states are able to make fully informed choices about accepting or not accepting funding (how would states have known when Medicaid was first introduced that they could lose their funding because of new, future requirements?), and (2) pressure to expand Medicaid in this instance is coercive ("the Roberts group determined this provision to be 'a gun to the head'") (Baker 2013, 78). Both the majority opinion and dissenters on the Supreme Court in this case determined that the funding involved in the Medicaid expansion provision crossed the line in terms of pressuring state choice in the matter. The majority opinion put these funds at "over 10 percent of a state's overall budget" while the dissenters indicated that states risked "21.86 percent of all state expenditures combined" (78).

Since the Supreme Court decision was handed down, states have been making the choice to expand Medicaid or not. Currently, twenty-five states have expanded the program, nineteen states are not expanding at this time, and in six, there is ongoing debate about the choice.[1] Though the federal government will provide funding for 100 percent of expanded coverage for the first three years, this funding drops to 90 percent after that. But many in states that have chosen not to expand believe that the federal government will not be able to follow through with such funding, given the estimated high costs associated with the program. Georgia Governor Nathan Deal has held firm to no expansion of Medicaid in his state thus far; state officials have estimated that expansion would cost $4.5 billion over ten years in Georgia (Malloy 2012). Presumably, the NFIB decision by the US Supreme Court has allowed the state to choose to avoid these costs, for now anyway.

Courts and Education

New Jersey has what some consider an unleashed judiciary that plays a strong policy role in the state. For example, in 2011, Governor Chris Christie lamented, "I don't think the [New Jersey] Supreme Court has any business being involved in setting the budget of the state government" (Malanga 2012). Steven Malanga (2012) describes the state's highest court as "the most activist state appellate court in America." Seemingly, this court determined early on to make its own rules rather than leave judicial rules of operation to the legislature. Malanga explains how the court's decisions regarding education funding, affordable housing, and state debt have led to suburbanization of previously small town communities, higher local taxes, substantial wealth redistribution, and a perpetually constrained state budget.

Yet in spite of substantial and expansive education spending, program results in the state lag behind individual expectations, national averages, or both. The New Jersey judiciary influences education policy in several ways—in its decisions addressing fiscal equity across school districts and fair share of affordable housing in local governments across the state, and also by changing the concepts of interest within policy areas. In particular, the court moved from ordering fiscal equity across school districts to requiring that all school districts provide an adequate education. This has led to "extravagantly funded" school districts with spending in some approaching $30,000 per student (Malanga 2012). "Judges don't merely determine levels of spending; they also initiate and monitor specific programs—policy details that, in most states, are left to elected officials," writes Malanga. One New Jersey chief executive who served as chief justice of the state's Supreme Court after his gubernatorial tenure ended "admitted that he wielded as much power as chief justice as he had in the governor's seat" (Malanga 2012).

A decision by the Kansas Supreme Court similarly forces that state to spend more on its public schools (Hanna and Milburn 2014). In this case, parents and school districts sued the state regarding local education expenditures and the court agreed that inequality among school districts violated the state constitution. The governor claims to be happy with this decision as it compels the legislature to come up with $125 million to accommodate the court's decision. In light of this decision, legislators now may have to address previous income tax cuts that were instigated as a pump on the state economy. Essentially, the state has been ordered by the courts to come up with more money to provide "an adequate education for every child" (Hanna and Milburn 2014, A3).

Courts and Public Pensions

Court decisions about public pensions illustrate how the judiciary can affect government policy and budgets, too. In fact, many state and local governments have turned to their retirement systems for fiscal relief. "As cities and states across the country attempt to reform their sometimes overly generous, underfunded, and expensive retirement plans, the ability to change future benefit accruals is critical to balancing their budgets" (Hinson, Godofsky, and Siegel 2013, 75).

Making changes to the promises that governments make to their workers is difficult as the legal protections associated with pensions are extremely complex. Legal conflicts about public pensions require courts to clarify benefits as contractual, property, or "gratuitous" (Brauer 2007, 71). States vary in the legal status they provide pensions, with most establishing the benefits as a contract between the employer (the government) and the employee. The US Constitution and most state constitutions have express protections of contracts, public or private, and so pensions that are understood legally as contracts are difficult to change. States with constitutional provisions regarding pensions as contracts cannot be changed without amending such constitutions.

Court decisions to date have determined that the core benefits of public pensions should be treated differently from cost-of-living adjustments (COLAs). States differ regarding their pension protections—in some, protections kick in only once benefits are vested; in others, when the employee is retirement eligible; and in still others, future benefits are protected. "States where the contract is found to exist at the time a worker is hired have little freedom to change benefits. States where the contract is found to exist at retirement have considerably more flexibility" (Munnell and Quinby 2012, 3). States have an easier time making changes to pensions that are considered to be property and challenges in these states to pension changes have met with little success. For most states, changing the future benefits of current employees, except the COLAs, is hard. Changes to COLAs have been approved by courts in Colorado, Minnesota, New Jersey, and South Dakota. In Minnesota, the court determined that COLA was not a core benefit and it needed to be changed to avoid the corrosion of the pension's fiscal health. Generally, the courts must sort out the core benefit—in this case specified COLAs and protections of accrued benefits—currently and in the future. "Protection of future accruals of core benefits serves to lock in any benefit expansions, limiting policymakers' ability to respond to changing economic conditions" (Munnell and Quinby 2012, 3).

In January, 2013, Florida's Supreme Court ruled in favor of legislated changes to the state's retirement system; the decision affects the state budget by almost $1 billion annually. The Florida Retirement System (FRS) includes the state and local governments that choose to participate; the system covers most public employees in the state. The FRS offers defined benefit and defined contribution plans as well as a hybrid one.[2] As of June, 2012, the system indicates an actuarial funding ratio[3] of 86.4 percent that compares well to the aggregated ratio for the 126 plans examined by the Public Fund Survey (2013) of 73.3 percent. The FRS indicates a ratio of 1.87 actives to annuitants, meaning there are 1.87 working, active, or preretirement members of the pension system for every one system retiree receiving benefits. This compares to the aggregated ratio for all pensions in the Public Fund Survey of 1.65 in 2012. This ratio was 2.0 or greater from 2001 to 2008; the ratio has declined in every year since 2008.

The plaintiffs in this case included public employees and unions who filed against the Florida governor, attorney general, chief financial officer, and the administrator of the pension plan. The plaintiffs complained that law passed in 2011 (to initiate cost savings) changed the pension and violated the state constitution. In 2011, the state was battling a budget shortfall of over $3.6 billion. Issues raised in the case related to two parts of the law: (1) for the first time, employees would have to contribute 3 percent of their gross compensation to their pension, going forward, and; (2) a change to the COLA. The Florida Supreme Court held to a previous decision made in *Florida Sheriffs Association v. Department of Administration* that provided for the ability of the state to modify "prospectively, the mandatory, noncontributory retirement plan for active state employees" (Hinson, Godofsky, and Siegel 2013, 78). The Florida Supreme Court upheld the constitutionality of the 2011 law that made changes to the state pension system; it held that governments under fiscal stress must have the ability to modify employee obligations, though without affecting prior earned benefits.

Courts and Corrections

Many court decisions have attempted to alleviate prison and jail overcrowding, advance the rights of inmates, and improve services provided to those incarcerated. An example of court influence on local budgets in this area involves Fulton County, Georgia. A 2006 federal consent order attempted to compel Fulton County to assuage overcrowding and understaffing, and to improve conditions in the county jail. Since 2006, county commissioners and the sheriff have periodically lobbed blame back and forth for lack of progress in complying with the order. In 2014, the US District Court Judge Thomas Thrash postponed a hearing about continuance of the consent decree to allow the county to complete compliance efforts that have been initiated. To reduce jail overcrowding, the county is spending $2 million in 2014 to rent beds in other local jails. Also, the board eased restrictions related to new hires, allocating $3.2 million for departing employee benefits that will allow for quicker hiring of new guards to fully staff the jail. The county is also following through on replacing faulty locks on cell doors, having budgeted $4.6 million for this project (Eloy 2013 and 2014).

The Courts and Agency Budget Behavior

Jeffrey Straussman (1986) analyzes how the threat of litigation and court decisions contribute to agency budgeting behaviors and affect the process itself. He explains that courts can influence the strategies used by agencies vis-à-vis the legislature in the budget-making process (an agency using the threat of litigation, for example, as indicative of funding need). However, the legislative response may not be changed—that is, the budget process and outcomes may remain incremental. Straussman notes, however, that courts can exacerbate the budget problem in periods of fiscal stress. Legislative response may be to invoke government-wide budget redirection, but more likely responses include pushing the agencies to conduct budget redirection internally to accommodate court decisions or to look to federal funding to fill the void. Also, agency budgeting behaviors are influenced by their agreement or disagreement with court decisions. For example, agencies might advocate court decisions to justify their funding needs given their agreement, or agencies might be obstructionist if the court decision requires a policy change or changes with which the agency does not agree. Further, the structure and comprehensiveness of the court decision—its level of specification of program changes, coverage government-wide (across a state prison system, for example, or related to just one facility), level of oversight, and the timeframe for compliance can all contribute to agency budget strategy (Fliter 1996). Court influence in agency operations and thus budgets potentially shifts budget power among the branches and can lessen popular control of the budget (Duncombe and Straussman 1993; Feeley 1989; Hale 1979; Harriman and Straussman 1983).

THE JUDICIARY AND THE BUDGET

The court system itself is part of a government budget; that is, it needs money to pay for judges and court staff and the technology, equipment, and infrastructure necessary to function. How the judiciary operates in the budget process and how much a government budget "spends" on this branch has an impact on public budgets. Also, level of government investment (or lack thereof) in the judiciary influences how well courts operate and, importantly, the degree of access that individuals, businesses, and other entities have to ways of resolving legal disputes. Usually, spending for the judiciary comprises only very small portions of total government budgets. Poor funding affects this branch significantly. In the words of the US Supreme Court Chief Justice John Roberts (2013), "unlike most executive branch agencies, the courts do not have discretionary programs they can eliminate or postpone in response to budget cuts" (5). Roberts also emphasizes that budgeting for the judiciary is especially difficult because its work is constitutionally and statutorily based. According to the Chief Justice, "We're not like the typical government entity that can slow down this program or cut this particular activity. When we face budget cuts, it means furloughing or laying off people" (Odendahl 2013, 3). And in spite of furloughs or layoffs, the judiciary must keep courts open for business.

The American Bar Association (ABA) has concluded that US state court systems "are being starved" (Robinson 2011, 34) and that inadequate funding of these systems negatively impacts their constitutional duties. US state governments fund and operate their own court systems, just as the federal government funds and operates the federal judiciary. As noted earlier, most judiciaries make up very small percentages (often 1 percent or less) of total government budgets, but in the case of the states, spending cuts remain consistently applied even since the official end of the Great Recession in June, 2009. A Utah Chief Justice announced at an ABA meeting in February, 2010 that "state courts are recognizing that the severity of this economic crisis may well mean that things are never going to return to 'normal'" (Derocher 2010). The implications of budget stringency afforded to court systems evolve from ad hoc, individual inconveniences such as a delay in processing a divorce case to systemic problems associated with significant staff furloughs and layoffs, delayed infrastructure, and technology advancements that have been brought to a standstill. Long term, such actions lead to a decline in court safety and that of judges, less accessibility to the courts, especially for the poor, and a demotion of the judiciary as a constitutionally equal branch of government with the legislature and executive.

At one point in the 1990s, then US Supreme Court Chief Justice William Rehnquist described an hourglass-shaped justice system that had resulted from US governments being stingy in funding their court systems. According to the Chief Justice, innumerable drug prosecutors were having to navigate their cases through the "bottleneck" of the court system (Wilson 2002, 356). Spikes in spending for personnel to arrest and prosecute perpetrators, and to build prisons to house offenders, had occurred but with no attendant spending for judges, court staff, or for support to resolve the increase in caseloads. More recently, Georgia Supreme Court Chief Justice Hugh Thompson (2014) discussed how investment in the judiciary can realize fiscal savings for governments, even in economically unstable times. He explained that the state judiciary has used its funds to implement over a hundred accountability courts, in spite of the fact that the state's "judges have not received a state pay raise for 15 years. At any given time, there are about 1,100 people participating in accountability courts who would otherwise be in the state prison system. These specialty courts save Georgia more than $20 million a year in state prison costs" (Thompson 2014, 5).

Budget Strategies of the Judiciary

Court systems, staff and judges themselves engage a variety of budget strategies. The US states indicate a number of ways that the courts manage their budgets through the process. The judiciary's budget may be centralized, with all courts submitting to a court administrative office before the budget is passed on to the legislature, executive, or both. Alternatively, separate courts might present their budgets directly to the legislature, executive, or both. The chief executive may or may not have the ability to make changes to judicial budgets before sending the request on to the legislature. Many defer to the judiciary by not making any changes to these requests. Most legislatures can change court budget requests. Also, the judiciary may be restricted in how it manages funds, once appropriated (Baar 1975; Douglas and Hartley 2001a, 2001b).

Jim Douglas and Roger Hartley (2004, 2003a, 2003b, 2001a, 2001b) have conducted extensive research about budgeting in US state court systems, the strategies courts engage during the appropriations process, and the threats to judicial independence of the budgetary process. They point out that courts are at a disadvantage compared to executive agencies in the politics of this process, given no ready constituency that the governor or legislators need to consider when making spending trade-offs across policy areas. Jim Douglas (2002) studied the Oklahoma judiciary and articulated a number of strategies engaged by the courts that are familiar executive agency budget strategies, including

- Testifying at legislative hearings by court officials and judges
- Lobbying legislators by court officials and judges
- Presenting justification of budget needs to the legislature
- Mobilizing political allies and building relationships among these allies, court officials, and the legislature
- Exploiting relationships between court officials and legislators
- Engaging budgetary rules and procedures advantageous to the courts
- Emphasizing to legislators the judicial powers available to force spending

Douglas also found budget success on the part of this judiciary to result from acquisitive behavior, by virtue of its independence from the other branches of government, its trustworthy reputation, and because of the expertise of the chief court administrator.

Douglas and Hartley (2001a) dig more deeply into court budgeting strategies in a study of US state judiciaries nationwide. They determine that the most important budget strategies of the courts include lobbying activity by the chief justice directly to the governor and individual legislators, lobbying by court officials to legislative committees, and the courts maintaining informal contacts with legislators throughout the year. Fiscally prudent strategies such as retaining the trustworthiness of budget requests, providing sufficient supporting documentation that justifies budget needs, and efficiency efforts are important for budget success, too. Supporting documentation is especially important to legislators when reviewing the budget requests of the judiciary. In terms of the use of budget games engaged for funding success, Douglas and Hartley (2001a) find that the courts tend to be less acquisitive than executive agencies in their budget requests, though legislatures tend to appropriate a greater proportion of judicial requests than those of executive agencies. High importance is placed on the submission of realistic budget requests by judiciaries. In fact, these scholars recommend that court systems probably need to be more strategic in framing their true budget needs in order to realize greater budget success. Their work concurs with earlier research at the federal level that determines that the judiciary traditionally provides conservative budget requests to Congress (Walker and Barrow 1985; Yarwood and Canon 1980).

Douglas and Hartley (2001a) find that moderately helpful budget strategies of the courts include mobilizing political allies, particularly attorney groups, judicial professional organizations, and (a bit less so) court staff. Stressing the importance of judicial independence is equally helpful, though there seems to be little need for this, as responses from those in the executive and legislative branches indicate a respect for judicial independence. Less important or unimportant strategies to improve budgets for the courts include pressing the power of the judiciary through threat of suit or issuance of writs to force spending. This has happened several times in New York, to assuage cuts to the judicial budget in 1991 and to improve the pay of judges in 2008 (Hartocollis 2008). Generally, it is more likely to heighten bad feelings across the branches for the judiciary to pull rank in such a fashion. Appealing to the public, distributing pork (such as court system benefits like video court across legislative districts) and lobbying for fees and fines to support the courts are not viewed as helpful to judicial budgeting.

Douglas and Hartley (2003) find in later work that judicial independence is threatened by two aspects of court budgeting. First, interbranch conflict can press the executive and legislature to use their budget powers to influence judicial decisions, and legislators are more active in this than governors. The judicial actions found "most likely to induce such behavior are rulings over the constitutionality or legality of laws or state actions that have budgetary implications and rulings that have a direct impact on the governor or legislators personally" (Douglas and Hartley 2003b, 452). Second, the courts are pressured, largely by legislatures, to raise their own revenues. This does have implications for equal access to legal recourse as the poor are less able to pay such fees and fines. Pushing fees also has the potential to bias court decisions; judges might be incentivized to stock their courts with cases that are paid for through fees (Tobin 1999). Douglas and Hartley (2003b) conclude that "the insulation of state courts from other political institutions is sometimes thin when it comes to budget politics" (452).

Budget Stringency in the US Federal Judiciary

The quote by US Supreme Court Chief Justice John Roberts (2013) that introduces this chapter is from his most recent year-end report on the federal judiciary. In this report, he emphasizes that "the independent Judicial Branch consumes only the tiniest sliver of federal revenues, just two-tenths of one percent of the federal government's total outlays." Still, the US federal judiciary has been receiving budget cuts for the last decade. Typical budget-cutting strategies of executive agencies are familiar to the judiciary. The federal court system has reduced spending on capital by stabilizing rents, limiting staff space, and holding off on new construction. Operating costs have been reduced by conducting staffing studies and cutting positions. Innovations using information technology have led to more efficient case docket maintenance, case processing, financial management, and administration of employee pay and benefits. Consolidation of financing and human resources among units within and across judicial districts and programs has supported tight budgets, too (Roberts 2013).

Chief Justice Roberts explained that the provisions of the Budget Control Act of 2011 went into effect on March 1, 2013, with the 5 percent across-the-board sequestration cut of almost $350 million to the Judiciary. To abide by the sequester, the Judiciary made across-the-board cuts to funding allocations to court units and staffing cuts followed (since 2011, federal court staff have been cut by 14 percent). In order to cover its constitutional and statutory duties, cuts were applied to discretionary areas of the Judiciary's budget. The Judiciary's request for fiscal 2014 of $7.04 billion (less than two-tenths of 1 percent of total federal outlays) is $180 million less than its original request for the year and $120 million less than the amount approved by the Senate. The Chief Justice emphasizes that if the Judiciary must live with the sequester, more court staff will have to be let go. The resulting delays in civil cases lead to "commercial uncertainty, lost opportunities, and unvindicated rights . . . [while delays in criminal cases] pose a genuine threat to public safety" (Roberts 2013, 9). Continued stringent judicial budgets foster reduced security of courts and judges, declining jurors' fees, and delays in civil and criminal trials.

JUDGES, COURTS, AND CORRUPTION

Transparency International (2007) defines judicial corruption as "any inappropriate influence on the impartiality of the judicial process by any actor within the court system" (xxi). Susan Rose-Ackerman (2007) discusses avenues to support judicial independence (freedom from influence) and competence (impartiality). Complete judicial independence without competence can lead to corruption; however, having highly competent judges who are vulnerable to the influence of others can lead to corruption as well.

A government's legal foundations—the rules regarding cases and their introduction into the courts, civil and criminal procedural rules, precedence, constitutional and statutory laws, and agency rules and regulations—all factor into judicial independence. The complexity of a system of laws can compromise judicial independence and competence. Rose-Ackerman distinguishes civil and common law judicial systems and how the differences can affect possible corruption. Judicial decisions in civil law governments are made according to code and statutes, whereas in common law governments judicial decision making supports the application of precedent. According to a civil law model, judges are professionals, apolitical, and usually serve for a lifetime; entry-level judges must have passed exams and then are moved up a career ladder from lower- to higher-level courts. Judicial selection in a common law model is more political; some may be elected, but others may be nominated by the executive and selected by the legislature, where political balance of the bench may be a consideration. Concerns about reelection can influence judicial decision making. In civil law systems, pay and benefits of judges are set by civil service rules. Judicial independence is also fostered by providing this branch control over its budget and the budgetary process of the courts. The ability of the judiciary to present its budget directly to the legislature (bypassing the executive) and to manage its own budget once approved supports independence.

Under the civil law model, there may be specialty courts, trials are decided mostly by individual judges, or panels of judges may be used, but jury trials are rare. The common law model engages juries (of peers) and public trials. Court management systems in civil law governments are likely to have rules that require losers to pay all legal fees in civil cases and "civil and criminal procedures that expedite court proceedings (for example, limited discovery, limited use of oral argument, no juries)" (Rose-Ackerman 2007, 20). Common law systems, however, engage procedures that prioritize the protection of individual rights; Rose-Ackerman points out that this delays case processing and incentivizes litigants to settle before trial.

How the court system is organized, the position of prosecutors in the structure of government, and the existence of specialty courts across levels of government are also factors that influence judicial independence. Rose-Ackerman explains that countries with written constitutions have national courts that are freestanding; lower courts appeal to these courts for redress of issues vis-à-vis conformity with the country's constitution. These courts may consider new laws for their constitutional conformity, too. Judges to these courts are selected by the legislature for "partisan balance" and in consideration of individuals' "strong commitment to the norms of the legal profession and the preservation of the constitutional order" (Rose-Ackerman 2007, 20). Opinions handed down by these courts can include dissents. In the United States (founded on common law), the prosecutor is located in the executive branch and acquiescence of appointed judges to the current administration might compromise judicial independence and can lead to corruption. In Italy (founded on civil law), the prosecutor is located in the executive branch as well. But, the prosecutor can be located in the judiciary or may be an independent entity altogether, separate from courts and the executive (Brazil has such a structure; this country's legal system is also founded on civil law) (Rose-Ackerman 2007).

Mary Pepys (2007) describes a corrupt judiciary as providing unequal access to the system and characterized by ad hoc decision making where those with power and money have an advantage. A judicial system is susceptible to corruption if it is open to influence peddling, bribery, intimidation, and extortion. As noted earlier, an independent judiciary requires that there be no undue influence on its work from the other branches of government, special interests, or individuals. The independence of judges necessitates their allegiance to the law and not to those in power, with power, or by virtue of their appointment of judges. Independence is promoted by objective, transparent nomination, and election/selection processes according to clear and specified eligibility criteria.

Other components that positively influence the independence of judges include professionalization of the judicial career through long terms of office, competitive salaries, objective case assignment among judges, their continuing education and the timely dissemination of new laws that keep judges up to date and support their comprehensive knowledge of the law (Pepys 2007; Rose-Ackerman 2007). Professional groups such as the Federal Judges Association, the American Judges Association, and the National Judges Association[4] offer support, education and training, research, and conferences to help judges in the United States remain current with their work and the law. Accountability of judges is enhanced through the development and continuing reflection on a professional code of ethics and by publishing judicial decisions. Judges should be required to make a declaration of assets and reveal any conflict of interest related to cases they are assigned; transparency of their personal wealth and their work in the courts supports accountability. Established and consistently applied disciplinary actions against corrupt judges and oversight of judicial behavior by more than just judicial peers help advance impartial and independent court systems. A high level of security afforded to judges can reduce their vulnerability to bribery and other activities that compromise independence. Judges must be rewarded for ethical, not corrupt behaviors (Pepys 2007; Rose-Ackerman 2007).

The work of judges is further advanced by attention to the qualifications and salaries of court staff; to the technology system(s) for case management, review, and processing; and to court infrastructure and capital space. Computerized case management systems and case assignments that are tamperproof can streamline the process. The pay and structure of court clerks and staffing, transparency of court proceedings, and the prevalence of written opinions and dissents also contribute to judicial independence and the vulnerability of judges and court staff to bribery and other corruption. Innovations such as alternative dispute resolution mechanisms to reach settlements outside of the courtroom and specialty courts (such as drug courts) can heighten efficiency. Greater access to courts through televised monitoring can open up the process to the public and help to improve their understanding of the law, individual rights, and the court system generally. Transparency of the court system is necessary to avoid corruption. The public should understand the case management process, judicial decisions should be publicized and accessible, and judges should disclose their assets and conflicts of interest. Media access to court proceedings and documents factors into this as well (Pepys 2007; Rose-Ackerman 2007).

Pepys explains many aspects of collective life that contribute to judicial independence or lack thereof. A cultural or social tolerance for corruption is difficult to dispel. If family or personal relationships overshadow the rule of law or, as is the case in some countries, if bribing government officials to receive or affect service delivery or goods is standard procedure, judicial independence will be compromised. Pepys (2007) presents an example of judicial collusion promoted in Zimbabwe where "the government allocated farms that had been expropriated under a fast-track land reform programme to judges at all levels of government, to ensure that court decisions would favour political interests" (6). In these circumstances, it is a Herculean task to effect change. If judges are beholden to those who appoint them, if they are susceptible to bribes, if they operate in fear for their home, family, or others by virtue of the decisions they hand down, they lack the independence necessary to rule by law. They will be making decisions based on fear or money or both. If judges are punished for making decisions according to law and not because of influence, the system shows new judges that corruption is endorsed. Low judicial and staff salaries also open up the entire court system to corruption. The Founding Fathers of the United States understood this and protect the salaries of federal judges in Article III, Section 1 of the US Constitution.

Giuseppe Albanese and Marco Sorge (2012) examine the role of the judiciary in public decision making and how the structure of the judiciary and court systems influences corruption of the policymaking process. These scholars develop a policy framework that presents the relationships of "a policy-maker who allocates public funds from a fixed budget between two groups, a judiciary that oversees the political process and investigates corruption charges and a lobby group that may bribe the policy-maker to bias the allocation of funds in its favor and/or the judiciary to exert less effort in investigating corruption in the allocation process" (2). They focus on the influences of judicial independence and judges' isolation from politics on the likelihood of corruption of politicians and judges and find that "preserving the efficiency of independent judiciaries can serve as an instrument for self-enforced judicial accountability, even in the presence of corrupt judges" (3). Still, they concede that a judiciary highly susceptible to bribery is "an insurmountable impediment" (17) to its ability to limit corruption. Important design elements for an independent judiciary include "insulating" the judiciary from political interference and from any "regime in power" (Albanese and Sorge 2012, 17).

Perceptions of Judicial Corruption around the World

Transparency International (TI) scores perceptions of government corruption in countries around the world using a collection of different studies, ratings, assessments and surveys.[5] Table 8.1 presents the 2013 results of the TI study that applies a scale of 0 to 100, where 0 indicates very high corruption and 100 very low corruption (or "clean") in government. TI findings indicate Australia (ranked 9th with Canada) and the United States (ranked 19th with Uruguay)

Table 8.1
Transparency International's Scores of Perceptions of Government Corruption, by Country for 2012 and 2013

Rank	Country	2013 Score	2012 Score	Surveys Used	90% Confidence Interval	
					Lower	Upper
1	Denmark	91	90	7	87	95
1	New Zealand	91	90	7	87	95
9	Australia	81	85	8	79	83
9	Canada	81	84	7	77	85
19	United States	73	73	9	66	80
19	Uruguay	73	72	6	71	75
69	Italy	43	42	7	39	47
69	Kuwait	43	44	5	37	49
69	Romania	43	44	9	38	48
72	Bosnia & Herzegovina	42	42	7	37	47
72	Brazil	42	43	8	36	48
72	Sao Tome & Principe	42	42	3	34	50
94	Algeria	36	34	6	31	41
94	Armenia	36	34	6	30	42
94	Benin	36	36	6	30	42
94	Colombia	36	36	7	33	39
94	Djibouti	36	36	3	22	50
94	India	36	36	10	32	40
94	Philippines	36	34	9	32	40
94	Suriname	36	37	3	31	41
111	Ethiopia	33	33	8	29	37
111	Kosovo	33	34	3	29	37
111	Tanzania	33	35	8	29	37
123	Belarus	29	31	5	22	36
123	Dominican Republic	29	32	6	23	35
123	Guatemala	29	33	6	25	33
123	Togo	29	30	5	23	35
175	Afghanistan	8	8	3	3	13
175	North Korea	8	8	3	2	14
175	Somalia	8	8	4	5	11

Source: Transparency International. Available at http://cpi.transparency.org/cpi2013/results/

Notes: The 2013 survey includes 177 countries and territories. Data for countries of interest are provided, along with any other countries similarly ranked and with highest and lowest ranked countries. The confidence interval provides some indication of the variability of the data associated with a specific country; the wider the interval, the greater the variation in the data regarding the specific country.

realizing scores above 50. Italy (ranked 69th) and Brazil (ranked 72nd) realized scores of 43 and 42, respectively. India realized a score of 36, Tanzania 33, and Guatemala has the lowest score at 29, representing the highest level of perception of government corruption of the countries of interest here. Comparing this year's scores to last year's, Australia, Brazil, Tanzania, and Guatemala lost ground, the United States and India stayed the same, and Italy realized some small improvement toward cleaner government.

TI also generates other measures of corruption that poke further into public perceptions of corruption countrywide, in the public sector and by institution.[6] In a 2013 survey presented to a sample of people in each country, TI asked, "To what extent do you think that corruption is a problem in the public sector in this country?" Responses range on a scale from 1, not a problem at all, to 5, a very serious problem. The global aggregated score for 107 countries is 4.1 on the 5-point scale. This suggests that generally, the public considers corruption in the public sector to be a problem. Rwanda, Denmark, Sudan, Switzerland, and Finland all realized scores less than 3.0; Australia realized a score of 3.6; United States, 4.0; India, 4.2; Italy and Tanzania, 4.4; and Brazil, 4.6.(Guatemala was not included in this study.) Liberia and Mongolia had the highest scores of 4.8; this suggests that the public in these countries consider corruption in government to be a very serious problem.

Table 8.2 presents the results from the 2013 study of perceived corruption by institution that indicate globally, over half of those surveyed consider political parties and government institutions, in particular, corrupt or extremely corrupt.

Remember that these results are not indicative of actual corruption in the various countries, only the perceptions of those surveyed about corruption in the different institutions and across sectors. Table 8.2 presents cells that are shaded in those instances where at least half or more of those surveyed consider an institution to be corrupt or extremely corrupt. In Australia, just two institutions, political parties and the media, reach the 50 percent threshold. But in India and Tanzania, seven institutions realize this threshold or higher. Examining perceptions of corruption related to the judiciary, in particular, 86 percent of those surveyed in Tanzania consider the branch to be corrupt or extremely so and 50 percent of those in Brazil regard their judicial branch to be corrupt. On the other hand, just 28 percent of those surveyed in Australia consider this branch to be corrupt and less than half of those surveyed in the United States (42 percent),

Table 8.2
Transparency International's Perceptions of Corruption by Institution

Country Institution	Global	Australia n=1,206	Brazil n=2,002	India n=1,025	Italy n=1,010	Tanzania n=1,001	United States n=1,000
	Percent of Those Surveyed Considering Institution Corrupt or Extremely Corrupt						
Political Parties	65	58	81	86	89	68	76
Police	60	33	70	75	27	87	42
Parliament/Legislature	57	36	72	65	77	53	61
Public Officials/Civil Servants	57	35	46	65	61	75	55
Judiciary	56	28	50	45	47	86	42
Business Private Sector	45	47	35	50	52	48	53
Medical and Health	45	20	55	56	54	79	43
Education System	41	19	33	61	29	74	34
Media	39	58	38	41	45	41	58
Military	34	25	30	20	25	38	30
Religious Bodies	29	44	31	44	39	23	35
NGOs	28	23	35	30	26	49	30

Source: Transparency International Global Corruption Barometer available at http://www.transparency.org/gcb2013

Notes: Guatemala is not included in this study. Global results are unweighted averages across 107 countries surveyed in 2013.

India (45 percent), and Italy (47 percent) feel likewise. In Denmark, just 5 percent of those surveyed consider the judiciary to be corrupt or extremely corrupt. Kyrgyzstan, Liberia, and Madagascar all are at the bottom using this score—89 percent of those surveyed in each of these countries consider the judiciary to be corrupt or extremely corrupt.

Courts in the United States

The United States is a federal system of government with a written constitution that maps limited powers of the national government with those left to the sovereign states. State governments have their own constitutions and their own court systems. This country operates a legal system based on common law. The United Nations Office of Drugs and Crime (UNODC 2012) determines that the United States had 10.6 judges per 100,000 inhabitants in 2009. The UNODC (2012) defines professional judges as "full-time and part-time officials as of 31 December authorized to hear civil, criminal and other cases, including in appeal courts, and to make dispositions in a court of law. Also includes authorized associate judges and magistrates."

Appointment of Federal Judges The US Constitution stipulates that the president nominate and the US Senate confirm appointments to the federal bench (US Supreme Court, Court of Appeals, and District Courts). The Constitution also specifies that federal judges hold the position during good behavior, and may not be removed except by impeachment. Thus, US federal judges have lifetime appointments. US laws require disclosure of assets by judges and strict limits on their activities on the bench (Rose-Ackerman 2007). There are no express qualifications for federal judges included in the Constitution and so the nomination process for these judges has evolved over time. With well over eight hundred judges that preside over the lower courts and including the nine Supreme Court justices, all of whom can serve for life, the president must have a means of generating nominations. The president may receive recommendations from those within any of the three branches of government, including the US Department of Justice or the Federal Bureau of Investigation, members of Congress, and current judges and justices. The American Bar Association provides recommendations and vetting of candidates as well. Senatorial courtesy allows a senator from the state with a judicial vacancy to recommend a candidate to the president. Candidates can self-nominate, too.

To get a sense of the factors considered regarding federal judicial appointments in the United States, go to the US Senate Committee on the Judiciary website,[7] access "Library" for the most recent Congress, and read through several committee questionnaires of candidates for current vacancies. It should be apparent that candidates are examined regarding their past legal experience and public service, their political orientation (liberal or conservative), their constitutional view (progressive or "originalist"), and past expressions of personal opinion indicated in books, articles, interviews, memos, or any other type of communication. Presidents do consider these factors as well as political party loyalty when thinking about candidates. Ethnicity and gender come into play as well to increase diversity in the federal bench, which has been traditionally and predominantly white and male.

But former US Senator Richard Lugar has stated that money and politics threaten the independence of the federal judiciary (Stafford 2013). He noted that his voters held him to account for his support of President Barack Obama's Supreme Court appointees, Sonia Sotomayor and Elena Kagan—against his party. He lost the 2012 Republican primary, and the winning Republican then lost to a Democrat in the general election that year. "It is no longer good politics to approach confirmation votes (of judicial nominees] from a non-political point of view," claimed Lugar (Stafford 2013, 23).

Selection of State Judges   State government constitutions dictate selection of state judges. The American Judicature Society[8] provides a summary of how judges are selected in the fifty states. Selection methods are numerous and include

- Gubernatorial appointment based on recommendation from nominating commission
- Gubernatorial appointment with judicial council approval
- Gubernatorial nomination based on recommendation from judicial selection commission and with appointment by executive council
- Gubernatorial nomination based on recommendation from judicial selection commission and with appointment by one or both houses of the state legislature
- Nonpartisan or partisan election
- A mix of methods across different courts (supreme, appeals, and district or circuit)

In South Carolina and Virginia, state judges are elected by the legislature. South Carolina's legislature has a three-pronged system for investigating candidates to the state bench. The state's Judicial Merit Selection Commission[9] (JMSC) investigates judicial candidates through interviews, exams, and research conducted by other committees. These committees include the state bar association's Judicial Qualifications Committee that vets candidates among bar association members, and regional Citizens Committees on Judicial Qualifications. By the time the JMSC report reaches the legislature, candidates have undergone numerous checks of their work experiences, legal career and knowledge, and character. The report indicates candidates as qualified or not qualified and can present up to three nominations per judicial vacancy. Once the report reaches the legislature, candidates may lobby individual legislators for support and legislators can indicate their support for particular candidates prior to a vote.

Qualifying characteristics for state judges vary among these governments but are generally more clearly specified than qualifications of federal judges. Requirements can include those related to citizenship, state residency, minimum or maximum age, years of practicing law, status as a licensed attorney and member of the state bar association.[10] Still, Minnesota's qualifications to be a judge of any state court include simply, "learned in the law", able to vote, and at least 21 years old with mandatory retirement at age seventy.

Corruption Susceptibility of State Judges In 2012, campaign contributions for high court candidates in all US state governments equaled more than $31 million.[11] This total includes over $4 million in Alabama, and over $3 million each in Michigan, Ohio, Texas, and West Virginia. Campaign contributions to appellate court candidates totaled more than $19.4 million in the same year; this includes $8.4 million in Texas alone, over $2 million each in Illinois and Louisiana, and over $1 million each in North Carolina and Ohio.[12] Roy Schotland (2007) discusses the vulnerability of state judges and court systems to bribery and other corrupting activities, given the number of judges and cases handled at this level of government. State judges manage twenty times as many cases as federal judges; there are almost 11,000 state appellate and general jurisdiction trial judges compared with 867 federal judges (Schotland 2007). Also, most state judges are elected—"60 percent of appellate judges and 80 percent of trial judges at state level face contested elections and only 11 percent face no elections" (27). The original intention of advancing judicial independence through elections was to keep the executive and legislature out of the process. Other strictures imposed, such as the inability of judges to run for other offices while in service, longer terms, and nonpartisan or retention elections were imposed to enhance independence, too.

Because some judicial elections involve high stakes money, judges are susceptible to undue influence. Schotland (2007) provides examples, such as a case in Illinois where judicial campaign contributions are not restricted. In this case, a panel of judges ruled in favor of the defendant whose employees and others affiliated with the company had provided significant campaign funds to one of the judges, the winner in an election the year before. Plaintiffs petitioned the US Supreme Court to consider the judge's participation in their case, but the Court denied their petition. In another example, two justices of the Ohio Supreme Court received significant campaign contributions from numerous members of the same family. Here the plaintiffs (family) brought a lower court decision to reduce their award from $25 to $15 million to the Ohio Supreme Court for redress and the justices ruled for the plaintiffs (to restore the full award). In this case, the defendant took the case to the US Supreme Court for review, but the petition was denied.

Recommendations that could help to remedy susceptibility to influence judgments in state courts include realistic and comprehensive limits on campaign contributions by all state governments. Most states do not have any limits; restrictions that exist are weak or lack coverage. Public funding of judicial elections is another suggestion. Half of states provide some public funding of elections of various state officials, but only a few have ever offered such a program for judges (Schotland 2007). In North Carolina, for example, public funding of judicial elections has been provided since 2002. The program was popular with voters and proved successful in reducing candidate reliance on private contributions. Fundraising by parties for judicial races all but disappeared; however, the program was repealed by the state legislature and the repeal signed into law by the governor in 2013 (Voss 2014). These programs can fall victim to budget wars pretty easily—their success depends upon maintaining funding from the government.

Other recommendations to reduce the likelihood of judicial corruption resulting from judicial elections suggested by Schotland (2007) include lengthening terms of office, thus reducing the number of times that a candidate must raise funds and campaign and influencing who seeks office in the first place.

Also, Schotland calls for the proliferation of "campaign conduct committees" (30) that can educate judges about legal campaigning, fundraising, and spending. Finally, he recommends that systems for appointing judges should be developed to completely avert elections.

The Judiciary in India

India is a union of states and territories with a parliamentary system of government. Its legal system is based on common law, though separate personal law codes apply to those of different faiths, and as you will read about in rural Guatemala, the application of customary laws (local traditional practice) is evidenced throughout rural India. India's Constitution, Chapter IV, establishes the central Supreme Court, its jurisdiction, the appointment of judges and the Chief Justice, and makes provisions for the officers, servants, and expenses of the Court. The Supreme Court includes a Chief Justice and a maximum of twenty-five justices, all appointed by the president. The president may refer matters to the Supreme Court for judicial review. Chapter V of the constitution provides for the jurisdiction and operations of High Courts in the States, judicial eligibility and their appointment, salaries, court officers, staff, and expenses. Chapter VI provides for subordinate courts and district judges. Supreme and High Court judges cannot be removed from office except by impeachment by the parliament. In India, there were approximately 1.4 judges per 100,000 inhabitants in 2008 (Timmons 2013).

Transparency International India (2007) finds spending for the judiciary in 2007 equaled 0.04 percent of the annual Union budget. There is little indication that spending on the courts throughout India is much improved today. According to a news report (Sarda 2013), a recent study by the India's court management system indicates that while states spend their total allocations from the Union government for health and education, they are stingy when it comes to the judiciary. Sarda (2013) explains that according to the court management study

> Eighteen state governments are spending less than 1 per cent of the total budget allocated to them for court services. Judicial independence cannot be interpreted only as a right to decide a matter without interference. It has become incumbent on the central government to make sufficient and appropriate provisions in budget,

keeping in view the central laws so as to share the burden of states.

The third pillar of democracy can't be ignored.

The report emphasizes that the legislative branch increases the judiciary's workload by passing new laws and that the executive induces stress on the third branch by holding back funding and infrastructure. "One branch of the Constitution should not ideally decline the needs of another parallel branch thereby creating difficulties in discharge of its constitutional responsibilities" (Sarda 2013).

Corruption in the legal system is high in India, especially in the lower courts. Case backlogs, delays, and inequitable access to the court system are almost insurmountable problems. In particular, the very low number of judges to 100,000 inhabitants (1.3 according to Transparency International India 2007; 1.4 according to Timmons 2013) has contributed to an overwhelming backlog of cases in courts at all levels. Judicial vacancies are numerous and filling these positions across the country is perpetually problematic. Significant and long-standing corruption means that the public tends to hold judges in low regard; judicial salaries and working conditions are poor. According to a professor at the National Law University in New Delhi, "There are various issues that lead to posts of judges not being filled, ranging from budgetary constraints, to the lack of qualified candidates, to just apathy" (Timmons 2013, 2). The complexity of laws and poor training of judges contributes to a lack of qualified candidates, and for current judges, a lack of competency in case deliberation.

Transparency International India (2007) commissioned a study that determined "the estimated amount paid [to lawyers, judges, court staff or middlemen] in bribes in a 12-month period at around R2,630 crores or US $580 million in 2005" (215). A significant problem associated with greasing the wheels of justice through bribes for speedy justice regards the building of unauthorized infrastructure projects that avoid construction and safety codes. Therefore, in addition to rule of law, public safety is compromised.

Transparency International India (2007) suggests a number of reforms that might chip away at this extremely complex and corrupt system of justice. Primarily, a stepped process for increasing the ratio of judges to 100,000 inhabitants should be conducted—India's own Supreme Court has called for raising this statistic from 1.2 to 5.0 over five years. This would involve another reform: better recruitment to the bench. Codes of conduct outlining judges' responsible behaviors, guidelines on cases that involve family members, ethical considerations related to gifts and contributions, and raising funds should be developed and the information disseminated to judges. The judiciary needs a greater share of the government budget and some flexibility to manage its funds; it currently has no spending autonomy with funding determined by the parliament and managed by the executive (Transparency International India 2007). Funding for capital, equipment, and operations is simply inadequate and contributes to substandard working conditions. Information technology and court management system upgrades exist in the higher courts, but are in their infancy in lower courts where tremendous backlogs mean long delays (years) to resolving legal disputes (Gupta and Thomas 2012). Without such investments, it is unlikely that the public conception that justice must be purchased can be dispelled.

The Judiciary in Guatemala

Guatemala is a constitutional democratic republic with a legal system founded on civil law. The Guatemalan Constitution spells out guarantees of the judiciary that include functional and economic independence, and nonremoval of judges and trial judges except in cases established by law and staff selection. Eligibility criteria of judges at various levels are outlined. Supreme Court justices are nominated by a commission and elected by the Congress and the Supreme Court makes lower-level appointments. Today, spending for the judiciary makes up approximately 4 percent of the total Guatemalan budget (Guatemala Ministry of Public Finances, Citizen Budget 2012). The government appropriates these funds because of constitutional strictures and to comply with the peace accords (that specified judicial spending at 6 percent of government revenues). In 2012, allocation to the judicial branch and Constitutional Court was less than that executed the previous year (Guatemala Ministry of Public Finances, Citizen Budget 2012). The United Nations Office of Drugs and Crime (UNODC 2012) determines that Guatemala had 0.7 judges per 100,000 inhabitants in 2009.

Jim Handy (2004) observes that Guatemala's history of using noninstitutional means of settling disputes, its exceptional and longstanding internal military conflict, the rise of civil patrols, and the ingrained application of customary law all reflect the lack of public trust in the judicial system and perpetuate vigilante justice. Handy emphasizes that customary law is a "body of ideas" that are understood by all within a particular community rather than a knowledge or practice domain; such law, "by its very nature, differs fundamentally from locale to locale" (2004, 553–554), and is itself dynamic over time. Handy explains that the extreme poverty of indigenous populations in rural Guatemala contributes to a strong attachment to customary law by locals. This severe rural poverty is replicated in India and Tanzania, two other countries where local customs, beliefs, and the application of customary law conflict with a national legal system.

The peace agreements in the 1990s that brought an end to civil war pressed national institutional reforms along with attention to indigenous populations and their application of customary law. National institutional reforms that conflict with local customs have contributed to the instability of this country's legal system and contributed to increasing violent crime (Replogle 2005). For example, the assignment of justices of the peace to rural areas "was anything but beneficial. Many of them could not function in the Mayan language of the district to which they were assigned; they had no history in the region, no understanding of the basis of customary law, no roots, and no way to understand the world view that needed to inform the application of justice" (Handy 2004, 560). The peace agreements prioritized national judicial reforms and created a justice commission that developed a report of the corrupt practices evidenced, including: judicial influence peddling, cronyism, extortion, bribery to speed the processing of cases as well as to avoid due process, loss of files, case materials, confiscated possessions, and evidence tampering. Prisons operated by organized crime, drug traffickers, and gangs, and significant corruption among police also compromise Guatemala's legal system (Peña 2007).

The Guatemalan Supreme Court has 12 judges, 72 court of appeals judges (with 48 substitute judges), 170 trial and sentencing judges, and 369 justices of the peace. Carlos Peña (2007) observes that the Guatemalan judicial branch has inadequate capacity to manage its workload efficiently, leaving it open to corruption. There are not sufficient judges, staff, equipment, or technology to process cases without delay, to allow for adequate deliberation, and to keep backlogs low. The Guatemalan Constitution specifies that higher court judges nominated by a council of judges are then elected by the national Congress. This process is highly political, however. Criteria for judicial eligibility are developed on an ad hoc basis, the criteria change over time, and the process for determining eligibility is not transparent. Votes on judicial candidates by the Congress are not made public. The council that nominates judges can remove them as well. The fact that this council is made up of judges reduces system accountability—judges are less likely to reprimand their own.

The political influences related to judicial service leads to the greater likelihood of the removal of truly independent judges and replacement with those who are progovernment. Peña (2007) points out that in Guatemala there are no "guarantees that judges will resolve matters without influence, incentives, pressures, threats or undue interference, be they direct or indirect, from any sector or for any reason" (213). He suggests better distribution of the Guatemalan budget to (1) add judges, staff, IT, and equipment necessary to advance case management efficiency and reduce the susceptibility of personnel to bribery; (2) professionalize the system through judicial training and career progression; (3) develop alternative dispute resolution mechanisms to relieve court dockets; and (4) implement other efficiency measures such as oral hearings and the use of writs against judicial decisions (214).

CONCLUSION

This chapter has exposed you to budgeting by and for the judicial branch of government. The foundations for rule of law rest with an independent and impartial judiciary that affords clear and timely access to all. Such a judiciary can contribute to a vibrant economy in which individuals and businesses are confident that laws will be upheld and legal disputes judged fairly and without prejudice. Modern courts and judgments contribute significantly to public policies and budgets—the decisions that judges hand down influence for what and how much governments are obligated to spend, the sources of revenue they can tap, and who has certain program and other responsibilities related to public budgeting and the provision of government goods and services. In spite of the tremendous responsibilities of this third leg of governance, the budget of the judiciary tends to be a small fraction of a total government budget. Judges and court staff engage traditional budgeting strategies to justify their appropriation requests; their long-established conservatism on the part of the courts during budget development, however, is one factor that may perpetuate budget stringency evidenced in this branch.

Corruption in the judiciary is a significant problem in governments all over the world and this has an impact on public policy and budgets as well. The court system in the United States is exposed by virtue of the elected status of most state judges. This requires judges to remain cognizant of periodically raising funds to get into and return to office; the consequences of being beholden to large donors can mean biased decision making in cases involving or related to such donors. India's judicial system is so overwhelmed with a backlog of cases, so poorly maintained, and so open to corrupt practices that the culture does not consider any alternative to the necessary purchase of justice. In Guatemala, customary laws, vigilante justice, and the significant lack of developing, recruiting, and retaining judges all work against a high-functioning judiciary. After reading this chapter, you should have a sense of (1) the vital importance of an independent and impartial judiciary for effective governance, (2) the ever-growing influences of this branch on public policy and budgets, and (3) the enduring fiscal stringency within which most court systems operate.

DISCUSSION QUESTIONS

1. What factors influence the independence of the judiciary? Explain why the independence and impartiality of judges is important to a national economy.

2. What does David Rosenbloom mean when he claims the judiciary is a senior associate in a partnership with the administrative state? Is this partnership evident today? Justify your response.

3. Pick a policy area other than health care, education, or corrections and explore how the judiciary has influenced government spending for or service provision in that area. Summarize the impact of courts on your chosen policy area.

4. How does judicial impact on agency operations and budgets shift budget power among the branches and change popular control of the budget?

5. What are the most important strategies that the courts can engage for budget success? How might these strategies change in periods of fiscal stress? In what ways might these strategies vary from those of executive agencies and why might such strategies differ?

NOTES

1. See the Henry J. Kaiser Foundation, *Status of State Action on the Medicaid Expansion Decision,* 2014, available at http://kff.org/health-reform/state-indicator/state-activity-around-expanding-medicaid-under-the-affordable-care-act/

2. In defined benefit (DB) plans, the employer provides the employee with a calculated and specified retirement benefit based on employee salary and years of service. The employee may be required to contribute to the plan, but regardless of this, the employer bears the funding and investment risks. These plans generally have longer vesting periods than defined contribution (DC) plans. In the case of a DB plan, the employer has the obligation to meet the promised benefited that has been determined upon hiring (and vesting of) the employee. In a DC plan, the employer and the employee contribute into a retirement account for the employee; the retirement benefit will be based on salary level, contributions made over time, investment earnings, and age at retirement. In this case, the employee bears the funding and investment risks. These plans allow the employee to direct investments and vesting is usually sooner than in DB plans. Also different from DB plans, DC plans are portable, meaning employees can take the fund with them if they leave their employer.

3. The actuarial funding ratio provides one indication of the fiscal health of a pension fund, though this measure should be used with care and rarely in isolation of other measures of these funds. The calculation of the ratio is total pension assets divided by total pension obligations. The figure provided here related to Florida's pension system is interesting for its comparison to the aggregated funding ratio for all state pension systems included in the Public Fund Survey in 2012, and given comparisons with the aggregated actuarial funding ratios of funds before December, 2007 (the onset of the Great Recession). That is, aggregated funding ratios were above 85 percent from 2001 to 2008, before beginning to decline in 2009 through 2012. The aggregated funding ratio of state pension systems in 2012 equals 73.5 percent (see The Public Fund Survey, Figure A, available at http://www.publicfundsurvey.org/publicfundsurvey/summaryoffindings.html).

4. See Federal Judges Association at http://www.federaljudgesassoc.org/, the American Judges Association at http://aja.ncsc.dni.us/index.html, and the National Judges Association at http://nationaljudgesassociation.org/

5. Data sources used to develop Corruption Perception Scores include: African Development Bank Governance Ratings 2012; Bertelsmann Foundation Sustainable Governance Indicators 2014 and Transformation Index 2014; Economist Intelligence Unit Country Risk Ratings; Freedom

House Nations in Transit 2013; Global Insight Country Risk Ratings; IMD World Competitiveness Yearbook 2013; Political and Economic Risk Consultancy Asian Intelligence 2013; Political Risk Services International Country Risk Guide; Transparency International Bribe Payers Survey 2011; World Bank—Country Policy and Institutional Assessment 2012; World Economic Forum Executive Opinion Survey (EOS) 2013; World Justice Project Rule of Law Index 2013.

6. TI's Global Corruption Barometer (GCB) methodology is based on data collected in surveys in 107 countries in which from 500 to 1,000 people were contacted between September 2012 and March 2013. Samples have been weighted to be nationally representative. Survey types used include face-to-face, computer-assisted telephone interviews, or online interviews. More information about the GCB is available at http://www.transparency .org/gcb2013/in_detail

7. Available at http://www.judiciary.senate.gov/

8. Available at http://www.judicialselection.com/

9. Available at http://www.scstatehouse.gov/JudicialMeritPage/JMSCMain Page.php

10. See the American Judicature Society website on selection of judges in the American states, available at https://www.ajs.org/

11. See National Institute on Money in State Politics, Follow the Money. Available at http://www.followthemoney.org/database/nationalview.phtml? l=0&f=J&y=2012&abbr=0

12. Ibid.

REFERENCES

Albanese, G. and Sorge, M. M. 2012. "The Role of the Judiciary in the Public Decision-Making Process." *Economics & Politics* 24 (1): 1–23.

Baar, C. 1975. *Separate but Subservient: Court Budgeting in the American States.* Lexington, MA: DC Health.

Baker, L. A. 2013. "The Spending Power after NFIB v. Sebelius." *Harvard Journal of Law & Public Policy* 37 (1): 71–81.

Brauer, M. A. 2007. "State and Local Government Pensions: In What Circumstances Can Governments Reduce Pension Benefits?" *Benefits Law Journal* 20 (4): 65–77.

Derocher, R. J. 2010. "Crisis in the Courts: Bars Take Steps to Stave Off Judicial Funding Cuts." The American Bar Association, *Bar Leader*, May-June 34 (5): 6–10.

Douglas, J. W. 2002. "Court Strategies in the Appropriations Process: The Oklahoma Case." *Public Budgeting, Accounting, and Financial Management* 14 (1): 117–136.

Douglas, J. W., and R. E. Hartley. 2004. "Sustaining Drug Courts in Arizona and South Carolina: An Experience in Hodgepodge Budgeting." *Justice System Journal* 25 (1): 75–86.

———. 2003a. "Budgeting for State Courts: The Perceptions of Key Officials Regarding the Determinants of Budget Success." *Justice System Journal* 24 (3): 251–263.

———. 2003b. "The Politics of Court Budgeting in the States: Is Judicial Independence Threatened by the Budgetary Process?" *Public Administration Review* 63 (4): 441–454.

———. 2001a. "State Court Strategies and Politics during the Appropriations Process." *Public Budgeting & Finance* 21 (1): 35–57.

———. 2001b. "State Court Budgeting and Judicial Independence: Clues from Oklahoma and Virginia." *Administration & Society* 33 (1): 54–78.

Duncombe, W. D., J. D. and Straussman. 1993. "The Impact of Courts on the Decision to Expand Jail Capacity." *Administration & Society* 25 (3): 267–292.

Eloy, M. 2014. "Judge Delays Hearing on Fulton Jail Conditions." PBA30, February 5. Available at http://wabe.org/post/judge-delays-hearing-fulton-county-jail-conditions

———. 2013. "Federal Judge Orders Contempt Hearing over Fulton Jail Conditions." PBA30, November 26. Available at http://wabe.org/post/federal-judge-orders-contempt-hearing-over-fulton-jail-conditions

Feeley, M. M. 1989. "The Significance of Prison Conditions Cases: Budgets and Regions." *Law and Society Review* 23 (2): 273–282.

Feld, L. P., and S. Voigt. 2003. "Economic Growth and Judicial Independence: Cross Country Evidence Using a New Set of Indicators." CESifo Working Paper, no. 906. Available at http://www.econstor.eu/bitstream/10419/76285/1/cesifo_wp906.pdf

Fliter, J. 1996. "Another Look at the Judicial Power of the Purse: Courts, Corrections and State Budgets in the 1980s." *Law and Society Review* 30 (2): 399–416.

Guatemala Ministry of Public Finances. January 2012. Citizen's Budget. Available at http://www.minfin.gob.gt/downloads/presupuesto_presupuesto_ciudadano/presupuesto_ciudadano2012/presupuesto_ciudadano12_ingles.pdf

Gupta, K., and S. Thomas. 2012. "Critical Analysis of Informational Technology Infrastructure in Indian Judicial System." Academia.edu. Available at http://www.academia.edu/3835623/Critical_Analysis_of_Informational_Technology_Infrastructure_in_Indian_Judicial_System

Hale, G. E. 1979. "Federal Courts and the State Budgetary Process." *Administration & Society* 11: 357–368.

Handy, J. 2004. "Chicken Thieves, Witches, and Judges: Vigilante Justice and Customary law in Guatemala." *Journal of Latin American Studies* 36(3): 533–561.

Hanna, J., and J. Milburn. 2014. "Kansas Forced to Spend More on its Public Schools." *The Atlanta Journal Constitution*, March 8: A3.

Harriman, L., and J. D. Straussman. 1983. "Do Judges Determine Budget Decisions? Federal Court Decisions in Prison Reform and State Spending for Corrections." *Public Administration Review* 43 (X): 343–351.

Hartocollis, A. 2008. "New York's Top Judge Sues over Judicial Pay." *The New York Times*, April 11. Available at http://www.nytimes.com/2008/04/11/nyregion/11judges.html?_r=0

Hinson, D., D. Godofsky, and R. Siegel. 2013. "Florida Supreme Court Upholds Right of Legislature to Prospectively Alter Public Employee Retirement Benefits." *Benefits Law Journal* 26 (2): 75–82.

Malanga, S. 2012. "New Jersey's Judicial Road to Fiscal Perdition." *The Wall Street Journal*, February 4. Available at http://online.wsj.com/news/articles/SB1000142405297020465 2904577190731461533606

Malloy, D. 2012. "Deal Rejects Expansion of Medicaid." *The Atlanta Journal Constitution*, August 28. Available at http://www.ajc.com/news/news/state-regional-govt-politics/deal-rejects-expansion-of-medicaid/nRMfK/

Munnell, A. H., and L/ Quinby. August 2012. "Legal Constraints on Changes in State and Local Pensions." Center for Retirement Research at Boston College, no. 25. Available at http://crr.bc.edu/wp-content/uploads/2012/08/slp_25.pdf

Odendahl, M. 2013. "Chief Justice Roberts Says Cuts to Judiciary Budget Becoming Too Deep." *Indiana Lawyer*, May 22–June 4, 3 and 23. Available at www.theindianalawyer.com

Peña, C. M. 2007. "Judicial Corruption and the Military Legacy in Guatemala." In *Global Corruption Report, Corruption and Judicial Systems*, 211–214. See Part Two: Country Reports on Judicial Corruption, available at http://archive.transparency.org/publications/gcr/gcr_2007

Pepys, M. N. 2007. "Corruption within the Judiciary: Causes and Remedies." In Transparency International, *Global Corruption Report: Corruption in Judicial Systems, 2007*. Available at http://archive.transparency.org/publications/gcr/gcr_2007

Replogle, J. 2005. "Citizens and Police Target Violent Gangs in What Some Charge is a 'Social Cleansing' Policy." *Christian Science Monitor*, October 6. Available at http://www.csmonitor.com/2005/1006/p06s01-woam.html

Roberts, J. 2013. "2013 Year-End Report on the Federal Judiciary." Supremecourt.gov, December 31. Available at http://www.supremecourt.gov/publicinfo/year-end/2013 year-endreport.pdf

Robinson, W. T., III. 2011. "The Real Costs of Shortchanged Courts." *National Law Journal*, August 1 33 (48): 34.

Rose-Ackerman, S. 2007. "Judicial Independence and Corruption." In Transparency International, *Global Corruption Report: Corruption in Judicial Systems, 2007*. Available at http://archive.transparency.org/publications/gcr/gcr_2007

Rosenbloom, D. H. 1987. "Public Administrators and the Judiciary: The "New Partnership." *Public Administration Review* 47 (1): 75–83.

Sarda, K. 2013. "Gross Injustice with Judiciary Budget." *The Sunday Standard*, December 22. Available at http://www.newindianexpress.com/thesundaystandard/Gross-Injustice-with-Judiciary-Budget/2013/12/22/article1958668.ece

Schotland, R. A. 2007. "Judicial Elections in the United States: Is Corruption an Issue?" In Transparency International, *Global Corruption Report: Corruption in Judicial Systems, 2007*. Available at http://archive.transparency.org/publications/gcr/gcr_2007

Stafford, D. 2013. "Lugar: I Paid the Price for Support of Obama Picks." *Indiana Lawyer*, May 22–June 4, 3 and 23. Available at www.theindianalawyer.com

Stinsky, B. 1993. "Why Lady Justice Is Wearing Rags: Budget Cutbacks Hit the Courts." *Judges' Journal* 32 (1): 12–36.

Straussman, J. D. 1986. "Courts and Public Purse Strings: Have Portraits of Budgeting Missed Something?" *Public Administration Review* 46 (4): 345–351.

The Public Fund Survey. 2013. Available at http://www.publicfundsurvey.org/publicfundsurvey/viewsystem.asp?SystemID=39

Thompson, H. P. 2014. "2014 State of the Judiciary Address." The Honorable Chief Justice Hugh P. Thompson, Supreme Court of Georgia, February 5. Available at http://www.gasupreme.us/press_releases/14JudiSpeech_1.pdf

Timmons, Heather. 2013. "Rape Trial Challenges a Jam in India's Justice System." *New York Times*, January 23, 1–2. Available at http://www.nytimes.com/2013/01/24/world/asia/gang-rape-trial-tests-indias-justice-system.html

Transparency International. 2007. "Indolence in India's Judiciary." In *Global Corruption Report, Corruption and Judicial Systems, 2007*, 214–217. See Part Two: Country Reports on Judicial Corruption, available at http://archive.transparency.org/publications/gcr/gcr_2007

Tobin, R. 1999. *Creating the Judicial Branch: The Unfinished Reform*. Williamsburg, VA: National Center for State Courts.

United Nations Office of Drugs and Crime. 2012. Statistics on Criminal Justice (UNODC), Criminal Justice System Resources. Available at https://www.unodc.org/unodc/en/data-and-analysis/statistics/data.html

Voss, G. 2014. "Stark Contrasts: The Effect of Public Campaign Funds on North Carolina Supreme Court Races." National Institute on Money in State Politics, February 6. Available at http://www.followthemoney.org/Research/index.phtml

Walker, T. G., and D. Barrow. 1985. "Funding the Federal Judiciary: The Congressional Connection." *Judicature* 69 (1): 43–50.

Wilson, S. H. 2002. *The Rise of Judicial Management in the U.S. District Court, Southern District of Texas, 1955–2000*. Athens: University of Georgia Press.

Yarwood, D. L., and B. C. Canon. 1980. "On the Supreme Court's Annual Trek to the Capital." *Judicature* 63 (7): 322–327.

The Bureaucracy, Citizens, the Media, and Public Budgets

A popular government without popular information or the means of acquiring it is but a prologue to Farce or Tragedy or perhaps both. Knowledge will forever govern ignorance, and a people who mean to be their own Governors must arm themselves with the power knowledge gives.

—James Madison to W. T. Barry, August 4, 1822

LEARNING OBJECTIVES

After reading this chapter, you should be able to

- Understand traditional theory about the budget behaviors of bureaucrats

- Distinguish bureaucratic budgeting today from traditional theoretical perspective

- Analyze the many components of the execution phase of public budgeting

- Compare budget execution activities among different systems and levels of government

- Understand how citizens, residents, and other stakeholders can have input into public budgets

- Understand the extent of participatory budgeting efforts conducted by governments around the world

- Understand modern media and how it influences public perceptions about budgets

- Explain how bureaucrats can better control their budget message by managing communication with the public

In this chapter, we consider budgeting in what has been termed the fourth branch of government. The influence of public program clients or customers, community residents, citizens, and taxpayers is assessed as well as the role of the media in determining budget allocations. The first part of this chapter reviews traditional theory about budget-maximizing bureaucrats and presents the different components of budget execution that are conducted by public agency heads, managers, and staff. The next section assesses public input in budgetary deliberations and allocation choices, with a focus on participatory budgeting. A final section explains the relationship of the media with bureaucracies and the public, and the impact that the media has on public budget priorities.

Once you have read this chapter, you may come away with a new appreciation for Rubin's theoretical perspective about public budgeting that was introduced in the first chapter. Real-time budgeting (RTB) considers the process a web of enduring, though nonsequential, decision streams. Each stream (revenues, process, expenditures, balance, and execution) involves specific stakeholders and occurs within a particular timeframe. In this chapter, the focus is on the influence and practices of agency officials, managers, and staff in securing their budgets and then implementing public policies and programs by managing their fiscal, human, and capital resources. The public is involved in all sorts of ways in the budgetary process and this is considered as well. The media can serve in an oversight capacity but can also provoke controversy that can compromise the budget process.

THE BUDGET-MAXIMIZING BUREAUCRAT

Budget execution is that phase in which budget resources are used by government managers, staff, and others to fulfill determined laws and policy. Today, administration in most large governments—what is referred to as the bureaucracy—is a complex and often confusing labyrinth, in spite of the fact that many governments have been downsizing and reorganizing, especially over the last decade. The US federal government employed 5.4 million people in 1962 but this number is down a million by 2011 to 4.4 million.[1] Government necessitates bureaucracy, even though the word itself often brings to mind a priori thoughts on the part of the public of slow, inefficient, and perhaps corrupt entities (Rainey and Bozeman 2000).

Because constitutions are usually much clearer about how governments can generate the means to carry out responsibilities (governments can tax and legislatures must pass appropriations for spending to occur legally) than they are about how the means should be managed, much of the framework for administrative practice has been developed by the executive branch. Government bureaucracies are the totality of the budget actions of bureaucrats over time, organizational arrangements, and the administrative processes, protocols, rules, and regulations that have been created up to this point to execute law.

William Niskanen's theory (1971) of the budget-maximizing bureaucrat no doubt contributes to the public's persistent suspicion about government bureaucracy and is rooted in Buchanan and Tullock's public choice theory (1962) of government growth that was introduced in the first chapter. Niskanen applies economic choice behavior to budgetary decision making in government, considering that the survival instincts of bureaucrats motivate them to expand the budgets that they control. These public servants exhibit classic utility-maximizing, monopolistic behavior within the agencies that they manage (Breton and Wintrobe 1975). The end result of such behavior is inefficiency—an overproduction of government output that is more than the public demands.

There are problems with the application of this theory to the actual budgetary decision making by government managers, especially today. Even Niskanen tempered his theory to account for the fact that bureaucrats do not have total control of their budgets. Critics of the theory have pointed out that bureaucrats may be incentivized to act and do so in ways different from Niskanen's model (Bartle and Korosec, 1996; Dolan 2002; Dunleavy 1985 and 1991; Loomis 1987; Sigelman 1986). Also, the application of this theory has been compromised by the advent of new ones, such as the New Public Management and New Public Service approaches to management.

Traditional public administration theory is founded upon political science and political power relationships of bureaucrats with their constituents or program clients. In such an environment, program managers and agency heads are expected to engage in protective and expansive budgeting behaviors. New Public Management springs from economic theory and in this case, bureaucrats relate to customers of public programs and services. Rather than conducting work through traditional hierarchies, market-driven options such as privatization and contracting out are engaged and organizational operations are decentralized. New Public Service engages democratic theory, determining the public interest through a dialogue of shared values. Bureaucrats engage with citizens regarding public programs and service; the organizational structure is collaborative with the engagement of networks and a public service motivation to work is emphasized (Denhardt and Denhardt 2000).

Today, government programs are less likely to be processed through a traditional hierarchical arrangement and bureaucrats need to be concerned with "doing more with less" over empire building. There is research that finds fault with Niskanen's conception of bureaucrats' utility functions—that is, that the conception of bureaucrat mobility (promotion) and other aspects of bureaucratic wealth and agency budget size do not hold water (Breton and Wintrobe 1975). Also, Donald Moynihan (2013) conducted an experiment that measures public service motivation in graduate students in public affairs, social work, and business to determine if such motivation explains budget-maximizing behavior—it does not.

In fact, in many modern government agencies, good managers are more likely to be recognized for their cost-cutting and efficiency measures rather than for budget and program expansion efforts. Today, public management and budget innovation is likely to generate positive recognition. For example, Wogan (2013) writes about José Cisneros, San Francisco's treasurer, who was recently recognized as an exceptional public leader by *Governing* magazine. San Francisco's treasurer is elected and serves the city as its banker, tax collector, and investment officer. Cisneros' innovations, particularly related to eradicating poverty, include

- Creation of college savings accounts for kindergartners in the public school system to incentivize parents to save and children to aspire to go to college
- Shepherding in a city tax credit for working families
- Persuading local banks to offer low-cost checking accounts to low-income residents

According to Cliff Johnson of the National League of Cities, Cisneros exhibits a public service motivation given his promotion of these antipoverty programs and that "most treasurers wouldn't think this was part of their job at all" (Wogan 2013). This local government finance officer is able to frame his decisions as not only a "street-level bureaucrat" but also as a representative of constituents who elected him into office. Cisneros claims that "Going through the election process gives me a different kind of visibility, a voice that is able to reach the people who need to hear this message" (Wogan 2013). In the end, two of Cisneros' innovations (savings accounts and low-cost checking accounts) involve leveraging external resources (parents and banks) rather than strict budget maximizing to effect a government policy (reduce poverty). Research that examines the budget preferences of state government agency heads across a quarter of a century provides good food for thought, too (Bowling, Cho, and Wright 2004). This study concludes that budget-maximizing behavior among agency heads does exist, but the degree of aggrandizement varies; bureaucratic preferences are nuanced and change over time and based on different contexts (Bowling, Cho, and Wright 2004). As in the preceding example, some executive agency heads are elected. For example, in many US state governments, governors' powers are tempered by the fact that heads of various executive agencies are similarly elected statewide. Elected status offers another perspective to such bureaucrats.

BUDGET EXECUTION PRACTICES

Budget execution is the third stage of the budget process in which agencies implement government programs and conduct government services. Agency heads, managers and staff must account for the flow of funds to get their work done. Agencies operating with annual appropriations have their limits so indicated with the new budget that has passed (ideally, on time). The following section examines budget execution strictures in different governments—first we discuss budget execution in the United States at the federal level and then compare execution practices in several of the sample countries. Consideration of budget execution in US state governments concludes the discussion about this stage of the budgetary process.

Budget Execution in the United States

Government budget execution is framed by rules and regulations of the process, accounting and record-keeping practices, and auditing standards and requirements—in addition to executive budgeting guidelines, budget formats, and funding compliance associated with other levels of government or donor institutions. As conducted, budget execution should support fund control, accuracy of fund accounting, and fund management flexibility. The components of budget execution involve periodic expenditure reporting, in-year reporting of expenditures, transparent and competitive procurement and contracting processes, routine and timely reconciliation of finances with bank records and publically available and accessible budget information and updates.

The US Department of Commerce provides an overview of all the legal and other strictures that bind federal government managers in the United States regarding the flow of fiscal resources through their agencies.[2] Specifically, the Commerce Department review confirms that US federal agencies are held to laws such as 31 U.S.C. 1301 requiring that appropriations "be applied only to the objects for which the appropriations were made," and that justifications be presented to the Appropriations Committees and appropriations laws and accompanying reports. Appropriations laws establish the purpose for spending, the time limits applicable for the expenditure, and the amount approved by Congress for the expenditure.

Other laws that affect modern US federal budget execution include the Government Performance and Results Act (GPRA) of 1993 that requires federal agencies to create multiyear strategic plans and link performance plans to budget program activities. This law represents a first attempt by Congress to legally require the development of strategic plans by federal agencies and the integration of performance and budget information.

GPRA was an effort to improve federal government efficiency and accountability by having agencies focus on, plan for, measure, and report on program results. The law was novel in providing a stepped process toward the integration of budgeting with performance. Agencies were initially required to establish strategic plans by 1997, develop performance plans with budget requests by 1999, and begin reporting on program results by 2000. The Government Accountability Office (US GAO 2004) found early efforts to adhere to GPRA problematic—agencies had difficulty linking goals, performance measures, and resources. Also, plan updates were awkwardly scheduled, conflicting with presidential elections in which leadership change might foster different agendas and foci.

The Program Assessment Rating Tool (PART) further influenced budgeting and management in US federal agencies. PART was an executive initiative used by the George W. Bush administration that transformed the original GPRA. President Bush, the only American president with an MBA degree, developed a management agenda that called for the integration of budgeting and performance by agency managers. According to Shelly Metzenbaum (2009), "PART shifted the focus from agency goals—to which many in an agency might contribute but for which no one but the most senior manager was wholly responsible—to program-level targets with clearer lines of responsibility" (11). PART required public managers to respond to questions in four areas that were weighted differently. An aggregated score inclusive of responses from all areas included measures of

1. **Program Purpose and Design (20 percent):** Does program have clear purpose and is it well designed?

2. **Strategic Planning (10 percent):** Does agency have valid annual and long-term goals for the program?

3. **Program Management (20 percent):** Explain agency program management, financial oversight, and program improvement efforts.

4. **Program Results (50 percent):** Is program performance related to goals and are goals justified?

Agencies and OMB collaborated on answering questions—OMB could overrule the agency (Joyce 2011). Total scores ranged between Effective (85–100), Moderately Effective (70–84), Adequate (50–69), and Ineffective (0–49). Agencies with problematic performance measures or with no performance data received an assessment of "Results Not Demonstrated."[3]

Research has indicated some positive management results to the PART effort (Joyce 2011; Shea 2008). Still, PART did not lead to dramatically changed budget decisions or management practice, and gaming was evidenced over time (Gilmour and Lewis 2006). It is helpful to remember that this was an executive initiative that did not have the full understanding much less the endorsement of Congress. As John Gilmour and David Lewis (2006) point out, "in one hearing held on Capitol Hill, a longtime appropriations staff member frankly acknowledged that he did not know what PART was" (185). PART use ended when George W. Bush left office.

The GPRA Modernization Act of 2010 is new law that reinforces and adds to components of GPRA, primarily tightening structure and better integrating plans with performance information for connection to budgets (Kaminsky 2010). The new structure requires development of multiyear, government-wide priorities with a requirement that federal agencies set their own goals within these overarching ones. OMB is responsible for coordinating agency goals around several crosscutting policy areas. GPRAMA also requires agencies to develop priority goals and periodically report on their attainment. In the end, a changed timeframe, input from Congress, and a centralizing focus of government-wide priorities may further strengthen federal efforts at integrating performance information with budgeting and budget results. In the meantime, the 2010 law does sustain a focus on developing performance information, thinking about and measuring program results and strategic planning to realize objectives.

Federal agency managers must also consult the 792 pages of the OMB Circular A-11 that presents detailed instructions about budget execution.[4] Part 4 of these instructions explains apportionment, reporting requirements regarding the flow of funds during execution, and agency operations in the absence of appropriations. Part 5 regards management and reporting related to federal credit. Part 6 presents information about strategic plans, annual performance plans, reviews, and reporting. If you return back to the US Department of Commerce and access their Chief Financial Officer's organizational chart for the office,[5] you will see several offices that have primary budgetary responsibilities during execution, including

- Office of the Budget:
  http://www.osec.doc.gov/bmi/budget/

- Office of Financial Management:
  http://www.osec.doc.gov/ofm/

- Office of Acquisition Management:
  http://www.osec.doc.gov/oam/

The day-to-day management of fund flow into and out of federal agencies requires attention to this complex web of parameters determined by law and developed within the executive branch. After appropriations have been determined, agencies are charged with committing funds—to purchase things, to pay employees, to contract for work to be completed. Effective budget execution requires continuously making comparisons and conducting analysis. Is spending tracking according to previously developed budget plans? What contingencies exist that compromise spending according to these plans? What happens in the case of an emergency? What if program costs are trending higher than estimated? Best practice in this phase requires that no one person be responsible for making obligations, letting contracts, and expending funds. Strong internal controls warrant a process of checks and balances within and across agencies.

This is evidenced in the several offices responsible for budget execution for the Department of Commerce mentioned earlier.[6]

Budget Execution in Governments Around the World

The International Monetary Fund (IMF) provides a guideline for public spending management that compares budget execution frameworks across different types of governments.[7] Table 2 of this guide presents stages of the spending process and the internal controls that exist across these different governments by stage. Note that control is influenced by the established role of the finance or treasury minister, the timing of expenditures and their reporting. This guideline also points out the current pressure for governments to conduct accrual accounting, a method of accounting that more accurately assesses the costs of government business, provides timely accounting of government resources and obligations, and better aligns with private sector accounting practice. The IMF reviews accounting gimmicks related to the timing of recording expenditures, billing tricks, and other practices that weaken internal controls and compromise budget execution. The guideline also discusses the benefits of the consolidation of funds in a central (treasury) account more likely to be found in industrialized countries versus the fragmentation of accounts often evidenced in developing countries.

The Public Expenditure and Financial Accountability Program[8] (PEFA) provides research, consultation, assessment, and outreach to governments for the improvement of budgeting practices and financial management system performance for purposes of strengthening economies and advancing government performance. The Program is a partnership of donor agencies and financial institutions that assesses the budgeting and financial management practices of countries to provide capacity-building advice, support, and action planning. The most recently completed countrywide PEFA assessments for Brazil, Guatemala, India, and Tanzania have been accessed here to describe the performance of some of the budget execution activities of the government ministries and departments of these countries that have been described earlier. PEFA assessments score government budgeting and financial management procedures and practices on a number of criteria: credibility of the budget; comprehensiveness and transparency; policy-based budgeting; predictability and control in budget execution; accounting, recording, and reporting; and external scrutiny and audit.

Examination of Table 9.1 indicates that of the budget execution, accounting, and auditing activities listed, most of these countries do best in recording

Table 9.1

PEFA Performance Indicators and Grades of Financial Management Practices by Country

	Year of Report	Effectiveness in Tax Collections	Predictability in the Availability of Funds for Commitment of Expenditures	Recording and Management of Cash Balances, Debt, and Guarantees	Effectiveness of Payroll Controls	Transparency, Competition, and Complaints Mechanisms in Procurement	Effectiveness of Internal Controls for Nonsalary Expenditure	Effectiveness of Internal Audit
Brazil	2009	B+	C+	A	B+	B+	A	A
Guatemala	2013	B+	C+	B	D+	D+	D+	D+
India	2010	D+	C+	A	C+	NR	D+	D+
Tanzania	2010	NR	C	C	NR	B	C+	C

Source: PEFA Assessment Portal Data, available at http://www.pefa.org/en/assessment_search. Assessments generated by country and most recent report accessed.

and management of cash balances, debt, and guarantees. Tanzania indicates the lowest grade of C for this activity. Effectiveness of tax collections—typically the work of a revenue department—is conducted equally well in Brazil and Guatemala (though the PEFA assessments for these countries were prepared four years apart), is compromised in India, and data problems preclude assessing tax collection performance in Tanzania. India's poor performance in this area is attributed to a very low collection of back taxes or tax arrears. According to Pratap Ranjan Jena (2010), the Government of India (GOI) can legally collect taxes, but collection is held up by tax disputes pending in the courts, with collection of arrears for income and corporate taxes trending at 8–9 percent. In this case, court backlog contributes to the cash flow inefficiency of tax collections.

All countries except Brazil indicate problems with accounting for payroll, procurement practices, internal spending controls, and internal auditing—India and Guatemala especially so. The PEFA assessment of India's procurement processes finds that although protocols are established and accessible through the General Financial Rules (GFR)[9] and the Manual on Policies and Procedures for Purchase of Goods,[10] internal ministry data is not available. Lack of such data did not allow for performance assessment related to competitive purchasing methods (if they exist and how they operate). The report explains that an avenue for making complaints regarding government purchasing does not exist, though procurement disputes can be arbitrated. Internal controls related to managing expenditures other than payroll is compromised in India by excessive year-end spending and shored-up balances (Jena 2010). Spiked year-end spending is a common public agency practice ("use it or lose it"), though many governments have tried to reduce this behavior by allowing agencies some flexibility in carrying over unused funds into the next year, or allowing them to keep a portion of savings realized through efficiency measures and other means conducted in the current year. Internal auditing of India's ministries and departments seems especially compromised. The internal audit in the GOI, "is not independent, has not developed standards, does not evaluate risks, and is conducted in a routine manner. The internal audit does not focus on systemic issues in helping the management to improve the efficiency and effectiveness of operations" (Jena 2010, 75).

PEFA's assessment of procurement in Guatemalan agencies determined that the majority of contracts are awarded noncompetitively and that there is no independent body to consider complaints about procurement. Though internal controls related to spending other than payroll are established in procedures and rules, the PEFA report explains that these are not relevant to issues of financial management risk nor program results. At the time of the assessment, Guatemala had not "developed risk maps and controls to improve outcomes and reduce costs" and breaches of internal controls system and legal regulations evidenced (Government of Guatemala 2013, 104–105). Internal audits are limited to transactions and do not cover areas of risk either.

Budget Execution in Subnational Governments

Budget execution in subnational governments involves the same activities as just discussed, though may be conducted on a different scale, especially in small local governments. (On the other hand, the economies of several US state governments, including California, Texas, and New York, compete with various countries around the world in size.) Subnational governments must manage their funds according to their own laws, rules, and regulations, but also must adhere to the constitutions, laws, rules, and regulations related to any funds received from higher levels of government, or to donor edicts (developing countries receive a significant amount of donor funds that support their budgets and these funds must be managed according to any prescriptions of the donor).

In the United States, new requirements for using and reporting on funds provided through the American Recovery and Reinvestment Act (ARRA) of 2009[11] (often referred to as "stimulus funding") were implemented to increase transparency and fund devolvement as well as to reduce the possibilities of corruption in securing and using the money. The Office of Management and Budget (OMB) provides guidance related to ARRA funding[12] and FederalReporting.gov provides extensive information and materials in a number of formats regarding the proper accounting of these funds by recipients.[13] Webinars on YouTube present video of some of these protocols and timing schemes for reporting, too.[14]

Anne Khademian and Sang Ok Choi (2011) explain the various implementation strategies, grant designs, management processes, and communication and collaboration strategies engaged by three cities in the State of Virginia that were possible because of characteristics of ARRA funding. They discuss how context and grants management structure affected realizing results in the different cities—one city oriented its funding management around its IT capacity; another, smaller government leveraged partnerships to fulfill ARRA projects; and a third engaged an "incident command system" to speed the process along. The rules of ARRA allowed for such accommodations.

Also in the United States, all entities that receive $500,000 or more in federally awarded funds must submit to an audit of the funds that corresponds to the Single Audit Act of 1984 and its subsequent amendments.[15] Examining the results of such an audit can help you to understand the bookkeeping and fund management undertaken by a public agency throughout the year that is necessary to properly account for public expenditures.[16]

Figure 9.1 provides the single audit results for the City of Little Rock, Arkansas, for 2012. The most important information to look for in such an

Figure 9.1
Single Audit for Little Rock, Arkansas, 2012

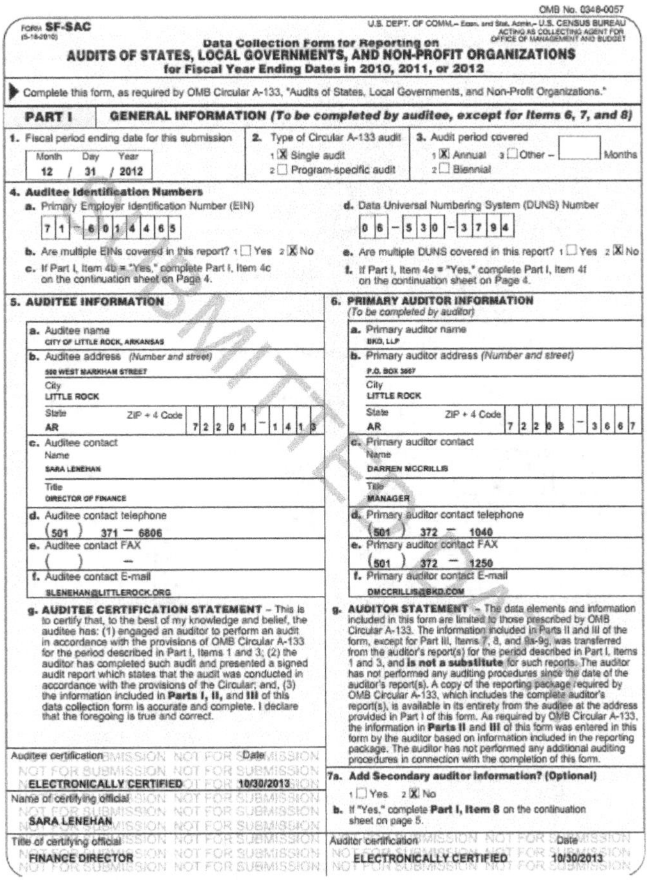

OMB No. 0348-0057

FORM **SF-SAC** (5-18-2010)

U.S. DEPT. OF COMM.– Econ. and Stat. Admin.– U.S. CENSUS BUREAU
ACTING AS COLLECTING AGENT FOR OFFICE OF MANAGEMENT AND BUDGET

Data Collection Form for Reporting on
AUDITS OF STATES, LOCAL GOVERNMENTS, AND NON-PROFIT ORGANIZATIONS
for Fiscal Year Ending Dates in 2010, 2011, or 2012

▶ Complete this form, as required by OMB Circular A-133, "Audits of States, Local Governments, and Non-Profit Organizations."

PART I **GENERAL INFORMATION** ***(To be completed by auditee, except for Items 6, 7, and 8)***

1. Fiscal period ending date for this submission
Month / Day / Year: 12 / 31 / 2012

2. Type of Circular A-133 audit
1 [X] Single audit
2 [ ] Program-specific audit

3. Audit period covered
1 [X] Annual 3 [ ] Other – ___ Months
2 [ ] Biennial

4. Auditee Identification Numbers

a. Primary Employer Identification Number (EIN): 71 – 6014465

b. Are multiple EINs covered in this report? 1 [ ] Yes 2 [X] No

c. If Part I, Item 4b = "Yes," complete Part I, Item 4c on the continuation sheet on Page 4.

d. Data Universal Numbering System (DUNS) Number: 06 – 530 – 3794

e. Are multiple DUNS covered in this report? 1 [ ] Yes 2 [X] No

f. If Part I, Item 4e = "Yes," complete Part I, Item 4f on the continuation sheet on Page 4.

5. AUDITEE INFORMATION

a. Auditee name
CITY OF LITTLE ROCK, ARKANSAS

b. Auditee address *(Number and street)*
500 WEST MARKHAM STREET
City
LITTLE ROCK
State: AR ZIP + 4 Code: 72201 – 1413

c. Auditee contact
Name
SARA LENEHAN
Title
DIRECTOR OF FINANCE

d. Auditee contact telephone
(501) 371 – 6806

e. Auditee contact FAX
( ) –

f. Auditee contact E-mail
SLENEHAN@LITTLEROCK.ORG

g. AUDITEE CERTIFICATION STATEMENT – This is to certify that, to the best of my knowledge and belief, the auditee has: (1) engaged an auditor to perform an audit in accordance with the provisions of OMB Circular A-133 for the period described in Part I, Items 1 and 3; (2) the auditor has completed such audit and presented a signed audit report which states that the audit was conducted in accordance with the provisions of the Circular; and, (3) the information included in **Parts I, II,** and **III** of this data collection form is accurate and complete. I declare that the foregoing is true and correct.

Auditee certification: **ELECTRONICALLY CERTIFIED** Date: **10/30/2013**
Name of certifying official: **SARA LENEHAN**
Title of certifying official: **FINANCE DIRECTOR**

6. PRIMARY AUDITOR INFORMATION
(To be completed by auditor)

a. Primary auditor name
BKD, LLP

b. Primary auditor address *(Number and street)*
P.O. BOX 3667
City
LITTLE ROCK
State: AR ZIP + 4 Code: 72203 – 3667

c. Primary auditor contact
Name
DARREN MCCRILLIS
Title
MANAGER

d. Primary auditor contact telephone
(501) 372 – 1040

e. Primary auditor contact FAX
(501) 372 – 1250

f. Primary auditor contact E-mail
DMCCRILLIS@BKD.COM

g. AUDITOR STATEMENT – The data elements and information included in this form are limited to those prescribed by OMB Circular A-133. The information included in Parts II and III of the form, except for Part III, Items 7, 8, and 9a-9g, was transferred from the auditor's report(s) for the period described in Part I, Items 1 and 3, and **is not a substitute** for such reports. The auditor has not performed any auditing procedures since the date of the auditor's report(s). A copy of the reporting package required by OMB Circular A-133, which includes the complete auditor's report(s), is available in its entirety from the auditee at the address provided in Part I of this form. As required by OMB Circular A-133, the information in **Parts II** and **III** of this form was entered in this form by the auditor based on information included in the reporting package. The auditor has not performed any additional auditing procedures in connection with the completion of this form.

7a. Add Secondary auditor information? (Optional)
1 [ ] Yes 2 [X] No

b. If "Yes," complete **Part I, Item 8** on the continuation sheet on page 5.

Auditor certification: **ELECTRONICALLY CERTIFIED** Date: **10/30/2013**

(Continued)

Figure 9.1 *Continued*

Primary EIN: `7 1 - 6 0 1 4 6 5`

PART II FINANCIAL STATEMENTS (To be completed by auditor)

1. Type of audit report
   Mark either: 1 ☒ Unqualified opinion **OR**
   any combination of: 2 ☐ Qualified opinion 3 ☐ Adverse opinion 4 ☐ Disclaimer of opinion

2. Is a "going concern" explanatory paragraph included in the audit report? 1 ☐ Yes 2 ☒ No

3. Is a significant deficiency disclosed? 1 ☐ Yes 2 ☒ No

4. Is a material weakness disclosed? 1 ☐ Yes 2 ☒ No

5. Is a material noncompliance disclosed? 1 ☐ Yes 2 ☒ No

PART III FEDERAL PROGRAMS (To be completed by auditor)

1. Does the auditor's report include a statement that the auditee's financial statements include departments, agencies, or other organizational units expending $500,000 or more in Federal awards that have separate A-133 audits which are not included in this audit? (AICPA Audit Guide, Chapter 13) 1 ☐ Yes 2 ☒ No

2. What is the dollar threshold to distinguish Type A and Type B programs? (OMB Circular A-133 § ___ .520(b)) $ 538,074

3. Did the auditee qualify as a low-risk auditee? (§ ___ .530) 1 ☒ Yes 2 ☐ No

4. Is a significant deficiency disclosed for any major program? (§ ___ .510(a)(1)) 1 ☐ Yes 2 ☒ No

5. Is a material weakness disclosed for any major program? (§ ___ .510(a)(1)) 1 ☐ Yes 2 ☒ No

6. Are any known questioned costs reported? (§ ___ .510(a)(3) or (4)) 1 ☐ Yes 2 ☒ No

7. Were Prior Audit Findings related to **direct** funding shown in the Summary Schedule of Prior Audit Findings? (§ ___ .315(b)) 1 ☐ Yes 2 ☒ No

8. Indicate which Federal agency(ies) have current year audit findings related to **direct** funding or prior audit findings shown in the Summary Schedule of Prior Audit Findings related to **direct** funding. (Mark (X) all that apply or None)

98 ☐ U.S. Agency for International Development	39 ☐ General Services Administration	89 ☐ National Archives and Records Administration
10 ☐ Agriculture	93 ☐ Health and Human Services	85 ☐ National Endowment for the Arts
23 ☐ Appalachian Regional Commission	97 ☐ Homeland Security	84 ☐ National Endowment for the Humanities
11 ☐ Commerce	14 ☐ Housing and Urban Development	47 ☐ National Science Foundation
94 ☐ Corporation for National and Community Service	03 ☐ Institute of Museum and Library Services	87 ☐ Office of National Drug Control Policy
12 ☐ Defense	15 ☐ Interior	59 ☐ Small Business Administration
84 ☐ Education	16 ☐ Justice	96 ☐ Social Security Administration
81 ☐ Energy	17 ☐ Labor	19 ☐ U.S. Department of State
66 ☐ Environmental Protection Agency	09 ☐ Legal Services Corporation	20 ☐ Transportation
	43 ☐ National Aeronautics and Space Administration	21 ☐ Treasury
		64 ☐ Veterans Affairs
		00 ☒ None
		☐ Other – Specify:

Page 2 FORM SF-SAC (5-15-2010)

(Page 3 – #2 of 4) Primary EIN: `7 1 - 6 0 1 4 6 5`

PART III FEDERAL PROGRAMS – Continued

9. FEDERAL AWARDS EXPENDED DURING FISCAL YEAR   10. AUDIT FINDINGS

CFDA Number Federal Agency Prefix (a)	Extension (b)	Research and development (c)	A R A? (d)	Name of Federal program (e)	Amount expended (f)	Direct award (g)	Major program (h)	If yes, type of audit report # (i)	Type(s) of compliance requirement(s) # (j)	Audit finding reference number(s) # (k)
1 6	.710	1☐Y 2☒N	1☐Y 2☐N	COPS	$ 81,284 .00	1☒Y 2☐N	1☒Y 2☐N	U	O	N/A
1 6	.710	1☐Y 2☒N	1☒Y 2☐N	ARRA COPS	$ 1,182,360 .00	1☒Y 2☐N	1☒Y 2☐N	U	O	N/A
1 6	.738	1☐Y 2☒N	1☐Y 2☐N	JUSTICE ASSISTANCE GRANT PROGRAM	$ 799,392 .00	1☒Y 2☐N	1☒Y 2☐N	U	O	N/A
1 6	.804	1☐Y 2☒N	1☒Y 2☐N	ARRA JUSTICE ASSISTANCE GRANT PROGRAM	$ 228,190 .00	1☒Y 2☐N	1☒Y 2☐N	U	O	N/A
1 6	.922	1☐Y 2☒N	1☐Y 2☒N	SPECIAL ASSET FORFEITURE	$ 21,249 .00	1☒Y 2☐N	1☐Y 2☒N		O	N/A
2 0	.205	1☐Y 2☒N	1☐Y 2☒N	HIGHWAY PLANNING AND CONSTRUCTION	$ 246,772 .00	1☐Y 2☒N	1☐Y 2☒N		O	N/A
2 0	.219	1☐Y 2☒N	1☐Y 2☒N	RIVERFRONT TRAIL	$ 37,680 .00	1☐Y 2☒N	1☐Y 2☒N		O	N/A
2 0	.600	1☐Y 2☒N	1☐Y 2☒N	SELECTIVE TRAFFIC ENFORCEMENT PROGRAM	$ 57,414 .00	1☐Y 2☒N	1☐Y 2☒N		O	N/A
4 5	.024	1☐Y 2☒N	1☐Y 2☒N	NEA OUR TOWN	$ 75,000 .00	1☒Y 2☐N	1☐Y 2☒N		O	N/A
4 5	.025	1☐Y 2☒N	1☐Y 2☒N	ARTISAN EDUCATION RESIDENCY MINI-GRANT PROGRAM	$ 1,521 .00	1☒Y 2☒N	1☐Y 2☒N		O	N/A

TOTAL FEDERAL AWARDS EXPENDED → $ 17,935,792 .00

1 See Appendix 1 of Instructions for valid Federal Agency two-digit prefixes.
2 Or other identifying number when the Catalog of Federal Domestic Assistance (CFDA) number is not available. (See Instructions)
3 American Recovery and Reinvestment Act of 2009 (ARRA).
4 If major program is marked "Yes," enter one appropriate letter (U = Unqualified opinion, Q = Qualified opinion, A = Adverse opinion, D = Disclaimer of opinion) corresponding to the type of audit report in the adjacent box. If major program is marked "No," leave the type of audit report box blank.
5 Enter the letter(s) of all type(s) of compliance requirement(s) that apply to audit findings (i.e., noncompliance, significant deficiency (including material weaknesses), questioned costs, fraud, and other items reported under § ___ .510(a)) reported for each Federal program.

A. Activities allowed or unallowed	E. Eligibility
B. Allowable costs/cost principles	F. Equipment and real property management
C. Cash management	G. Matching, level of effort, earmarking
D. Davis – Bacon Act	H. Period of availability of Federal funds

I. Procurement and suspension and debarment	L. Reporting
J. Program income	M. Subrecipient monitoring
K. Real property acquisition and relocation assistance	N. Special tests and provisions
	O. None
	P. Other

N/A for NONE

Source: US Federal Audit Clearinghouse, available at https://harvester.census.gov/facweb/Default.aspx

audit can be found in Part II, Financial Statements. An "unqualified opinion" means that there are no important qualifications (or problems) that the audit has uncovered. In this case, if you look at the answers by the City of Little Rock to the next few questions, you will note that no "significant deficiency" is disclosed. Part III of the audit, beginning on page 3, lists the different federal awards by type expended in 2012 by Little Rock, with audit findings and type of compliance problem, if evidenced. If any audit compliance problems are evidenced, they are indicated by letter in this section and defined at the bottom of the page. City officials and agency managers are then responsible for ferreting out any breaches, addressing the problem, and following through with determined solutions.

CITIZENS AND BUDGETS

Efforts to advance citizen participation in government budget deliberations and allocation choices are worldwide and ubiquitous. Proponents of participatory budgeting proclaim that the process heightens democracy and equity, promotes transparency and advances efficiency (Baiocchi and Lerner, 2007). Public participation in developing government budgets and public input throughout the budget process can help coalesce multiple priorities and values with budgetary decisions. Amy Franklin, Alfred Ho, and Carol Ebdon (2009) provide a comprehensive assessment of methods of public engagement in American city budgets, including surveys, budget simulations, citizen budget committees, focus groups, special budget meetings, public hearings, televised budget hearings with call-in features, neighborhood district meetings, and direct citizen interaction. These methods engage micro-level (individual) and macro-level (public or community-wide) interests and can be used to support various goals spanning improved education and communication; to support government programs, services, and funding; to influence decision making, generally; to support community building; and to enhance public trust in government (Franklin, Ho, and Ebdon 2009).

In their study of 261 midwestern cities in the United States, these scholars find the most popular means that city officials use to engage citizens in budgeting is through regular public hearings, special budget meetings, and by direct contact with citizens. Neighborhood meetings, televised focus groups, and special citizen budget committees are used by 10 percent or fewer of these cities and none indicated using budget simulation. The authors determine that elected officials place higher value on methods of participation that provide them with closer interaction with citizens, but these methods also tend to emphasize micro-level or individual, not community-wide, interests (Franklin, Ho, and Ebdon 2009).

The Instituto Brasileiro de Análises Sociais e Económicas (Ibase) in Brazil has developed educational programs to advance citizen input into government budgets in that country. A nongovernmental institution with a mission to build citizen capacity to understand and analyze public budgets, Ibase created online distance-learning modules that include topics such as "Mayor for a Day," effective citizenship, and elementary budgeting. Participants engage in formulating hypothetical budgets that require them to respond "to pressures from different constituencies and complying with federal regulations and guidelines" (de Renzio and Krafchik 2007, 7). Also concerned about the lack of transparency regarding some typically off-budget government expenditures, Ibase has introduced Brazilian citizens to the work of Brazil's National Economic and Social Development Bank (BNDES), which makes significant investments into country projects and infrastructure and has a strong hand in national development strategies (de Renzio and Krafchik 2007).

The Development Initiatives for Social and Human Action (DISHA) in India is similar to Ibase in Brazil. DISHA has pushed for the political and economic advancement of some of India's poorest citizens through budget analysis. Specifically, the institution examines state government budgets to determine whether spending outcomes equate with expenditure plans, with a special focus on programming and resources that have been allocated in the budget process to address the problems of poor and marginalized populations. For example, after a budget has been approved, DISHA contacts village officials to determine whether the money has been received and projects have been started. If not, DISHA works through the government bureaucracy to compel funding as approved. DISHA has been successful in getting funding streams unclogged and a higher percent of resources released to these villages. The work of DISHA has fostered the development of numerous budget groups around the country and advanced the use of budget analysis and education to heighten government accountability (deRenzio and Krafchik 2007).

Porto Alegre, Brazil, has used a participatory budgeting process in the past with success. Remember from chapter 2 that municipal structure and operation is provided in the 1998 Brazilian Constitution, though cities have the power to determine their budgets. Porto Alegre has a mayor and a Chamber of Deputies (legislature). Two executive offices—planning and community relations—developed and managed citizen input into the budget through multiple discussion assemblies from each of the sixteen regions of the city (Wagle and Shah 2003). The process covers five budget themes, citizen ranking of budget desires and a coupling of rankings with measures of need, access, and population size. Citizen demands are fed to a Council of Participatory Budgeting (COP) that navigates these through Chamber debates on the budget later in the budget development process. The success of this initiative has been evidenced in government benefits distributions across rich and poor regions of the city and in light of water and sewer system improvements and better education across the city. Swamim Wagle and Parmesh Shah (2003) point out that as the process becomes institutionalized, there is fear that citizens will be co-opted as "participatory citizens" or professionals who revert back to parochial interests and horse-trading. They also explain that the city legislature (Chamber of Deputies) has become "increasingly insecure" as participatory budgeting gains strength, perhaps fearing loss of budgetary influence (Wagle and Shah 2003).

Brazil has been recognized for its advancement of participatory budgeting throughout the nation. Cities in Brazil can choose to use the reform and, between 1990 and 2008, over 120 of Brazil's largest cities adopted it (Wampler and Touchton 2014). As noted earlier, citizens determine how to spend public funds. "The funding amounts can represent up to 100 percent of that for all new capital spending projects and generally fall between five and 15 percent of the total municipal budget" (Wampler and Touchton 2014). Boise State University professors Brian Wampler and Mike Touchton (2014) have blogged that Brazilian cities have realized good results from implementing participatory budgeting, including greater public investment in education and sanitation services and decreased infant mortality rates. "Infant mortality drops by almost 20 percent for municipalities that have used participatory budgeting for more than eight years" (Wampler and Touchton 2014). These scholars find that the reform gains traction with strong and consistent leadership (which has occurred in some cities when the mayor is from the Workers' Party) and with time. This coincides with the work of Yi Lu and Katherine Willoughby (2012) regarding performance budgeting—the reform yields better results the longer it is consistently engaged.

Gianpaolo Baiocchi and Josh Lerner (2007) discuss participatory budgeting in four Canadian cities and explain that "each process adapted popular education and facilitation approaches to the participants, allowing different people to learn how to participate in different ways" (10). For example, some efforts used cartoons, colors, and low-tech visual aids that helped people understand budgets and have an easier time talking about their budget priorities. Another component of success regards the collaborative nature of each venture—partnering with other communities or groups with similar interests in knowledge building and the expansion of deliberation about city funds and budget priorities. Finally, these scholars recognize the incremental flavor of the efforts—the participatory budgeting efforts of these cities often grew from meetings of civil society groups or activities outside of political parties, from the ground up and over time to generate a momentum for application to specific budgets and processes.

Baiocchi and Lerner (2007) emphasize that implementation success rests on context. Specifically, these scholars suggest that the relative wealth of cities in North America compared to those in South America may be a real hindrance to participatory budgeting efforts in Canada and the United States. These scholars highlight the significant legal distinctions across continents. For example, the powers of US local governments differ widely across and within state governments (remember the discussion of incorporation and home rule in chapter 5), whereas Brazil's Constitution prescribes local government powers in that country uniformly. Also, according to Baiocchi and Lerner (2007), in the United States, the rich can leave the poor inner city for the suburbs, exacerbating issues of wealth and race that hinder developing a participatory approach.

A new city movement in the State of Georgia provides an interesting attenuation of citizen-determined governance and budget making that may lend some credence to issues mentioned earlier. In 2005, Sandy Springs incorporated in Fulton County, Georgia. Proponents lobbied thirty years for cityhood. Since 2005, there have been a rash of incorporations—six new cities in Fulton County and two neighboring counties, DeKalb and Gwinnett. "Today, 44 of the 46 elected officials in those cities are white. . . And in the history of those cities, of the 66 people elected since their inception, just one was black" (Torpy and Edwards 2014, A1). Currently, there are a number of proposals for more new cities.[17]

Many of these efforts have been couched in terms of improved democracy, better services, and even cheaper government. The home county of these communities and its leadership is predominantly Black and there is concern that the incorporation movement, if successful, will decimate the county budget. Incorporation proponents, however, argue that as taxpayers they deserve a stronger voice in determining budget allocations, which services they want, and levels of program delivery. These proponents have also cited corruption in the county school system and on the part of county leadership as reasons for wanting to carve out their own governments separate from the county.

In countries with little budget transparency and accountability, there is often "massive leakage of scarce public resources into unnecessary projects, corruption, and ineffective service delivery, undermining efforts to reduce poverty, improve governance, and consolidate democracy" (de Renzio and Krafchik 2007, 2). In India, constitutional provisions reserve portions of local representation to previously marginalized groups including women, scheduled casts, and tribes. There have been efforts to familiarize these elected officials with the budgeting process and arm them with the ability to articulate budget priorities and choices. Traditionally, these groups have been left out of the budgeting process and thus they have very little experience with public budgets or analyzing them or making allocation trade-offs. Efforts to improve these individuals' contributions to budget making have included focus groups to compare normative budgets (what the budget should look like given good governance) and actual budgets (what the budget looks like as traditionally prepared).

Ahalya Bhat and colleagues (2004) find that these elected Indian women have "the capacity to participate in directing fiscal policy, but lack sufficient training to enable them to participate effectively" (4809). Most especially, these women did not understand the costs associated with the budget priorities that they supported and thus the policies they were likely to push for remain unfulfilled. These scholars emphasize that revenue scarcity hampers true and effective participation in the budget process in Indian local governments. That is, even with self-governance, these communities do not have adequate resources to carry out responsibilities. To address this, the GOI minister for local governments has called for quicker funneling of national monies to the local level and also asked state governments to better communicate with localities about restricted and unrestricted transfers in comparison to the revenues that the locals are expected to raise on their own through taxes (Bhat and colleagues, 2004).

Katherine Willoughby and Juan Luis Gómez (2011) examined budgeting in nine rural local governments in the State of West Bengal, India. They find that an upward flow of budget development that should include neighborhood input is prescribed in state rules.[18] These rules specify that local budgets be prepared by village development committees and sectoral (policy area) committees after holding community discussions about program and funding schemes and recording these discussions. Presumably, budgets are developed based on committee meetings and with input from local residents. However, delays in meeting the budget schedule and often a lack of commitment from sectoral committee members were cited as problematic to gathering effective community input to budgets. Rather than communities coming together and determining budgets, it is more likely that a facilitating team considers local stakeholder priorities and presents written comments in a final version of the local budget which would take note of social maps, or analyses conducted every two years that identify all households in a village and the development needs of each (Willoughby and Gomez 2011).

There are other ways that have opened up for citizens to have input to public budgets in India. The Indian Parliament passed a Right to Information law in 2005 requiring government agencies to create public information officers and open up agency information to public scrutiny. "Less than a decade ago, Indians had little access to information about how their government was being run and their tax rupees spent" (Kapur 2010). Now government officials must respond to citizen requests for information within thirty days or they incur penalties or can be dismissed from the job. Publication of budget and other information occurs in newspapers, online, on chalkboards, or is painted on government building walls. The law has also fostered "institutional competition" or stronger checks and balances across the branches of government (Kapur 2010).

Also, in the State of Andhra Pradesh, social audits are used to ferret out waste, fraud, and abuse. Thousands of young people who have been trained by a nongovernmental organization (NGO), the Society for Social Audit, Accountability, and Transparency, review public documents and travel to the thousands of villages across the state (35,000) to check on public programming and expenditures (Mandhana 2012). Community meetings tease out and confirm corruption, if it exists. Andhra Pradesh is using social audit results to clean up government. Approximately "$4 million lost to corruption has been recovered in the last six years, and nearly 15,000 officials have been dismissed, says Sowmya Kidambi, who runs the program" (Mandhana 2012).

Tanzania has experience with an initiative called "Voices of Citizens" that gathers citizen input for government budget and policy development (Wild 2013).[19] This initiative is a monthly survey whereby citizens are called on their mobile telephones; half of the surveys concentrate on education, health, and water services and half consider other issues, those of interest to citizens or those in which politicians and government officials are interested in learning more about the public perspective. The data collected through these surveys are compiled into short reports with visual displays to provide quick and simple feedback to government officials about the public mood on considered issues. The timeliness and direct connection with citizens is considered a strength of the project. Elected officials must now respond to real-time data and current public interest and cannot base their budget and policy initiatives on outdated information. This method was recently used by the Tanzanian government to gauge the public's consideration of a new draft constitution to replace the 1984 one.

CITIZEN PARTICIPATION IN US STATE BUDGETING

Most of the research about public input to government budgets regards local levels. The following section considers these efforts in the fifty American states, considering data and research based on the 2008 Government Performance Project (GPP), a survey of the management capacity of these governments that was defined previously in chapter 7. In the survey, state officials were asked about provisions for citizens to have input into state budgets. Seven states received the highest scores for this variable. The citizen input variable is one component of the measurement of state budgeting used by the GPP to determine level of transparency, understandability, and inclusiveness. States that received the highest scores for this variable by the GPP in 2008 included Georgia, Iowa, Michigan, Minnesota, Vermont, Virginia, and Washington. These states engaged multiple methods to develop and heighten citizen input into state budget deliberations and budget and policy outcomes. Unique aspects employed included

- Virginia's Office of Constituent Services served as a conduit between state residents and the governor about budget and policy interests.

- Iowa's governor and lieutenant governor used *Purchasing Results* to develop budgets; citizens reviewed agency budget requests and ranked them in order of significance to support the governor's budget development.

- Two of Iowa's largest agencies (Human Services and Corrections) used citizen boards to approve each department's budget request.

- Georgia's governor created a "Commission for New Georgia" made up of task forces including over 400 private citizens responsible for reviewing state operations and making recommendations for improvement.

- Georgia's governor created a customer service program that initiated surveys of state residents to determine issues of major concern to the public. Individuals were encouraged to contact the governor directly through e-mail, letter, and telephone to make suggestions about issues and spending priorities.

- Several governors (Michigan, Vermont, and Virginia) held town hall meetings (some televised) across their respective states to discuss state budgets and futures.

- Governors (Michigan and Minnesota) provided for citizen input about state budgets on their homepages online. (A majority of voters in Minnesota responded to one governor's survey about the budget and endorsed an increase to the cigarette tax one year.)

- A Minnesota legislative commission added citizens to the body to make funding recommendations regarding state investment in the environment.

- The Washington legislature passed a law requiring the governor to seek public involvement and input on the priorities to be used for budget development.

- Virginia Senate Finance and House Appropriations Committees are statutorily required to seek input on the budget from citizens across the state. Code of Virginia (§2.2–1510 B) requires at least four regional public hearings on the governor's proposed budget prior to the convening of the legislative session.

- Virginia and neighboring states listened to citizen complaints about the condition of the Chesapeake Bay and developed a multistate agreement to reduce point source pollution in the Bay. Citizen push back regarding a general tax increase to address the state's surface transportation problems led to the development in Virginia of a combination of user fees, land use proposals, accountability measures, and long-term funding solutions to heed public concerns and address the transportation problems.

- Washington's budget director and senior staff held town hall meetings around the state to generate dialogue about government priorities, performance and accountability. In half a dozen cities, fifty citizens were selected at random to represent each community. These citizens met and discussed, designed, and prioritized performance measures to track progress in critical services, such as health care, the economy, transportation, and education. This citizen engagement process also included community leader lunches and open-forum town hall meetings where the governor asked citizens about what the state should be accountable for delivering.

Milena Neshkova and David Guo (2012), in their research about the effects of public participation on agency performance, examined data from an earlier 2005 GPP online survey that posed the following question to state transportation department officials:

> We are interested in any strategies that your agency has used to generate input from citizens concerning budget priorities, development and/or assessment. Specifically, if your agency has engaged in any of the strategies below to gain citizen input, indicate if the strategy has been useful in terms of the outcomes listed. (Check all that apply for each strategy.)

Respondents indicated which of seven strategies they used across different budget process stages (information sharing, budget discussion, budget decision, and program assessment), including: citizen surveys, budget simulations, focus groups, open forums, public hearings, citizen advisory boards, and telephone hotlines. These strategies span simple consultation (surveys and telephone hotlines) to involvement (focus groups, forums, and hearings) to collaborative (advisory boards).

These scholars emphasize their expectation of a negative association between public input in budgeting and agency performance, given that the values underscoring democratic decision making (equity and voice) conflict with those associated with administrative decision making (efficiency and effectiveness).

Neshkova and Guo (2012) measure transportation agency performance with several variables of efficiency and effectiveness. Cost efficiency is annual operating expenditures for vehicle mile traveled per state. Effectiveness is measured by road quality and safety (highway fatality rate per 1,000 million vehicle miles traveled). In several models, the scholars control for bridge and road condition, safety, urban/rural context, and program resources. Their results indicate that states are most likely to engage citizens in the budget process for information sharing, though efforts are made to engage citizens throughout the other stages. Budget simulation and contingent valuation are the least likely strategies to be used. Citizen advisory boards, citizen/client surveys, public hearings, and open forums are most likely to be engaged by these agencies across all budget process stages. Regression findings support that citizen participation in state budgeting advances organizational performance. Specifically, Neshkova and Guo (2012) find that "transportation agencies that are more open to the public and more actively seek its input achieve higher results in terms of efficiency and effectiveness" (282). This work provides statistical proof that participatory budgeting has real value for public agency performance beyond educating citizens and increasing their trust in government.

THE MEDIA AND PUBLIC BUDGETS

US Bill of Rights: Amendment I reads:

> ***Congress shall make no law*** respecting an establishment of religion, or prohibiting the free exercise thereof; or ***abridging the freedom*** of speech, or ***of the press***; or the right of the people peaceably to assemble, and to petition the Government for a redress of grievances

According to one (former) newspaper editor, "The First Amendment was given to us specifically to watchdog government" (Dorrah 2009, 26). The media exposes government information, activities, and program results to the public. The complexity of modern government organizations and the amounts of money spent by governments requires full attention by reporters to provide complete, unbiased, and timely coverage. Rachel Smolkin (2004) discusses news coverage of federal government departments in Washington, DC and quotes one reporter:

> There's no way, if you're not covering a beat fulltime, that you can keep up with what's going on and maintain sources. A lot of reporting is just keeping up with sources and decisions and policies that are under development at the departments. (46)

In the Information Age, however, traditional newspapers have been decimated and media coverage of government affairs has changed. Both of these trends have compromised the watchdog role that the media can play. Since 2007, at least two hundred newspapers around the nation have closed or stopped publishing paper copy and let go of reporting staff.[20] Jennifer Dorrah (2009) explains that many newspapers in Arizona cut reporters to the state capitol beat, leading to less coverage of state government activities. Given this, important budget and policy issues being debated in the state legislature were not brought to the public's attention. Elected officials may act differently, if out of the media spotlight. Dorrah (2009) points out that a digital news start-up comprised of several laid-off reporters eventually provided a shot in the arm for state government reporting, with one newspaper editor confirming that now, "More flashlights keep it brighter in the halls of the Legislature" (24).

Though hardcopy newspapers are folding, there are an ever-growing number of ways that the public can get news online—through any major news press organization (ABC, AP, CNN, and so forth), by social media venues, and via blogs. News can be fed into handheld devices 24/7/365 via mobile apps. The beat reporters of yesterday are today's independent bloggers, who have greater flexibility regarding what they write about as well as how they present the story to the public. Still, according to Mordecai Lee (1999), this has only empowered the media as policy entrepreneurs on par with bureaucrats and citizens—the media have become the primary venue for promoting public discourse on policy issues.

In spite of the fact that the number of ways to get the news has exploded, public perception about media credibility has tanked. In 2012, a Gallup poll found that just 40 percent of Americans claimed to have a great deal or fair amount of trust and confidence in the mass media. This increased slightly to 44 percent in 2013. Americans' trust in the media has tracked lower that it was a decade ago, with the decline in confidence evidenced in Democrats, Independents, and Republicans. The poll also found that most Americans believe that the media maintain a liberal bias (Mendes 2013).

What gets covered has changed, too. Reporters talk about having to become "ruthless" in determining story priorities and being constricted to covering the big issues of the day, which might be the budget. Even so, coverage of the budget will suffer as news stories by local reporters focus on community interests only. According to one longtime reporter in the State of Georgia:

> Papers are looking for local stories, and almost all of that is going to revolve around the [local legislative] delegation. Maybe we'll look at what the state highway folks are doing in our local area. But there will not be a lot of time to look at their overall spending plan or how

well the agencies are run. If it doesn't have a local angle, we're not going to be able to get it in the paper. (Dorrah 2009, 25)

Thus, it is not just the volume of media coverage that influences the public's knowledge about government budget and policy issues. "The breadth of coverage and the prominence of the story are equally powerful predictors of knowledge and are more important that demographic characteristics or indicators of socioeconomic status [of individuals]" (Barabas and Jerit 2009, 86). The media gravitate to high-conflict issues. John Maltese (1994) conducted an extensive study of communications and press relationships of the White House. Maltese (1994) quotes Dick Cheney regarding the hardships of governing in a society in which the media is more interested in highlighting disagreements over "the dry details of the budget" (1–2):

> It's much easier for [the media] to get into covering and focusing upon an alleged personnel clash between the secretary of defense and the secretary of state over what the arms control policy is going to be than it is to talk about the policy itself, which most of them don't understand. (1–2)

Cheney had a long career in government, including serving as chief of staff to President Gerald Ford, representative from Wyoming in the US House, secretary of defense under President George H. W. Bush, and vice president to President George W. Bush. Maltese (1994) writes about the efforts of American presidents to control the media rather the other way around—explaining that to be successful, the White House must control the president's agenda by being disciplined and unified. The media will crush a president if they get wind of disunity, confusion, or fragmented lines of communication.

Amy Jasperson and her colleagues (1998) concur regarding the influence of high-conflict issues and government budget agendas. They study the 1996 federal budget impasse that occurred in fall of 1995 to explain how the quality and quantity of news coverage influences the issues important to the American public. During this period, Republicans dismissed Democratic interest in budget balance as insincere; Democrats claimed Republicans just wanted an end to social welfare spending. Budget battles between Democratic President Bill Clinton and the Republican Congress resulted in a government shutdown November 14–19, 1995, and then from December 16, 1995 to January 6, 1996;

stop-gap funding was provided in between the shutdowns and after January 6 to get federal employees back to work.

Public polling at the time indicated a 15 percent increase in the proportion of Americans believing the federal budget deficit to be "the most important problem" of the country (from 5 percent in October to 20 percent in January). These scholars distinguish levels of intensity of budget discussions—from talks, fights, impasse, to crisis. Their findings indicate that public perception of the budget as the most important issue during the period of study shifted according to how the media framed budget events, with only the "fight" frame having significant impact on public opinion. When this frame was used, the public placed the budget deficit at the top of the list of the nation's most important problems. Salience and persuasiveness of content rises as conflict around the issue grows (Jasperson et al. 1998).

News stories about government are usually of two types. According to Lee (1999):

> [News] stories generally imply that the public administrator is a martinet who is rigidly applying a regulation or requirement instead of making an exception based on decency and reasonableness. Or, the story tends to depict a situation in a manner that suggests that this is a "problem" that the government is currently doing nothing about. The stories insinuate bureaucratic incompetence or indifference to what the authors of the stories identify as a problem. (455)

For example, in response to a news article about the pensions of bus and train drivers of the local public transportation system, a reader responded in the *Atlanta Journal-Constitution* (Letter to the Editor 2014, A12):

> The article "MARTA pensions costly" (News, January 19, 2014) was very troubling. Not because MARTA workers have a pension, but because the slant of the article implied that they did not deserve one! How many workers today can save enough money for a secure retirement considering the costs of health care, ever-rising utilities and rents or mortgages? Social Security alone does not meet the cost of bare necessities. Frankly, I am tired of articles that point to teachers, public employees and others who own or control very little as the source of our economic problems. CEOs of big companies now

earn over 354 times more than the average worker. Let's see some finger-pointing at them!

Because of the power that the media has as a policy entrepreneur that shapes public opinion, Lee (1999) suggests that bureaucrats become savvy about their relationships with reporters. He explains that the agency message should be concise, easy to report about and understand, and communicated in multiple ways and through a variety of venues. Bureaucrats should put a human face to the issue whenever possible. Also, agencies need to generate relationships with reporters to foster better understanding about the context within which agencies must manage. Lee's suggestions (1999) coincide with those of Maltese (1994) in that public agencies must get out in front of stories, be proactive about communicating with the public about ongoing activities as well as future plans—that is, they need to control the agency's agenda rather than having the media control it.

Two examples describe efforts in other countries to improve media understanding and communication about governments and budgets. Australia sequesters journalists in the early afternoon of "Budget Night" each May when the treasurer presents the budget to the Parliament. This effort, called "media lock-up," is to provide better, clearer, more consistent communication about the budget in news stories that will be published after the budget speech. Throughout the day, Treasury and Finance officials provide information to reporters and answer their questions. At a 5:00 p.m. press conference, the treasurer outlines key components of the upcoming speech. Until the treasurer begins the budget speech later that evening, journalists cannot communicate with the outside world—at the start of the speech, reporters are able to publish their stories (Blöndal et al. 2008).

In the Indian State of Gujarat, DISHA has worked in the past to make the budget more transparent and understandable to legislators, the media, and the public.[21] When budget information has not been provided by the government to DISHA, the organization has secured the information from opposition members in the legislature on the day the budget is presented. DISHA then has analyzed the information and distilled it into concise, clear, more easily understood material made accessible to all of these stakeholders (de Renzio and Krafchik 2007).

CONCLUSION

This chapter has shown you how agencies implement budgets, how citizens contribute to and collaborate on budget priorities and allocations, and what role the media plays in influencing public perceptions of government budget and policy foci. Bureaucracies are complicated organizations that have innumerable constraints regarding their activities and the individual actions of managers and staff. Bureaucrats today operate within intricate organizational networks to get work done; they must conduct continuous analyses of information—tabulating, comparing, reporting, justifying, explaining, and reacting—to navigate successfully through budget execution.

Modern governments offer many ways for citizens and community residents to have input into their budgets. Efforts are being made in developing and industrialized countries to provide these avenues for purposes of education, to empower and include people directly in the determination of government resources and spending. Doing so can improve government performance.

Public confidence in the media as a source of comprehensive and unbiased information remains extremely low. The production of news has changed dramatically and bureaucrats, especially, need to adapt to such change in order to succeed in conducting work that they are legally required to do.

DISCUSSION QUESTIONS

1. Explain Niskansen's characterization of bureaucrats as budget maximizing, as well as critiques of that view. How have changes in the current economy and modern management practices altered the budget behavior of bureaucrats since Niskansen first presented his theory?

2. Why has the US federal government attempted to link strategic planning and budget execution through GPRA and other laws? Justify your response.

3. Discuss methods of public participation in government budgeting. What are the benefits and challenges associated with these different approaches?

4. Of the participation approaches employed in India and Tanzania, which one captured your interest the most? Conduct some research to find out about other methods of citizen input into public budgets that have been used in developing countries.

5. How do you become informed about important public budgeting and policy issues? That is, does the news you access come from journalists, bloggers, political consultants, or entertainers? Explain and compare the ways you think these news sources filter the information that you are receiving.

6. Discuss the strategies that agency officials should use to engage the media to communicate about their budgets and policies.

NOTES

1. See http://www.opm.gov/policy-data-oversight/data-analysis-documentation /federal-employment-reports/historical-tables/total-government-employment-since-1962/

2. See http://www.osec.doc.gov/bmi/BUDGET/HANDBOOK/Chp5.pdf

3. See http://www.whitehouse.gov/omb/expectmore/part.html

4. See http://www.whitehouse.gov/sites/default/files/omb/assets/a11_current_ year/a11_2013.pdf

5. See http://www.osec.doc.gov/cfo/documents/Current_CFOASA_Organization _Chart.pdf

6. To learn more about the US federal financial management architecture, see http://www.whitehouse.gov/omb/financial_ffs_financial/

7. See http://www.imf.org/external/pubs/ft/expend/guide4.htm

8. See www.pefa.org

9. To view rules and updates, see http://finmin.nic.in/the_ministry/dept_ expenditure/gfrs/index.asp

10. See http://finmin.nic.in/the_ministry/dept_expenditure/acts_codes/index .asp

11. The Recovery Act of 2009 attempted to provide substantial federal funding relief, more quickly and directly, to state and local governments to combat the effects on their budgets of the Great Recession that officially began in December, 2007. Recipients of these federal contracts, grants and loans were held to extensive requirements related to fund use, accounting, and reporting. Reporting of funds received is provided at www.recovery.gov

12. See http://www.whitehouse.gov/omb/recovery_default/

13. Available at: http://www.recovery.gov/arra/FAQ/Pages/RecipientReporting.aspx

14. See http://www.youtube.com/watch?v=9z24mGAJAVM&feature=c4-overview -vl&list=PL7381987D89AA7ABD

15. See http://www.whitehouse.gov/omb/financial_fin_single_audit. A quick search of US federal domestic assistance programs indicates the billions of federal dollars provided to subnational governments, universities, colleges and schools, non-profits and other entities. This money must be accounted for through periodic reporting during budget execution and through pre-scribed audits. Search the Catalog of Federal Domestic Assistance by going to https://www.cfda.gov/

16. For example, to search the US Federal Audit Clearinghouse to find audit information for a recipient government, agency or other entity, go to https://harvester.census.gov/facweb/Default.aspx. Tap onto the link, "Find Audit Information," Federal Audit Clearinghouse IDDS and under search options, tap onto number 4: Entity Search. In the first space of the next page, type in any US local government and state and you will be provided with all the single audits associated with that government and relegated to the federal single audit process.

17. See City of Lakeside, Georgia, http://lakesidecityalliance.org/wp-content/ uploads/2013/02/lakeside-final_112013.pdf; City of Briarcliff, Georgia, http://briarcliffga.org/wp-content/uploads/Briarcliff_Report_-_Final_12_ 17_13.pdf; and City of Tucker, Georgia, http://tucker2014.com/docs/City_ of_Tucker_Feasibility_Study.pdf

18. The West Bengal Gram Panchayat Accounts, Audit and Budget Rules of 2007; see Chapter XIII, p. 39 at http://www.siprd.org.in/upload_file/pri_ rd_acts/WB%20Panchayat%20GP%20Accounts%20Audit%20budget%20 %20rule_07.pdf

19. See http://www.odi.org.uk/opinion/7859-service-delivery-information- communication-technology-tanzania-twaweza-citizen-voice

20. See *Paper Cuts* at http://newspaperlayoffs.com/

21. Today there is more budget information available at the Gujarat Finance Department website. See http://financedepartment.gujarat.gov.in/budget/ budget13-14.php

REFERENCES

Baiocchi, B., and J. Lerner. 2007. "Could Participatory Budgeting Work in the United States?" *The Good Society* 16 (1): 8–13.

Barabas, J., and J. Jerit. 2009. "Estimating the Causal Effects of Media Coverage on Policy-Specific Knowledge." *American Journal of Political Science* 53 (1): 73–89.

Bartle, J. R., and R. L. Korosec. 1996. "Are City Managers Greedy Bureaucrats?" *Public Administration Quarter* 20 (1): 89–102.

Bhat, A. S., S. Colhar, A. Chellappa, and H. Anand. 2004. "Building Budgets from Below." *Economic and Political Weekly* 39 (44): 4803–4810.

Blöndal, J. R., D. Bergvall, I. Hawkesworth, and R. Deighton-Smith. 2008. "Budgeting in Australia." *OECD Journal on Budgeting* 8 (2): 1–64.

Bowling, C. J., C.-L. Cho, and D. S. Wright. 2004. "Establishing a Continuum from Minimizing to Maximizing Bureaucrats: State Agency Head Preferences for Governmental Expansion—A Typology of Administrator Growth Postures, 1964–1998." *Public Administration Review* 64 (4): 489–499.

Breton, A., and R. Wintrobe. 1975. "The Equilibrium Size of a Budget-Maximizing Bureau: A Note on Niskanen's Theory of Bureaucracy." *Journal of Political Economy* 83 (1): 195–208.

Buchanan, J. M., and G. Tullock. 1962. *The Calculus of Consent: Logical Foundations of Constitutional Democracy.* Ann Arbor: University of Michigan Press.

De Renzio, P., and W. Krafchik. 2007. "Lessons from the Field: The Impact of Civil Society Budget Analysis and Advocacy in Six Countries." International Budget Project. Available at http://www.internationalbudget.org/wp-content/uploads/Lessons-from-the-Field-The-Impact-of-Civil-Society-Budget-Analysis-and-Advocacy-in-Six-Countries.pdf

Denhardt, R. B., and J. V. Denhardt. 2000. "The New Public Service: Serving Rather than Steering." *Public Administration Review* 60 (6): 549–559.

Dolan, J. 2002. "The Budget-Maximizing Bureaucrat? Empirical Evidence from the Senior Executive Service." *Public Administration Review* 62 (1): 42–50.

Dorrah, J. 2009. "Statehouse Exodus." *American Journalism Review,* April/May, 22–29.

Dunleavy, P. 1985. "Bureaucrats, Budgets and the Growth of the State: Reconstructing an Instrumental Model." *British Journal of Political Science* 15 (3): 299–328.

Dunleavy, P. 1991. *Democracy, Bureaucracy and Public Choice: Economic Explanations in Political Science.* London: Harvester Wheatsheaf.

Franklin, A. L., A. T. Ho, and C. Ebdon. 2009. "Participatory Budgeting in Midwestern States: Democratic Connection or Citizen Disconnection?" *Public Budgeting & Finance* 29 (3): 52–73.

Gilmour, J. B., and D. E. Lewis. 2006. "Assessing Performance Budgeting at OMB: The Influence of Politics, Performance, and Program Size." *Journal of Public Administration Research and Theory* 16 (2): 169–186.

Government of Guatemala, Minister of Public Finance. February 2013. "Report of the Performance of the Management of Public Finance, PEFA Final Report." Assessment Report available at http://www.pefa.org/en/assessment/gt-feb13-pfmpr-public-en

Jasperson, A. E., D. V. Shah, M. Watts, R. J. Faber, and D. P. Fan. 1998. "Framing and the Public Agenda: Media Effects on the Importance of the Federal Budget Deficit." *Political Communication* 15 (2): 205–224.

Jena, P. R. 2010. "India Public Expenditure and Financial Accountability Public Financial Management Performance Assessment Report." New Delhi: National Institute of Public Finance and Policy, March 19. Assessment Report available at http://www.pefa.org/en/assessment/mar10-pfmpr-public-en

Joyce, P. G. 2011. "The Obama Administration and PBB: Building on the Legacy of Federal Performance-Informed Budgeting?" *Public Administration Review* 71 (3): 356–367.

Kaminsky, John. 2010. "GPRA Modernization Act of 2010 Explained." IBM Center for the Business of Government. Available at http://www.businessofgovernment.org/report/gpra-modernization-act-2010-explained

Kapur, A. 2010. "Prying Open India's Vast Bureaucracy." *The New York Times*, June 17. Available at http://www.nytimes.com/2010/06/18/world/asia/18iht-letter.html?_r=0

Khademian, A. M., and S. O. Choi. 2011. "Virginia's Implementation of the American Recovery and Reinvestment Act: Forging a New Intergovernmental Partnership." IBM Business of Government. Available at http://www.businessofgovernment.org/article/virginia%E2%80%99s-implementation-american-recovery-and-reinvestment-act-forging-new-intergovernment

Lee, M. 1999. "Reporters and Bureaucrats: Public Relations Counter-Strategies by Public Administrators in an Era of Media Disinterest in Government." *Public Relations Review* 25 (4): 451–463.

Letter to the Editor. 2014. "Re: MARTA Pensions Costly." *Atlanta Journal-Constitution,* January 23, Editorial Page, A12.

Loomis, J. B. 1987. "Economic Efficiency Analysis, Bureaucrats, and Budgets: A Test of Hypotheses." *Western Journal of Agricultural Economics* 12 (1): 27–34.

Lu, Y., and K. Willoughby. 2012. "Performance Budgeting in the States: An Assessment." IBM *The Business of Government*, Fall/Winter 71–75.

Maltese, J. A. 1994. *Spin Control: The White House Office of Communications and the Management of Presidential News.* Chapel Hill: University of North Carolina Press.

Mandhana, N. 2012. "How India's 'Right to Information' Laws Put Power in the People's Hands." *Time.com*, June 14. Available at http://world.time.com/2012/06/14/how-indias-right-to-information-laws-put-power-in-the-peoples-hands/

Mendes, E. 2013. "In U.S., Trust in Media Recovers Slightly from All-Time Low." Gallup, September 19. Available at http://www.gallup.com/poll/164459/trust-media-recovers-slightly-time-low.aspx?version=print

Metzenbaum, S. H. 2009. "Performance Management Recommendations for the New Administration." IBM Center for the Business of Government. Available at http://www.businessofgovernment.org/sites/default/files/PerformanceManagement.pdf

Moynihan, D. P. 2013 "Does Public Service Motivation Lead to Budget Maximization? Evidence from an Experiment." *International Public Management Journal* 16 (2): 179–196.

Neshkova, M. I., and H. D. Guo. 2012. "Public Participation and Organizational Performance: Evidence from State Agencies." *Journal of Public Administration Research and Theory* 22 (2): 267–288.

Niskanen, W. A., Jr. 1971. *Bureaucracy and Representative Government.* Chicago: Aldine-Atherton.

_____. 1986. "Economists and Politicians." *Journal of Policy Analysis and Management* 5 (2): 234–244.

Rainey, H. G., and B. Bozeman. 2000. "Comparing Public and Private Organizations: Empirical Research and the Power of the A Priori." *Journal of Public Administration Research and Theory* 10 (2): 447–470.

Shea, R. T. 2008. "Performance Budgeting in the United States." *OECD Journal on Budgeting* 8 (1).

Sigelman, L. 1986. "The Bureaucrat as Budget Maximizer: An Assumption Examined." *Public Budgeting & Finance* 6 (1): 50–59.

Smolkin, R. 2004. "Covering Federal Agencies." *American Journalism Review*, February/March: 46–49.

Torpy, B., and J. Edwards. 2014. "New Cities Reignite Debate About Race." *Atlanta Journal-Constitution*, January 26 A1 and A14.

U.S. Government Accountability Office. 2013. "Results-Oriented Government: GPRA Has Established a Solid Foundation for Achieving Greater Results." GAO-04–38, March. Available at http://www.gao.gov/new.items/d0438.pdf

Wagle, S., and P. Shah. 2003. "Case Study 2-Porto Alegre, Brazil: participatory Approaches in Budgeting and Public Expenditure Management." Participation and Civic Engagement Group, The World Bank, March, Note No. 71. Available at https://openknowledge.worldbank.org/bitstream/handle/10986/11309/274620PAPER0snd71.txt?sequence=2

Wampler, B., and M. Touchton. 2014. "Brazil Lets Its Citizens Make Decisions About City Budgets. Here's What Happened." *Washington Post,* January 22. Available at http://www.washingtonpost.com/blogs/monkey-cage/wp/2014/01/22/brazil-let-its-citizens-make-decisions-about-city-budgets-heres-what-happened/

Wild, Leni. 2013. "Using Information and Communication Technologies to Improve Service Delivery." Leni Wild interviews Mushi Elvis Leonard, September 30. Available at http://www.odi.org.uk/opinion/7859-service-delivery-information-communication-technology-tanzania-twaweza-citizen-voice

Willoughby, K., and J. L. Gomez. June 2011. "GP Financial Management Capacity and PRI Financial Management Reform Efforts in West Bengal." International Studies Program Working Paper 11-16.

Wogan, J. B. December 2013. "The People's Banker: 2013 Honoree: José Cisneros San Francisco Treasurer." *Governing*. Available at http://www.governing.com/topics/mgmt/gov-2013-poy.html

Budget Mechanics and Reforms

Reforms are innovations prompted by disparities between existing conditions and preferred states that actors believe are attainable.

—Matthew Dull, 2006

LEARNING OBJECTIVES

After reading this chapter, you should be able to

- Discern various budget types used by governments to budget

- Access government budgets, determine budget format(s), and understand the information included in budget documents

- Understand public budgeting cycles and distinguish timelines by level of government

- List some current best practices related to public budgeting; articulate one or two components relevant to each practice

- Distinguish and characterize different public budgeting reforms

- List various components of modern performance budgeting; investigate a government budgeting system to determine if it engages any of these components

---

Thus far, we have explained public budgeting in terms of the legal frameworks established for governance. These frameworks provide for the budgeting powers, roles, and responsibilities of public officials charged with governing. Previous chapters discussed political and other influences of those in the legislative, executive, and judiciary branches of government on the budgetary process and budget outcomes. Bureaucratic influences, the input of citizens, and media sway about government activities and budgets have also been introduced. This chapter explains public budgeting mechanics—the different types of budgets that exist and the accounting of various types of public expenditure. In addition, the chapter describes government budget cycles and timelines. This is followed by a review of best practices of public budgeting that are promoted by professional organizations, standards setting boards, and governments themselves. The chapter ends with an overview of several budget reforms that have been attempted by governments around the world and at every level.

BUDGET TYPES

Governments employ people to provide multiple services and to implement programs; governments build roads, hospitals, university dormitories, and parking decks. The following section explains how spending is accounted for in these different circumstances. Operating and capital budgets are distinguished and various types of budget format are compared. Governments must use a variety of budget types and most engage a hybrid budget format to track and manage revenues and expenditures for the conduct of these diverse activities and projects.

Operating and Capital Budgets

Governments spend for routine operations (operating budgets). Spending may be to pay for the provision of housing or health services, or environmental, recreational, and educational programs. Entitlement spending involves making transfer payments from government(s) to the individuals or entities eligible—a subnational government might receive funding for an entitlement program that is passed through from the central government, administered by the subnational government, then sent to and received by those eligible. Spending for operations also includes the salaries of government employees to carry out the work associated with determined policies and programs. Fund flows in the operating budget account for the day-to-day recurring costs of conducting government business.

Governments also pay to build infrastructure—roads, bridges, buildings, sewage treatment plants, water utilities, recreational facilities, and the like. Spending for these kinds of long-term, expensive projects, which will provide benefits to the public well into the future, necessitates the conduct of capital budgeting. A capital budget separates the financing of capital or investment expenditures from current or operating expenditures and excludes them from the calculation of any operating deficit or surplus. Capital financing by governments may include cash (pay as you go), debt issuance, intergovernmental grants or loans, or funds from a reserve or sinking fund (or some combination of these methods). Debt financing requires an assessment of the time value of money, to account for debt servicing (payback) over time. The Congressional Budget Office (CBO 2008) defines depreciation as "the systematic method for assigning cost of asset to each period of its useful life" (8) and contrasts straight-line depreciation with spending on intangible investments. According to the CBO (2008):

- In straight-line depreciation, an item costs $1 million to purchase and has ten-year useful life and is depreciated at $100,000 a year; depreciation is reported as expense (amortized) at that annual rate for the life of the asset.

- Alternatively, spending on intangible federal investments appears as an expense in the period in which it occurs, rather than amortized over time.

To learn more about different types of public budgets, simply search for one online, download the document and read it. Government budgets provide a wealth of information and they are available at your fingertips. For example, you can access almost any government website, search for the budget or finance office, and quickly find agency budget requests and the chief executive budget recommendation. You can also go to the website of a government legislature and search for budget laws, then download end-of-year financial reports from government auditor offices. The following documents are provided by the State of Wyoming:[1]

- 2015–2016 Agency Budget Requests: https://sites.google.com/a/wyo.gov/ai/budget-division/budget-fiscal-years/2015-2016-budget/bfy1516-individual-agency-budgets

- 2015–2016 Biennium Governor's Budget Submitted to the Legislature: https://drive.google.com/file/d/0B9L2AFFD9o_LbXJvZTlILTRMd28/edit?pli=1

- An Appropriations Bill: http://legisweb.state.wy.us/2014/Enroll/HB0001.pdf

- 2012 Comprehensive Annual Financial Report: sao.state.wy.us/CAFR/cafr_report.htm#cafr2012

The Wyoming Governor's Budget Recommendation provides a good reader's guide to the state's budget that is replicated in Figure 10.1. The various descriptions provide ways of tabulating budgets—in dollars for Division total, object of expenditure, and source of funding, and numerically for employees. The object series relates to the government's chart of accounts; spending for specific lines, such as personal services (0100), can be aggregated for all agencies and tracked through the government's financial information management system and accounting structure for management and reporting purposes.

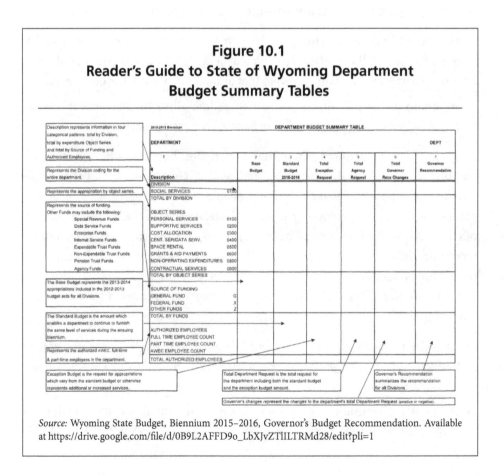

Figure 10.1
Reader's Guide to State of Wyoming Department Budget Summary Tables

Source: Wyoming State Budget, Biennium 2015–2016, Governor's Budget Recommendation. Available at https://drive.google.com/file/d/0B9L2AFFD9o_LbXJvZTlILTRMd28/edit?pli=1

Budget Formats

The most elementary type of budget format is the line item or object of expenditure. Appropriations by line item afford the legislative branch the greatest amount of control over executive agency spending because legislation spells out specific spending amounts or limits for individual objects by agency. Usually, all of these documents exhibited from Wyoming—agency requests, the chief executive's recommendation, the legislative appropriation and accounting records—are provided in multiple formats. If you examine a portion of Wyoming's appropriation bill (Figure 10.2), you will notice the total appropriation of +$56 million is broken down by programs, not objects of expenditure. Program budgets include information about revenues and expenditures for the major

---

Figure 10.2
State of Wyoming, 2014 Budget Appropriation, Section 007, Military Department

SIXTY-FIRST LEGISLATURE OF THE STATE OF WYOMING
2012 BUDGET SESSION

APPROPRIATION FOR	GENERAL FUND $	FEDERAL FUND $	OTHER FUNDS $	TOTAL APPROPRIATION $
Section 007. WYOMING MILITARY DEPARTMENT				
PROGRAM				
Military Dept Operations	14,466,055			14,466,055
Air National Guard	815,105	10,212,972		11,028,077
Camp Guernsey	79,187		800,200 AG	879,387
Army National Guard [1,2]		21,834,403	4,629,126 85	26,463,529
Veterans' Services	2,171,603	165,223	7,500 SR	2,344,326
Oregon Trail Cemetery	573,181		20,000 SR	593,181
Mil Support to Civilians	183,006			183,006
Civil Air Patrol	213,459			213,459
TOTALS	18,501,596	32,212,598	5,456,826	56,171,020

AUTHORIZED EMPLOYEES

Full Time	226
Part Time	47
TOTAL	273

1. Notwithstanding W.S. 19-9-704, the national guard youth challenge program is hereby authorized to continue operating until June 30, 2014.

2. Notwithstanding W.S. 19-9-702, for every forty cents ($0.40) of federal funds appropriated to the national guard youth challenge program, the department may expend state funds appropriated for this program in an amount not to exceed sixty cents ($0.60), or such other minimum amount as necessary to qualify for the appropriation of federal funds.

Source: Original Senate Enrolled Act No. 29, 61st Legislature of the State of Wyoming, 2012 Budget Session, 10. Available at http://legisweb.state.wy.us/budget/2013/2012SF0001.pdf

activities of an agency. This format helps managers focus on resources and costs of programs for good comparability.

Other types of budget formats include lump sum (appropriation for an entire agency or division); performance (measures of agency program and service performance or results included in budget documents and linked to budget numbers); and zero- or target-based (necessitate the preparation of budget requests at various levels of spending, within spending ceilings or targets or levels of accomplishment). Budget format specifies what kinds of information must be included in required budget documents throughout the budgeting process, including agency requests, executive recommendations, the budget legislation (appropriation), budget execution (expenditure) reports, and end-of-year evaluations and audits. Budget formats should not be confused with reforms related to the budget process (these are considered later in this chapter). For example, current Georgia Governor Nathan Deal has emphasized zero-based budgeting for the state.[2] This type of budgeting is not a budget format, but a process implemented for the purpose of assessing the efficiency and effectiveness of state programs vis-à-vis their legal requirements, purposes and costs. This is a type of evaluation of program expenditures, efficiency, and effectiveness that is conducted currently in Georgia for selected agencies each year and by the governor's budget office, which helps in the development of the governor's budget that is submitted to the General Assembly.

Other budget concepts highlighted in the reader's guide from Wyoming's budget include the budget base—in this case, the previous year's appropriation. Incrementalism is founded on the concept of budget base and agreement on the base. Although budget base is defined in this instance as previous appropriation, it just as easily could be defined as "standard budget," or what is defined by Wyoming as spending necessary to provide the same level of service as the previous fiscal year (in the case of Wyoming, the previous biennium). Problems with budget deliberation and agreement surface when considerations of the budget base are different among the responsible decision makers.

Figure 10.1 also highlights an "exception" budget, as budgets often present a continuation (status quo) and expansion (new spending) budget. The continuation budget regards budget base or the standard budget (as defined here) or maybe some other calculation based on last year's budget. An expansion budget would include requests for new or added spending. Undoubtedly, a public agency or program today that seeks expansion, given the fiscal environment (muted economic growth almost five years out of the Great Recession), would need to indicate some sort of trade-off of the added spending with increased revenues, borrowing, expenditure cuts, or some combination of these strategies for success. Mandated expenditures, however, may not be held to such strictures.

BUDGET CYCLES AND TIMELINES

Originally, governments established their fiscal years to accommodate farming schedules and crop cycles. Legislatures would meet during the months of the year in which members had no harvesting commitments and the start of the budget year would occur some months following the close of legislative sessions (hence legislative sessions occurred in the winter and fiscal years began in the summer). Many governments have changed their original fiscal year to (1) provide more time for budget deliberations (an initial thought behind the Congressional Budget and Impoundment Control Act of 1974 in the United States); (2) better coordinate with upper-level governments (a few years ago, the City of Atlanta changed its budget year, in part, to coincide with the state's July to June fiscal year); and (3) coincide with the fiscal years of donors (as in Papua New Guinea, where donor funds greatly influence the economy) (Tarschys 2002).

Among the countries of interest here, Brazil, Guatemala, and Italy have fiscal years that begin January 1 and end December 31. Guatemala presents a schematic of its budget cycle in its 2012 Citizen Budget (see Figure 10.3). India's fiscal year begins April 1 and ends March 30. Australia and Tanzania have fiscal years that begin July 1 and end June 30. The United States' fiscal year was changed by the 1974 Congressional Budget and Impoundment Control Act, originally July 1–June 30 to October 1–September 30. Each budget cycle follows a somewhat similar path that includes revenue and expenditure estimate development, deliberation and reestimating within the executive branch, then presentation by the executive of the budget to parliament or the congress. In India, the Union Budget is presented to parliament the last day of February, just one month before the fiscal year begins, thus constricting legislative deliberation. In Tanzania, the start of the fiscal year is overlaid by legislative debate about the budget, so that the fiscal year begins before the budget is passed.

Table 10.1 presents the budget cycles for the City of New York, the State of Georgia, and the US federal government. What should be immediately apparent

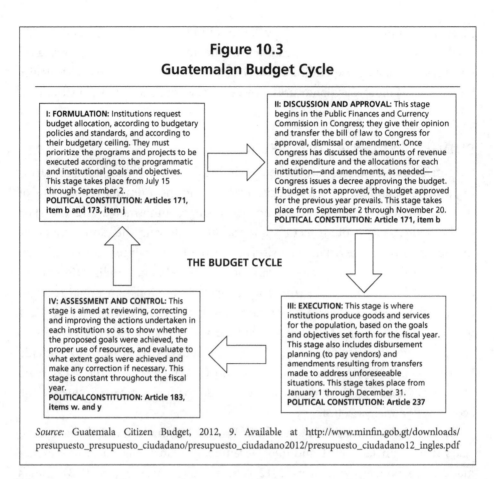

Figure 10.3
Guatemalan Budget Cycle

I: FORMULATION: Institutions request budget allocation, according to budgetary policies and standards, and according to their budgetary ceiling. They must prioritize the programs and projects to be executed according to the programmatic and institutional goals and objectives. This stage takes place from July 15 through September 2.
POLITICAL CONSTITUTION: Articles 171, item b and 173, item j

II: DISCUSSION AND APPROVAL: This stage begins in the Public Finances and Currency Commission in Congress; they give their opinion and transfer the bill of law to Congress for approval, dismissal or amendment. Once Congress has discussed the amounts of revenue and expenditure and the allocations for each institution—and amendments, as needed—Congress issues a decree approving the budget. If budget is not approved, the budget approved for the previous year prevails. This stage takes place from September 2 through November 20.
POLITICAL CONSTITUTION: Article 171, item b

THE BUDGET CYCLE

IV: ASSESSMENT AND CONTROL: This stage is aimed at reviewing, correcting and improving the actions undertaken in each institution so as to show whether the proposed goals were achieved, the proper use of resources, and evaluate to what extent goals were achieved and make any correction if necessary. This stage is constant throughout the fiscal year.
POLITICALCONSTITUTION: Article 183, items w. and y

III: EXECUTION: This stage is where institutions produce goods and services for the population, based on the goals and objectives set forth for the fiscal year. This stage also includes disbursement planning (to pay vendors) and amendments resulting from transfers made to address unforeseeable situations. This stage takes place from January 1 through December 31.
POLITICAL CONSTITUTION: Article 237

Source: Guatemala Citizen Budget, 2012, 9. Available at http://www.minfin.gob.gt/downloads/presupuesto_presupuesto_ciudadano/presupuesto_ciudadano2012/presupuesto_ciudadano12_ingles.pdf

upon careful analysis of this table is the short timeframe for budget development and passage at the local level of government relative to that at state or federal levels. Local budget executive development and legislative deliberation in New York City takes about six months; the process at the state level takes about twelve months and at the federal level it takes about eighteen months. Of course, these timelines do not account for periodic breakdowns in negotiations, political gridlock, or crises that can stall movement from one phase to the next, such as a natural disaster or international conflict. Also, at least in the United States, a local government may have a January 1–December 31 fiscal year, its home state's fiscal year might be July 1–June 30, and the federal fiscal year is October 1–September 30. Three different fiscal years can wreak havoc on budget planning by lower-level governments regarding programming dependent upon intergovernmental grants, loans, and other funds.

Table 10.1

Budget Timelines of United States Governments

Month	New York City	State of Georgia	U.S. Federal Government
1	Mayor releases preliminary budget for FY1 Community Board review of preliminary budget (FY1 budget)	Agencies are spending FY budget, preparing to spend FY1 budget that begins in 6 months, and yet to receive guidelines for FY2 budget Governor's Office of Planning and Budget (OPB) issues strategic plan guidelines to agencies	Agencies are spending FY budget, preparing to spend FY1 budget that begins in 8 months, and yet to receive guidelines for FY2 budget
2	Borough Boards submit their priorities for FY1 budget to the Mayor and City Council	Agencies review and develop strategic plans	President submits FY1 budget to Congress Office of Planning and Budget (OMB) issues planning guidance to agencies for FY2 budget For next 8 months, congressional phase of FY1 budget deliberations; agencies will interact with Congress, justifying and explaining President's FY1 budget
3	City Council submission of the Operating Budget of the Council Borough President's recommendation on the FY1 budget City Council holds FY1 budget hearings and recommendations		Agencies begin and continue preparing FY2 budget requests Congressional deliberation of FY1 budget

(Continued)

Table 10.1 *Continued*

Month	New York City	State of Georgia	U.S. Federal Government
4	Mayor's submission of 10-Year Capital Strategy (odd years) Mayor's Executive Budget and Message submitted for FY1 Expense and Capital Budget Borough allocation recalculated	Incorporate laws passed and fiscal notes (from current legislative session) into preparation of FY1 budget plans	
5	City Council hearings on the Executive Budget for FY1	Agencies' 4 year strategic plans due to OPB OPB prepares budget development instructions for FY2	
6	FY1 budget Adopted Tax Fixing Resolutions	Agency annual operating budgets (AOB) for FY1 budget are approved by OPB	President submits midsession review to Congress re: FY1 budget Agencies continue preparing FY2 budget requests
7	*New Fiscal Year Begins* (FY1 budget starts)	*New Fiscal Year Begins* (FY1 budget starts) OPB and agencies discuss strategy for FY2 budget	OMB issues annual update to Circular A-11, with detailed instructions for submitting budget data and material for agency FY2 budget requests
8		By end of the month, agency budget requests for FY2 are due to OPB FY budget actuals are fed into the system for OPB to use to review FY2 budget requests	Agencies submit apportionment requests to OMB for each budget account re: FY1 budget

#			
9	Community Boards release their budget priorities for FY2 to the Mayor and Borough Presidents Mayor submits Capital Commitment Plan	OPB analyzes agency FY2 budget requests OPB continues to monitor FY1 budgets through review of AOBs and expenditure analyses	OMB apportions available funds to agencies by time period, program, project, or activity re: FY1 budget Agencies submit FY2 budget requests to OMB
10		Prepare OPB FY2 budget recommendation	OMB reviews FY2 agency budget requests re: President's priorities, program performance, and budget constraints *New Fiscal Year Begins* (FY1 budget starts)
11	Comptroller's Report on Actual Revenues for Previous Year	OPB develops Governor's FY2 Budget Recommendation	President decides on FY2 agency budget requests
12	Draft 10-Year Capital Strategy by City Planning Commission (CPC) and Office of Management and Budget (even years)	Program assessments and quarterly expenditure analyses are fed into OPB budget analyses OPB finalizes Governor's FY2 budget Recommendation Financial audit of FY budget should be complete by end of month	OMB informs agencies of FY2 decisions (called OMB "passback") Agencies can appeal FY2 "passback" to OMB director and sometimes President directly
13	Mayor releases preliminary budget for FY2 Community Board review of preliminary budget (FY2 budget)	Governor's FY2 Budget Recommendation submitted to state legislature General Assembly members analyze legislation, attend committee meetings and track appropriations and deliberate about FY2 budget	Agencies are spending FY2 budget, preparing to spend FY2 budget that begins in 8 months, and yet to receive guidelines for FY3 budget
14	Borough Boards submit their priorities for FY2 budget to the Mayor and City Council	Amended budget for FY1 is passed	President submits FY1 budget to Congress Office of Planning and Budget (OMB) issues planning guidance to agencies for FY2 budget For next 8 months, congressional phase of FY1 budget deliberations; agencies will interact with Congress, justifying and explaining President's FY1 budget

(Continued)

Table 10.1 Continued

Month	New York City	State of Georgia	U.S. Federal Government
15	City Council submission of the Operating Budget of the Council	FY2 budget is passed	Agencies begin and continue preparing FY3 budget requests
	Borough President's recommendation on the FY2 budget		Congressional deliberation of FY2 budget
	City Council holds FY2 budget hearings and recommendations		

Sources: For New York City Budget Cycle, go to http://www.nyc.gov/html/omb/html/about/cycle.shtml; for State of Georgia Budget Cycle, go to http://opb.georgia.gov/sites/opb.georgia.gov/files/imported/vgn/images/portal/cit_1210/44/31/162982494ga_budget_cycle.pdf; for US Federal Government Budget Cycle, go to https://www.fas.org/sgp/crs/misc/98-721.pdf

BEST PRACTICES

The Government Finance Officers Association (GFOA) that was introduced to you in chapter 4, provides guidance on "best practices" of public budgeting and financial management. As noted in the introductory chapter of this book, there is no one best way to budget and no one government budgets best. Still, governments consult associations such as GFOA, as they are mindful of professional standards in managing and advancing their budgeting systems. If you review the very lengthy list of budget processes covered by the GFOA,[3] you should get a sense of the innumerable parts to these systems.

The Government Performance Project[4] that has been described in earlier chapters was a periodic survey conducted by The Pew Charitable Trusts that focused on a number of these best practices to measure management capacity in US state governments. Management practices related to budgeting and financial management are highlighted in this section.

Multiyear Perspective

Budgets are plans and a foundational aspect of governmental functioning regards the engagement of a long-term planning orientation to reach budget and policy goals. In the budgeting arena, and at a most basic of level, this means accurately forecasting revenues and estimating expenditures. Governments must determine where they will get the money to pay their employees, to pay for equipment and supplies necessary to conduct services and programs, to build roads and bridges, and essentially, to honor the fiscal obligations inherent in policies and laws established to date. Best practices suggest the conduct of making estimates that are thorough, accurate, and transparent and for multiple years. Making thorough revenue forecasts requires assessment of all revenue sources engaged and using realistic assumptions about the economic, fiscal, demographic, and legal circumstances related to those resources over a determined period of time.

Analysts in legislatures often draw up notes or briefs that measure the fiscal costs associated with legislation being considered. Most state governments today prepare tax expenditure or exemption reports or budgets that attempt to quantify concessions in tax code that represent foregone revenue by the government; the tax code is used to promote a specific policy outcome or activity.[5] In the US Congress, all bills reported out of committee are analyzed to determine their effect on federal revenues and expenditures. Former director of the

Congressional Budget Office (CBO) Rudolf Penner (2003) explains that "the Joint Committee on Taxation considers bills that affect major revenue sources, while the Congressional Budget Office scores bills' spending impact along with revenues from less important sources like import tariffs" (27). In this briefing, Penner discusses the intricacies of the scoring process, often conducted by numerous analysts in both offices, focusing on different provisions of the same bill and accounting for a multitude of factors. The process, not surprisingly, is often politicized as members of Congress and others push for preferred numbers. Penner also explains that the call for and use of dynamic scoring—analyses that incorporate macroeconomic effects—is no panacea for unrealistic or incomplete results. Determining how human beings will behave in light of government fiscal policy changes is both art and science, and not an exact science, at that.

Regarding revenue forecasts, accuracy requires consistently looking back to check if past estimates equate well with actual revenues collected or spending that has occurred. Variances between estimates and actuals need to be investigated and explained. According to Kerry Jacobs (2008), "the most interesting aspect of the budget process is not the budget itself but the deviations from the budget (known as the variances)" (75). These variances can alert to problems with meeting policy goals, cost issues, or even that a policy issue meant to be addressed with the spending has begun to disappear or already has. Certainly, consistently overestimating revenues means trouble later on in the budget process. Appropriations that have been based on inflated revenue forecasts inevitably lead to fiscal belt tightening; there will only be losers and no winners in this situation. Surprisingly, consistently underestimating revenues can be problematic, too. Craig Kammholz and Craig Maher (2008) point out that consistently underestimating revenue usually leads to replenishment and even overstocking of reserves. Many governments have rainy day or budget stabilization funds to help smooth the way in periods of fiscal stress. Once these reserve funds are fully stocked, as tax receipts exceed expectations, Kammholz and Maher (2008) suggest that the "risk of underestimating revenues is often excessive taxation" (286). Should taxpayers get wind of overstocked reserves, or consistently high unrestricted fund balances, there will be calls for tax cuts or increased spending for new or expanded programs.

Planning for and calculating reliable and valid estimates of long-term liabilities falls into this area of best practice as well. Governments are responsible for significant capital infrastructure as well as for the retirement benefits of their employees and thus need to consider realistic and timely valuations of these long-term obligations. Management of a reasonable level of debt means maintaining low credit risk. As indicated in earlier chapters, subnational governments in the United States have legal ceilings on the amounts and types of debt that they can incur. Governments that borrow are subjected to credit risk assessments; higher credit scores mean lower borrowing costs.

Results-Oriented Budgeting

Best practices suggest that governments should strive to develop budgeting systems that are "results oriented." This is reminiscent of Georgia Governor Deal's effort to employ a zero-based approach to the evaluation of a sample of state agencies each year. A results orientation means consideration of the impacts of government spending, activities, services, and programs. Often, the question asked is, "What is the return on [government] investment?" The city of Norfolk, Virginia, provides a performance "dashboard" with statistics on a number of capital projects and the status of each.[6] This dashboard can be quickly scanned to find projects that are completely or almost completely constructed versus those just out of design and into the contracting phases. In the state of Missouri, Governor Jay Nixon has tied funding for higher education to targeted goals for student retention, progression, and graduation, with an eye toward improving student learning and increasing institutional fiscal responsibility and efficiency.[7] Colleges and universities in Missouri that provide evidence of meeting targets have the chance to increase their state funding through the governor's performance-based funding model.

Other best practices related to budgeting for results include passing the budget on time (before the start of the fiscal year) and providing opportunities for citizen input into the budgeting process. The previous chapter provided a number of examples of citizen influence and involvement in the budget process and a few more will be examined in this chapter in the section on budgeting reforms. Regarding passing the budget on time, we only need to recall the gridlock of the US federal government to understand the problems associated with deferring budget decisions and the uncertainty of contingency budgeting that ensues.

Budgeting for results regards the accessibility and understandability of budget information. The Center for Digital Government presents an annual award to US governments for Web and digital achievements. In 2013, the Center picked the State of Tennessee (http://www.tennessee.gov/), Alameda County in

California (http://www.acgov.org/), and Austin, Texas (http://austintexas.gov/) as digital leaders. Generally, the websites of these governments avoid clutter and present information clearly and concisely. It should be simple for individuals to navigate government portals and access documents and services easily; this is particularly essential for government budget documents and financial reports.

Structural Balance

Best practices of budgeting and financial management inherently regard reaching and maintaining balance between ongoing revenues and expenditures. Usually, a government needs to maintain a diversified tax structure that is flexible and can accommodate both up and down economies. Governments that can reach and maintain structural balance are more likely to have and use countercyclical or contingency planning devices, such as budget stabilization or shortfall funds, to combat economic downturns as well. Best practice in this area dictates little dependence of a government on windfalls, "one-time" revenues, debt, or accounting gimmicks to finance current or operating expenditures. Processes examined in the states that fall into this area of financial management include

- Fund balances as a percent of expenditures greater than 5 percent
- Strong financial position (unrestricted net assets/annual revenues)
- Strong cash position (current assets/current liabilities)
- Balanced tax structures (dependent upon at least two major tax sources)
- Conduct of strategies for speeding receipt of tax revenue into state coffers
- Conduct of strategies for decreasing tax delinquencies
- Comprehensive auditing processes to enhance tax compliance
- Consistently stocked budget reserve/stabilization funds

Tax policy and administration will be discussed in more detail in the next chapter.

Procurement and Contracting

Best practices in purchasing and contracting suggest that these activities should be supported to advance efficiency and equity, streamlining vendor relationships and leveraging the buying power of governments through collectives. Purchasing and contracting processes should strive to balance internal controls and managerial flexibility for effective program results. Efforts here should offer some flexibility for agency staff in purchasing supplies and for engaging in contractual work, though with adequate internal controls and caps. Adequate oversight of transactions equates with many of the reporting activities mentioned in the previous chapter regarding budget execution. Digital-age governance calls for streamlining the transaction process and open access to request for proposal (RFP) and bidding processes through information technology, electronic, and online features (Dunleavy et al. 2006). Nonetheless, this should not loosen the strings of oversight required of public budgeting, accounting, and auditing offices vis-à-vis the agencies that carry out government work.

Financial Reporting

Finally, the best practices reviewed here include government preparation of timely annual financial audits in line with generally accepted accounting principles (GAAP). Governments ascribing to these practices prepare their annual financial audits in accordance with GAAP and routinely receive clean audit opinions—for both own-source and other funds. These practices also support government reporting on linkages between financial costs and operational performance.

Pew's *Grading the States 2008* was the fourth in a series of government surveys about management capacity. This survey represents a type of effort to measure government capacity to attempt and conduct best practices in various management areas. The Government Performance Project, *Governing* magazine, and academic and state government experts conducted surveys and research to analyze state performance in budgeting and financial management, human resources, information, and infrastructure. Table 10.2 presents the state leaders in budgeting and financial management that were graded using the best practices highlighted above.

These "best performers" are presented from highest to lowest in terms of GPP budget management scores, with highest scores indicating better state performance of the specific practice noted. Shaded cells indicate that states received the same score for the practice indicated. Nonetheless, each of these states performed well across the five budget management practices. For example, regarding structural balance, these states, compared with all others, indicated

- Balances as a percent of expenditures greater than 5 percent
- Strong financial positions (unrestricted net assets/annual revenues)
- Strong current ratios (current assets/current liabilities)

Table 10.2

Government Performance Project, 2008: State Government Leaders in Money Management

Long-Term Outlook	Budget Process	Structural Balance	Procurement	Financial Reporting
Delaware	Washington	Utah	Virginia	Utah
Nebraska	Virginia	Delaware	Minnesota	Indiana
Minnesota	Delaware	Indiana	Delaware	Washington
Utah	Utah	Nebraska	Georgia	Virginia
Washington	Georgia	Georgia	Nebraska	Delaware
Virginia	Nebraska	Virginia	Utah	Minnesota
Georgia	Minnesota	Minnesota	Indiana	Nebraska
Indiana	Indiana	Washington	Washington	Georgia

Source: *Governing*, "Measuring Performance: The State Management Report Card for 2008," Governing.com, March, 2008.

- Balanced tax structures (dependent upon at least two major tax sources)
- Conduct of strategies for speeding receipt of tax revenue into state coffers
- Conduct of strategies for decreasing tax delinquencies
- Comprehensive auditing processes to enhance tax compliance
- Consistently stocked budget reserve/stabilization funds

BUDGET REFORMS

In the past century, US federal budget reforms have been

- Centralizing (the Budget Act of 1921)
- Activity-based (performance budgeting of the 1950s)
- Focused on program evaluation (PPBS in the 1960s)
- Management-oriented (MBO in the early 1970s)
- Bottom-up (ZBB in the mid-1970s)
- Draconian (Gramm-Rudman-Hollings of the 1980s)
- Results oriented (GPRA in the 1990s)

Each of these attempts alludes to some disappointment with the system of budgeting in practice, the hopefulness for improving budgeting, and an effort to inject rationality into a highly political process. Modern performance budgeting reforms are no different, though current versions of performance budgeting reforms attempt to refocus budgeting and decision making by

- Shifting attention from the means of accomplishment to the accomplishments themselves

- Transferring the focus of government budgets from the traditional line-item approach to the classification of expenditures by government functions, activities, costs, and accomplishments

- Presenting performance information alongside budget amounts, introducing a different rationality into budgetary decision making

- Focusing funding choices on results rather than on political bartering

New Public Management, Performance Measurement, and Budget Reform

In chapter 7 it was noted that New Public Management precepts as touted by David Osborne and Ted Gaebler (1992) pushed government managers in a new direction—that is, to anticipate problems and promote a competitive environment for getting work done in more cost-effective ways. Applicability to resource management included expenditure control budgeting or mission-driven budgeting, which Osborne and Gaebler (1992) explain offers greater budget flexibility to public managers. The innovation involves doing away with line items, providing agencies with a determined budget amount for the fiscal year, and asking them to manage toward agreed-upon goals within this total—mindful that any savings can be fed back into the agency. In the past, Iowa implemented a form of mission-driven budgeting using what are called "charter agencies," which were able to avoid the traditional appropriations process by making agreements to conduct determined levels of work and reach certain goals within a set budget. The city of Trillium, Oregon, provides a recent example of a city government applying the full force of expenditure control budgeting to manage through the Great Recession. According to Scott Lazenby (2013), city manager of Sandy, Oregon, and adjunct associate professor at Portland State University,

Instead of having departments go through the game-playing of a competitive budget request process, the city manager gave each department director a set amount of general tax resources (based on a projection of how much would be available to balance the budget). They were then free to build their own budgets, adding any departmental revenues (fees, grants, etc.) they could, along with 100 percent of any savings carried over from the previous year. They were given complete control over line items and were encouraged to set aside reserves in departmental contingency accounts to handle emergency repairs or cyclical revenues.

Such efforts take agencies out of the politics of budget development: gamesmanship is unnecessary; just manage within your budget and you can reap rewards for your agency, and perhaps for the entire government.

Another aftereffect of the entrepreneurial approach encouraged by Osborne and Gaebler (1992) was a new focus on government performance and its measurement. Robert Behn (2003) articulates eight purposes for measuring government performance. These purposes align well with the phases and decision requirements of the public budgeting process—to help determine what to fund and at what level, for justification and promotion about operations, services, and programs to important stakeholders and decision makers, for control and evaluation during program execution, and at year-end to learn and improve service delivery and program results. Behn also suggests the use of performance measurement to celebrate, asking "What accomplishments are worthy of the important organizational ritual of celebrating success?" He cautions, however, that public managers must carefully consider the purpose(s) for using performance measures prior to establishing a performance management system. If those working in government do not adequately understand why performance measures are being introduced and what ends the reform is expected to address, any system is unlikely to take hold, yield insight on government performance, or clarify results from public programs, services, activities, or operations.

Performance budgeting is defined here as a performance measurement system to support budgetary decision making. The Governmental Accounting Standards Board (GASB) defines "managing for results" as the focus of governments on missions, goals, and objectives requiring the development, use, and reporting of performance measures "so that management, elected officials, and the public can assess the degree of success the organization has in accomplishing its mission goals and objectives" (GASB 2012). But a comprehensive *performance budgeting system* requires much more than simply developing and reporting performance measures. Such a system would incorporate performance measurement into all phases of the budgetary process timeline, from executive budget development and analysis to legislative budget deliberation and agreement (passage of the budget), through budget implementation, budget and program evaluation, and audit. Also, a truly comprehensive system should be integrated with the government's financial management information system (FMIS).

Research indicates, however, that most government performance budgeting systems today are more aptly titled performance-*informed* budgeting rather than performance-*based* budgeting (Robinson and Last 2009; see also Joyce 2003). Ronald McGill (2001) explains that "performance based allocations will be dependent on specific performance tests" (381) and though it may very well be a goal of a performance budgeting reform it is an unrealistic one for many, if not most, governments. Also, substantial research exists about the use of measures for management and budgeting in executive agencies and by program managers, though there is scant proof that government performance metrics are used by legislators and other policymakers for making resource allocation decisions—that is, for making the trade-offs often necessary in the annual budget process (Ho 2011, Hou et al. 2011, and Joyce 2011).

Patria de Lancer Julnes and Marc Holzer (2002) point out distinctly different factors that affect the adoption of performance measurement as a reform versus those that affect the actual use of measures for decision making. Matthew Andrews (2006) assesses efforts at performance budgeting reform in seven governments around the world (including two US state governments) and finds their success falls along a continuum.[8] Highly formalized budget systems with strong controls presented "robust reform progress" (in Florida and Virginia) whereas weak budget controls limited reform progress in Ghana. Andrews (2006) found the greatest progress with the reform in governments with budget processes that incorporated strong reporting systems where decision makers had data that was accessible, dependable, and high quality. Still, this research illuminates the complexities of successfully implementing performance budgeting. A strong budget basics legacy—including strong line item control, cash accounting, reliable financial reporting, and effective financial and compliance auditing—can advance a performance budgeting reform. Such a legacy, however, can impede implementation of reform, if, for example, the effort is not sequenced well or accommodated along the way with managerial flexibility.

Given the confusing nature of public budgeting, it should not be surprising that numerous challenges hinder engaging a performance budgeting approach successfully or even adequately. Consistent leadership and championing of the effort is necessary. Developing valid and reliable measures is difficult, staff need to be trained and retrained in measurement development and choice, and in data collection and reporting. Responsibility for measures may not be clarified in law or policy (Lu, Willoughby, and Arnett 2009 and 2011). Coordinating the performance information system with a medium-term framework and linking performance information and its reporting with both the budget process and the accounting system are problematic. Indeed, in a study of performance budgeting efforts in twenty-eight OECD countries, Teresa Curristine (2005) finds that "the main explanation for non-use of performance information is the lack of a process to integrate it into the budget process. . . to encourage budget officials to use it if they are not already doing so"(125).

Miekatrien Sterck and Bram Scheers (2006) explain that the seemingly ubiquitous application of performance measurement and management for budgeting has arisen globally (and predominantly) from pressures for greater internal and external accountability. They define accountability in terms of transparency. Previous chapters have discussed the push for transparency that has pressured public officials to provide clear and measured justification for their budget decisions. Internal accountability regards understanding and communication about executive programs, agency and department budgets, and operations among these entities and with the central (executive) budget office. External accountability regards understanding and communication about program, agency, and department operations between the executive and legislative branches and with the public.

Budget Transparency

Experts point out that greater transparency of budget documents by governments supports the checks and balances of the budgetary processes, puts a damper on corruption, can enhance the credibility of policy and its prioritization, and contributes positively to program management. Yet, even with technological advancements and the fact that many governments around the world have embraced a performance budgeting approach, budget transparency around the world is "not impressive."[9] In a survey of 100 countries, "only 23 provide significant budget information, yielding an Open Budget Index (OBI) or score that exceeds 60 [out of 100]. A disturbing 26 countries provide scant or no budget information, with scores of 20 or less. . . And, even when [budget] documents are published, they frequently lack sufficient detail" (McCullough 2012, 4). These researchers also find that "higher-income, more democratic countries tend to have higher OBI scores while oil-dependent autocracies tend to have lower OBI scores. Also, aid-dependent countries like Afghanistan, hydrocarbon revenue–dependent countries such as Mexico, and countries in the Middle East and sub-Saharan Africa have relatively transparent budget systems" with higher OBI scores than their cohorts (4).

Table 10.3 lists the OBI scores for the countries of interest here. This table refers to a number of different budget documents that may be accessible to the public across budget phases. The *pre-budget statement* includes assumptions used in budget development; the *executive's budget proposal* is the chief executive's budget recommendation to the legislative branch; a *citizen's budget* presents budget information is an easy, clear, and simple way; the *enacted budget* is the appropriation or appropriations passed by the legislature; *in-year, mid-year, and year-end reports* are those provided throughout budget execution; and the *audit report* is the financial (and sometimes performance) evaluation of expenditures at the end of the fiscal year. As indicated, all of these countries provide budget documents across the budget process timeline, though accessibility to all documents by the public does not necessarily contribute to a high overall OBI score. That is, none of the countries listed received an OBI score indicating provision of extensive budget information. The United States, Brazil, and India have scores recognizing public access to a significant amount of budget information; Italy, Guatemala, and Tanzania have scores indicating less transparency and public access to some budget information. Essentially, the guts of these documents (the details of each) are important for true budget transparency.

Table 10.3 also indicates the strength of various transparency-related practices, including the ability of the public to have input into the budget process throughout a fiscal year—from development to deliberation, during execution, and evaluation. Of these countries, the United States scores highest, then Brazil followed by Italy. The scores for public input are very poor for India and Tanzania; in Guatemala, although not completely shut out of budgeting

Table 10.3
Open Budget Index for Countries of Interest*

Countries of Interest	Public Availability of Budget Documents**							Public Engagement and Strength of Oversight			Overall OBI Score in 2012
	Pre-Budget Statement	Executive's Budget Proposal	Citizens' Budget	Enacted Budget	In-Year Reports	Mid-Year Review	Year-End Report	Audit Report	Public Engagement	Legislative Strength	Supreme Audit Institution	
Brazil	2	2	2	2	2	0	2	2	36	61	100	73
Guatemala	2	2	2	2	2	0	2	2	3	42	100	51
India	0	2	2	2	2	2	2	2	17	76	100	68
Italy	2	2	2	2	2	2	2	2	25	70	67	60
Tanzania	2	2	2	2	2	0	0	2	14	43	67	47
United States	0	2	0	2	2	2	2	2	58	87	100	79

Source: The Open Budget Survey conducted by the International Budget Partnership, available at http://internationalbudget.org/wp-content/uploads/OBI2012-Report-English.pdf

* Australia not included in this survey.

**Stoplight color coding document availability recoded numerically: 0=document not produced; 1=document available for internal use within government; 2=document available to the public.

decisions and monitoring, practically speaking, the public does not have a say in decisions about revenue generation or allocation.

Like the research examined in chapter 7, the Open Budget Survey reformulated its measure of legislative budget oversight and strength of practice to include (1) this branch's involvement in budgeting prior to delivery of the executive's budget proposal, (2) legislative research and analytic support, (3) amendment powers and time for deliberation about amendments prior to budget approval, and (4) legislative powers of fiscal management during budget execution and for supplemental budgets and contingency funds (Open Budget Survey 2012, 37). The United States Congress receives the highest score of these countries, then India. The rest of the countries indicate rather weak oversight capacity on the part of national legislatures—in Italy and Brazil legislative oversight falls between the United States and India (highest scores of group) and Tanzania and Guatemala (lowest scores of group). Also, the OBS examines the provision of independent oversight of government budgeting (by a "Supreme Audit Institution" or, in the United States, the Government Accountability Office). Of this group of countries, only Italy and Tanzania are lagging in auditor strength and independence.

Performance Budgeting Reforms

Curristine (2005) explains about performance measurement and budgeting[10] that "in the majority of OECD countries, efforts to assess the performance of programmes and ministries are now an accepted normal part of government" (89). Curristine finds that by 2005, most of these countries have developed a combination of output and outcome measures and many use more detailed evaluations to determine how well programs are operating and about the results generated from them. An assessment by Andrews (2006) of budget basics (legacies) and performance reforms in seven governments yields the conclusion that that even "governments without basics (or at least without basics first) could indeed adopt a performance based approach, especially when political, managerial and other factors are in line" (159).

The OECD (2007a) has surveyed its member countries periodically about budget laws and processes, and the use of performance information for budgeting, in particular. The survey data examined here includes results from the 2007 OECD survey of budget practices and procedures in member countries, the 2007–2008 World Bank/OECD survey of budget practices and procedures in Asia and other regions, and the 2008 CABRI/OECD survey of budget practices and procedures in Africa.[11] Responses were received from 97 countries. A more recent survey was conducted in 2012, but these data are yet to be made accessible on the OECD website.

The OECD distinguishes performance based budgeting from performance informed budgeting for survey respondents. According to its glossary of terms that accompanies the OECD Budget Practices and Procedures Database (2007a), *performance budgeting*

> strictly defined, is only a budget that explicitly links each increment in resources to an increment in outputs or other results. Broadly defined, a performance budget is any budget that presents information on what Government organisations have done or expect to do with the money provided to them. The latter is also sometimes referred to as performance-informed budgeting. (5)

Question 74 of the 2007 OECD Budget Practices and Procedures Survey is, "In which year was the first Government-wide initiative to introduce performance measures (outputs and/or outcomes)?"[12] According to the results of the survey, most countries introduced a government-wide performance measurement initiative within the last dozen years. Table 10.4 presents country responses to question 74 as posed by the OECD. Of the 97 countries responding, 50 countries began government-wide efforts in 2000 or after. Just 23 indicate introducing performance measurement government-wide by or before 2000. Twenty-four countries had either missing responses or indicated "not applicable" to this question.

Comparing countries based on year of government-wide PMI provides an interesting contrast. Table 10.5 presents responses by group to a question about the types of nonfinancial performance information produced in these governments. Note that countries introducing their PMIs in 2000 or later are less likely to produce any of the different measures or evaluation reports than countries introducing their PMIs before 2000. This may speak to the evolutionary quality of reform execution. Countries with initiatives in place by 2000 have had more time to collect measures, choose different types of measures, and to set targets. Especially interesting is the far greater likelihood that countries with older initiatives are more than twice as likely to engage in benchmarking as other countries. This may suggest that the build-up of measures in-country and across years provides the basis for benchmarking; that is, those countries with older PMIs have more data and opportunity to make comparisons.

Table 10.4
Year of First Government-Wide Initiative Introducing
Performance Measures*

Year	Country Introducing PMI	N
1970s	Canada, Hong Kong (pre-1970s)	2
1980s	Finland, Norway, Qatar, Sweden	4
1990s	Argentina, **Australia**, **Brazil**, Chile, Denmark, Germany, Iceland, Ireland, Latvia, Malawi, Mali, Namibia, New Zealand, Papua New Guinea, Spain, United Kingdom, **United States**	17
2000s	Albania, Austria, Benin, Bolivia, Botswana, Bulgaria, Burkina Faso, Cambodia, Fiji, France, Guinea, Indonesia, **Italy**, Japan, Jordan, Kenya, Liberia, Lithuania, Madagascar, Malta, Mauritius, Mexico, Moldova, Mongolia, Morocco, Netherlands, Nigeria, Peru, Philippines, Poland, Portugal, Republic of Serbia, Romania, Russian Federation, Rwanda, Sierra Leone, Slovak Republic, Slovenia, South Africa, Korea, Taiwan, Tunisia, Turkey, Uganda, Ukraine, United Arab Emirates, Uruguay, Venezuela, Zambia, Zimbabwe	50
N/A or Missing	Belgium, Bosnia/Herzegovenia, Congo, Costa Rica, Croatia, Cyprus, Czech Republic, Ethiopia, Ghana, Greece, Haiti, Hungary, Israel, Kyrgyzstan, Lesotho, Luxemburg, Mozambique, Solomon Islands, Surinam, Swaziland, Switzerland, Tajikistan, Thailand, Vietnam	24

Source: OECD Budget Practices and Procedures Survey, Question 74 (2007).

*Of the countries of interest in this book, Guatemala, India, and Tanzania are not included in this survey.

Results from the survey provide some insight into budget roles and responsibilities. That is, the central (executive) budget authority is more likely to be involved in the commissioning or conducting of evaluations of every kind for countries with older PMIs, while the legislature is more likely to be commissioning or conducting evaluations in countries that have more recently initiated performance measurement. The Supreme Audit Institution is more likely to conduct reviews of ongoing programs and sectoral (ministry) reviews in countries with older initiatives, whereas the Ministry of Finance is more likely to conduct reviews of new programs and sectoral evaluations in countries with more recent

Table 10.5
Types of PI Produced by Year Government-Wide Initiative Introduced

Year First Government-Wide Performance Measures Initiative Introduced		What Types of Performance Information Are Produced to Assess the Government's Nonfinancial Performance? $n = 73$
<2000	**>2000**	
***n* = 23**	***n* = 50**	
95.7%	56.0%	Performance measures
82.6%	70.0%	Evaluation reports (program, sectoral, efficiency, or cost reviews)
78.3%	60.0%	Performance targets
39.1%	14.0%	Benchmarking
13.0%	8.0%	Other
0.0%	15.1%	None
0.0%	0.0%	Missing answer

Source: OECD Budget Practices and Procedures Survey, Question 71 (2007).

PMIs. For all types of evaluations, the role of line ministries is consistent across countries, and this squares with research that regularly finds that performance information and its evaluation are more likely to be used for micro-level management decisions than for macro-level allocation decisions.

Regarding the use of information for budgeting decisions, 91.3 percent of countries with older PMIs responded that evaluation reports are used as part of budget discussions and negotiations between the Central Budget Authorities and line ministries. This compares with 60 percent of countries with more recent PMIs; 36 percent of these countries responded that evaluation reports are not used in such discussions. A series of questions then asked about the use of performance information by Central Budget Authorities and line ministries. Just 4.3 percent of countries with older PMIs indicated no impact on decisions of line ministries; 6.0 percent of countries with more recent PMIs indicated no impact on the decision making of the Central Budget Authority.

The data from the 2007 survey by the OECD of its members, coupled with that of the other surveys of Latin American and Asian countries, seems to square with past research and expectations regarding the use of performance information for budgetary decision making by governments. Responses indicate that although chief executives and legislatures do commission evaluation studies, performance reports, and reviews, these top-level budget- and policy-makers are less likely to use performance information when making budget allocation decisions. The use of performance information for budgeting and management seems to hold for relevant administrators of ministries and executive agencies. Also, Ministers of Finance and Central Budget Authorities are likely to *at least sometimes* use performance information when making budget allocation decisions.

A comparison of countries according to year of introduction of performance measurement initiative suggests that those with older initiatives have benefited from a longer settling-in period; their systems have had more time to develop than those of countries with more recent initiatives. The development and use of performance information for budgeting is more likely to occur more often and by more decision makers in countries with older PMIs than in countries with initiatives introduced in 2000 or later. This makes sense and is hopeful. PMIs provide a foundation for system development and execution. Time provides for reform practice and retooling and system entrenchment, allowing a government more time to continue what works, consider innovations, and to tweak or discard that which does not work.

In a recent report that provides preliminary results of the 2012 OECD survey[13] about budget procedures and practices Christian Kastrop (2012) explains that applications of performance budgeting in governments around the world are "numerous but structures vary." The survey data indicate, according to Kastrop (2012), that performance information use is still more common "for management and accountability purposes, than for allocation of resources." Kastrop (2012) also points out that efforts in countries are "generally decentralised within the central government (to line ministries and agencies), with the exception of spending reviews." That there seems to be status quo in terms of the use of performance measurement for budgeting across these countries in spite of the global recession is heartening. Given this update and the findings here, the best recommendation to governments regarding the use of performance information for budgeting might be to just get started—that is, governments without performance measurement initiatives should introduce them. Future research will dig deeper into the components of the PMIs that exist in these countries, how they fit with budget laws, and other factors that influence the allocation decisions in these governments.

Gender Budgeting

The United Nations Entity for Gender Equality and the Empowerment of Women[14] provides data and information about gender budgeting applied internationally. Gender budgeting, like performance budgeting, comes in many forms and has multiple definitions. Broadly, efforts attempt to integrate the female perspective into public budgeting decisions and public policy discussions, and to understand government impacts on women. Restricted definitions seek to measure reform results in terms of women and employment in government.

Marilyn Rubin and John Bartle (2005) discuss a comprehensive, integrative reform that would overlay the four budget phases with a gender-attuned perspective, necessitate research and data collection about government policies and activities and their impacts on women, present the woman's perspective within agencies, and apply this perspective to budgeting (and management) decisions, in addition to hiring women to meet equity goals. These scholars (2005) provide a matrix of gender perspective integration into different budget formats, indicating the various ways that such a perspective can be infused into public budgeting. With an object of expenditure budget format, relevant data may include the proportion of personal services spending directed to women employees or the proportion of contracts awarded to woman-owned firms. A performance format would require that measures account for gender specific goals and objectives. Program budgets include measures of program impact on women and on gender equity priorities. Zero-based budgeting formats would include gender analyses at each decision level. Edward Hiza Mhina (2007) notes that "gender budgeting challenges traditional planning processes and opens them up into being more participatory, democratic and increasingly accountable" (4).

Rubin and Bartle (2005) describe the first gender budgeting initiative that occurred in Australia's federal government beginning in 1984. To address what was considered to be significant gender inequality in government operations and program results, federal agencies and departments submitted reports with evidence of the impact of their programs on women, and detailed their methods of improvements to meet women's needs. These scholars suggest, however, that the most lasting impact of the reform occurred at the state and not federal level in Australia.

Tanzania This country engaged a comprehensive approach to gender budgeting, "to target resources and services to improve the quality of life for the most marginalised women, men and youth, to protect poor men and women against social adversity, expand the concept of poverty as more than lack of income, and to increase the incomes as well as improve access to other resources of these populations" (Mhina 2007, 11). Tanzania conducted a multilayered effort at gender budgeting reform to reorient budgets via gender perspective. This country engaged additional research on gender; developed and conducted training and seminars about gender budgeting, progress, and ongoing commitment to policy efforts; engaged in partnerships with an NGO; and piloted gender budgeting in selected government ministries. The central government worked with local governments and networks to integrate gender policy with budgets as well as increase the political representation of women in governments at the local and central levels. This initiative sought to identify the cultural, structural, and other impediments to making progress in advancing the female perspective.

India Bhumika Jhamb, Yamini Mishra, and Nvanita Sinha (2013) find that gender budgeting in India may be lip service. Discrimination and violence against women in that country in December 2012 in particular, exposed a culture of such crimes against women. Legislation passed in 2013 included stricter anti-rape law and a ban on sexual harassment at the workplace. In the budget speech by India's Minister of Finance, Palaniappan Chidambaram, on February 28, 2013, he discussed the plight of women, suggesting the following budgetary remedies:

- Women belonging to the most vulnerable groups must be able to live with self-esteem and dignity. Young women face gender discrimination everywhere. Ministry of Women and Child Development asked to design schemes that will address these concerns. I propose to provide an additional sum of `200 crore to that Ministry to begin work. (4)

- The handloom sector is in distress. A very large proportion of handloom weavers are women and belong mainly to the backward classes. I propose to accept their demand for working capital and term loans at a concessional interest of 6 percent. (14)

- Can we have a bank that lends mostly to women and women-run businesses, that supports women SHGs and women's livelihood, that employs predominantly women, and that addresses gender related aspects of empowerment and financial inclusion? I think we can. I therefore propose to set up India's first Women's Bank as a public sector bank and I shall provide `1,000 crore as initial capital. (15)

- We pledge to do everything possible to empower them and to keep them safe and secure. A number of initiatives are under way and many more will be taken by Government as well as non-government organisations. These deserve our support. As an earnest of our commitment to these objectives, I propose to set up a fund—let us call it the Nirbhaya Fund—and Government will contribute `1,000 crore. (20)

Jhamb, Mishra, and Sinha (2013) present data, however, indicating reductions in budgetary support specific to women from the 11th to the 12th Five-Year Plans; such funding as a percentage of the total expenditure of the Union budget represents a decrease from 5.9 to 5.8 percent.

US Local Governments

The cities of San Francisco, California, and Fulton County, Georgia are the only two known US local governments to have experimented with gender budgeting, to date. In 1998, San Francisco passed a local ordinance founded on the principles of the United Nations Convention on the Elimination of All Forms of Discrimination Against Women (CEDAW). The law pressures for gender analyses to thwart discrimination against women. This city conducted piloted agency gender analysis reports, though this initiative was related to city personnel and hiring of women, predominantly.[15] The initiative in Fulton County, Georgia, was similar to San Francisco's, with an emphasis on women and employment, the use of analysis to understand issues of equality and discrimination of women, and the impacts of public policy on women. Training about the female perspective was another component of Fulton's reform.[16]

CONCLUSION

This chapter has introduced you to various mechanics of public budgeting. Governments spend for different things and across different time periods. These various types of spending require accounting nuances. Examination of budget documents can help you to conceptualize distinctive funds. Public budgeting documents differ across budget phase—executive agency budget requests may include program goals, objectives, and performance measures as well as a multiyear accounting of line-item expenditures. A chief executive's budget recommendation often includes substantial narrative, numerous summary tables, and budget recommendations by department, activity, or line. Appropriation bills may represent a line-item, program or other orientation. Most governments engage hybrid budget formats—it is rare today to find a government that employs a budget format that is strictly object of expenditure.

Budget timelines vary among governments and by level. A short timeframe from budget executive development to submission to the legislature and passage of the budget has implications for the deliberative process. Also, passing the budget after the start of the fiscal year fosters an atmosphere of uncertainty that heightens budget process complexity.

Budget reforms by governments are too numerous to count or fully describe. Although reforms differ in their definition, focus, and components, each attempts to change the budget process with new or different information and protocols. For lasting value, reforms necessitate (1) buy-in and commitment from both government and the public; (2) support for subnational governments should the central government mandate the reform (or a state to local mandate); (3) a political environment that contributes to integration of the reform into current systems; and (4) ample time for settling in.

DISCUSSION QUESTIONS

1. Discuss the potential advantages and disadvantages of various budget formats for different audiences (e.g., legislators, chief executives, agency managers, and citizens). For example, compare a line-item with a performance format in terms of contributing to citizen understanding about government budgeting and services.

2. Having a multiyear perspective and a structural balance are identified as two best practices in budgeting. How do these two practices complement each other? How are they advanced by governments through budget rules and formats?

3. Discuss the concept of the base budget. Why might it be useful for policymakers to rely on the base budget in decision making? What are the potential pitfalls to considering only the base when making budget allocation decisions for future years?

4. Explain Robert Behn's reasoning for measuring government performance. How does the need to measure government performance relate to public budgeting?

5. Define gender-based budgeting. Why might a government pursue this type of budgeting? Explain and compare the benefits and challenges of gender-based budgeting in industrialized versus developing countries.

NOTES

1. A good place to access most US state government budgets is through the NASBO website: http://www.nasbo.org/resources/states-proposed-enacted-budgets

2. See http://opb.georgia.gov/zero-based-budgeting

3. See the Association's Committee on Governmental Budgeting and Fiscal Policy Best Practices at http://www.gfoa.org/index.php?option=com_content&task=view&id=120&Itemid=134

4. This research project was introduced in earlier chapters. Information about the project is available at http://www.pewstates.org/projects/government-performance-project-328600

5. For example, see tax expenditure reports produced by the state of Georgia at http://opb.georgia.gov/tax-expenditure-reports

6. See http://www.norfolk.gov/index.aspx?NID=1173

7. See http://governor.mo.gov/newsroom/2013/Gov_Nixon_outlines_performance_based_funding_model_for_higher_education_during_visit_to_Missouri_State_University

8. Andrews scores governments using the Government Performance Project, Managing for Results (MFR) measure. In 2001, the MFR measure was based on the following criteria:

    i. Does the state have a strategic plan? Do agencies have plans? If so, are they effectively used?

    ii. Are citizens, unions, businesses, and other stakeholders involved in development of strategic plans?

    iii. To what extent has the state developed and used performance indicators and evaluative data by which progress toward results can be measured? Is it relying on measures of output or is it moving toward outcome measures that track results?

    iv. How effectively are performance measures used for policy making, management, and evaluation of the government's progress toward its goals?

    v. Are performance results communicated to citizens, elected officials, and any other stakeholders? If so, how often?

    See Moynihan and Ingraham (2003) for more information about this measure and the GPP methodology.

9. The Open Budget Survey conducted by the International Budget Partnership calculates an "Open Budget Index" (OBI), the average of quantified responses for 95 survey questions regarding budget transparency; scores range from 0 (not transparent) to 100 (very transparent). See D. McCullough, D. (Ed.), *The Open Budget Survey: Open Budgets, Transform Lives* (Washington, DC: International Budget Partnership, 2012). Accessible online at http://internationalbudget.org/wp-content/uploads/OBI2012-Report-English.pdf

10. This section examines the efforts to initiate performance budgeting government-wide by countries around the world. A compendium of surveys conducted by the Organization for Economic Cooperation and Development (OECD) and the World Bank in 2007 and 2008 provide data for 97 countries regarding their budget laws and performance initiatives. This section compares countries by their performance budgeting efforts and according to the year of these countries' first government-wide initiative to introduce performance measures (PMI).

11. The information presented here uses data made publicly available by the Organisation for Economic Co-operation and Development (OECD) but in no way represents the views of the OECD or the World Bank. According to the OECD, the "database contains the results of the 2007 OECD survey of budget practices and procedures in OECD countries, the 2008 World Bank/OECD survey of budget practices and procedures in Asia and other regions, and the 2008 CABRI/OECD survey of budget practices and procedures in Africa." Dataset available at http://webnet. oecd.org/budgeting/Budgeting.aspx

12. The year of the country's introduction of the government-wide performance measurement initiative is used here as a proxy for government adoption of a system in which performance measures are applied to the budget process (performance informed budgeting) and is referred to as the PMI (introduced either before 2000 or in 2000 or after) of each country.

13. Data from this survey is not yet publicly available.

14. See http://www.unwomen.org/

15. An update of San Francisco's gender analysis reports by department can be found at http://www.sfgov3.org/index.aspx?page=108

16. Information about this effort can be found at http://www.fultoncountyga. gov/gep-home

REFERENCES

Andrews, M. 2006. "Beyond 'Best Practice' and 'Basics First' in Adopting Performance Budgeting Reform." *Public Administration and Development*, 26, 147–161.

Behn, R. D. 2003. Why Measure Performance? Different Purposes Require Different Measures. *Public Administration Review* 63 (5): 586–606.

Chidambaram, P. 2013. "Budget 2013–2014 Speech." Minister of Finance to Madam Speaker, February 28. Available at http://timesofindia.indiatimes.com/budget-2013-full-text-of-P-chidambaram-speech/photo/18728750.cms

Curristine, T. 2005. Performance Information in the Budget Process: Results of the OECD 2005 Questionnaire. *OECD Journal on Budgeting* 5 (2): 88–131.

De Lancer Julnes, P., and M. Holzer. 2002. "Promoting the Utilization of Performance Measures in Public Organizations: An Empirical Study of factors Affecting Adoption and Implementation." *Public Administration Review* 61 (6): 693–708.

Dull, M. 2006. "Why PART? The Institutional Politics of Presidential Budget Reform." *Journal of Public Administration Research and Theory* 16 (2): 187–215.

Dunleavy, P., H. Margetts, S. Bastow, and J. Tinkler. 2006. "New Public Management Is Dead—Long Live Digital-Era Governance." *Journal of Public Administration Research and Theory* 16 (3): 467–494.

Government Accounting Standards Board (GASB). 2012. "About SEA Reporting—Performance Management." Accessed November 30, 2012. Accessible online at http://www.seagov.org/aboutpmg/managing_for_results.shtml

Ho, A. T-K. 2011. "PBB in American Local Governments: It's More than a Management Tool." *Public Administration Review* 71 (30): 391–401.

Hou, Y., R. S. Lunsford, K. C. Sides, and K. A. Jones. 2011. "State Performance-Based Budgeting in Boom and Bust Years: An Analytical Framework." *Public Administration Review* 71 (30): 370–388.

Jacobs, K. 2008. "Budgets—An Accountant's Perspective." In *Legislative Oversight and Budgeting: A World Perspective,* edited by R. Stapenhurst, R. Pelizzo, D. M. Olson, and L. von Trapp, 67–78. WBI Development Studies, 45627. Washington, DC: The World Bank.

Jhamb, B., Y. Mishra, and N. Sinha. 2013. "The Paradox of Gender Responsive Budgeting." *Economic & Political Weekly*, May 18, 48 (2): 35–38. Available at http://www.epw.in/system/files/pdf/2013_48/20/The_Paradox_of_Gender_Responsive_Budgeting.pdf

Joyce, P. G. 2003. *Linking Performance and Budgeting: Opportunities in the Federal Budget Process.* Washington, DC: IBM Center for The Business of Government.

————. 2011. "The Obama Administration and PBB: Building on the Legacy of Federal Performance-Informed Budgeting?" *Public Administration Review* 71 (30): 356–367.

Kammholz, C. D., and C. S. Maher. 2008. "Does Revenue Forecasting Responsibility Matter: The Case of Milwaukee, Wisconsin." In *Government Budget Forecasting Theory and Practice*, edited by J. Sun and T. D. Lynch, 282–302. Boca Raton, FL: Taylor and Francis.

Kastrop, C. 2012. Preliminary Results of the OECD 2012 Performance Budgeting Survey. PowerPoint Slide Show at the OECD 50 Better Policies for Better Lives Conference. Updates accessible online at http://www.oecd.org/gov/budgeting/34thannualmeetingofoecdseniorbudgetofficialssbo.htm

Lazenby, S. 2013. "The Human Side of Budgeting." *PA Times*. Available at http://patimes.org/human-side-budgeting/

Lu, Y., K. Willoughby, K., and S. Arnett. 2011. "Performance Budgeting in the American States: What's Law Got to Do with It?" *State and Local Government Review* 43 (2): 79–94.

————. 2009. Legislating Results: Examining the Legal Foundations of PBB Systems in the States. *Public Performance and Management Review* 33 (2): 266–287.

McCullough, D. ed. 2012. *The Open Budget Survey: Open Budgets, Transform Lives.* Washington, DC: International Budget Partnership. Accessible online at http://internationalbudget.org/wp-content/uploads/OBI2012-Report-English.pdf

McGill, R. 2001. "Performance Budgeting." *International Journal of Public Sector Management* 14 (5): 376–390.

Mhina, E. H. August, 2007. Paper on Financing for Gender Equality and the Empowerment of Woman: Experiences from Tanzania. Tanzania Gender Networking Programme. Available at http://www.gender-budgets.org/index.php?option=com_joo mdoc&view=documents&path=resources/by-region-country/africa-documents/tanzania&Itemid=540

Moynihan, D. P., and P. W. Ingraham. 2003. "Look for the Silver Lining: When Performance-Based Accountability Systems Work." *Journal of Public Administration Research and Theory* 13 (4): 469–490.

OECD. 2007a. "Budget Practices and Procedures Survey." The World Bank and OECD. Accessible online at http://webnet.oecd.org/budgeting/Budgeting.aspx

_____. 2007b. "Performance Budgeting in OECD Countries." Available at http://www.oecd.org/gov/budgeting/performancebudgetinginoecdcountries.htm

Open Budget Survey. 2012. "Open Budgets. Transform Lives." International Budget Partnership. Available at http://internationalbudget.org/wp-content/uploads/OBI2012-Report-English.pdf

Osborne, D. E., and T. Gaebler. 1992. *Reinventing Government: How the Entrepreneurial Spirit Is Transforming the Public Sector.* Reading, MA: Addison-Wesley.

Penner, R. G. 2003. "The Dynamics of Scoring: A Congressional Tale." Tax Policy Center, August 1. Washington, DC: The Urban Institute and Brookings Institution. Available at http://www.taxpolicycenter.org/

Robinson, M., and D. Last. 2009. "A Basic Model of Performance-Based Budgeting." Technical Notes and Manuals. A publication of the PFM of the IMF accessible online at http://blog-pfm.imf.org/files/fad-technical-manual-1.pdf

Rubin, M. M., and J. R. Bartle,. 2005. "Integrating Gender into Government Budgets: A New Perspective." *Public Administration Review* 65 (3): 259–272.

Sterck, M., and B. Scheers. 2006. "Trends in Performance Budgeting in Seven OECD Countries." *Public Performance and Management Review* 30 (1): 47–72.

Tarschys, D. 2002. "Time Horizons in Budgeting." *OECD Journal on Budgeting* 2 (2): 77–103.

US Congressional Budget Office. May 2008. "Capital Budgeting." Available at http://www.cbo.gov/publication/41689

chapter ELEVEN

Funding with Taxes and Other Revenues

Money is, with propriety, considered as the vital principle of the body politic; as that which sustains its life and motion, and enables it to perform its most essential functions. A complete power, therefore, to procure a regular and adequate supply of it, as far as the resources of the community will permit, may be regarded as an indispensable ingredient in every Constitution.

—Alexander Hamilton, The Federalist Papers, Number 30

LEARNING OBJECTIVES

After reading this chapter, you should be able to

- Understand components of sound tax policy
- Distinguish taxes in terms of efficiency, equity, transparency, and adequacy
- Compare revenue structures across governments
- Understand modern methods of tax administration to advance revenue flow into governments
- Understand intergovernmental fiscal relationships and the importance of donor assistance in developing countries

---

Governments need money to function and must be empowered to raise funds to pursue agreed-upon policies. Governments engage their policing powers to generate revenues, passing tax laws that taxpayers must follow or suffer penalty. Paying taxes is not voluntary. This, in part, explains the mix of taxes, fees, charges, grants, loans, and other resources of a particular government. A government's revenue structure—the totality of types and individual characteristics of the fiscal resources that a government engages—is influenced by constitutions; laws; court decisions; history and culture; past policies and current rules, regulations, and mandates; intergovernmental relationships; economics; and voter preferences.

John Mikesell (2011) reminds us of the principles of sound tax policy in a market economy espoused by Adam Smith in *The Wealth of Nations* (1776) that include fairness, efficiency, transparency, and adequacy. The public is generally suspicious of government—taxpayers generally believe that they are paying too much in taxes and receiving too little in return. Thus, deliberations about taxes and consideration of these principles swirl around how taxes can be made more palatable to taxpayers. The decision to create a new tax or increase the rates or the base of an existing one is never taken lightly by politicians. Tax policies, which include both the imposition of taxes as well as the exception from tax liability (tax expenditures) are used by governments to provide for public service delivery and infrastructure development, to incentivize certain behaviors, and to assist certain individuals or groups. Be aware, however, that the principles of sound tax policy can and do conflict with the politics of tax policy—resulting systems are highly complex and are often full of loopholes that compromise equity, efficiency, transparency, and adequacy.

This chapter introduces the principles of sound tax policy. Tax administration as conducted in US states is highlighted to understand modern means of advancing the flow of revenues into government coffers. Taxes on wealth and consumption are examined and the predominant tax sources evidenced in a developed and developing country are described. A final section reviews intergovernmental grants evidenced in the United States and the role of donor funds in developing countries is explained. After reading this chapter, you should have a better understanding of how governments fund public programs and services through taxes, the characteristics of various tax sources that are often tapped, and the factors relevant to sound tax policy.

EQUITY

Considerations of tax equity are founded upon the "benefits received" or "ability to pay" principles (Lewis and Hildreth 2013). Generally, government market- or business-like services and operations such as utilities operate on the benefits received principle—those receiving the benefit or service pay the costs. In the purest sense, if you do not choose to receive a particular good or service, you do not pay for it. Governments impose fees and charges for many public goods and services; these can include park entrance or recreational fees, charges to use government buildings or spaces, and fees for licenses of all sorts (for example, hunting, business, and driver's licenses). Fees and charges are imposed to recoup the costs of these activities, but they are also used to regulate behaviors—for instance, governments may impose charges on industries according to the pollution emitted during production. These charges incentivize companies to develop clean technologies.

Fees and charges make up a significant portion of government budgets. In US local governments, current charges and utilities revenues (from water, electricity, gas, and transit services) comprised 22.9 percent of total revenues in 2010–2011 (US Census Bureau 2010–2011). Generally, the public is more amenable to government use of fees and charges, given the usual assignment of resulting receipts to the specific services or goods received. Even if earmarked, however, fees and charges, rarely if ever cover the full costs associated with the conduct of the government service or production. More important, governments conduct services and programs that are not amenable to market-like transactions. Thus, the provision of public goods and the purposes of government require engaging the ability-to-pay principle in terms of tax policy.

The ability-to-pay principle applied to taxation essentially means that household wealth determines tax liability. Applying this principle requires determination of what "equitable" means, commonly considering that the highest tax burdens should be borne by households of the greatest wealth. (Tax burden equates with total taxes paid by an individual or entity as a proportion of individual or entity income for a prescribed period.) The constitutions of Brazil, Guatemala, and Italy explicitly state this principle as a foundation for government tax policy:

- Article 145 of the Brazilian Constitution: Whenever possible, taxes will have personal character and will be graded according to the economic capacity of the taxpayer and the tax administration, especially to give effect to these objectives, identifying, respecting individual rights and in accordance with law, equity, income and economic activities of the taxpayer.

- Article 243 of the Guatemalan Constitution: The principle of capacity to pay the tax system must be fair and equitable. Tax laws will be structured according to the principle of ability to pay.

- Article 53 of the Italian Constitution: Every person shall contribute to public expenditure in accordance with their capability. The tax system shall be progressive.

Thus, under this principle, household wealth must be defined. Wealth is most often defined in terms of income and property. Considerations of tax equity then regard how to treat households according to similar or different capabilities to pay (or wealth). Horizontal equity in tax policy regards imposing similar tax burdens on individuals with similar capacities to pay. For example, if imposing some sort of wealth tax, should the same rate apply to an individual with total wages earned of $45,000, to another who received a bequest of $45,000, and to yet another who won $45,000 on a TV game show?

Vertical equity related to tax policy regards the treatment of individuals differently, given their various capacities to pay. For example, sliding scale fees applied to health clinic visits recognize that some are able to pay the full or partial amount of service, whereas others have no capacity to pay for these services. Table 11.1 provides a very elementary illustration of progressive, proportional, and regressive tax rate structures on taxable incomes of $20,000, $40,000, and $80,000. This table illustrates that those with higher incomes indeed pay more income taxes using any of these rate structures. But in a progressive tax structure, where those in higher income categories pay a greater proportion of their income in taxes, presumably greater tax burdens are applied to households with greater wealth. A proportional structure applies the same tax rate to each income level; a regressive rate structure imposes higher tax rates on lower incomes—those with low incomes are paying a greater share of their income in taxes than those with higher incomes.

If you examine incomes as a share of total income, pre- and post-tax, you should see the effects of proportional versus regressive tax structures more clearly. Before imposition of the tax, the low-income individual ($20,000) holds 14.3 percent of total taxable income ($140,000). The middle-income individual

Table 11.1
Progressive, Proportional, and Regressive Tax Rate Structures

Taxable Income	Tax Rate and Tax Liability					
	Progressive		Proportional		Regressive	
$20,000	10%	$2,000	10%	$2,000	10%	$2,000
$40,000	17%	$6,800	10%	$4,000	7%	$2,800
$80,000	25%	$20,000	10%	$8,000	5%	$4,000

holds 28.6 percent of total income, and the high-income individual 57.1 percent of total taxable income. After taxes under the progressive structure, these shares are 16.2 percent (low-income proportion of total income, after taxes are imposed), 29.9 percent (middle-income) and 54 percent (high-income). But after taxes under the regressive structure, the shares are 13.7 percent (low-income), 28.4 percent (middle-income) and 57.9 percent (high-income).

Table 11.2 compares marginal with effective tax rates. This table regards US federal income tax rates for 2012 and taxable income of unmarried individuals, assuming the standard deduction noted. The tax rate applied to income in excess of the taxable income floor is provided for each income bracket. Consider the individual with taxable income of $30,000. The amount of income greater than the income floor of $8,700 is $21,300; this excess is multiplied by the marginal tax rate of 15 percent to yield $3,195. This amount is added to $870 (10 percent of income floor in this bracket) to yield total tax liability of $4,065. Total tax liability is divided by total taxable income ($30,000) which indicates an effective tax rate of 13.6 percent—the effective tax rate may be different from the statutory rate.

EFFICIENCY

Evaluating tax options requires answering questions about the purpose of the tax, its political feasibility, and the expected consequences of the policy. Considering the economic efficiency of a tax means determining its distorting effects. That is, how will people and businesses react to certain tax policy? Will increasing the income tax incentivize individuals to work more or work less?

Table 11.2

Comparison of Marginal and Effective Income Tax Rates by Taxable Income Levels

Unmarried Individuals
(other than surviving spouses and heads of households)
Standard deduction: $5,950

If Taxable Income Is:	The Tax Is	A Taxable Income	B Excess Over	C Excess Over x Marginal Tax Rate	D Tax Amount + C	E Effective Tax Rate
≤ $8,700	10% of the taxable income	$7,500	-0-	-0-	$750	10.0%
> $8,700 and ≤ $35,350	$870 plus **15%** of excess > $8,700	$30,000	$21,300	$3,195	$4,065	13.6%
> $35,350 and ≤ $85,650	$4,867.50 plus **25%** of excess > $35,350	$62,000	$26,650	$6,663	$11,530	18.6%
> $85,650 and ≤ $178,650	$17,442.50 plus **28%** of excess > $85,650	$143,000	$57,350	$16,058	$33,501	23.4%
> $178,650 and ≤ $388,350	$43,482.50 plus **33%** of excess > $178,650	$222,000	$43,350	$14,306	$57,788	26.0%
> $388,350	$112,683.50 plus **35%** of excess > $388,350	$500,000	$111,650	$39,078	$151,761	30.4%

Will a change to business taxes incentivize businesses to increase their demand for labor or reduce it? How will sales taxes affect buying behaviors? How will tax liabilities affect private investment and individual savings rates? Collectively, these behaviors have an impact on the health of the economy. Determining tax policy means conducting research about the mix of taxes currently used across all levels of government, their rates and bases, and how imposition of another tax or change to a current tax will affect behaviors. Calculations of tax burdens (the cost to the individual or household by paying the tax) and excess burdens (the cost to society from imposition of the tax, or "deadweight loss") attempt to estimate the true costs on taxpayers and society with the imposition of a tax in order to predict impact (Auerbach and Hines 2001).

Andrew Chamberlain and Gerald Prante (2007) examine government taxing and spending in the United States for a fifteen-year period. They explain that studies that consider only one side of the equation (just the taxes that governments impose or just government spending) are incomplete because real tax burdens are much greater than the revenue lost by taxpayers and collected by the government. Mikesell (2011) explains and Rubin (2010) illustrates that true tax incidence cannot be legislated, given the highly charged political process of taxation.

ADEQUACY

Taxes must bring in sufficient revenue to warrant levying; they must balance this adequacy with acceptability on the part of taxpayers. If rates are too high, taxpayers will make choices to evade the tax legally (quit buying cigarettes, consume less gasoline, move out of the taxing jurisdiction) or illegally (hide income). Determining tax rates is complicated given this balancing requirement. Arthur Laffer, who espouses supply side economics and for whom the "Laffer Curve" is named, modeled this behavioral relationship between tax rates and government revenue (see Laffer 2004). An accommodation of his curve is provided in Figure 11.1. In this figure, the straight line presents a strict, linear relationship between tax rates and government revenue—as the tax rate is increased, government revenue increases and proportionally so. Laffer suggested, however, that tax rates at zero (0 percent) and 100 percent yield zero government revenue, that the relationship between rates and revenue is really curvilinear. After reaching a certain rate (t^*), government revenue resulting from the tax

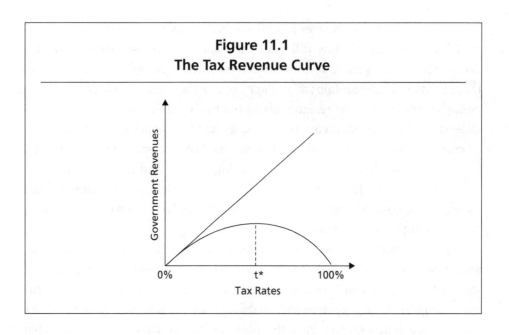

Figure 11.1
The Tax Revenue Curve

actually declines. Sometimes termed "trickle-down economics," supply-side economics is a macroeconomic theory pitted against demand-side or Keynesian economics. Supply-side economics considers that reducing government's footprint in terms of taxes and spending will foster and energize a free and competitive market, promoting savings and business investment, thereby advancing the economy. US President Ronald Reagan's cuts to taxes, government regulations, and expenditures (except for defense) rested on this reasoning, which is often associated with conservative, Republican fiscal policy. However, although inflation was kept in check during the Reagan administration, the federal deficit grew dramatically and the national savings rate declined.

TRANSPARENCY

In determining the feasibility of a tax, it can be very hard to buffer the decision-making process from special interests seeking tax benefits (tax expenditures). Discussions of taxes are complicated and lots of misinformation is often bandied about—especially if there is a wide gulf between potential taxpayers and their understanding of how and for what the money will be used by the government. If receipts from a tax will pay for projects or services that benefit a relative few, or if the receipts are *perceived* as benefiting a relative few, the tax initiative will be a very hard sell on the part of politicians. Consider the two following cases regarding local option sales taxes[1] in Georgia and Atlanta and voter decisions on two separate tax issues:

- In 2004, Atlanta voters agreed to add a 1 percent Municipal Option Sales Tax (MOST) to fund water and sewer renovations. The tax applies to food, but WIC and food stamp purchases are exempt, as are car purchases. Sold as a temporary tax with receipts earmarked for water and sewer repairs, it has been estimated that 30 percent of these taxes are paid by visitors to the city. Residents approved of the tax, in part, because outsiders would pay some of the tax, because it was billed as temporary, and because the tax would forestall increases to water and sewer bills to pay for the planned improvements (City of Atlanta 2014).
- In Georgia in 2012, a statewide referendum was put forward to voters for a Special Purpose Local Option Sales Tax (SPLOST) to be applied to transportation projects. The referendum was voted on by twelve regions and passed in only three of them—Central Savannah River, Heart of Georgia Altamaha, and the River Valley districts. The Atlanta district voted overwhelmingly "No" (63 percent) on increasing local sales taxes by a penny. The tax was highly controversial among voters because money from the tax was to be applied to transportation projects decided upon by local communities all around the state. One opponent of the tax claimed the outcome of the vote to be "the people's victory," given her group's battle against increasing taxes statewide that would benefit local projects. Many proponents of the tax claimed voters did not fully understand how the added revenues would benefit transportation across the state (Wallace 2012).

Transparency implies an open process for taxes under consideration, clear explanations of tax components (rate and base) to expect, tax liability calculations that are objective and clear, and administration that is simple and convenient. Mikesell (2011) explains that tax transparency is perhaps most important for promoting trust in government in that taxpayers must be able to see a direct link between the taxes that they pay and the government services and goods provided. Taxpayers need confirmation that their taxes are being used as intended and applied to the costs associated with conducting government work.

Winners in tax wars are those who are able to secure some sort of benefit—an abatement, exemption, credit, deferral, or incentive. These sorts of benefits complicate tax systems and compromise transparency. Such benefits are termed tax expenditures and are often pushed as efforts to redistribute the tax burden or to provide incentives for behaviors considered worthy, such as development of an impoverished community. Tax expenditures mean revenue losses to government because a tax is not applied or the tax liability of individuals or corporations is reduced. This revenue loss affects the overall equity and efficiency of the revenue structure of a government and concerns the transparency of a government tax structure.

The Pew Charitable Trusts (2013) studied the US federal tax expenditure that allows homeowners who itemize deductions when filing their taxes to deduct the interest paid on their mortgage from their gross income. The Pew Trusts (2013) estimates that the federal government lost $72 billion in income tax revenue in fiscal 2011 from this tax expenditure. This tax policy is expected to incentivize individuals to purchase homes, with the benefits of home ownership considered to include the development and stability of neighborhoods, improved community health and well-being, and strong and growing economies. The Pew Trusts (2013) finds wide disparities among states in deduction claims and thus in the benefits from this particular tax policy. The report warns that tax reform going forward must account for how changes to this tax expenditure will affect individual tax burdens.

The Government Accountability Office (US Government Accountability Office 2005) estimates that tax expenditures in the United States are growing in number and dollar value—the total value of these expenditures for fiscal year 2011 has been estimated at $1 trillion. The GAO (2005) also explains that individual taxpayers have benefited more than corporations from federal tax expenditures—the most significant of these expenditures are in the form of employer-provided medical premiums, the mortgage deduction, exclusion of pension and 401k earnings, and deductibility of state and local taxes. Finally, the GAO presses for greater scrutiny of these expenditures, given their growth but also because the Government Performance and Results Modernization Act of 2010 (GPRAMA, discussed in chapter 9) requires an accounting and assessment of tax expenditures and their contributions to the government's crosscutting goals. The GAO provides an overview of how to analyze tax expenditures.[2]

COLLECTABILITY

The US Internal Revenue Service (2012) collects about $2 trillion annually in taxes. In tax year 2006, the IRS estimated an 83.1 percent compliance rate for its taxpayers, resulting in a gross tax gap between tax liabilities and collections of $450 billion. After accounting for tax enforcement and penalties, this gap shrank to $385. A study by Richard Cebula and Edgar L. Feige (2011) calculated the gap closer to $500 billion. These researchers determine that income tax evasion goes up with the average effective federal income tax rate, unemployment, public dissatisfaction with government, and per capita real GDP. Their results indicate some support that tax reform afforded by the Tax Reform Act of 1986 reduced evasion and slight indication that IRS audits also suppress evasion.

In a *Time* magazine article, "The Lying Game," Christopher Matthews (2013, D2) compares "shadow economies" across countries to see if the United States is much different in terms of tax receipts lost. His unscientific comparison of the percentage of a country's GDP that is "illegally untaxed" (D2) indicates the United States and Switzerland at ~8.5 percent; United Kingdom and Germany, ~12–16 percent; Korea, Italy and Greece at ~27 percent and Mexico at 30 percent. Matthews speculates lax penalties (Korea), the existence of organized crime (Italy), a culture of noncompliance (Greece), and the ability of businesses to hide profits during an explosive export market (Mexico) as reasons for the higher rates of evasion in these countries. He claims that those in the United States may feel more of a moral obligation to pay their taxes, given his measure of the country as "more religious" (D2) than some of the others.

Nick Devas, Simon Delay, and Michael Hubbard (2001) write that "tax policy reform can achieve relatively little without reform of tax administration" (211). Improving the efficient flow and amount of money into government supports not only the conduct of public programs and services, but also can improve taxpayer understanding of the connection between tax dollars and government service. As noted above, tax evasion results in significant dollars lost by governments. And, taxpayers need clarity about what government is doing with the money it receives through taxes.

Public entities responsible for tax administration are usually viewed as the hidden infrastructure of government, conducting services for a reluctant client, the taxpayer. Today, these agencies are often charged not only with the management of the flow of revenue into and out of the government treasury, but also to advance the amount of funds and the pace of their delivery into the treasury.

Given the political realities of elections, these offices are, more often than not, understaffed and revenue starved in terms of their own budgets. Elected officials would rather fund services that more directly benefit their constituents, such as education or transportation. There is often a mismatch between the needs of a Department of Revenue (DOR) to do its job efficiently and effectively and the legislative support it receives in the form of appropriations. Govind Iyer, Philip Reckers, and Debra Sanders (2010) explain that US state government revenue departments, in particular, "do not have the resources to aggressively enforce compliance with tax laws" (29). This happens in spite of the fact that investment in a DOR can realize significant and quick fiscal results. For instance, Florida's state DOR conducted upgrades costing $60 million in the early 2000s and, as a result of this investment, realized "$320 million in increased revenue through 2004 alone" (Chen 2005, 36). Massachusetts DOR indicated that an initial investment of less than $6 million in state funds for data warehousing resulted in increased collections of nearly $500 million. For this reason and particularly in periods of economic decline, chief executives often look to their revenue agencies for support to bridge and close budget gaps by bringing needed revenues into the state more quickly and in larger amounts.

The distinctive work of revenue agencies imposes many challenges to assessing their performance. Optimum performance would include 100 percent compliance for all revenue sources and no delinquencies. Access to the office and staff by taxpayers must be convenient, the information provided must be correct, and processing of transactions should be quick and simple. Taxpayers, the revenue agency's customers, must understand how to calculate their tax liabilities and how to comply with tax laws.

The 2008 GPP survey of state management capacities that has been discussed in previous chapters examined the performance of revenue departments in US states. The survey asked these governments about their strategies for speeding receipt of tax revenue into the government, for decreasing tax delinquencies, and their comprehensive auditing processes to enhance tax compliance. Customer-based measures include timeliness of processing returns and quality of taxpayer interaction (taxpayer satisfaction with office and staff accessibility, expertise, accuracy, and timeliness). Management-based measures of revenue agency performance include dollars collected per revenue agent per month for individual tax sources, overall tax collection rates, tax cases closed per revenue agent, percent of returns filed electronically, employee training hours per year, and so on.

Survey results indicate strong performers in this area to be Delaware, Georgia, Indiana, Minnesota, Nebraska, Utah, Virginia, and Washington.

Table 11.3 presents state responses to a question in the online survey of the GPP completed by state administrators of strategies used to speed receipt of tax revenue into the state. (As explained in chapter 10, speeding tax receipts into government coffers is one measure used by the GPP to assess the strength of structural balance that is managed by states.) Of forty states responding to this question, 97.5 percent indicated that the electronic funds transfer (EFT) option

Table 11.3

US State Government Strategies to Speed Tax Receipts into Government, in Percents ($N = 40$)*

Management Strategy	Very Effective	Effective	Somewhat Effective	Not Effective	Not Used
Electronic funds transfer option	67.5	30.0	2.5	0	0
Online filing of returns	57.5	35.0	2.5	0	2.5
Online payment of taxes	47.5	40.0	5.0	0	5.0
Mandated electronic filing	35.0	20.0	2.5	2.5	37.5
Bar coding of income tax returns	25.0	37.5	10.0	0	25.0
Credit card payment of taxes	20.0	37.5	25.0	2.5	15.0
Online filing of liens	12.5	7.5	7.5	2.5	67.5
Additional personnel to work with taxpayers	12.5	30.0	5.0	0	45.0
IVR payment of taxes	10.0	12.5	15.0	2.5	57.5
Telephone filing of returns	7.5	12.5	30.0	7.5	40.0

Source: The Government Performance Project, online survey, Money section, Question 9: *In the last two years, which of the following strategies have been effective in speeding the receipt of tax revenue into your state?*

*The ten states not responding to this question included: Alaska, California, Florida, Hawaii, Kentucky, Nevada, New York, Rhode Island, South Dakota, and Texas.

for tax and other payments to the state was effective or very effective. All states indicated that they use this strategy for improving DOR operations. Online filing of returns and payment of taxes are found to be effective or very effective by 92.5 percent and 87.5 percent of states, respectively. Over half of states indicated that mandated electronic filing, bar coding of income tax returns, and credit card payment of taxes are effective in increasing the pace of revenue collection. It is interesting to note that although 42.5 percent of states responded that adding personnel to work with taxpayers is effective or very effective to tax administration, 45 percent indicated that they did not use this strategy. Certainly, this speaks to the gap between funding support provided to DORs and their effective operations.

Table 11.4 presents state responses to another question in the GPP online survey to state managers regarding tax administration strategies. Many of the strategies listed were considered to be effective or very effective by just over one-third to

Table 11.4
US State Government Strategies to Reduce Tax Delinquencies or Increase Compliance, in Percents (*N* = 40)*

Management Strategy	Very Effective	Effective	Somewhat Effective	Not Effective	Not Used
Data mining	30.0	32.5	17.5	0	20.0
Taxpayer education program	22.5	50.0	25.0	0	2.5
Debit payment option	22.5	32.5	7.5	0	32.5
Outside collection agency	17.5	27.5	25.0	5.0	25.0
Reduce EFT threshold on tax payments	17.5	20.0	2.5	2.5	55.0
Public notice of delinquent taxpayers by name	15.0	20.0	15.0	2.5	45.0
Tax amnesty program	5.0	2.5	12.5	5.0	72.5

Source: The Government Performance Project, online survey, Money section, Question 10: *In the last two years, how effective have any of the following strategies been in your state in decreasing tax delinquencies or increasing the proportion of taxpayers who pay state taxes completely and on time?*

*The ten states not responding to this question included: Alaska, California, Florida, Hawaii, Kentucky, Nevada, New York, Rhode Island, South Dakota, and Texas.

almost three-quarters of states in reducing tax delinquencies or increasing compliance. Several strategies would appear to be cost effective, such as the reduction of the EFT threshold on tax payments and public notice of delinquent taxpayers by name and debit payment. Yet, from one-third to over half of states responding indicated that they did not use these strategies to improve tax administration.

States indicate a number of ways for determining who or what entities to audit for tax compliance, the types of audits conducted and offered, and regarding the support available to those who choose self-auditing. Ways for determining audit candidates include using technology and data warehousing, as well as by collaborating with other states, professional groups, and national commissions. Automation and data warehousing offer states cost-effective ways to manage the audit process, allowing for the analysis of payment trends to look for unusual patterns of deductions or exemptions compared to past years or to peer-group profiles. Such systems also allow cross-referencing queries that focus on aberrations and mismatches. For example, a DOR might match liquor distributor records of customer sales against sales reported by those customers and use tax returns to identify audit leads. Or property sales records can be used to identify nonresident, nonfilers with capital gains from real estate sales. Mineral royalty payment records can be used to identify nonfilers with mineral royalty income. Finally, modern automation and data storage also allow for queries between and among a number of entities such as the US Internal Revenue Service and other state agencies, such as the Division of Motor Vehicles.

Methods of selecting who will be audited include: statistical sampling or random selection of candidates from databases; referrals or complaints about tax scofflaws or under-reporters; and regular, periodic audits of particular taxpayers such as larger accounts with high probability of noncompliance or those with the highest potential revenue. Some states indicated using the services of such companies as Dun & Bradstreet to identify entities likely making sales in the state but not complying with state tax laws.

Manual auditing is made more efficient with computer-assisted audit support or laptop audit worksheet programs. These systems can be used to extract, analyze, verify, and manage taxpayer data electronically. Multijurisdictional auditing may involve ad hoc coordination between two or more states or it may involve coordination with the Multistate Tax Commission (MTC), an intergovernmental entity created in 1967 to work "on behalf of states and taxpayers to administer, equitably and efficiently, tax laws that apply to multistate and multinational enterprises."[3] The Commission works to avoid duplicative taxation, helps multistate taxpayers determine their tax liabilities, presses for uniformity of significant components of tax systems, and promotes taxpayer convenience in filing returns to pump up compliance.

States may also work with regional or national professional associations that provide referrals for audits. Also, voluntary disclosure programs exist that allow taxpayers an avenue to come forward and remit past liabilities rather than having to contact each government in which they may owe taxes. States may also hire auditors in other states to audit taxpayers within their specific geographic region. This assists the taxpayers in completing audits more quickly. Finally, managed or self-audit programs exist in which certain categories of taxpayers are identified for voluntary participation in a self-audit. Targeted taxpayers are provided information regarding the voluntary audit process and they can choose to conduct a self-audit within a prescribed schedule; assistance from the DOR can be onsite or by telephone or electronic communication. Audit responses are checked for accuracy and processed. Questionable or nonresponses can be referred for a more in-depth field audit. Often, states offer relief from penalties and assessments if these targeted groups conduct a self-audit, which saves the DOR in manpower and other costs associated with a full, field audit.

Similarly, states may send targeted educational mailings to encourage self-review and correction by specific taxpayers whose returns are at high risk for error or who may be inclined not to report income from sources outside the state (such as municipal bond interest), or who claim excessive noncash charitable contributions, losses from activities not engaged in for profit, or dependent-based exclusions and credits to which they may not be entitled. Or, states might send audit alerts to employees and educational tax alerts to the taxpaying public to educate staff and citizens about tax changes, new laws, court decisions, or other issues to raise awareness and improve collections.

A well-working performance measurement system applied to DORs would engage both customer-based and management-based measures; multiple measures should be engaged regarding the different components of tax administration—taxpayer communications and satisfaction, management efficiency and effectiveness, and revenue results. According to the GPP, Minnesota indicates leadership in tax administration. Regarding selecting and managing tax audits, Minnesota devotes substantial resources to high-touch (as opposed to high-volume) compliance efforts focusing on issues shared with the US IRS, such as unreported gross receipts, overstated business expenses, tax deferred exchanges and losses from not-for-profit activities, for example, and other issues that are Minnesota's alone, such as residency and refundable credits. The state makes extensive use of its data warehouse, which includes information from other state and local agencies, to enhance its selection of personal income tax audits. Also, Minnesota uses the kinds of targeted educational mailings discussed earlier to encourage self-review and correction by taxpayers whose returns are at high risk for error.

On the collections front, the state's DOR Collection Division indicated implementing an automated bank and wage levy process. If there is an identifiable bank or wage asset for a debtor that meets certain criteria, the state will automate the levy process instead of having a collector touch each of these cases. As part of the department's workforce planning, the Collection Division has undertaken to document its collection procedures. The division shared templates and style guides for doing this with another state to help them begin to develop their own process. Minnesota also offered technical assistance to help in this effort. These templates and guides were demonstrated and presented at a national professional tax administrators' conference. Finally, all of these efforts, including audit selection and the management of the audit process, have been greatly improved with the installation of a new integrated tax processing system recently authorized and funded by the Minnesota Legislature. This system will provide more accurate, consistent, and timely tax return and taxpayer account data and will enable the state to detect patterns of noncompliance more quickly.

In 2010, Terri Steenblock explained the tax administration transformation in Minnesota's DOR. The department invested in personnel, process, and technological improvements to strengthen its performance and results. Human capital has been enhanced primarily through rebudgeting and redirection within compliance support areas—for example, trading supplies and mail for workforce refinements such as providing personnel with detailed procedural manuals to build knowledge base and allow for expansive assignment of auditors across different tax compliance cases. "By shifting workforce and budget, the DOR has effectively created an institution that is flexible and prepared for changing demands" (Steenblock 2010, 65–66). The department holds employees accountable to a performance model that incorporates qualitative (competency) and quantitative measures that are weighted equally. For example, in compliance, employees assume ownership of a case and manage it from start to finish. This provides taxpayers with a one-stop shop for resolving problems, advances employee expertise, and pushes employees to close cases. Calls are monitored to measure accuracy of information provided and cases are randomly selected and checked for completion and accuracy.

Minnesota's DOR better manages incoming calls for more efficient service across seasonal peak times. Also, as noted earlier, the Collections Division was reorganized and processes redesigned or done away with. For example, a traditionally conducted call campaign was ended and collectors were reassigned to research the assets of debtors to offset delinquencies. In terms of technological advancements, the department found that some upgrades were available but not being used. In addition, after an examination of processes, the need for additional programs and upgrades surfaced in order for the department to more effectively serve the needs of its customers. For instance, since implementation of an automated wage and bank levy program, $40 million has been collected without human intervention. Minnesota's DOR also considers its more robust data warehouse and the introduction of online filing and payment to have advanced its performance markedly. Essentially, better use of existing technology and upgrades allowed for redirecting of human capital elsewhere.[4] This state's transformation in the DOR represents an example of digital-era governance in action as described by Patrick Dunleavy and his colleagues (2006)—using technology to improve government processes, access, transparency, performance, and results.

TAXES IN THE UNITED STATES AND GUATEMALA

The following section examines tax choices in the United States and Guatemala. Tax policy in the United States is interesting in that the national and subnational governments have relatively strong capacity to raise their own revenues. In a developing country, subnational governments, especially local governments, have little capacity to raise their own revenues—the tax base is weak or does not exist. In the United States, each level of government depends predominantly on a specific revenue source, though there is some overlap of tax dependency across levels and for some governments this is more the case than others. Certainly compared with subnational governments in other countries, US state and local governments have significant revenue-raising capabilities. The comparison of tax dependence across the countries highlighted here is stark—a personal income tax is the predominant tax of the United States national government, whereas Guatemala depends mostly on a national sales tax.

Taxing Wealth and Consumption in the United States

Table 11.5 presents tax revenue as a percent of gross domestic product (GDP) by the countries of interest (excepting Tanzania) and for the last decade. The table also presents this measure for all OECD member countries[5] and as classified by income according to the World Bank (WB). This table clarifies the United States as having the lowest tax revenues as a percent of GDP in this group of countries, lower by more than half when compared to both Australia and Italy. Relative to other nations around the globe, United States taxes are low.

Tax dependence by US governments is distinctive by level and type. The US federal government is almost solely dependent upon income and wage taxes. State tax structures are diverse; these governments use a variety of taxes, with strong dependence on sales and income taxes. Local governments are highly dependent upon the property tax. The United States tax system is a bit unique when compared to other countries in that the national government does not employ a sales tax or value added tax (VAT). The following section describes taxes in the United States, an industrialized nation, in comparison to Guatemala, a developing one.

US Federal Income Taxes   In 2012, US federal personal income tax receipts made up 46 percent of total federal revenues and corporate income tax receipts made up 10 percent of these revenues (US Office of Management and Budget 2013a). Payroll tax receipts that fund social security and retirement programs made up 35 percent of total federal revenues. Of tax sources, the US federal government relies on these income and wage-related sources almost exclusively; together they make up 96 percent of total federal tax receipts in 2012 (US Office of Management and Budget 2013a). Other sources of US federal revenues include excise taxes, estate and gift taxes, customs, duties and fees, and miscellaneous revenues (including deposits of earnings by the Federal Reserve) (US Office of Management and Budget 2013a).

Personal income taxes cover both earned and unearned income. Earned income includes wages, salaries, tips, and commissions. Unearned income includes interest earned, dividends, capital gains, rent, and royalties. Inheritance and gifts generally are taxed separately. Business income tax includes that of proprietary, unincorporated, or small businesses and professions (net profits and gross income) and corporations (net income). The US Internal Revenue Service (IRS) provides information for taxpayers that define what to include as income as well as what

Table 11.5
Tax Revenues as a Percent of GDP, by Country and Year*

Country Name	2001	2002	2003	2004	2005	2006	2007	2008	2009	2010	2011
United States	12.0	10.0	9.5	9.6	10.8	11.4	11.5	10.0	8.2	8.9	9.7
India	7.9	8.5	9.0	9.4	9.9	11.0	11.9	10.8	9.6	10.1	10.4
Guatemala	10.9	11.9	11.7	11.6	11.2	11.9	12.1	11.3	10.3	10.4	10.8
Brazil	14.7	15.8	15.4	15.9	16.7	16.5	16.2	15.9	14.8	14.6	15.7
Australia	24.8	23.5	24.3	24.4	24.9	24.6	24.2	24.3	22.2	20.7	20.5
Italy	22.7	22.0	22.0	21.5	21.1	22.6	22.9	22.4	23.0	22.7	22.5
OECD Members	16.0	14.8	14.8	15.0	15.0	15.7	15.9	15.1	13.6	14.0	14.5
High Income	16.0	14.7	14.7	14.9	15.0	15.6	15.9	15.0	13.5	13.9	14.4
Upper Middle Income		11.5	11.9	12.5	12.9	14.1	14.1	14.2	13.5	13.7	
Lower Middle Income	9.8	10.7	11.1	10.6	11.1	11.7	12.2	12.0	11.5	11.4	11.9
Low & Middle Income		11.2	11.7	11.9	12.4	13.4	13.6	13.6	13.0	13.1	
Low Income		9.8	9.9	10.4	10.7	10.7	10.7	11.5	11.1	11.7	

Source: The World Bank, Tax Revenue as a Percent of GDP, by Country, OECD membership, and country income classification. Indicator code: GC.TAX.TOTL. GD.ZS. Available at http://data.worldbank.org/indicator/

*From the World Bank definition of tax revenue that refers to compulsory transfers to the central government for public purposes. Certain compulsory transfers such as fines, penalties, and most social security contributions are excluded. Refunds and corrections of erroneously collected tax revenue are treated as negative revenue. Data for Tanzania not provided.

classifies as exclusions, deductions, credits, and the like. You can access numerous publications and guidelines about specific taxes at the IRS website at www.irs.gov.[6]

Income taxes are highly elastic to the economy and tax policy changes. Elasticity related to the economy means that as the economy shifts, receipts resulting from the tax shift as well (all other things, like tax policy, held constant). Specifically, an economic downturn (and no tax law changes) means reduced income tax receipts and, alternatively, in an economic surge, income tax receipts increase. Changes to tax policy illustrate such elasticity of this tax source as well. President Reagan's tax cuts in 1981 reduced federal marginal income tax rates, especially for high-income taxpayers. Tax reform in 1986 cut rates again. Tax reforms under Presidents George H. W. Bush in 1990 and Bill Clinton in 1993 raised marginal income tax rates. Examining individual income taxes as a percent of GDP from 1980 to 2000 in five-year blocks is telling. From 1980 to 1984, average individual income taxes as a percent of GDP equals 9.0; from 1985 to 1989, the average is 8.1; from 1990 to 1994, 7.8; and then from 1995 to 1999, 8.9 (US Office of Management and Budget 2013b). Government revenues from the income tax shrink and swell following tax policy changes—after rate cuts, receipts declined; after rates were increased, receipts increased. Other factors come into play to explain these changes, of course, but the elasticity of the income tax is one reason for US federal government's strong dependence on it for revenue.

Sales Taxes in the States US state governments have more diversified tax structures than the US national government. In 2012, states general and selective sales and gross tax receipts made up 47 percent of these governments' tax revenues and 23 percent of their total general revenues. State income tax receipts made up 40 percent of state tax revenues (personal income taxes make up 35 percent of state tax receipts and corporate income taxes make up 5 percent) and 20 percent of state total general revenues in this same year (US Census Bureau 2012). State revenues make up 66 percent of total subnational government revenues in the United States in 2010–2011; state tax receipts compose 57 percent of total subnational tax receipts in this same year (US Census Bureau 2010–2011).

As noted, states depend mostly on sales taxes, then income taxes. Sales taxes may be applied universally or generally on consumption (often with exemptions for food or medicines) or selectively (excise). Benefits-received sales taxes include those on utilities, hotel/motel, and motor fuels taxes. Sumptuary or "sin" taxes include those on alcohol and tobacco. These are all examples of excise taxes. Sales taxes are less elastic than income taxes—when the economy slides, people still need to heat their homes and purchase essentials like food and clothes.

The states are distinctive for their diversified tax structures, though there are efforts to streamline taxing across borders. Specifically, in two US Supreme Court decisions in *Bellas Hess v. Illinois* and *Quill Corporation v. North Dakota*, it has been determined that without physical presence in a state, a seller cannot be compelled by the state to tax on sales in the state. Rather, the Court ruled that the US Congress has the power to allow states to compel remote sellers to collect such taxes. Outcome from these judgments include an effort by states to work together to simplify sales and use tax administration across borders and reduce tax compliance burdens. The Streamlined Sales and Use Tax Agreement has fostered a governing board that serves as a centralizing force to generate and disseminate information about uniformity and simplification of sales and use taxes across state borders. There are currently twenty-four member states that have adopted simplification measures.[7]

Property Taxes of Local Governments Receipts from property taxes or ad valorem taxes are the most significant own-source revenue of US local governments. US local government tax structures are less diversified than those of the states but more so than the US national government. Local property tax revenues made up 74 percent of total tax receipts at this level of government and 47 percent of total general revenue from own sources in 2010–2011; property tax receipts made up 26 percent of total revenue of US local governments in this same year (US Census Bureau 2010–2011). Property taxes are levies on wealth, broken down into real and personal property. Real property includes land that may be farm- or timberland, open spaces and minerals, or gas and oil lands; real property includes improvements made to residential, commercial, industrial buildings, infrastructure, and any subsurface improvements (such as a gas tank or lines underground). Personal property is defined as tangible or intangible—tangible includes inventory, equipment, vehicles, jewelry, furniture, and artwork; intangible property includes stocks and taxable bonds and notes, insurance policies, bank deposits, patents, copyrights and trademarks, and accounts receivable. Compared to income and sales taxes, property taxes are inelastic and regressive. Assessments of properties are conducted only periodically (and, in fact, the value of property should appreciate with time) (Bland 2005).

In the United States, millage rates are determined annually by calculating total local government operating expenditures, subtracting out revenue from all sources other than the property tax, then dividing remaining expenditures by the total assessed value of all taxable property of the government (the tax digest). In Georgia, state revenue rule 560–11–2–.58 requires governments to rollback millage rates, if increases of existing real property values occur because of inflation and not because of new or improved properties. In the case of increased values because of inflation, "rollback millage rate must be computed that will produce the same total revenue on the current year's new digest that last year's millage rate would have produced had no reassessments occurred" (Georgia Department of Revenue 2014).

The most important component of the property tax calculation for the taxpayer is the assessed value of the property. Assessed value is a proportion of the property's market value that the government has determined is the value of the property that will be used for taxation purposes. Property tax rates are percentages of assessed value, expressed in mills. A mill is 1/10th of a percent. A one mill tax rate yields $1 for every $1,000 assessment. For example, a 44.1 millage rate applied to a home with a market value of $150,000 and assessed at 40 percent equals $2,646.

$$\$150,000 \times 0.40 \times 0.0441 = \$2,646$$

This calculation does not include any exemptions or credits provided by the government, however. Examine the sample Atlanta, Georgia tax bill provided in Figure 11.2.

This sample tax bill presents property tax levies of the state of Georgia, Fulton County, and Atlanta. All three governments provide exemptions.[8] Exemptions are tax liability reductions of a specific amount or a calculated proportion of the original tax liability. Property owners usually must apply and be approved to receive property tax exemptions. As indicated in this display, net assessment upon which the millage rate will apply is determined by the assessed value of the property's fair market value minus any exemptions. The assessment rate in Georgia is 40 percent. The state millage rate is 0.150; the county rate is 10.481, the Atlanta city rate is 11.85, and Atlanta schools rate is 21.64. This sample tax bill also illustrates how property tax receipts are used, adding to the transparency of taxes—in this case,

Figure 11.2
Sample Atlanta, Georgia Property Tax Bill

Detailed Tax Summary
City of Atlanta/Fulton
Tax Year 2013

Owner Name
Smith, Jane

Parcel Identification
00-1111-XX-222-3

Account Number
1234567

Property Location
45 James Road

Fair Market Value
$150,000.00

Assessed Value
$60,000.00

Tax District
05-Atlanta

City Exemption: Atlanta Homestead Reg
County Exemption: Fulton Homestead Reg

Levies	Assessment	Exemptions	Net Assessment	X	Net Rate	State Credit	TAX
Fulton Cycle							
FULTON BONDS	$ 60,000.00	$ -	$ 60,000.00	X	0.000270	$ -	$ 16.20
FULTON OPERATING	$ 60,000.00	$ 30,000.00	$ 30,000.00	X	0.010211	$ -	$ 306.33
STATE	$ 60,000.00	$ 2,000.00	$ 58,000.00	X	0.000150	$ -	$ 8.70
INTEREST							
PENALTIES/FEES							
			Total Amount Billed			$	331.23
			Less Amount Paid			$	-
			Total Due			**$**	**331.23**
City of Atlanta/Fulton Cycle							
ATLANTA BONDS	$ 60,000.00	$ -	$ 60,000.00	X	0.00120	$ -	$ 72.00
ATLANTA GENERAL	$ 60,000.00	$ 30,000.00	$ 30,000.00	X	0.01005	$ -	$ 301.50
ATLANTA PARKS	$ 60,000.00	$ 30,000.00	$ 30,000.00	X	0.00050	$ -	$ 15.00
ATLANTA SCHOOL BOND	$ 60,000.00	$ -	$ 60,000.00	X	0.00010	$ -	$ 6.00
ATLANTA SCHOOL	$ 60,000.00	$ 30,000.00	$ 30,000.00	X	0.02164	$ -	$ 649.20
INTEREST							
PENALTIES/FEES							
			Total Amount Billed			$ 1,043.70	
			Less Amount Paid			$	-
			Total Due			**$ 1,043.70**	

Property owners with current legal matters, such as bankruptcy or foreclosure, must contact the
Tax Commissioner's Office at: (404)-730-6100 for the official balance due on their parcel(s).

to pay back bonds issued to build schools, parks, and other infrastructure as well as for the general operations of the governments and the school district.

Taxes in Guatemala

Guatemala is a developing country with primary dependence on a national sales tax, though it applies income taxes, too. In this country, the Superintendence of

Table 11.6
Guatemalan Tax Revenues, 1995 and 2012,
Tax Type as a % of Total Tax Revenues

Total Tax Revenues (in millions of Quetzales)	1995	2012
	$6,775.1	$42,819.8
	Tax Type as % of Total $	
Direct Taxes	20.7	31.4
Income	20.1	24.7
Real Estate on Other	<1.0	<1.0
Solidarity Extraordinary and Temporary	<1.0	-0-
Commercial and Agricultural Business	-0-	-0-
Extraordinary Temporary Support of PeaceAccords	-0-	-0-
Solidarity Tax	-0-	6.6
Excise	79.3	68.6
Value Added Tax	36.0	48.8
Customs Duties on Imports	23.6	5.4
Distribution of Oil and Derivatives	8.9	4.9
Stamp Tax	2.8	2.0
Vehicle Traffic	1.9	1.3
Iprima	-0-	<1.0
Oil and Hydrocarbons	<1.0	2.5
Leaving the Country	<1.0	<1.0
Beverage Distribution	2.1	1.3
Snuff	2.1	<1.0
Distribution of Cement	-0-	<1.0
Others	1.6	<1.0

Source: Guatemala Ministry of Public Finance, available at http://www.minfin.gob.gt/

Tax Administration (SAT) manages tax administration for the government and debt is managed by the Ministry of Finance.

Table 11.6 presents tax types as a percent of total taxes in Guatemala for 1995 and 2012. In the 2012 budget, 73.2 percent of revenues come from taxes; 12.6 percent from treasury bonds; 8 percent from loans by international organizations;

4 percent from fees, charges, and leases; 1.7 percent in donations from international agencies and foreign governments; and 0.5 percent from cash balances (Common Fund). What is immediately apparent when examining Table 11.6 is the increase in dependence on direct taxes over this period—the income tax and a solidarity tax—and decreasing dependence on excises overall. Still, the national sales tax or value added tax (VAT) remains the largest single tax source for this government. A 12 percent tax is applied to sales of goods and services conducted in country, to imported goods, leasing contracts, first sale real estate transfers, and insurance and bonding. Exports of goods and services are exempted from the VAT. The decrease in excise taxes as a portion of total taxes results from the decline in customs duties on imports by 77.1 percent for the period. In addition to the VAT, Guatemala imposes selective sales taxes on cement, tobacco, alcoholic beverages, and fuels. The politics of taxation in this developing country is evidenced in the recent court challenge to the creation of the Iprima, a first car plate tax. Suit has been brought by importers of used vehicles to do away with this tax. The head of collections at SAT has indicated that the suspension of the 5 percent tax has resulted in $63 million in lost revenues to the government (inShare 2013).

Remember from chapter 2, the Guatemalan Constitution restricts government spending to specific policy areas, functions, and institutions. According to the Guatemalan Citizen Budget (2012):

> The Constitution of the Republic of Guatemala mandates that State revenues should allocate 10% to the country's municipalities, 5% to the University of San Carlos of Guatemala, 4% to the Judicial Branch, 5% to the Constitutional Court, 1.5% for sport federations, 0.75% for non-federated sport; 0.75% to physical education in schools, and 0.5% the Supreme Electoral Tribunal.

Guatemala's budget is highly rigid due to constitutional stipulations for spending noted earlier, because of requirements of the peace accords, and given that large portions of spending are for government employees (teachers, police officers, and general government), public employee retirement benefits, and debt repayments.

INTERGOVERNMENTAL REVENUES

Research about fiscal federalism examines fund flows from central to subnational governments and seeks to explain how lower-level governments react to these revenues. That is, how do central government monies affect local budgeting decisions (Oates 1999)? Grant determination may be based on a measure of a government's own potential revenue-raising capacity, and for equalization purposes by the central government to correct horizontal and vertical imbalances.[9] Intergovernmental grant structures effect federal policy implementation by lower-level governments, providing a means for central governments to carry out macroeconomic policies of economic stabilization, allocation, and redistribution.

The "flypaper effect"—that money sticks where it lands—characterizes the use of these funds by lower-level governments. James Hines and Richard Thaler (1995) conclude from a meta-analysis of numerous studies about this effect that local government spending behavior is different depending upon the nature of the funds (own-source revenue or grants). Intergovernmental transfers influence the mix of services, programs, and projects provided by the governments receiving these monies.

Table 11.7 presents US federal grants to state and local governments, comparing 1940–1941 to 2010–2011. Several things stand out. First, federal grants are over a third of state and local government expenditures from own sources by 2010, indicative of their importance to state and local budgets. Federal grants as a share of total federal outlays have almost tripled from 1941 to 2010 and, as a percent of GDP they have more than quadrupled. Types of grants have changed as well—federal grants to individuals as a share of total grants have increased by 20.8 percent from 1941 to 2011.

In the United States, the Catalog of Federal Domestic Assistance presents data on all federal assistance to state and local governments.[10] The top five federal agencies issuing federal assistance programs include Health and Human Services (38 percent of programs), Interior (22 percent), Agriculture (20 percent), Housing and Urban Development (10 percent) and Justice (10 percent). These represent federal transfers for a range of activities to individuals for health, welfare, housing, and economic sustenance as well as those for subnational government programming in these policy areas. Objectives may be explicit or vague and applicant eligibility varies with award processes that include statutory formulas, federal agency discretion, or some combination of the two. Applications may be required or be entitlement grants if eligibility criteria are met. Grant continuation may be time-limited or renewable. As explained in chapter 10, grant recipients have reporting and auditing requirements to grant dispensing

Table 11.7

Federal Grants-in-Aid to State and Local Governments,1940 to 2011

	Current Dollars		Grants to Individuals			Grants as a Percent		Constant (2005) Dollars	
Year	Total Grants ($ million)	Annual Percent Change	Grants to individuals, total ($ million)	Percent of total grants	State and Local Government Expenditures from Own Sources	Federal Outlays	GDP	Total Grants ($ billions)	Annual Percent Change
1940	872	NA	298	34.2	NA	9.2	0.9	13.2	NA
1941	847	-2.9	356	42.0	NA	6.2	0.7	13.3	0.8
2010	608,390	13.1	384,480	63.2	37.5	17.6	4.2	527.1	10.6
2011, est.	625,211	2.8	392,506	62.8	NA	16.4	4.1	532.7	1.1

Source: US Office of Management Budget, Budget of the United States, Historical Tables, annual. Also available from the Statistical Abstract at http://www .census.gov/compendia/statab/2012/tables/12s0431.pdf

Notes: Annual percent change from prior year shown; NA = not available; State and local government expenditures from own sources as defined in the national income and product accounts. In this table, 135,325 represents $135,325,000,000, except as indicated. Data for fiscal year ending in year shown. Minus sign (–) indicates decrease.

agencies, Congress, and the Government Accountability Office (GAO) regarding the fair, efficient, and legal expense of the funds. The following is a list of the types of grants that are explained in more detail by the US Government Accountability Office (2012) and that range in restrictions on use and recipient discretion for application:

- **Project Grants:** fund specific project or service for fixed period of time; most restricted of all grants; funding to address policies Congress defines as problematic

- **Categorical Grants:** fund specific, narrowly defined purposes; funding amounts based on formula or discretionary on the part of federal agencies; outnumber block grants in program reach and amount of funding

- **Formula Grants:** fund according to formula; may be broad or narrow in scope; usually to support ongoing activities, not specific projects

- **Matching Grants:** fund with requirements that recipient contribute cash, services, or facilities to match some portion of grant; used to incentivize efficient management of federal program

- **Block Grants:** fund for broad range of eligible activities; recipient has flexibility in use of funds and regarding problems addressed

- **Entitlement Grants:** fund pays benefits to individual or government meeting eligibility requirements established in law

In developing countries, the central government generates tax revenues, devolving these monies to local governments for service delivery and infrastructure purposes. Intergovernmental fiscal structures in these countries may be general purpose, sectoral, or policy based (block), or for a specific purpose. Amounts may be formula based and passed down or may engage a cost reimbursement scheme (Schroeder and Smoke 2003). Factors affecting intergovernmental fiscal schemes in developing countries regard single or multitiered government, the urban-rural subnational government landscape, grant stability, and flexibility,[11] and whether funding is to support routine expenditures (services and operations) or capital development.

Richard Bird and Michael Smart (2003) emphasize that there is no one best way to design intergovernmental fiscal schemes, though principles for sound taxation come into play. For example, for general purposes, grants should be established for stability, simplicity, and transparency—offering subnational governments some discretion in use and reliability in terms of expectations of support annually. For special purpose matching funds, Bird and Smart find it best that matching requirements vary with the type of spending and fiscal capacity of the recipient government. As with taxes, development of intergovernmental fiscal structures necessitate consideration of the adequacy of the revenue, its predictability, simplicity, and transparency and the incentives that may be fostered by lower-tiered recipient governments.

Maarten Allers and Lewis Ishemoi (2011) examine central to local government fiscal transfers in Tanzania, a developing country. They confirm that typically in developing countries, the overwhelming influence of politics in final allocations means that overrepresented localities in the national congress receive a greater share of funds. They discuss means of reducing political influence on fund allocations via tighter funding formulas or centralizing grant allocation (as is conducted in India through the Planning Commission).

Tanzania has a unitary governance structure with a dominant central government; local governments were reestablished in the country in 1984 with passage of the Local Government Act in 1982, after having been abolished about fifteen years prior. Local governments in Tanzania are substantially constrained by the central government; that is, local government authorities (LGAs) are restricted in their abilities to meet local needs by the central government, which dictates the guidelines and conditions for service provision and funding (Boex and Martinez-Vazquez 2003). According to Allers and Ishemoi (2011), own-source revenues of LGA's comprise less than 10 percent of expenditures for services. Jamie Boex (2003) confirms that most revenues for local government recurring expenditures are from intergovernmental transfers. In this country, "approximately 19 percent of on-budget government spending (or 2.7 percent of GDP) is done at the local level with resources provided to them through the transfer mechanism" (Boex and Martinez-Vazquez 2003, 9). The central government, with significant funding from external donors, funnels money to local governments for the provision of determined services and projects.

Political representation across districts throughout Tanzania is uneven and grant allocations to LGAs are extremely uneven and inequitable—the poorest areas do not necessarily receive the most funds. Among the central government transfers to LGAs, there are (1) block grants that support education, health, water, agriculture, and roads, (2) general purpose grants that replace revenues lost given that some LGA taxes are no longer available, and (3) capital development grants that support infrastructure projects. The central government commissioned a study to examine its grant structure; the results were that new formulas were established to account for the different expenditure needs but not revenue capacities of LGAs. Allers and Ishemoi (2010) then analyze whether political influence on grant allocations continues in Tanzania, given this new formula grant structure and the fact that one-party politics still predominates in the country.

Allers and Ishemoi find that under the new scheme, LGAs with more poor residents do not receive more grant money than other LGAs. Also, these scholars do not find a difference in grants among urban and rural LGAs. They determine that the new allocation system has not forestalled the politics of intergovernmental grants in Tanzania. In fact, they estimate that if LGAs were represented proportionally in the national parliament, there would be a dramatic shift in grants from currently overrepresented LGAs to underrepresented ones. Nonetheless, the grant formula reform has improved transparency. According Allers and Ishemoi (2010), "in the case of Tanzania, where the central government depends heavily on European donors to finance its budget, allocation formulas cannot be blatantly unfair" (1795).

Regarding external donor support, which makes up much of the funding for local services and capital in low-income countries, Table 11.8 presents ten-year averages of per capita development assistance to the several developing countries of interest here, with amounts by year for 2010 and 2011. Results indicate growth patterns of assistance to these countries; assistance has spiked in Tanzania; assistance has indicated consistent growth in Guatemala; there has been growth and decline in India; and assistance in Brazil has maintained the status quo, with recent slight growth. Donor assistance can be a double-edged sword. The infusion of funds allows governments to conduct services and address infrastructure project needs. However, donor interests and restrictions may direct monies to services and projects not highly prioritized by the home country. Most donors have significant fiscal and performance reporting and auditing requirements that developing countries may not have the administrative capacity to fully meet. The proportion of the budget made up in donor assistance and the structure of use of these monies contribute to budget complexity, opaqueness, and can even exacerbate existing fiscal inequities in recipient governments.

Table 11.8
Net Official Development Assistance Per Capita, Average by Decade*

	1960s	1970s	1980s	1990s	2000s	2010	2011
Tanzania	2.8	1.3	1.3	1.1	1.3	65.8	52.5
Guatemala	2.9	6.8	16.2	22.4	26.1	27.4	26.6
Brazil	2.0	1.8	2.4	2.0	1.4	2.3	4.2
India	3.4	14.0	32.9	35.0	47.4	2.3	2.6
Heavily indebted poor countries	0.7	1.3	2.2	2.2	0.4	72.3	69.6
Least developed countries: UN classification	1.1	1.4	3.2	4.9	7.5	53.3	52.9
Low income	1.1	1.4	3.2	4.9	7.5	50.3	52.3
Low and middle income	2.0	3.5	5.8	8.0	9.8	23.2	24.8
Lower middle income	2.2	4.7	9.0	12.1	16.9	14.8	14.3
Middle income	2.8	6.0	8.7	10.9	11.7	10.7	11.3
Upper middle income	2.3	7.5	18.8	23.1	31.1	5.8	7.6
OECD members	2.3	7.5	18.8	23.1	31.1	1.4	3.5
High income	4.2	11.3	28.8	38.2	48.7	0.4	0.2

Source: The World Bank Development Indicators, available at http://data.worldbank.org/indicator/DT.ODA.ODAT.PC.ZS

*The World Bank defines net official development assistance (ODA) per capita as disbursements of loans made on concessional terms (net of repayments of principal) and grants by official agencies of the members of the Development Assistance Committee (DAC), by multilateral institutions, and by non-DAC countries to promote economic development and welfare in countries and territories in the DAC list of ODA recipients. The per capita amount is calculated by dividing net ODA received by the midyear population estimate. ODA includes loans with a grant element of at least 25 percent (calculated at a rate of discount of 10 percent).

CONCLUSION

After reading this chapter, you should have insight into the complexities of government revenue generation by taxing. There is no perfect tax—the public unwillingly yields to the requirements to pay taxes and pushes hard against efforts to increase rates, expand bases, or create new ones. Sound tax policy rests on considerations of tax equity, efficiency, adequacy, and transparency. These principles can and do conflict with each other and so establishing a tax that meets all tenets well is impossible. Government administrative and technical capacities to bring in revenues quickly and comprehensively are an advantage, but this requires investments in revenue departments that are often overshadowed by the direction of funds to the more visible work of government—education, health and welfare services, public safety, and economic development.

Governments exhibit different revenue structures, given that developing countries rely on significant donor investment. The tax choices of the United States national government compared to Guatemala's are distinctive. The US federal government depends almost solely on income and wage taxes whereas Guatemala depends predominantly on its national sales tax. Intergovernmental fiscal arrangements are complex and morph in structure for different reasons, generally to effect central government fiscal policy initiatives. These structures are especially prone to political allocation in developing countries where local fiscal capacity is low or nonexistent. Finally, in addition to all the strictures thus far noted that box in government budgets, donor assistance adds complexity to the process as well as further restrictions on funding levels and final expenditures.

DISCUSSION QUESTIONS

1. Explain the implications for a government with a constitutional provision that the tax system abide by the principle of ability to pay.

2. Distinguish between horizontal and vertical tax equity.

3. What is the difference between marginal and effective tax rates and why is this difference important?

4. Discuss why tax incidence is difficult to measure.

5. What is meant by the transparency of a tax? Provide an example of how transparency of taxes can be improved.

6. Define a tax expenditure. Why have tax expenditures of the US national government increased in number and dollar value? Should we be concerned about these tax expenditures? Why or why not?

7. Describe modern methods of tax administration used by governments. Why might government chief executives look to revenue departments to help close budget gaps?

8. Discuss the tax structures you would expect to find in industrialized versus developing countries. Investigate the tax structures of one industrialized and one developing country that have not been examined in this chapter. Are your expectations on the mark?

9. Explain why donor fiscal assistance may further compromise budgets and budgeting in a developing country. How would you measure the performance and results of this type of assistance?

NOTES

1. US local governments are more restricted as "creatures of the state" than US state governments as sovereign vis-à-vis the federal government in terms of determining their revenues and tax structures. In 1975, the Georgia General Assembly passed law allowing local governments to impose a 1 percent local option sales tax (LOST) on the purchase, sale, rental, storage, use, or consumption of tangible personal property and related services, if approved by voters. The LOST was passed to provide local governments the ability to keep property taxes low and to be able to pay for any government services allowed as articulated in the Georgia constitution (and listed in chapter 5). LOST revenues are second only to property tax receipts in importance to Georgia's local governments today. "In 2008, cities collected in excess of $510 million in LOST revenues. Statewide, LOST revenues account for 16 percent of municipal general fund revenues" (Georgia Municipal Association 2011, 1).

2. See http://www.gao.gov/assets/660/654155.pdf

3. See The Multistate Tax Commission website at http://www.mtc.gov/About.aspx?id=40

4. See http://www.revenue.state.mn.us/Pages/default.aspx

5. The Organisation for Economic Co-operation and Development (OECD) is an institution of thirty-four member nations that works to advance public policy and economies worldwide. Of the countries here, Australia, Italy, and the United States are members and Brazil and India are partners, yet to join as members. Read more about the OECD and find data and statistics for countries at www.oecd.org

6. For example, read about how business income is defined for small business owners at http://www.irs.gov/pub/irs-pdf/p334.pdf

7. See http://www.streamlinedsalestax.org/

8. To read about standard homestead and other exemptions offered by the state and available to local governments, go to Georgia's Department of Revenue at https://etax.dor.ga.gov/ptd/adm/taxguide/exempt/homestead.aspx

9. Horizontal fiscal imbalance is defined as the difference between the resources available to governments at the same level; vertical fiscal imbalance is defined as the difference between own-source revenue capacity and expenditure responsibility assignment at different levels of government.

10. See https://www.cfda.gov/

11. Administration of grants may be through sectoral ministries, such as a national government health department, or by a central unit, such as India's Planning Commission that oversees local government grants in that country. See http://planningcommission.nic.in/ and also, the Ministry of Panchayati Raj: http://www.panchayat.gov.in/

REFERENCES

Allers, M. S., and L. J. Ishemoi. 2011. "Do Formulas Reduce Political Influence on Intergovernmental Grants? Evidence from Tanzania." *Journal of Development Studies* 47 (12): 1781–1797.

Auerbach, A. J., and J. R. Hines, Jr. 2001. "Taxation and Economic Efficiency." NBER Working Paper Series, Working Paper 8181, March. Available at http://www.nber.org/papers/w8181

Bird, R. M., and M. Smart. 2002 "Intergovernmental Fiscal Transfers: International Lessons for Developing Countries." *World Development* 30 (6): 899–912.

Bland, R. L. 2005. *A Revenue Guide for Local Government*, 2nd ed. Washington, DC: ICMA.

Boex, J. 2003. "The Incidence of Local Government Allocations in Tanzania." *Public Administration and Development* 23 (5): 381–391.

Boex, J. and Martinez-Vazquez, J. March 2003. "Local Government Reform in Tanzania: Considerations for the Development of a System of Formula-Based Grants." Working Paper 03–05. International Studies Program, Andrew Young School of Policy Studies, Georgia State University.

Cebula, R., and E. L. Feige. 2011. "America's Underground Economy: Measuring the Size, Growth and Determinants of Income Tax Evasion in the U.S." Madison: University of Wisconsin.

Chamberlain, A., and G. Prante. March 2007. "Who Pays Taxes and Who Receives Government Spending? An Analysis of Federal, State and Local Tax and Spending Distributions, 1991–2004." Tax Foundation Working Paper No. 1, The Tax Foundation. Available at http://taxfoundation.org/sites/taxfoundation.org/files/docs/wp1.pdf

Chen, A. 2005. "CRM Pays Off for Florida DOR." *eWeek,* May 23: 34–38.

City of Atlanta. 2014. "MOST Important." Available at http://www.atlantaga.gov/index.aspx?page=755

Devas, N., S. Delay, and M. Hubbard. 2001. "Revenue Authorities: Are They the Right Vehicle for Improved Tax Administration." *Public Administration and Development* 21: 211–222.

Dunleavy, P., H. Margetts, S. Bastow, and J. Tinkler. 2006. "New Public Management Is Dead—Long Live Digital-Era Governance." *Journal of Public Administration Research and Theory* 16 (3): 467–494.

Georgia Department of Revenue. 2014. "Property Tax Guide for the Georgia Taxpayer: Taxpayer Bill of Rights." Local Government Services Division. Available at https://etax.dor.ga.gov/ptd/adm/taxguide/rights.aspx

Georgia Municipal Association. January, 2011. "Local Option Sales Tax (LOST): Definitions, Legal Requirements, and FAQ." Available at http://www.gmanet.com/Assets/PDF/LOST_guide_2011.pdf

Guatemalan Citizen Budget. 2012. Ministry of Public Finances. Available at http://www.minfin.gob.gt/downloads/presupuesto_presupuesto_ciudadano/presupuesto_ciudadano2012/presupuesto_ciudadano12_ingles.pdf

Hines, J. R., and R. H. Thaler. 1995. "The Flypaper Effect." *Journal of Economic Perspectives* 9 (4): 217–226.

inShare. 2013. "First Car Plate Tax $63 Million Lost in Tax Reform Challenges." Business to Business, CentralAmericaData, February 20. Available at http://en.centralamericadata.com/en/search?q1=content_en_le%3A%22First+Car+Plate+Tax+(Guatemala)%22

Iyer, G. S., P. M. J. Reckers, and D. L. Sanders. 2010. "Increasing Tax Compliance in Washington State: A Field Experiment." *National Tax Journal* 6 (1): 7–32.

Laffer, A. 2004. "The Laffer Curve: Past, Present and Future." The Heritage Foundation, Backgrounder 1765, June 1. Available at http://news.heartland.org/sites/all/modules/custom/heartland_migration/files/pdfs/15245.pdf

Lewis, C. W., and W. B. Hildreth. 2013. *Budgeting: Politics and Power*, 2nd ed. New York: Oxford University Press.

Matthews, C. 2013. "The Lying Game." *Time*, April 15, 181 (14): D2.

Mikesell, J. L. 2011. *Fiscal Administration,* 8th ed. Boston: Wadsworth, Cengage Learning.

Oates, W. E. 1999. "An Essay on Fiscal Federalism." *Journal of Economic Literature* 37 (3): 1120–1150.

Rubin, I. S. 2010. *The Politics of Public Budgeting*, 6th ed. Washington, DC: CQ Press.

Schroeder, L., and P. Smoke. 2003. "Intergovernmental Fiscal Transfers: Concepts, International Practice and Policy Issues." Chapter 2 in *Intergovernmental Fiscal Transfers in Asia: Current Practice and Challenges for the Future,* edited by Paul Smoke and Yun-Hwan Kim. Asian Development Bank.

Steenblock, T. 2010. "The Minnesota Department of Revenue Fine-Tunes Its Systems." *Government Finance Review* April: 65–68.

The Pew Charitable Trusts. 2013. "The Geographic Distribution of the Mortgage Interest Deduction." April 30. Available at http://www.pewtrusts.org/en/research-and-analysis/reports/0001/01/01/the-geographic-distribution-of-the-mortgage-interest-deduction

US Census Bureau. 2012. "2012 Annual Survey of State Government Finances. US Department of Commerce. Available at http://www.census.gov/govs/state/

US Census Bureau. 2010–2011. State and Local Summary Tables by Level of Government, US Summary, Table 1. State and Local Government Finances by Level of Government and by State: 2010–2011. US Department of Commerce. Available at https://www.census.gov//govs/local/

US Government Accountability Office. 2005, "Government Performance and Accountability: Tax Expenditures Represent a Substantial Federal Commitment and Need to Be Reexamined." GAO-05-690, September 23. Washington, DC.

_____. 2012. "Grants to State and Local Governments: An Overview of Federal Funding Levels and Selected Challenges." GAO-12-1016, September. Washington, DC.

US Internal Revenue Service. 2012. "IRS Releases New Tax Gap Estimates: Compliance Rates Remain Statistically Unchanged From Previous Study." IR-2012–4, Jan. 6. Available at http://www.irs.gov/uac/IRS-Releases-New-Tax-Gap-Estimates;-Compliance-Rates-Remain-Statistically-Unchanged-From-Previous-Study

US Office of Management and Budget. 2013a. Historical Tables. Table 2.1—Receipts by Source: 1934–2018 and Table 2.5—Composition of "Other Receipts": 1940–2018. Available at http://www.whitehouse.gov/omb/budget/historicals

_____. Historical Tables. 2013b. Table 2.3—Receipts by Source as Percentages of GDP: 1934–2018. Available at http://www.whitehouse.gov/omb/budget/historicals

Wallace, P. 2012. "TSPLOST Results Are In." GPB News, August 1.

The Results of Government Spending

*Governments have an "obligation of result," which speaks to
[an] obligation to ensure that their actions—policies, plans, budgets,
programs—actually result in an increase in people's enjoyment of their
rights. Work of groups that assess the impact of government expenditures
is an important way to analyze compliance with this obligation of result.*

Ann Blyberg, "The Case of the Mislaid Allocation: Economic
and Social Rights and Budget Work"

LEARNING OBJECTIVES

After reading this chapter, you should be able to

- Define human rights budget work

- Compare government expenditures across countries and governments

- Describe quality of life across governments using social indicators

- Measure country competitiveness and consider its relationship to public
  institutions, government budgets, and quality of life

- Conduct your own investigation of government expenditures and the
  results of such spending for social advancement

- Understand how budget institutions and context affect government results

---

This chapter considers the results of government expenditure. It begins by defining human rights budget work that involves research about how government budgets affect human lives. The next section compares governments across a number of indicators, beginning with government spending for social protection that includes cash transfers and aid to individuals and households to lift them from poverty, for life sustenance, and to improve their health, knowledge, and skills. Specifically, we present government spending by function among OECD countries as compared to that of a developing country, focusing on the countries of interest in this book. Social indicators that measure quality of life among governments and an index of country competitiveness are described and compared. We discuss budget and management reform in Italy, a member of the European Union, given the country's significant expenditures for social programming, very high public debt to GDP ratio, and lackluster competitiveness score when compared to the other two industrialized countries of interest here. Italy's recent experience with health reform is explained. The chapter ends with a forecast of the big budget issues that governments face into the future. In spite of the many institutions that constrain public budgeting, governments are improving—as indicated by movement from developing to developed noted in chapter 2. Also, modern governments spend tremendous amounts of money, launch and maintain innumerable programs, and conduct an exceptional variety of services to advance civil society and improve individual circumstances. Still, much remains to be done.

HUMAN RIGHTS BUDGET WORK

Human rights budget work extends the focus on the results of government expenditure from shorter term activity and output of public programs to their long term impact. Ann Blyberg (2009) defines human rights budget work as research that exposes and analyzes the connections of government expenditure to the adherence and advancement of human rights, particularly related to those most vulnerable in society. Human rights budget work has evolved because of (1) democratization among countries globally that emphasizes public acceptance of government legitimacy; (2) decentralization within countries that concentrates on street-level services and projects attuned to local needs and desires; (3) good governance efforts that press budget transparency and accountability by international agencies like the World Bank; (4) support of the work of civil society organizations by donors like the Open Society Institute; (5) legislative interest to advance human rights through budgets; (6) and technological advancements, especially personal computing, that allow individuals to search government budget and other data and analyze such data (Blyberg 2009).

Blyberg (2009) explains that human rights budget work is evidenced across a variety of governments via improvements in public budget transparency, and attempts at participatory, gender, and children budget reforms. Human rights budget work considers substantive versus process rights-based budget foci—this means a heavier concentration on how government activities, services, and programs affect human lives (and positively enhance human rights) compared with the degree of access and inclusion in the budget making process. A roadmap to human rights budget work occurs when macroeconomic policies indicate "sensitivity" to these rights in budgets as developed. Blyberg (2009) points out that rights-based budget work relies "both on national constitutions and laws, and on international standards related to specific rights" (128). International standards related to this kind of budgeting can be found in the International Covenant on Economic, Social and Cultural Rights and in commentary by the United Nations Committee on Economic, Social and Cultural Rights. Blyberg highlights the following examples of human rights budget work:

- The Muslims for Human Rights nongovernmental organization in Kenya successfully exposed information to the public about fund management and project results of the Constituency Development Fund, through which Kenyan MPs (Members of Parliament) could funnel money to their constituents with little transparency.

- The Instituto Brazileiro de Análises Sociais e Econónomicas (described in chapter 9) has developed and disseminated educational materials to the public countrywide to improve citizen knowledge of and skills related to public budgetary analysis.

- The United Nations' Convention on the Elimination of All Forms of Discrimination against Women (introduced in chapter 10) has been at the forefront of efforts like gender responsive budgeting in Tanzania.

- Women's Dignity, an organization in Tanzania, has spearheaded better allocation of funding to support prenatal and birthing programs for poor women, improve budget transparency of these programs, and improve the delivery of supplies to those populations with the greatest need.

- The Children's Budget Unit of the Institute for Democracy in South Africa has applied human rights provisions in the South African Constitution to its research about government funding for health, education, housing, and social development of children as well as educated children about government budgets and how to be involved.

- The Centro Internacional para Investigaciones en los Derechos Humanos in Guatemala focused on the country's ill-conceived milk delivery program, finding that delivery of milk to less food-secure areas, as compared to other areas, was erratic and milk often arrived spoiled. The investigation also found that the government was not receiving the best price for milk and, most important, that the program clients, mostly indigenous, tend to be lactose intolerant.

- The Brazilian National Food and Nutrition Security Council conducted an examination to equate social and economic rights to food with government budget line items; the study conducted in 2005 focused on the national budget and food security and assessed 43 public programs and 143 government activities.

This last effort at human rights budget work in Brazil is somewhat similar to the recent examination of poverty and the national budget in the United States conducted by the US House Budget Committee Majority Staff (2014). This analysis endeavors to measure the extent of poverty and to explain the complexity of poverty in the United States in light of government attempts to address the problem. The report claims a current poverty level in the United States of 15 percent, which equates to approximately 47.7 million people. Further, the report calculates that the level of "deep poverty" (households earning less than 50 percent of the poverty line) today is the highest recorded.[1]

This report attributes poverty in the United States to a number of factors, including the breakdown of family structure, a low marriage rate, labor force participation changes, lack of education and affordable education, and education achievement gaps due to differences in income and race. The report hones in on the duplicative and confusing array of national government programs that exist to combat poverty that it deems as partially to blame, as well. Similar to many other governments in attempting to solve a complex problem, the United States federal government has attempted to alleviate poverty in an ad hoc, chaotic way, with little strategic vision.

[I]t has expanded programs and created new ones with little regard to how these changes fit into the larger effort. Rather than provide a roadmap out of poverty, Washington has created a complex web of programs that are often difficult to navigate. . . . Because the federal government created different programs to solve different problems— at different times—there's little to no coordination among them. (US House Budget Committee Majority Staff 2014, 4, 6)

According to the Budget Committee report, in fiscal year 2012, the US federal government spent $799 billion across ninety-two programs to battle poverty. Federal support to those in low-income categories comes in the form of direct cash assistance, subsidies, tax expenditures, food supplies, housing vouchers, education and job training programs, energy supply programs, health care, programs specific for veterans, and social services that include community and urban development, communications, and legal services, and transportation support.

Having presented numerous examples of the burgeoning worldwide focus on human rights budget work, Blyberg explains that this work is compromised in several ways. Government budgets must be available; information must be transparent and accessible for study. Chapter 10 presented scores for the countries of interest here generated by the Open Budget Survey regarding public access to budget information. Access to this data is better today than in the past. For example, many governments do offer "citizen budgets," which provide budget information in an easy-to-read format. Still, examining Tanzania's Citizen Budget[2] for the financial year 2013–2014 indicates that it does take some skill and knowledge to analyze the data and Blyberg emphasizes that this is another challenge to pursuing human rights budget work. For example, it would be necessary to convert the fiscal data presented in narrative form in the Tanzanian Citizen Budget into a spreadsheet format to conduct even the simplest analysis of government revenues and expenditures. Other documents and data would need to be gathered and assessed; discussions with government officials and program clients would be necessary too for a complete assessment of how the Tanzanian budget affects human life in that country.

Blyberg explains that determining standards for human rights and then linking these standards to government budgets (i.e., the levels of spending associated with attainment of standards) is the most difficult aspect of this type of budget work. In the following section, we review government presence and prosperity among the countries of interest, consider government spending and quality-of-life indicators, and then examine country competitiveness. We review Italy's budget reform efforts and then consider results and reforms in the country's spending for health.

GOVERNMENT PRESENCE AND PROSPERITY

Understanding the long-term impact of government spending requires examination of numerous economic, social, and other indicators. We start with measures of government presence in the economy and national prosperity. Table 12.1 provides several government indicators that should be familiar to you. Considering the World Bank's classification of countries by income that was presented in chapter 2, it is interesting to compare the developing and industrialized countries we've discussed. The countries fall along an expected continuum regarding gross domestic product (GDP) per capita (a measure of national prosperity) that was noted in chapter 2. That is, the high-income countries (Australia, United States. and Italy) indicate higher standards of living than developing countries—low-income Tanzania indicates the lowest standard of living. High inflation relative to the other countries is evidenced in Tanzania and India. However, country GDP as a percentage of world production indicates the influence of the emerging markets of lower-middle-income India and upper-middle income Brazil that surpass high-income countries Italy and Australia. The data about national savings rates is interesting, too; lower-middle-income India and low income Tanzania are ahead of high-income United States and upper-middle-income Brazil. Gross general government debt as a percent of GDP presents Italy's high public debt status compared to other countries; lower-middle-income Guatemala indicates the lowest measure of debt. This country's credit rating helps to explain this—Guatemala received the lowest credit rating from Standard & Poor's of these countries (BB). However, the higher-rated countries, India (BBB) and Italy (BBB), received a negative outlook, while all others are regarded as stable. We consider government spending by function in the following section, concentrating on the government budget and spending in Italy. It is notable that Italy stands out with the highest percentage of general government expenditure as a percent of GDP (50.6 percent). Remember from the last chapter that Italy indicates the highest tax revenues as a percent of GDP relative to our sample countries, too. Guatemala indicates the lowest government expenditures as a percent of its production at 14.1 percent.

Table 12.1
Government Indicators by Country, 2012

Government Indicators (all data for 2012)	Australia	Brazil	Guatemala	India	Italy	Tanzania	United States
GDP per capita in current US dollars	67,723	12,079	3,302	1,492	33,115	599	49,922
GDP based on PPP as percentage of world GDP	1.17	2.83	0.10	5.63	2.21	0.09	18.87
General government expenditures as a percentage of GDP	37.1	40.4	14.1	27.3	50.6	26.9	38.8
General government budget balance as a percentage of GDP	−2.9	−2.8	−2.4	−8.3	−3.0	−5.0	−8.5
Gross national savings as a percentage of GDP	25.2	15.4	11.0	29.8	17.1	23.6	13.1
Annual percent change in consumer price index (year average)	1.8	5.4	3.8	9.3	3.3	16.0	2.1
Gross general government debt as a percentage of GDP	27.2	68.5	25.1	66.8	127.0	41.4	106.5
Unemployment rate (percentage of total labor force)	5.2	5.5	—	—	10.7	—	8.1
Country Credit Ratings by S&P	AAA-Stable	BBB Stable	BB Stable	BBB-Negative	BBB Negative	nr	AA+Stable

Source: Schwab, K. editor. *World Economic Forum: The Global Competitiveness Report 2013–1014, Full Data Edition.* Geneva: World Economic Forum, 2013. Available at http://www3.weforum.org/docs/WEF_GlobalCompetitivenessReport_2013–14.pdf; General government expenditures as a percentage of GDP and Unemployment Rates are from International Monetary Fund, World Economic Outlook Database, October 2013. Available at http://www.imf.org/external/pubs/ft/weo/2013/02/weodata/index.aspx; Country credit ratings by Standard &Poor's available at http://www.tradingeconomics.com/country-list/rating

GOVERNMENT SPENDING BY FUNCTION

Data about government spending, to some extent, illustrates the relative value that various countries place on public functions. The Organization for Economic Cooperation and Development (OECD) provides comparative data about government spending by functions for its member countries. Table 12.2 presents the most recent data from the OECD for thirty member countries. This information allows for some comparison across industrialized countries; information from India is provided by the United Nations and serves as a comparison of industrialized countries with a lower-middle-income or developing country.[3] Of the government budgets of interest here, note that general government expenditures for social protection—general social benefits and transfers of cash to provide living sustenance—varies quite a bit among the OECD member countries alone. In Italy, 41 percent of general government expenditures support such aid; in Australia, this figure is 27.1 and in the United States, 21.3. Such spending as a portion of total general government expenditure is lowest in Korea (13.1 percent). Comparison with a developing country is stark; in India, the portion of government final consumption expenditure applied to this type of individual and household aid is 5.2 percent.

Australia indicates government spending above OECD averages across many of the functions (seven of ten); the United States in five of ten—spending for defense is over three times larger as a proportion of general government expenditures than the OECD average. Italy's focus on social expenditures is evidenced in higher than average government spending proportions for social protection and health; its spending for general public services is relatively high. This includes spending for government employees. This functional area also includes spending for "financial and fiscal affairs, external affairs and foreign economic aid, basic research and expenses related to debt."[4]

SOCIAL INDICATORS: QUALITY OF LIFE

Numerous measures can be used to describe quality of life in different countries, relating the specific challenges of certain governments as well as any results of government intervention to date in boosting quality. Table 12.3 presents social indicators that provide some measure of quality of life for the countries of interest. India's population is more than eight times that of Guatemala. The United States is the second most populous country of those here, followed by Brazil,

Table 12.2
General Government Expenditures by Functions, OECD Member Countries, 2011[a]

	Social Protection	Health	General Public Services	Education	Economic Affairs	Public Order and Safety	Defense	Recreation, Culture, and Religion	Housing and Community Amenities	Environmental Protection
Denmark	43.8	14.5	13.7	13.5	6.1	2.0	2.4	2.8	0.6	0.7
Germany	43.3	15.5	13.6	9.4	7.8	3.5	2.4	1.8	1.2	1.5
Luxembourg	43.2	11.4	11.4	12.1	9.9	2.5	1.0	4.0	1.8	2.8
Finland	43.1	14.2	13.3	11.6	8.8	2.7	2.6	2.2	1.0	0.5
Japan	42.7	17.3	11.0	8.4	9.8	3.1	2.2	0.8	1.8	2.9
France	42.6	14.7	11.5	10.8	6.3	3.1	3.2	2.5	3.4	1.9
Austria	41.6	15.3	13.1	11.0	10.5	2.9	1.4	2.0	1.2	1.0
Italy	41.0	14.7	17.3	8.5	7.1	4.0	3.0	1.1	1.4	1.8
Sweden	40.5	13.7	14.4	13.3	8.2	2.7	2.9	2.2	1.5	0.7
Norway	39.8	16.5	9.7	12.6	9.6	2.2	3.6	2.9	1.6	1.5
Greece	39.3	11.6	24.6	7.9	6.2	3.3	4.6	1.2	0.4	1.0
Switzerland	39.0	6.1	9.9	17.9	13.7	5.0	2.9	2.6	0.6	2.3
Spain	37.4	14.1	12.5	10.5	11.6	4.8	2.3	3.3	1.3	2.1
Slovenia	37.3	13.5	12.4	13.2	11.4	3.3	2.3	3.7	1.3	1.6
United Kingdom	36.8	16.5	11.6	13.4	5.3	5.3	5.1	2.1	1.8	2.0
Portugal	36.7	13.8	17.1	12.9	8.2	4.0	2.7	2.2	1.3	1.1
Belgium	36.6	14.8	15.0	11.6	12.3	3.4	1.8	2.4	0.7	1.4
Poland	36.6	10.9	13.4	12.8	13.0	4.2	2.7	3.0	2.0	1.6
Ireland	35.9	15.6	11.4	10.9	16.4	3.7	0.9	1.8	1.3	2.1
Netherlands	34.5	17.0	11.2	11.6	10.9	4.2	2.7	3.5	1.2	3.3
Hungary	34.5	10.4	17.5	10.5	14.4	3.9	2.3	3.5	1.6	1.5

(continued)

Table 12.2 (continued)

	Social Protection	Health	General Public Services	Education	Economic Affairs	Public Order and Safety	Defense	Recreation, Culture, and Religion	Housing and Community Amenities	Environmental Protection
Estonia	34.2	13.3	8.4	16.9	12.0	5.6	4.1	5.0	1.6	-0.9
Turkey	31.9	12.1	16.4	11.4	11.9	5.2	4.1	2.3	3.5	1.1
Czech Republic	31.7	18.1	10.7	11.4	13.9	4.3	2.1	2.9	1.9	3.1
Slovak Republic	31.3	15.5	15.4	10.6	9.8	6.4	2.7	3.0	2.6	2.7
Australia	27.1	19.2	12.5	14.5	11.4	4.8	4.1	2.1	1.8	2.6
Israel	25.9	12.3	14.7	16.5	5.8	3.8	14.7	3.9	1.0	1.5
Iceland	24.6	16.1	17.8	17.1	12.4	3.1	0.1	7.0	0.7	1.3
United States	21.3	21.4	12.4	15.5	9.4	5.5	11.7	0.7	2.1	0.0
Korea	13.1	15.2	15.2	15.8	20.1	4.2	8.6	2.2	3.3	2.4
Average OECD	35.6	14.5	13.6	12.5	10.5	3.9	3.6	2.7	1.6	1.6
(2010) India	5.2	8.1	30.0	21.1	8.9		23.5	0.8	1.8	0.1

Source: OECD iLibrary, Structure of General Government Expenditures. Based on data availability for thirty OECD member countries. Available at http://www.oecd-ilibrary.org/governance/government-at-a-glance_22214399 November 14, 2013. Data from OECD National Accounts Statistics (database). Data for Australia are based on Government Finance Statistics provided by the Australian Bureau of Statistics. Data are not available for Canada, Chile, Mexico, and New Zealand. Information on data for Israel: http://dx.doi.org/10.1787/888932315602. Data for India (2010) from UN data, "Table 3.1 Government final consumption expenditure by function at current prices," for 2010. Available at http://data.un.org/Search.aspx?q=government+expenditures. According to UN data, government final consumption expenditure "consists of expenditure, including imputed expenditure, incurred by general government on both individual consumption goods and services and collective consumption services." Data for India do not include 0.3 percent noted for "Other Functions." No data or category listed for "Public Order & Safety."

^aPercentages add to 100 by country and across rows for OECD countries.

Table 12.3
Social Indicators by Country

Social Indicator	Time Period	Australia[a]	Brazil[b]	Guatemala	India	Italy[c]	Tanzania[d]	United States[e]
Total population in millions	2012	22.3	196.7	14.8	1,241.5	60.7	46.2	311.6
Population growth rate (average annual %)	2010–2015	1.3	0.8	2.5	1.3	0.2	3.1	0.9
Urban population growth rate (average annual %)	2010–2015	1.5	1.2	3.4	2.5	0.5	4.8	1.1
Rural population growth rate (average annual %)	2010–2015	–0.1	–1	1.6	0.8	–0.4	2.4	–0.6
Urban population (%)	2012	89.4	84.9	50.2	31.6	68.6	27.2	82.7
Population aged 0–14 years (%)	2012	19.0	24.5	40.8	29.9	14.1	44.9	20.1
Population aged 60+ years (females and males, % of total)	2012	20.6/18.5	11.9/9.9	6.7/6.2	8.6/7.4	29.8/24.1	5.4/4.4	21.0/17.2
Sex ratio (males per 100 females)	2012	99.5	96.8	95.1	106.7	96.1	99.9	97.6
Life expectancy at birth (females and males, years)	2010–2015	84.3/79.9	77.4/70.7	75.1/68.0	67.6/64.4	84.6/79.2	60.3/58.2	81.3/76.2

(continued)

Table 12.3 (continued)

Social Indicator	Time Period	Australia[a]	Brazil[b]	Guatemala	India	Italy[c]	Tanzania[d]	United States[e]
Infant mortality rate (per 1,000 live births)	2010–2015	4.5	19	26.3	47.9	3.4	53.7	6.5
Fertility rate, total (live births per woman)	2010–2015	2.0	1.8	3.8	2.5	1.5	5.5	2.1
Contraceptive prevalence (ages 15–49, %)	2006–2010	70.8	80.3	43.3	56.3	62.7	34.4	78.6
International migrant stock (% of total population)	mid-2010	21.9	0.4	0.4	0.5	7.4	1.5	13.5
Intentional homi-cides (females and males, per 100,000)	2008–2010	1.2/3.3	5.4/54.7	10.0/84.5	1.5/3.9	0.5/1.6	3.4/45.7	1.9/6.6

Source: UN Data, World Statistics Pocketbook, United Nations Statistics Division, generated for each country. Accessible from: http://data.un.org/; for example, US report available at http://data.un.org/CountryProfile.aspx?crName=United%20States%20of%20America

[a]First 12 indicators include Christmas, Cocos (Keeling), and Norfolk Islands.

[b]Contraceptive prevalence is from 2002; International migrant stock includes refugees.

[c]Contraceptive prevalence age group 20–49 years, 1995–1996.

[d]International migrant stock includes refugees; Education Primary-Secondary gross enrollment ratio is UNESCO estimate; intentional homicides are estimates based, for the most part, on cause-of-death modeling and death registration data from other countries in the region.

[e]Contraceptive prevalence age group 15–44 years; international migrant stock estimates include persons born in other US territories and American citizens at birth who were born abroad and reside in the US; Refugees and others of concern to the UNHCR excludes individuals whose decision on their asylum claims with the Executive Office for Immigration Review are pending; seats held by women in national parliaments total refers to all voting members of the US House.

Italy, Tanzania, Australia, and Guatemala. Among these countries, population growth rates are highest in Tanzania and Guatemala; these two countries have the highest fertility rates and indicate lowest prevalence of contraceptive use. Infant mortality rates are highest in the three developing countries—Tanzania, India, and Guatemala. Urban and rural growth rates are highest in these three countries; rural populations are declining in all the other countries examined here. In India and Tanzania, most of the population lives in rural areas. High proportions of the population in Tanzania (45 percent) and Guatemala (41 percent) are very young (aged 0–14 years); not so in Italy (14 percent) where over half (53.9 percent) of the population is 60+ years old. Life expectancy for women is greatest in Italy; for men, in Australia. The lowest life expectancy for both sexes among these countries is evidenced in Tanzania. Migrant stock is greatest in Australia and the United States and very low, comparatively, in Brazil, Guatemala, and Tanzania. Considering intentional homicide rates, safety of men and women is most compromised in Guatemala and then Brazil. Such social indicators and their evidenced trends are compared to government promises (in law and as practiced) and thus impact future public policies and budgets.

COUNTRY COMPETITIVENESS

The World Economic Forum (WEF) has developed a global competitive index (GCI) that incorporates twelve measures including country governance institutions and infrastructure; macroeconomic policies; health, education, goods, and labor market efficiencies and financial market development; technological advancements; market size; and business sophistication and innovation. The WEF points to country competitiveness as being "widely accepted as the key driver for sustaining prosperity and raising the well-being of its citizens" (Schwab 2013, 5). The GCI aggregates the scores of various criteria into subindices that encompass basic requirements, efficiency enhancers, and innovation and sophistication measures. Different weights are applied to the criteria within each subindex. However, weights of the subindices that make up the global index are not fixed and depend upon level of development stage reached by individual countries (Schwab 2013). The three subindices and their criteria are displayed in Figure 12.1.

The WEF assesses advancing stages of competitiveness, with a country meeting basic requirements indicative of stage 1, or a factor-driven economy, which indicates existence of basic governance institutions and infrastructure, a

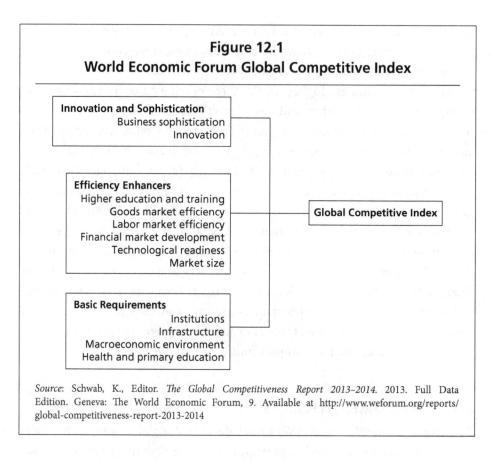

Figure 12.1
World Economic Forum Global Competitive Index

Innovation and Sophistication
  Business sophistication
  Innovation

Efficiency Enhancers
  Higher education and training
  Goods market efficiency
  Labor market efficiency
  Financial market development
  Technological readiness
  Market size

Global Competitive Index

Basic Requirements
  Institutions
  Infrastructure
  Macroeconomic environment
  Health and primary education

Source: Schwab, K., Editor. *The Global Competitiveness Report 2013–2014*. 2013. Full Data Edition. Geneva: The World Economic Forum, 9. Available at http://www.weforum.org/reports/global-competitiveness-report-2013-2014

structure for the macroeconomic environment, and spending for health and primary education. Stage 2 countries, termed efficiency-driven economies, indicate stronger labor and financial market development, technology readiness, spending for higher education and training, and a more robust market economy. Countries reaching stage 3, or innovation-driven economies, indicate business sophistication and innovation not evidenced in countries in earlier stages of competitiveness (Schwab 2013). Stage of development considers GDP per capita (wage proxy) and the level of resource extraction (mineral exports) exhibited in a country. Although the wage proxy provides some indication of national prosperity, the WEF points out that a very high level of resource extraction and export indicates a factor-driven economy (Schwab 2013). Higher scores on the global competitive index thus do not necessarily equate with stage of development.

The 2013–2014 GCIs for the countries of interest are presented in Figure 12.2. The assessment determines that Switzerland is ranked first of the 148 countries

Figure 12.2
World Economic Forum Global Index, 2013–2014, by Country

	Rank	Country	WEF Global Competitive Index
Best Performers	1	Switzerland	5.67
	5	**United States**	
	6	Sweden	5.48
	21	**Australia**	
	22	Luxembourg	5.09
	48	Lithuania	
	49	**Italy**	
	50	Kazakhstan	4.41
	56	**Brazil**	4.33
	60	**India**	4.28
	86	**Guatemala**	4.04
	125	**Tanzania**	
	126	Côte d'Ivoire	
	126	Ethiopia	3.50
Worst Performers	148	Chad	285

Source: Schwab, K., Editor. *The Global Competitiveness Report 2013–2014.* 2013. Full Data Edition. Geneva: The World Economic Forum. Available at http://www.weforum.org/reports/global-competitiveness-report-2013-2014

examined. Of the sample countries here, the United States realized the same score as Sweden and is ranked fifth, having improved by two spots in ranking from last year. Australia and Luxembourg have the same GCI score; Australia dropped one place from last year. Italy ranks within the top fifty countries in terms of competitiveness, but dropped seven spots from last year; Brazil declined in ranking by eight places. India declined from 59th to 60th while Guatemala dropped by three spots. Tanzania fell five spaces from last year to 125th. Guatemala and Tanzania fall below the GCI country average of 4.18.

Of the countries studied, the WEF determines an even split between factor-driven (38) and innovation-driven economies (37); 20 countries are transitioning from stage 1 to stage 2, 31 fall into stage 2, and 22 are transitioning from stage 2 to stage 3. The WEF assesses India and Tanzania as stage 1, factor-driven economies. Guatemala is recognized as stage 2, efficiency-driven, and Brazil is assessed as transitioning from stage 2 to stage 3. Australia, Italy, and the United States are determined as stage 3, innovation-driven economies (Schwab 2013).

The WEF uses primary and secondary data to compile the GCI. The Forum has conducted an annual Executive Opinion Survey for more than thirty years, collecting the opinions of numerous business leaders in each country (Schwab 2013). This year's survey generated responses from 148 countries; an average of 85.5 persons responded from each country. Table 12.4 presents survey data about public institutions that is part of the basic requirements subindex and regards many of the concepts of import here—property rights, ethics and corruption in government, public trust in politicians, judicial independence, public security, efficiency of the legal framework for business transactions and government policymaking, and government efficiency and wasteful spending.

Australia and the United States meet or exceed the country average for most items presented in Table 12.4 that concern the public institutions component of basic requirements of the GCI. Australia only trails regarding the item, *How burdensome is it for businesses to comply with government administrative requirements?* The United States scores lag behind country averages for this same item and two others, *How efficiently does the government spend public revenue?* and *To what extent does the incidence of crime and violence impose costs on businesses?* At the other end of the spectrum, Italy and Tanzania do not meet the country averages for 14 of the 17 items. The focus on Italy's budgeting and health expenditures (to be presented later in this chapter) is further informed by this data. Italy scores poorly regarding level of corruption related to public budgeting (diversion of funds) and the ethics of politicians as well as corporations in terms of their interactions with government. Those interviewed in this survey from Italy determine that the government is inefficient in providing goods and services, and this item receives the lowest score of the countries compared here. Finally, Italy indicates that its financial auditing and reporting standards are relatively weak as compared to the other countries—its score is the sixth lowest (4.0), just above Tanzania's (3.7).

Overall, the WEF determines Switzerland to be the most effective and transparent in the world (5th). Its governance structures provide for equal opportunity; strong confidence in legitimate business practice; an independent, corruption-free judiciary; strong rule of law; and responsible government. Switzerland is ranked 75th for public and private institutions. The WEF finds the United States economy gaining a bit of steam since the end of the Great Recession, with financial markets stabilizing, a relatively flexible labor market; and recognition of the country's strong higher education system that fosters

Table 12.4

World Economic Forum GCI Subindex, Basic Requirements: Public Institutions

World Economic Forum Global Competitiveness Index:

Sub-Index Basic Requirements

Items regard *Public Institutions* (mean score for item)

(all data for 2012)	Australia	Brazil	Guatemala	India	Italy	Tanzania	United States
How strong is the protection of property rights, including financial assets? (4.3) [1 = extremely weak; 7 = extremely strong]	5.2	4.6	3.8	4.4	4.3	3.8	5.2
How strong is the protection of intellectual property, including anti-counterfeiting measures? (3.8) [1 = extremely weak; 7 = extremely strong]	5.3	3.5	2.9	3.7	3.7	3.2	5.2
How common is diversion of public funds to companies, individuals, or groups due to corruption? (3.5) [1 = very commonly occurs; 7 = never occurs]	5.2	2.3	2.3	2.8	2.8	2.9	4.6
How would you rate the ethical standards of politicians? (3.1) [1 = extremely low; 7 = extremely high]	3.8	1.9	2.0	2.2	1.8	2.8	3.3
Regarding irregular payments and bribes. (4.1)[a]	5.7	3.9	3.9	3.2	3.8	3.9	4.9
To what extent is the judiciary independent from influences of members of government, citizens, or firms? (3.9) [1 = heavily influenced; 7 = entirely independent]	5.7	3.9	3.0	4.7	3.7	3.2	5.0
To what extent do government officials show favoritism to well-connected firms and individuals when deciding upon policies and contracts? (3.2) [1 = always show favoritism; 7 = never show favoritism]	4.0	2.9	2.8	2.8	2.4	3.1	3.3

(continued)

Table 12.4 (continued)

World Economic Forum Global Competitiveness Index:

Sub-Index Basic Requirements

Items regard *Public Institutions* (mean score for item)

(all data for 2012)	Australia	Brazil	Guatemala	India	Italy	Tanzania	United States
How efficiently does the government spend public revenue? (3.2)	3.4	2.2	2.4	3.0	2.0	3.0	3.1
[1 = extremely inefficient re: goods and services; 7 = extremely efficient re: goods and services]							
How burdensome is it for businesses to comply with governmental administrative requirements (e.g., permits, regulations, reporting)? (3.5)	2.8	2.0	3.5	3.1	2.2	3.7	3.4
[1 = extremely burdensome; 7 = not burdensome at all]							
How efficient is the legal framework for private businesses in settling disputes? (3.8)	4.6	3.3	3.3	3.8	2.3	3.6	4.7
[1 = extremely inefficient; 7 = extremely efficient]							
How easy is it for private businesses to challenge government actions and/or regulations through the legal system? (3.5)	4.3	3.5	3.5	3.8	2.5	3.3	4.3
[1 = extremely difficult; 7 = extremely easy]							
How easy is it for businesses to obtain information about changes in government policies and regulations affecting their activities? (4.2)	4.4	3.7	4.5	4.2	3.0	3.7	4.4
[1 = extremely difficult;7 = extremely easy]							
To what extent does organized crime (mafia-oriented racketeering, extortion) impose costs on businesses? (5.0)	5.9	4.0	2.4	4.8	3.6	5.0	4.8
[1 = to a great extent; 7 = not at all]							

To what extent does the incidence of crime and violence impose costs on businesses? (4.5) [1 = to a great extent; 7 = not at all]	5.4	3.4	2.0	4.7	4.5	4.6	4.3
To what extent can police services be relied upon to enforce law and order? (4.3) [1 = cannot be relied upon at all; 7 = can be completely relied upon]	6.0	4.3	2.8	4.0	5.0	3.5	5.7
How would you rate the corporate ethics of companies (ethical behavior in interactions with public officials, politicians, and other firms)? (4.1) [1 = extremely poor—among the worst in the world; 7 = excellent—among the best in the world]	5.5	3.7	3.9	3.7	3.6	3.4	4.9
How strong are financial auditing and reporting standards? (4.6) [1 = extremely weak; 7 = extremely strong]	5.8	5.3	4.7	4.9	4.0	3.7	5.3

Source: Schwab, K., Editor. *The Global Competitiveness Report 2013–2014.* 2013. Full Data Edition. Geneva: The World Economic Forum. Available at http://www.weforum.org/reports/global-competitiveness-report-2013-2014

university connections with business and technology firms for research and development. Business remains suspect of politicians, however, and bureaucratic red tape is a considered problem. Those interviewed consider that government spends inefficiently. According to the WEF (Schwab 2013), "the macroeconomic environment continues to be the United States' greatest area of weakness (117th of 148), although the deficit is narrowing for the first time since the onset of the financial crisis" (23). The United States is ranked 35th for its public and private institutions. Australia has maintained its competitiveness, according to the WEF. It is 7th in financial market development, strong in higher education and training, with improving macroeconomics with a reduced deficit, inflation under 2 percent, and public debt as a percent of GDP ranking the third lowest of advanced economies. On the other hand, WEF cites the country's rigid labor market and burdensome government regulation as slights on an otherwise cheery outlook (Schwab 2013). This country ranks ahead of the United States on public and private institutions at 23rd.

The WEF indicates that Italy's competitiveness "deteriorated across the board" (Schwab 2013, 30) this year. Lack of political leadership has increased uncertainty in the country's business community. Italy offers a relatively sophisticated market—it produces some of the best value products across a number of areas. Its market size is 10th among the 148 countries studied. Like Australia, however, this country has a rigid labor market and its financial markets are underdeveloped. Factors related to problems with conducting business in Italy include tax rates, access to financing, and an inefficient government bureaucracy (Schwab 2013). Its greatest problem in achieving competitiveness, however, relates to high corruption and organized crime, and a judiciary considered more influenced than independent. Collectively, these components place Italy at 102nd regarding its public and private institutional environment.

Brazil indicates some deterioration in several macroeconomic indicators, including a constricted financial market, heightened concerns about government efficiency and corruption, and little trust in political leaders. High-quality infrastructure is elusive in Brazil. The business community, however, is innovative and research driven, and the country has a large market size relative to its competitors (Schwab 2013). Brazil's public and private institutions rank ahead of Italy's at 80th.

WEF finds that India is losing a competitive edge evidenced in years past. It currently lags behind Brazil, South Africa, and China, and Russia is on its heels. Poor infrastructure, transport, telecommunications, and energy, hold this country back in terms of its competitive potential. The country maintains a tremendously burdensome bureaucracy, politicians are little trusted, and corruption is "deeply rooted" in the culture. India also scores low on public health and education; the education measure tends toward poor technology readiness. Labor market efficiency in India is low; "the most salient problem remains the dismally low participation of women in the workforce" (Schwab 2013, 36). India's macroeconomic indicators are poor—inflation and public debt-to-GDP ratios are high relative to its BRICS competitors. Still, India's public and private institutions are ranked ahead of both Brazil and Italy at 72nd.

Guatemala has well-functioning markets, open trade, and a solid banking system, but high corruption and crime are significant barriers that compromise competitiveness in this country. This country scores low on its educational system and the digital gap is substantial, given large proportions of the population that live in rural areas (indigenous groups) (Schwab 2013). Guatemala's public and private institutions are ranked 111th of 148. WEF ranks Tanzania's competitiveness lowest (125th) of the sample countries. As in India, infrastructure in this country is poorly developed and unreliable. Primary education enrollment rates are high, but those in secondary and higher education are the lowest in the world. Quality of education is lacking and again, as in India, contributes to lagging technological readiness. Health is a major issue; the very low proportion of the population that reach 60+ years of age is partially indicative of the high incidence of HIV. High rates of HIV and malaria in the workforce further compromise advancement in this country. This country's public and private institutions are ranked just ahead of Italy's and Guatemala's at 97th.

BUDGET REFORM IN ITALY

This section examines budget reform in Italy, its applicability to national health expenditures, and its impact on health services in one locality of the country. Italy presents a good example of a country that adheres to incremental budgeting yet illustrates the possibilities for innovation that results in improved services and lower costs. As noted in chapter 2, Italy has a prime minister, appointed by the president and confirmed by Parliament, who serves as the head of government. A Council of Ministers (cabinet), selected by the prime minister and confirmed by the president, is responsible for assisting with budget and policy development and execution. Italy's constitution[5] provides for individual rights yet imposes expectations on citizens to contribute "to the material or spiritual progress of society." An extensive social safety net is implicit in constitutional provisions for individual welfare and health support, free education, and financial assistance for higher education. The Italian Constitution is definitive regarding the budget process. Article 81 provides for reaction of the Parliament to the government (executive) budget by making appropriations as providing "the legal foundation" for accounting control. Continuity of the budget, revenue and spending limits, and budget balance are also stipulated in 81. Articles 100 and 103 of the constitution provide for the Corte dei Conti, the independent accounting control office that reports to Parliament based on its financial and management oversight of the central government and any institutions that the central government supports fiscally. Italy has reformed central to sub-central relationships via fiscal decentralization, at different times affording, retracting, and then reinforcing local fiscal autonomy. This system is recognized as highly complex, legalistic, and rulebound; a majority of Italy's public spending and programming occur through these subcentral governments, as is noted in the discussion later in this chapter of Italy's national health service.

Italy has undergone, however, several significant public budgeting and management reform periods to centralize budgeting, apply a multiyear budgeting perspective, improve forecasting, implement performance-oriented budgeting, and advance transparency (Ranalli and Giosi 2011; see also, Di Mascio, Natalini, and Stolfi 2013). As presented in chapter 2, problems in the mid-1970s related to an ever-expanding social safety net provided through central government social welfare spending, budget gaps funded through debt, high tax evasion, corrupt public management, and local governments strongly dependent upon the central government to finance public services and projects (Pacifico and Sequiti 2000). Budget law passed in 1978 required the Italian Parliament to develop a framework for budget decisions early in the budget process (the Finance Act). At this time, an Enlarged Public Sector Account, using modified cash basis, accounted for autonomous firms (for example, Italian railway, post office, and telecommunications), municipal companies (for production of transportation services, electricity, gas, and water), and the country's electrical energy monopoly (Mussari, Ruggiero, and Monfardini 2011). In 1988, new budget law placed limits on the Finance Act and attempted to focus on current account budget balance. Then, privatization in the early 1990s changed these autonomous firms into joint stock companies that employed accrual accounting.

In 2001, new laws increased the central government role in the development of strategy, consolidated eighteen ministries into twelve newly streamlined ones, and promoted the coordination of budget and program implementation through the cabinet and by ministries. New offices replaced legislative ones to foster collaboration with ministries for purposes of centralized (political) policy development. The reorganization marked departments as a funnel between political ministry heads and operational managers and staff. The functional devolution of government services to subcentral governments was streamlined as well (Mussari, Ruggiero, and Monfardini 2011; Di Mascio, Natalini, and Stolfi 2013).

Italy, as a member of the European Union (EU), is constrained to some degree by its rules for membership in good standing. Chapter 2 indicated that the Stability and Growth Pact of the Maastricht Treaty requires member states to adhere to a budget deficit not in excess of 3 percent of GDP and a ratio of public debt to GDP not in excess of 60 percent. But George Guess and Lance LeLoup (2010) illustrate that Italy (with Greece, Malta, Germany, and Portugal) exceeded both of these requirements in 2005. These scholars explain that although the EU has some ability to impose an "excessive deficit procedure" (106) on any country that does not meet the deficit criteria, the Union "is limited in its ability to sanction member states that do not abide by these budget guidelines" (2010, 106). Still, such visible accounting does impose some pressure upon errant governments to work toward meeting these criteria.

Teresa Ter-Minassian and colleagues (2007), in a report about Italy's budget system, enumerate its problems:

- Budget development is incremental with limited reflection on government priorities or linkage of priorities with budget choices
- Parliament votes on a budget of more than 1,500 line items that "bear no clear relation to the objectives of public spending" (5)
- There is no multiple-year budget perspective; forward projections are not real baselines for future budgets
- Thousands of amendments accompany budget approval by Parliament
- Multiple controls on budget execution constrain budget managers and heighten attention to legal compliance over efficient program delivery
- The cost data about program expenditures are weak
- There is a lack of focus on budget results and little accountability for performance

Riccardo Mussari, Pasquale Ruggiero, and Patrizio Monfardini (2011) discuss reforms that Italy imposed for the 2008 budget that sought to address some of these problems. A program budget format was established by law that requires aggregation of spending information into missions that represent main functions and strategic objectives for expenditures, and programs that are the collection of activities conducted within ministries to reach mission objectives (Mussari, Ruggiero, and Monfardini 2011). Ministries must fit their budget into missions and programs. Parliament now deliberates about and approves programs; programs are made up of basic budget units that include current expenditures, capital expenses, and loan reimbursements. Basic budget units are further broken into responsibility centers through which financial resources are managed. Revenues are reclassified into several levels as well. This reclassification of the budget into a program format reduced Parliament's consideration of line items from 1,656 in 2007 to 690 in 2008.

In 2009, Law No. 196 established numerous changes to the budget system that were expected to be enforced by 2011 (Di Mascio, Natalini, and Stolfi 2013). The law changed the budget cycle whereby the report on the economy and government finance was pushed to April 15. This report includes national economic trends, assessment of economic and cash accounts, and macroeconomic forecast updates. A public finance decision, which includes updated budget forecasts and variances of forecasts with current macroeconomic indicators, replaces the economic and financial planning documents and must be submitted to Parliament by September 15. Law No. 196 calls for clearer development of general economic objectives, definition of sector objectives that link central and local governments and national agencies, explanation of strategies to reach sector objectives, and a three-year spending plan. Accounting systems and spending are expected to equate with the classification of the functions of government; accrual-based accounting and performance indicators are introduced and whole-of-government accounts are to be prepared. Mussari, Ruggiero, and Monfardini (2011) are in agreement with others (Ranalli and Giosi 2011) that despite new law, the Italian budget remains in flux. Several decrees were passed in 2010 to further change budgeting in Italy.

Noel Hyndman and colleagues (2014) assess accounting and budgeting reforms in Austria, Italy, and the United Kingdom. They consider reforms as contributing to "sedimentation" rather than dramatic change—that is, as a layering of elements that might transform current structures and practices, but rarely displaces them. They agree that legal foundations and the context within which a government operates flavors reform implementation. Essentially, a reform "hits the wall" of a government, its context, and administrative and legal structures, and is changed. They view successful reform as one having the ability to settle into the current sediment of governmental functioning and influence activities going forward. These scholars are interested in the variability in government adoption of reforms and why some governments are more aggressive adopters than others. They discuss that governmental systems with more attention paid to rules and formality are less likely to integrate reforms well, as are those with cultures that have greater power distance, high uncertainty avoidance, and a short-term orientation to budget and policy outcomes. They expect that governments with multiple political parties will be slower to reform than others.

These scholars study reform in the United Kingdom (Anglo-Saxon), Austria (Germanic/Continental Europe) and Italy (French/Napoleonic/Southern European) from 1980 to 2010 to distinguish degree of reform sedimentation. In addition to interviewing central government officials, the authors analyzed documents including laws, technical commentaries to bills, and debates in parliaments and committees. Information collected was coded as positive (supportive) or negative (critical or challenging) about specified reforms; they also considered reforms in terms of traditional public administration (PA), new public management (NPM), and public governance (PG) (Hyndman et al. 2014).

These authors list the budget reforms in Italy (at least on paper) as moving from the 1980s—with a focus on budget control, compliance, and financial accounting—to the next decade with the reclassification of revenues and expenditures and introduction of accrual and cost accounting, to parallel the traditional cash budget. By the 2000s, reform reorganizes the budget to focus on missions and programs, but in 2009, these scholars determine that commitment-based budgeting is abandoned. Across the decades, Italy holds to a traditional public administration orientation that is rules based (Hyndman et al. 2014). Discourse addressed PA predominantly throughout the 1980s, with consideration of NPM and PG much less in evidence. Reference to NPM peaks in the 1990s, however, given the focus on cost and accrual accounting system reforms. This period indicates an increase in the combination of PA and PG codes as well. Reform during this decade sought to focus on the nonfinancial results of government expenditure. Perhaps it is surprising that these scholars find that the PA discourse remains strong in the 2000s in Italy. Different from discourse in the UK and Austria, discussion of PG hardly ever occurs and, if mentioned, it mostly relates to PA. In fact, Hyndman and colleagues (2014) determine that in Italy, traditional public administration arguments remain prevalent throughout the time period studied because there is little pressure to replace old ideas; NPM types of accounting changes "are marginal rather than embedded" (101).

HEALTH CARE IN ITALY: CHANGING BUDGET ORIENTATION

How much of Italy's budget is focused on health care? Also, what are the results of this country's investments in health services, given its budget process sedimentation just described? Compared to other industrialized nations presented in Table 12.2, Italy falls exactly in the middle in terms of the proportion of its general government expenditures applied to public health. What are health services like in Italy and how has spending for health services changed in this country, if at all? This section describes the result of Italy's government expenditures for health and gives an example of how budget and accounting reform has affected health services in at least one region of the country.

Italy operates a National Health Service that is financed through earmarked corporate and value-added taxes, in addition to general and regional tax revenues. Copayment is established for outpatient care and limited copayment applied to drugs. Low-income protections and other exemptions exist to accommodate the elderly, children, pregnant women, and those with specified disabilities and diseases (Thomson et al. 2013). Doctors in Italy are self-employed and sign contracts to work in the system (though reforms will be explained later in this chapter), whereas hospitals are predominantly public. Fixed fee for service is employed with costs per capitation; hospital payments engage global budgets and case-based payments that include physician costs. Patients must register with a general practitioner (GP); GPs provide a "gatekeeping" role, meaning that patient referrals are required for specialized care (Thomson et al. 2013, 9).

In a comparison of health care metrics across fourteen industrialized nations, Italy is the sixth most populous country of the group (United States is the most populous and New Zealand is least). As noted earlier, Italy has a large portion of the population over the age of 60. This report indicates that Italy has the second-highest proportion of the population over the age of 65 (21 percent); of this group of countries, Japan has the highest proportion of age 65 or over (23.3 percent) and the United States the lowest (13.2 percent). Italy indicates the second-lowest GDP spending on health care (9.2 percent); Australia's is the lowest

(8.9 percent) and United States the highest (17.7 percent). Italy has realized the lowest average annual growth rate of real health care spending per capita from 2000 to 2011 (1.2 percent) whereas the Netherlands has the highest (4.7 percent). Italy has the highest number of practicing physicians per 1,000 people (4.1); Japan indicates the lowest number (2.21), though data is missing for several countries. Italy falls in the middle of the pack regarding number of acute care hospital beds per 1,000 (2.75), the highest is 7.95 in Japan and the lowest is 1.73 in Canada. Of two health risk factors—Italy scores poorly on one and well on the other. Italy and France have the highest proportion of adults who smoke daily (22.5 and 23.3, respectively). Sweden has the lowest percentage of daily smokers (13.3 percent). However, Italy is second lowest in prevalence of obesity (10 percent); Japan has the lowest rate (4.1 percent) and United States has the highest (36.5 percent) (Thomson et al. 2013).

Italy provides centralized financing of a decentralized health care system. The central government defines national standards of care; nineteen regions and two autonomous provinces provide the structure of care and service delivery. Health care is provided through local health units (LHUs) that are managed by chief executive officers (CEOs) appointed by regional governors. General practitioners (GPs) are independent contracted workers with the system based on three-year agreements determined by the government and GP unions. Italy changed its public health care system in 1978, modeling it on the British system, to provide coverage that is "automatic and universal" (Donatini 2013, 66) for citizens and legal foreign residents. Illegal immigrants can access basic services and visitors can pay for services. Individuals can purchase additional private health insurance, and approximately 15 percent of the population purchases coverage to be able to use private health facilities and services. Levels of care are prescribed and positive and negative lists of services delineated by the central government. Positive lists include services offered to all; negative lists indicate services not offered, covered on a case-by-case basis, and those in which hospital stays are not considered necessary. The central government provides reference rates for hospital stays, outpatient payments and drugs; regions determine their own rates, considering such references. Regions must finance any services that they choose to provide over and above the level of care specified by the central government. Level of care does not necessarily indicate type of services provided but rather services covered. This health system does have ceilings for individual payment responsibilities that are provided in law. Still, in the last few years, Italy has added copayments for services and drugs, and to avert overuse of emergency rooms (Donatini 2013).

Public financing accounts for over three-quarters of total health care spending in 2012, with a corporate tax collected nationally, then parceled to regions. Value-added tax revenue is also collected centrally and then distributed to regions, accounting for disparate fiscal capacities among the regions. A conference of regional and central government representatives determines criteria for fund allocation to provide the determined levels of service across all regions. Inequity across regions related to financing remains a concern; financial law passed in 2008 determining regional health care financing based on actual costs "is not operating yet" (Donatini 2013, 68).

In the last two decades, Italy's health care system has attempted to incorporate new public management accountability principles to improve health care services and reduce costs. For example, the Italian Ministry of Health has a number of institutions, councils, and committees that provide research, advice, and technical support to help with decisions about benefits, services, and appropriate levels. Andrea Donatini (2013) of the Emilia-Romagna Regional Health Authority, writes that determinations of benefits and service levels "are based mainly on clinical effectiveness and appropriateness rather than cost-effectiveness. At the regional level, some governments have established agencies to evaluate and monitor local health care quality and provide technical comparative effectiveness assessments and scientific support to regional health departments" (70–71). Quality of care has been addressed through accreditation and continuing education of national service doctors and staff. Plans developed in the mid-1990s and work in 2003 and 2007 (1) expanded and improved patient screening guidelines to support evidenced-based diagnostics, (2) pressed for greater transparency of patient care and hospital service quality metrics, and (3) promoted a pilot project related to patient safety. Better coordination among health care providers and government has produced 24-hour access to care with no additional costs, though regional differences in service remains uneven. Also, GPs today are likely to work in networks rather than independently, allowing for freer flow of communication and information sharing about patient care, technologies and diagnostics.

Iris Bosa (2010) writes about the application of new public management to the National Health Service in Italy by concentrating on changes made between 1999 and 2004 at one local "social-health care authority (LSHA) located in the Veneto region of northeastern Italy" (77). She conducts interviews and collects and analyzes data about the authority from 1996 to 2004. This authority realized the biggest deficit of all local health authorities in the region in 1992; the period is marked by leadership change and service cuts. The creation of chief executives in regions to manage health care brought about pressures for budget balance, but the pressure was framed in terms of quality of care through management accounting. "This dialogue encouraged GPs to adopt a wider understanding of the concept of 'quality of service'—that is, to look beyond the individual patient to the societal context of resource distribution" (78).

In many ways, this effort represents participatory budgeting (Bassoli 2012). In this case, doctors were included in the process of change by creating twice weekly meetings in which a pilot group developed a budget allocation for each GP within the authority, "based upon equity and objective criteria" (Bosa 2010, 78). This group concentrated on changing the conversation from one of doctor-illness to doctor-patient. "Dialogue regarding equity of access and service quality led the group to begin speaking of the concept of an ethical budget" (78). The process required the doctors to gather and assess cost data and the distribution of disease patterns. Doctors learned that most health spending was applied to just 15 percent of the population. Insights like this "socialized" (79) doctors to the benefits of statistical information (Bosa, 2010).

Relationships were fostered between doctors and the hospitals as well to better understand costs and investigate efficiency. In 1997, regional management held a conference to expose results from the work of the pilot group and recognize the budget not merely in terms of finances, but as an ethical tool (Bosa 2010). After this, the local health authority began to establish incentives for GPs to engage in specified activities. Also, contracts with GPs required (1) their participation in quality circles, (2) stated performance objectives, (3) attendance at refresher courses, and (4) more comprehensive reporting to accompany referrals to hospitals. Hospital admissions for the piloted local health authority fell from 215 in 1997 to 146 in 2004, a drop of 32 percent; and by 2004, the authority drug unit expenditure was 18.4 percent below the average for the region (Bosa 2010). The results of this innovation to a local health authority included improved services and cost reductions. In addition and as noted earlier, most GPs today are working in networks rather than independently and they are held to various performance metrics. Bosa emphasizes that GP training, advanced reporting requirements, and continual feedback were important components for making changes in budgeting for health services in this particular Italian locality. "The concept of budget is now accepted as part of a new framework of medical ethics in which cost awareness plays a legitimate role" (2010, 80). The reform started small and has required changing the perspective of professionals (GPs) over time to consider how financing and their medical expertise can coalesce to advance public health.

On the other hand, Fabrizio Di Macio, Alessandro Natalini, and Franscesco Stolfi (2013) find in their study of Italy's past budget reforms a layering of reactions to fiscal crisis, based partially on history and partially on budget institutions; these factors temper the above consideration of reform in health services at the local level with changing central government roles. "Law 196/2009 provided for the harmonization of accounting systems at all levels of government and the reform of the financial planning cycle as essential prerequisites for greater involvement of subnational governments in setting budget objectives. However, the reform is still on paper since the adoption of the mandated implementing legislation has encountered obstacles and opposition" (27). Over the last twenty years, the Italian Minister of Finance has gained power and holds more centralized control over government spending. "The containment of healthcare expenditure [the largest regional area spending] has been defined within the framework of the transversal approach in place since 2000. The framework has been made more robust for regions with healthcare deficits, which must undergo restructuring plans to be agreed with and under the control of the Finance Ministry" (27).

BUDGET INSTITUTIONS, REFORM, AND RESULTS

James Savage (2013) explains the vital link between the budget and effective governance in his book about statebuilding and reconstruction of a budgetary system in Iraq. He brings up the importance of transparency and inclusiveness of process to effect democratic governance. In the case of Iraq, in 2003, a US-led coalition helped the country develop budgets for the first time in over a dozen years. The coalition worked with the Iraqi government to develop law (Coalition Provisional Authority Order 95) for a reformed budgetary process in which the parliament would vote on the budget, the Ministry of Finance would coordinate the process, and fiscal federalism was structured. Benchmarks were established that pushed Iraqis to work toward budget objectives. Savage explains that budgeting in Iraq still suffers tremendously (corruption is high) in spite of this strengthening of its budget institutions. His assessment indicates, however, that a sedimentation has occurred in this country brought about, in part, from Iraqi ownership of the budget process. The new institutions that were developed layered onto traditional ones rather than fully replaced them. The evolution of budgeting in Iraq over this period speaks to an ever-changing process, but one that is incremental and holds fast to administrative culture. Especially now, given the upsurge in violence, unstable governing institutions, and lack of rule of law in Iraq, expect it to take decades and tremendous effort for this country to lurch toward a strong and stable budgetary system.

This chapter has presented an emerging consideration of public budgeting related to human rights. This type of "budget work" determines how government budgets influence human lives or the results of government budgets. We would expect that government budgets that advance the human condition and community living would spend heavily for social protection, health and education, community development, and housing, and for such programs that work directly to lift people from poverty to lead healthful and productive lives. Comparison of the governments that have been considered throughout this book indicates that several measure as industrial or developed and several rank as lower income or developing. Yet all of these governments attempt human rights budgeting—examples abound of efforts to promote greater inclusion and transparency of operations and funding, to improve health and knowledge building, to promote equal social and economic rights, and to avert poverty. These efforts occur in spite of tight budgets, lagging or lack of resources, internal and international conflicts, natural disasters, and other events that compromise well-functioning public institutions.

The consideration of Italy in this chapter is instructive, given this government's traditional adherence to rules versus results. This country's detailed constitution provides for a relatively expansive social welfare program, yet constricts budget making. The country's social protection spending is high compared to the other governments examined here; government presence relative to the country's economy is larger than the other governments as well. Social indicators are important for tracking current government policies and determining new ones for the future. Italy's government expenditures for social protection undoubtedly attempt to account for the high proportion of elderly that make up the country's population. Life expectancy is high for both men and women in Italy, as compared to other countries. The country's low fertility rate has implications for the government when analyzing financing capacity. Low birth rates mean fewer future workers, which can compromise a country's economic health and growth. The WEF noted that tax rates are one problem related to Italy's competitiveness; competitiveness is a contributor to country prosperity and the well-being of society. Even though the World Bank and other organizations have indicated that more countries are advancing toward industrialized status, Italy presents us with an example of some backtracking in an industrialized country.

On the other hand, a more detailed examination of Italy's budget process, particularly related to its spending for health care, indicates that reform is possible and a rule-bound government can change, even if incrementally and on a small scale. Italy has undergone some budget and management reforms that have stretched decision makers to reorient their focus—from budget control to programming and even spending results. Mussari, Riggiero, and Monfardini (2011) predict that in spite of the legal strictures of the country's constitution and laws, and those related to EU membership, and pressures to accommodate best practices, Italy will continue to layer its budget system to support clarity, simplicity, accountability, and timeliness. Hyndman and colleagues emphasize Italy's steadfast incrementalism, though even these authors recognize a changing conversation over time with each budget reform, in spite of little real traction.

Still, Italy's changing national health system offers an example of change over time to realize human rights budgeting. Bosa's research (2010) finds public management reforms in one Italian local health authority revised the health budget by refocusing the dialogue of professionals (doctors) with management for improved service delivery at reduced costs. In fact, the reform provided for participatory budgeting by doctors, allowing them ownership of the process to effect change. This is similar to what Savage found related to changes in how Iraq budgets. This case provides support for the ability to improve the results of government spending through budget reform.

CONCLUSION

This book began by presenting different definitions of budgets—resource bound, yet strategic, and providing for control and accountability. These concepts remain front and center of public budgeting as does clarity, timeliness, accuracy, comprehensiveness, and unity. Subsequent chapters have provided a look at the institutions and components that structure government taxing and spending. Constitutions and laws establish responsibilities, set schedules, and frame processes that occur routinely but during ever-changing circumstances. Governments are bound by these institutions, yet must accommodate to these changing circumstances. Chief executives can provide a government-wide focus and set the strategy for future operations. Legislatures determine and approve budgets, setting laws that establish what will be done. The judiciary influences government budgets by interpreting such law and the activities and results of government taxing and spending. Bureaucrats execute the budget, interpreting guidelines and rules for budget implementation, and considering new and different ways to carry out budgets to reach strategic goals within the strictures of budget laws and rules. Citizens through participation and the media through exposure influence what governments budget for and how governments follow through on promises.

In the current climate and for the foreseeable future, expect governments to be in a perpetual state of rebudgeting—that is, continually reassessing their fiscal status and accommodating this status to the current crisis of the day. Significant and enduring challenges for governments include tapping revenue (tax) sources acceptable to the public to pay for continually growing needs associated with quality-of-life measures. Expect the public to hold governments responsible for the conduct of rights-based budget work in order to reach higher standards of quality of life (however these are determined) and continual economic progress. Reforms can occur over time in governments to carry out this work, but these reforms take time, often start small, and require ownership and consistent championship. Expect incrementalism and real-time budgeting to be prominent, realistic explanations of public budgeting, though reforms will continue to be layered on top of such processes in attempts to engender positive results.

DISCUSSION QUESTIONS

1. What is human rights budgeting? Research an example of human rights budgeting in a government that has not been mentioned here.

2. Consider the social indicators presented for selected countries in Table 12.2. How might this information inform government about public policy and public spending, specifically?

3. Analyze the general government expenditures by function for an OECD country other than Australia, Italy, or the United States. What do expenditures indicate to you about government and civil society in this country?

4. What is country competitiveness? How does competitiveness as defined by the WEF affect civil society? Explain the relationship between competitiveness and government budgets.

5. Do you think that incrementalism and reform can coexist in governmental budgeting? Explain your response.

NOTES

1. To view updated US federal poverty guidelines can be found at http://familiesusa.org/product/federal-poverty-guidelines

2. To see example of citizen budgets, go to Australia's Budget website at http://www.budget.gov.au/2014-15/index.htm; Guatemala's at http://www.minfin.gob.gt/index.php/presupuesto-ciudadano; and Tanzania's at http://www.mof.go.tz/index.php?option=com_content&view=category&layout=blog&id=21&Itemid=206r

3. Complete and comparable data for Brazil, Guatemala, and Tanzania was unavailable from UN data (http://data.un.org/) at the time of this study.

4. See the European Commission, Eurostat Glossary, available at http://epp.eurostat.ec.europa.eu/statistics_explained/index.php/Main_Page

5. See US Library of Congress, http://www.loc.gov/law/help/guide/nations/italy.php or see, Costituzione Della Repubblica Italiana, http://www.camera.it/application/xmanager/projects/camera/attachments/upload_file/upload_files/000/000/002/costituzione.pdf.

REFERENCES

Bassoli, M. 2012. "Participatory Budgeting in Italy: An Analysis of (Almost Democratic) Participatory Governance Arrangements." *International Journal of Urban and Regional Research* 36 (6): 1183–1203.

Blyberg, A. 2009. "The Case of the Mislaid Allocation: Economic and Social Rights and Budget Work." *International Journal on Human Rights* 6 (11): 123–139.

Bosa, I. M. 2010. "Ethical Budgets: A Critical Success Factor in Implementing New Public Management Accountability in Health Care." *Health Services Management Research* 23: 76–83.

Di Mascio, F., A. Natalini, F. Stolfi. 2013. "The Ghost of Crises Past: Analyzing Reform Sequences to Understand Italy's Response to the Global Crisis." *Public Administration* 91 (1): 17–31.

Donatini, A. November 2013. "The Italian Health Care System, 2013." In Thomson, S., Osborn, R., Squires, D. and Jun, M., Editors. *International Profiles of Health Care Systems, 2013*, edited by S. Thomson, R. Osborn, D. Squires, and M. Jun. The Commonwealth Fund. Available at http://www.commonwealthfund.org/~/media/Files/Publications/Fund%20Report/2013/Nov/1717_Thomson_intl_profiles_hlt_care_sys_2013_v2.pdf

Guess, G. M., and L. T. LeLoup. 2010. *Comparative Public Budgeting.* Albany: SUNY Press.

Hyndman, N., M. Liguori, R. E. Meyer, T. Polzer, S. Rota, and J. Seiwald. 2014. "The Translation and Sedimentation of Accounting Reforms. A Comparison of the UK, Austrian and Italian Experiences." *Critical Perspectives on Accounting:* 35 (4–5): 388–408. Available at http://dx.doi.org/10.1016/j.cpa.2013.05.008

Mussari, R., P. Ruggiero, and P. Monfardini. 2011. "Italian Central Government Budgeting: Future Hopes and Past Disappointments." In *Comparative Public Budgeting: A Global Perspective*, edited by C. E. Menifield, 151–176. Sudbury, MA: Jones and Bartlett Learning.

Pacifico, L., and M. L. Sequiti. 2000. "Reform: Budgeting and Financial Management." *International Journal of Public Administration* 23 (2–3): 367–381.

Ranalli, F., and A. Giosi, A. 2011. "New Perspectives on Budgeting Procedures in Italy." *International Journal of Public Administration* 34 (1–2): 32–42.

Savage, J. D. 2013. *Reconstructing Iraq's Budgetary Institutions: Coalition State Building after Saddam.* New York: Cambridge University Press.

Schwab, K., Ed. 2013. *The Global Competitiveness Report 2013–2014.* Full Data Edition. Geneva: The World Economic Forum. Available at http://www.weforum.org/reports/global-competitiveness-report-2013-2014

Ter-Minassian, T., J. Daniel, A. Fedelino, M. Robinson, J. Tyson, and M. Keating. May 2007. "Italy: Budget System Reforms." International Monetary Fund, Fiscal Affairs Department. Available at http://www.rgs.mef.gov.it/_Documenti/VERSIONE-I/Pubblicazioni/Analisi_e_valutazione_della_Spesa/Documenti/Italia—-Riforme-del-sistema-di-bilancio—-Testo-integrale-in-lingua-inglese.pdf

Thomson, S., R. Osborn, D. Squires, and M. Jun, Eds. November 2013. *International Profiles of Health Care Systems, 2013.* The Commonwealth Fund. Available at http://www.commonwealthfund.org/~/media/Files/Publications/Fund%20Report/2013/Nov/1717_Thomson_intl_profiles_hlt_care_sys_2013_v2.pdf

US House Budget Committee Majority Staff. 2013. *The War on Poverty: 50 Years Later.* March 3. Available at http://budget.house.gov/waronpoverty/

LIST OF ABBREVIATIONS AND ACRONYMS

AB1	Appropriation Bill 1 of Australia
AB2	Appropriation Bill 2 of Australia
ABA	American Bar Association
ACA	Patient Protection and Affordable Care Act
ANAO	Australian National Audit Office
AOB	Agency Annual Operating Budgets of US State of Georgia
ARRA	American Recovery and Reinvestment Act
BBA	Balanced Budget Act of the US federal government
BCA	Budget Control Act of the US federal government
BEA	Budget Enforcement Act (Title XIII of the Omnibus Budget Reconciliation Act of 1990)
BNDES	Brazilian National Economic and Social Development Bank
BOB	Bureau of the Budget of the US federal government
BRICS	Brazil Russia India China and South Africa
CAFR	Comprehensive Annual Financial Report
CBA	Congressional Budget Act (Congressional Budget and Impoundment Control Act of 1974)
CBO	Congressional Budget Office
CEDAW	United Nations Convention on the Elimination of All Forms of Discrimination Against Women

CEO	Chief Executive Officer
CFO	Chief Financial Officer
CHIP	Children's Health Insurance Program
CIA	Central Intelligence Agency
CMO	Planning, Budget and Oversight Joint Committee of Brazilian Congress
COLA	Cost-of-Living Adjustment
COO	Chief Operating Officer
COP	Council of Participatory Budgeting of Brazil
CPC	City Planning Commission of New York City
CR	Continuing Resolution
DAC	Development Assistance Committee
DB	Defined Benefit Pension Plan
DC	Defined Contribution Pension Plan
DFID	Department for International Development of United Kingdom
DISHA	Development Initiatives for Social and Human Action of India
DOR	Department of Revenue
EFT	Electronic Funds Transfer
EOP	Executive Office of the President
EOS	World Economic Forum Executive Opinion Survey
EPA	Environmental Protection Agency
ERC	Expenditure Review Committee
EU	European Union
FASAB	Federal Accounting Standards Advisory Board
FRS	Florida Retirement System
FSIO	Financial Systems Integration Office
FY	Fiscal Year
GAAP	Generally Accepted Accounting Principles

GAO	Government Accountability Office
GASB	Governmental Accounting Standards Board
GCB	Global Corruption Barometer
GCI	Global Competitive Index
GDP	Gross Domestic Product
GFOA	Government Finance Officers Association
GFR	General Financial Rules of India
GNI	Gross National Income
GNP	Gross National Product
GNRU	Guatemala National Revolutionary Unity
GO	General Obligation bonds
GOI	Government of India
GP	General Practitioner
GPP	Government Performance Project
GPRA	Government Performance and Results Act
GPRAMA	GPRA Modernization Act of 2010
GRH	Gramm-Rudman-Hollings (Public Law 99–177)
HDI	Human Development Index
HPSCI	House Permanent Select Committee on Intelligence
IAS	International Accounting Standards
IASB	International Accounting Standards Board
Ibase	Instituto Brasileiro de Análises Sociais e Económicas
IBP	International Budget Partnership
ICGFM	International Consortium on Governmental Financial Management
ICMA	International City/County Management Association
IFAC	International Federation of Accountants
IFRS	International Financial Reporting Standards

IMF	International Monetary Fund
IPSAS	International Public Sector Accounting Standards
IRS	Internal Revenue Service
IVR	Integrated Voice Response (telephone activated)
JCPAA	Joint Committee of Public Accounts and Audits of Australia
JFMIP	Joint Financial Management Improvement Program
JMSC	Judicial Merit Selection Commission
LBB	Legislative Budget Board of the US State of Texas
LDO	Law of Budget Directives (Lei de Diretrizes Orcamentarias) of Brazil
LGA	Local Government Authorities of Tanzania
LGLB	Local Government Loan Board
LOA	Lei do Orcamento Anual of Brazil
LOST	Local Option Sales Tax
LSHA	Social Health Care Authority of Italy
MBO	Management by Objective
MFR	Managing for Results
MOST	Municipal Option Sales Tax
MTC	Multistate Tax Commission
MTEF	Medium-Term Framework
NASBO	National Association of State Budget Officers
NBER	National Bureau of Economic Research
NCSL	National Conference of State Legislatures
NFIB	National Federation of Independent Business
NGO	Non-governmental Organization
NPM	New Public Management
NPR	National Performance Review (National Partnership for Reinventing Government)

OBI	Open Budget Index
OBS	Open Budget Survey
OCGA	Official Code of Georgia
ODA	Official Development Assistance
OECD	Organization for Economic Cooperation and Development
OMB	Office of Management and Budget
OPB	Office of Planning and Budget of the US State of Georgia
OPEB	Other Post Employment Benefits
PA	Public Administration
PART	Program Assessment Rating Tool
PAYGO	Pay-As-You-Go
PBO	Parliamentary Budget Office of Australia
PEFA	Public Expenditure and Financial Accountability Program
PG	Public Governance
PI	Performance Information
PM	Prime Minister
PMI	Performance Measurement Initiative
PPA	Plano Pluri-Annual of Brazil
PPBS	Planning Programming Budgeting System
PPP	Purchasing Power Parity
PRS	Poverty Reduction Strategy
RTB	Real Time Budgeting
SAT	Superintendence of Tax Administration of Guatemala
SHG	Self-Help Group
SSCI	Senate Select Committee on Intelligence
TAD	Tax Allocation District
TARP	Troubled Asset Relief Act
TEL	Tax and Expenditure Limitation

TI	Transparency International
UN	United Nations
UNDP	United Nations Development Programme
UNESCO	United Nations Educational, Scientific and Cultural Organization
UNHCR	United Nations High Commissioner for Refugees
UNODC	United Nations Office of Drugs and Crime
US	United States
VAT	Value Added Tax
WB	World Bank
WEF	World Economic Forum
WGI	Worldwide Governance Indicators
WIC	Women Infants and Children
WJP	World Justice Project
ZBB	Zero-Based Budgeting

INDEX

Governors: agenda setting, 172–174; as budget and policy leaders, 170–172; governor's party, 176–179; impact of party on gubernatorial agenda, 176–182; issues expressed by governors as priority, 175; overview, 169–170; percent of governors mentioning an issue as priority, 180. *See also* U.S. state government budgeting

GPRA Modernization Act of 2010, 273–274

Gramm-Rudman-Hollings (GRH), 77–78, 212

Grants, 369

Great Recession, 79–80; percent of governors mentioning an issue as priority before, during, and after, 180; state of state addresses before, during, and after, 174–176

Greer, Robert, 110

Grodzins, Morton, 133

Guatemala, 44–47; budget cycles, 310; judiciary, 258–260; taxes, 364–366

Guess, George, 33, 401

Guo, David, 289–290

Gupta, Anand, 48

H

Hallerberg, Mark, 210

Handy, Jim, 258–259

Hartley, Roger, 241–244

HDI. *See* Human Development Index (HDI)

Health care: and the courts, 234–236; in Italy, 404–408

Health care expenditures, 5, 6

Heniff, Bill, 80–81, 212

Herrara, Richard, 172–173

Herzik, Eric, 172, 173

Ho, Alfred, 281

Holcombe, Randall, 98

Holzer, Marc, 323

Home rule, 135–136, 139–140

Horizontal equity, 344

Hubbard, Michael, 351

Human Development Index (HDI), 26–28

Human rights budget work, 380–384

Hyndman, Noel, 402–404

I

IMF. *See* International Monetary Fund (IMF)

Income tax, 70, 359–361

Incrementalism, 13–16, 308

India, 47–49; citizens and budgets, 285–286; gender budgeting, 333–334; judiciary, 256–258; presidents and prime ministers, 161–162

Industrialized countries: vs. developing countries, 26–32. *See also individual countries*

Inman, Robert, 112

Institute for Democracy in South Africa, Children's Budget Unit, 382

Instituto Brasileiro de Análises Sociais e Económicas, 282, 381

Intergovernmental revenues, 366–372

International City/County Management Association (ICMA), 183–184

International Monetary Fund (IMF), 26; World Economic Outlook Database, 11–13, 29–30

Iraq, 408–409

Ishemoi, Lewis, 370, 371

Italy, 49–52, 409–410; budget reform, 399–404; health care, 404–408

Iyer, Govind, 352

J

Jacobs, Kerry, 316

Jail overcrowding, reducing, 239

Jasperson, Amy, 292–293

Jefferson County, Alabama, 145–147

Jena, Pratap Ranjan, 277

Jhamb, Bhumika, 333–334

Johnson, Cliff, 270

Johnson, Loch, 211–212

Joint Committee of Public Accounts and Audits (JCPAA), 208

Jones, Bryan, 16

Joyce, Philip, 85, 162–163, 165–166, 167, 214, 215

Judiciary: appointment of federal judges, 252–253; and the budget, 240–244; budget strategies, 241–244; budget stringency in U.S. federal judiciary, 244; and corruption, 245–260; corruption susceptibility of state judges, 254–256; and the economy, 232–233; in Guatemala, 258–260; in India, 256–258; perceptions of judicial corruption around the world, 248–252; and public policy, 233–240; selection of state judges, 253–254. *See also* courts

Julnes, Patria de Lancer, 323

K

Kagan, Elena, 253

Kammholz, Craig, 316

Kastrop, Christian, 331

Katz, Daniel, 100–104

Keynes, Maynard, 73

Keynesian theory, 73

Khademian, Anne, 278

Rosenbloom, David, 233–234
RTB. *See* real-time budgeting (RTB)
Rubin, Irene, 4, 34, 85–86, 170, 182–183, 347
Rubin, Marilyn, 332
Rueben, Kim, 112
Ruggiero, Pasquale, 402
Rule of law, 35–37; Australia, 41; Brazil, 44; Guatemala, 47; India, 49; Italy, 52; Tanzania, 55; United States, 86–87
Rybicki, Elizabeth, 80–81

S

Sabato, Larry, 170
Sales tax, 361–362
Samuel, Peter, 96–97
Sanders, Debra, 352
Savage, James, 408–409
Scheers, Bram, 324
Schemes, 48
Schotland, Roy, 254–256
Searcy, Cynthia, 188
Sector working groups, 55
Segal, Geoffrey, 96–97
Sequester, 81, 244
Sequiti, Maria Laura, 51
Services as a percent of GDP, 31
Shafer, Karen, 172–173
Shah, Parmesh, 283
Siena Research Institute, 168–169
Single Audit Act of 1984, 279–281
Sinha, Nvanita, 333–334
Smart, Michael, 369
Smith, Adam, 342
Smith, Harold, 20–21
Smolkin, Rachel, 290
Sobel, Russell, 98
Social indicators, by country, 386–391
Sorge, Marco, 248
Sotomayor, Sonia, 253
Souza, Saulo, 42
Special districts, 136
Special purpose governments, 132, 133
Specification, 20
Stages of the budget process, 159
Stallman, Judith, 112–113
State budget institutions and rules: balanced budget rules, 107–108, 109; debt limitations, 108–110; overview, 106–107; supermajority voting requirements, 111–113; tax and expenditure limitations, 110–111; tax and expenditure limitations (TELs), 112–113

State constitutions, 100–104; Missouri, 104–105; South Carolina, 105–106; Wisconsin, 106
State governments. *See* U.S. state government budgeting
State legislatures, 214–215; Georgia, 217–218; New York, 218–221; Texas, 215–217
State of Louisiana's Revenue Estimating Conference, 19
State of state addresses, 174–176
Steenblock, Terri, 357
Sterck, Miekatrien, 324
Stimulus funding. *See* American Recovery and Reinvestment Act (ARRA)
Stolfi, Francesco, 408
Strategic planning, and the budgeting process, 158–159
Straussman, Jeffrey, 239–240
Successive limited comparisons, 15. *See also* branch and root method of decision making
Supermajority voting requirements, 111–113
Supply-side economics, 76
Swan, Wayne, 160

T

Tanzania, 52–55; citizens and budgets, 287; gender budgeting, 333; presidents and prime ministers, 160; semipresidential system, 157–158
Target-based budgets, 308
Tax and expenditure limitations (TELs), 110–111, 112–113
Tax revenue curve, 348
Taxes: in Guatemala, 364–366; property taxes of local governments, 362–364; sales taxes in the U.S., 361–362; taxing wealth and consumption in the U.S., 359–364; U.S. federal income taxes, 359–361. *See also* collectability; property tax
Ter-Minassian, Teresa, 401
Testa, Cecilia, 162
Texas, state legislature, 215–217
Thompson, Hugh, 241
Thrash, Thomas, 239
Timelines, 309–314; of U.S. governments, 311–314
Tollestrup, Jessica, 85
Tollini, Helilo, 209
Tools, 20
Touchton, Mike, 283
Town meeting government, 184
Transparency, 33, 324–327, 348–350
Transparency International, 245, 248–250, 251, 256–257
Troubled Asset Relief Act (TARP), 80

CPSIA information can be obtained
at www.ICGtesting.com
Printed in the USA
LVHW101157270820
664241LV00049B/428

9 781118 509326